Divine Grace and Human Agency
A Study of the Semi-Pelagian Controversy

Divine Grace and Human Agency

A Study
of the Semi-Pelagian Controversy

Rebecca Harden Weaver

North American Patristic Society
Patristic Monograph Series
15

MERCER UNIVERSITY PRESS

ISBN 0-86554-619-3   MUP/P178

Divine Grace and Human Agency.
A Study of the Semi-Pelagian Controversy.
Copyright ©1996
Mercer University Press, Macon, Georgia 31210
All rights reserved
Printed in the United States of America
First printing, March 1996
Perfectbound edition, November 1998

———————

The paper used in this publication meets the minimum requirements
of American National Standard for Information Sciences—
Permanence of Paper for Printed Library Materials, ANSI Z39.48-1984.

———————

Library of Congress Cataloging-in-Publication Data
[Original, casebound edition; perfectbound CIP pending.]

Weaver, Rebecca Harden, 1944–   .
Divine grace and human agency :
a study of the Semi-Pelagian controversy / Rebecca Harden Weaver.
xii+264 pp. 6x9″ (15x23cm.) — (Patristic monograph series ; no. 15).
Includes bibliographical references and indexes.
ISBN 0-86554-491-3 (alk. paper) [casebound first edition].
ISBN 0-86554-619-3 (alk. paper) [perfectbound edition].
1. Semi-Pelagianism.   I. Title.   II. Series.
    BT1460.W43   1996
    273'.5—dc20   96-5042

                                                    CIP

Contents

To my parents

Oscar Burford Harden
Dorothy Blaylock Harden

Preface

The relationship between divine grace and human agency has been the source of recurrent dispute throughout the history of the Western church. The controversies surrounding Pelagius in the early fifth century, the Semi-Pelagians in the fifth and early sixth centuries, Gottschalk in the ninth century, the Jesuit Molina and the Dominican Báñez in the De Auxiliis controversies in the sixteenth and early seventeenth centuries, and the Jansenists in the seventeenth and eighteenth centuries are only the most prominent instances of a debate for which the church has never found a satisfactory resolution.

The purpose of this study will be to examine one of the more notable outbreaks of the argument, the Semi-Pelagian controversy which began around 426 in Hadrumetum in North Africa and reached its official conclusion in 529 at the second Council of Orange in South Gaul. This controversy is of particular significance for several reasons. First, in establishing his own position in the argument, Augustine set the terms for debate of the issue in the West. Second, the views of the Semi-Pelagians, in their inherent balance and moderation, have offered a persistently attractive alternative to the extreme Augustinian teachings on grace. Like Augustine, his adversaries in this controversy acknowledged the necessity of grace but believed that it was equally important to affirm the significance of human agency. They insisted that human persons have a genuine role in shaping their own lives and destiny; therefore, they objected to the teaching of a sovereign, predestinating grace that severely diminishes or even denies human agency. The church officially rejected much of their argument at the Council of Orange in 529, but in subsequent centuries variations of their teaching have functioned as the operative theology of the church. Third, the canons adopted at the Council of Orange have continued to serve as the most nearly definitive statement that the church offers on the question of grace and human agency. Although the canons were the work of only a regional council and have never been considered entirely satisfactory, the church in the West has failed to formulate a statement that would supersede them.

In its basic elements, therefore, the Semi-Pelagian controversy provides a window onto the church's prolonged struggle to define the relation of grace and human agency. An examination of this debate should illuminate, at least to a limited degree, the difficulties that the church has encountered in this effort.

I have sought to explore the dynamics of the controversy from three perspectives. First, I have attempted to clarify the difference between the Semi-Pelagian and the Augustinian positions by suggesting that the need to safeguard the rela-

tionship between human action and human destiny determined the former and the
need to safeguard the sovereignty of grace determined the latter. The overlap
between the two positions was sufficient to have caused confusion and misunderstanding, but in reality each side operated from a different framework with its
own sets of issues.

Second, I have tried to demonstrate that the social contexts of the participants in the debate, specifically the monastic and congregational settings, affected
the issues that were raised and the positions that were taken. Third, I have
attempted to establish a distinction between the traditions to which each party
appealed for substantiation of its arguments. The Semi-Pelagian heritage derived
from the Eastern, Origenist tradition of the desert fathers; the Augustinian tradition was new, Western, and almost entirely self-constructed. The sources of
authority and the directions of their emphases were markedly different.

In the last decade the Semi-Pelagian controversy has received renewed attention. As well as I can determine, however, it has never been examined as a conflict between two different sets of issues, two different social contexts, and two
different theological traditions. This new approach should offer a fresh access to
the occasion for the emergence of the debate, the passion and character of its
evolution, and its eventual resolution.

My work on this project has been made possible through the assistance and
encouragement of many people. I owe a deep debt of gratitude to William S.
Babcock, who provided painstaking guidance during the years that I developed
this project into a dissertation. Jeremy DuQ. Adams and John Deschner also provided invaluable suggestions, as did Schubert M. Ogden. The rewriting of this
material would not have been possible without the warm encouragement and
helpful counsel of Fredrick M. Norris and J. Patout Burns. Patout Burns offered
suggestions both with regard to the general argument and its specific detail for
which I am profoundly thankful. In the time spent on the Gallic material I have
benefitted from the help of William E. Klingshirn and Thomas A. Smith. F.
Douglas Ottati provided useful suggestions regarding both style and content.
Joseph T. Lienhard of the Patristic Monograph Series and Edd Rowell of Mercer
University Press deserve my warm thanks.

I am also indebted to the administration of Union Theological Seminary in
Virginia, particularly T. Hartley Hall, IV, William V. Arnold, Charles M.
Swezey, and Robert Norfleet, who provided both the resources of the school and
time for my writing. The seminary library staff, especially Patsy Verreault,
Hobbie Bryant, John Trotti, and Elaine Christensen, have consistently supported
my efforts. Fairfax Fair, David Duquette, Jeremy Grant, and David Nash proved
to be able research assistants. Sally Hicks and Kathy Davis provided efficient
secretarial assistance combined with enormous patience and good humor.

Finally, I wish to thank my parents for a lifetime of encouragement and my
husband for his unfailing grace.

Abbreviations

Ad Simpl.	Augustine, *Ad Simplicanum de diversis quaestionibus* (*Responses to Various questions from Simplicianus*)
Auct.	Prosper, *Praeteritorum episcoporum sedis apostolicae auctoritates de gratia Dei et libero voluntatis arbitrio* (*Official Pronouncements of the Apostolic See on Divine Grace and Free Will*)
CCSL	*Corpus Christianorum*, Series Latina
C. Coll.	Prosper, *Contra collatorem* (*Against the Conferencer*)
C. duas ep. Pel.	*C. duas ep. Pel.*: Augustine, *Contra duas epistulas Pelagianorum* (*Against Two Letters of the Pelagians*)
Coll.	Cassian, *Collationes* (*Conferences*)
Comm.	Vincent of Lérins, *Commonitorium primum Peregrini pro catholicae fidei antiquitate et universitate adversus prophanas omnium haereticorum novitates* (*Commonitory*)
De bapt.	Augustine, *De baptismo contra Donatistas* (*On Baptism, against the Donatists*)
De corr. et gr.	Augustine, *De correptione et gratia* (*On Rebuke and Grace*)
De div. quaest.	Augustine, *De diversis quaestionibus* (*Responses to Various Questions*)
De don. pers.	Augustine, *De dono perseverantiae* (*The Gift of Perseverance*)
De gr.	Faustus, *De gratia* (*On Grace*)
De gr. et lib. arb.	Augustine, *De gratia et libero arbitrio* (*On Grace and Free Will*)
De gr. Chr.	Augustine, *De gratia Christi* (*On the Grace of Christ*)
De gub. Dei	Salvian, *De gubernatione Dei* (*On the Government of God*)
De nat. et gr.	Augustine, *De natura et gratia* (*On Nature and Grace*)
De orat.	Evagrius, *De oratione* (*On Prayer*)
De orat.	Origen, *De oratione* (*On Prayer*)
De praed. sanct.	Augustine, *De praedestinatione sanctorum* (*The Predestination of the Saints*)
De spir. et litt.	Augustine, *De spiritu et littera* (*The Spirit and the Letter*)
De princ.	Origen, *De principiis* (*On First Principles*)
De ver.	Fulgentius, *De veritate praedestinationis et gratiae Dei* (*On the Truth of Predestination and the Grace of God*)
De voc.	Prosper, *De vocatione omnium* (*The Call of All Nations*)
Dial.	Sulpicius Severus, *Dialogi* (*Dialogues*)
Ep.	*Epistola* (*Letter*)
Ep. ad Ruf.	Prosper, *Epistola ad Rufinum* (*Letter to Rufinus*)
Exp. ep. ad Rom. inch.	Augustine, *Epistolae ad Romanos inchoata expositio* (*Unfinished Exposition of the Epistle to the Romans*)

GCS   *Die griechischen christlichen Schriftsteller*
Inst.   Cassian, *De coenobiorum institutis* (*Institutes of the Cenobia*)
Inst.   Cassiodorus, *Institutiones* (*Institutes*)
Prop. ad Rom.   Augustine, *Expositio quarundam propositionum*
         ex epistula ad Romanos (*Exposition of Certain Propositions*
         from the Epistle to the Romans)
Resp. Gall.   Prosper, *Pro Augustino responsiones*
         ad capitula objectionum Gallorum calumniantium
         (*Response to the Objections of the Gauls*)
Resp. Gen.   Prosper, *Pro Augustino responsiones ad excerpta*
         Genuensium (*Response to the Extracts of the Genoese*)
Resp. Vinc.   Prosper, *Pro Augustino responsiones ad capitula*
         objectionum Gallorum calumniantium
         (*Response to the Vincentian Articles*)
Retr.   Augustine, *Retractationes* (*Reconsiderations*)
Serm.   Caesarius, *Sermones* (*Sermons*)
VCaes.   *Sancti Caesarii Arelatensis Vita*
         (*Life of St. Caesarius of Arles*)
VMart.   Sulpicius Severus, *Vita Martini* (*Life of St. Martin*)

Chapter 1

North Africa:
An Amicable Disagreement

Introduction

About 426, in a monastery at Hadrumetum (now Sousse, Tunisia) in North Africa, a seemingly innocuous disagreement arose among several of the monks. The occasion for the disagreement was the anti-Pelagian teaching on grace of the North African bishop Augustine. Augustine's insistence that human salvation is the gift of an utterly unmerited grace appeared to call into question the significance of human striving. Augustine's teaching had been designed to safeguard the operation of grace, but some of the monks at Hadrumetum perceived it as a challenge to the connection between human works performed over a lifetime and divine reward or punishment received in eternity.

Although the focus of disagreement among the monks at Hadrumetum was the nature of the operation of grace, by implication these monks were also questioning the relationship between a person's actions in this life and the outcome of those actions in eternity. The difficulty of this relationship quickly became apparent: to the extent that the intervention of divine grace, apart from merit, determines a person's ultimate destiny, the character of a person's actions does not affect that determination. Furthermore, to the extent that grace shapes a person's actions, it is not human agency but the divine operation upon human agency that determines the person's destiny.

The problem was a crucial one for these monks. Their monastic ideal rested on the notion that, by one's own agency, although not without grace, one can so shape one's life according to the monastic discipline as ultimately to attain to God. The questioning, therefore, of the relationship between actions and their outcome, between the pattern of one's life and one's ultimate destiny, was a challenge to the entire monastic undertaking.

I propose in this study to examine that dispute, usually but unsatisfactorily labeled the Semi-Pelagian controversy. It had its beginnings at Hadrumetum, later spread to southern Gaul, attracted the attention and involvement of the Roman see, and finally reached a somewhat uncertain resolution at the Council of Orange in 529. A particular question will govern the inquiry into the controversy: In what way did the participants view the connection between a person's actions and the outcome of these actions?[1] The pursuit of this question, however, entails the examination of two secondary issues that affected the outworking of the controversy and its final resolution: the character of the monastic life and the related issue of authority.

Basic to the monastic undertaking was a particular understanding of how human effort and divine grace are related. The monks believed the goal of life is union with the divine and that in order to achieve such a union, one's life must be shaped to conform with deity. Accordingly, the advantage of monasticism was that it provided a social context appropriate to the formation of the human person in perfection. That context was a community in which individual striving was regulated according to a discipline. The aim of such a discipline was the development of love for God. A basic assumption, of course, was that human beings, assisted by grace, can in fact live such a life and perhaps achieve such a goal.

A fundamental challenge to the entire monastic undertaking arose, therefore, when several monks began to question, in effect, whether there is any connection between actions and ultimate destiny. The source of this challenge was the teaching of Augustine which presented a very different account from that provided by monasticism of the means by which persons attain salvation or restoration to God. According to the bishop of Hippo, such restoration rests on God's grace, given freely and without regard to human merit, rather than on the pattern of the person's life or the character of the person's actions. One effect of this view is the severance of the linkage between a person's actions and that person's ultimate destiny, since restoration depends entirely on God's grace and not at all on human moral achievement.

Yet not only would the actions of the monks have seemed unrelated to their eternal destinies, but also the very reality of these actions would have appeared dubious, for Augustine's teaching on the sovereignty of grace challenged the genuinely human character of various kinds of behavior. The effect of such actions as prayer, exhortation, and rebuke, that is, behavior that has to do with the interaction between human persons and God or among human beings themselves, is controlled from outside the human sphere. What determines the result of such interactions is not the interaction itself but some prior decision of God; thus prayer, rebuke, and exhortation are effective only when they originate in God and not in the human agent, for the genuineness of these actions depends on the divine influence.

---

[1]It should be noted that the language employed here differs from the actual language used by the participants. The intent is to provide a perspective for interpreting the disagreement.

Augustine's teaching called into question the monastic way of life, for as just described, it presupposed a theological complex involving human freedom and divine judgment. Freedom serves as a guarantee that human beings determine their own actions and that they are morally responsible, that is, able to choose either good or evil. Divine judgment guarantees that God is just, rewarding or punishing according to the actual character of human actions and not according to totally unknowable standards. Moreover, it guarantees that human choices make a real difference: They do affect persons' destinies. The Augustinian doctrine of grace called into question this complex of human freedom and divine judgment with regard to both of its elements. The emphasis on the gratuity of grace suggested, first, that the gift of salvation is not correlated with human action; thus no freedom is required. Second, it suggested that this gift is not given according to any relevant moral difference among persons; thus both human agency and divine justice are jeopardized.

The scheme of human freedom and divine justice proved to be a recurrent theme throughout the course of the controversy. Actually, the existence of this scheme far predated the controversy. It had been present in the Christian tradition from at least the second century.[2] In one form or another it was part of the authoritative heritage of all the disputants and had to be dealt with accordingly. To deny it or at least to denigrate its significance, as Augustine and his followers were thought to be doing, was to cast doubt on one's adherence to the tradition. All parties, therefore, included the complex in their exposition of the interaction of divine grace and human effort, although the weight of emphasis tended to vary according to whether it was their intent to underscore the significance of grace or of human responsibility.

Accordingly, a second factor to be considered, along with the nature of the monastic undertaking, is the matter of authority. Of specific importance are the authority of the tradition and of Scripture, as interpreted by the tradition, as well as the authority of particular individuals or councils that were understood to have made a crucial contribution to the shaping of the tradition. Of course, the tradition of the church was hardly monolithic. This situation was particularly true with regard to the question of the interaction of divine and human efforts in the accomplishment of salvation. The crucial issue here is to discover the ways in which the various disputants in the debate made use of particular passages of Scripture and specific teachings of recognized fathers and councils of the church in order to reshape the tradition to support their own argument. Significantly, over the course of a century, the list of authorities would undergo transformation,

---

[2]An example would be Irenaeus's *Adv. haer.* 4.37; 4.4.3; 4.15.2. This early church background will be discussed below, 78-88.

particularly as changes in the geographical location of the dispute would affect the prestige granted to various figures.

Ironically, this challenge to the monastic scheme of divine grace, human effort, final judgment, and reward arose from the writings of one of the authoritative teachers of the church. It was not pagan teachings of fatalism or of an utterly random universe but Augustine's teaching on the sovereignty of grace that called into question the very logic of the monk's life.

The works of Augustine that are pertinent to this controversy show the final development of his thinking on the role of grace. At the conclusion of the Pelagian debate, Augustine had written a letter to Sixtus, who was later to become Pope Sixtus III. In this letter the bishop of Hippo had stressed his views regarding human nature and divine grace. He had insisted that the human condition as fallen in Adam is incapable of attaining merit on its own. Furthermore, he had argued that grace is utterly gratuitous; it is given totally apart from any human deserving to those whom it chooses. Somewhat in contrast to his position in this letter is the argument that he made in the *De gratia et libero arbitrio*. In this treatise, the first of two that he sent to the monks of Hadrumetum, Augustine tried to maintain the reality of the human free will, and he insisted that divine reward is given to human merit. He did argue, however, that the operation of the human free will and of the divine reward were both to be understood in the context of the overriding operation of grace. In the second treatise, *De correptione et gratia*, the incapacity of the human condition and its utter dependence on grace for salvation once again came to the fore, as in the letter to Sixtus.

The purpose of this chapter will be to explore the course of this debate sparked by the monks of Hadrumetum, a debate in which all the issues surveyed above began to emerge, only to develop in significance and evolve in shape as the controversy spread to southern Gaul and then continued in its course for more than a century.

Epistula ad Sixtum

What was finally to become a bitter theological controversy began more in the spirit of inquiry than of acrimony. In 427 a monk named Florus, who was from the monastery at Hadrumetum, was visiting the library of Evodius, bishop of Uzalis, a longtime friend and colleague of Augustine. Here Florus found a copy of Augustine's letter to the priest Sixtus.[3]

---

[3]*Ep.* 194; see Peter Brown, *Augustine of Hippo* (Berkeley: University of California Press, 1967) 399; B. R. Rees, *Pelagius: A Reluctant Heretic* (Suffolk: Boydell Press, 1988) 101-103.

In this letter, which had been written in 418 and marked the conclusion of the Pelagian controversy, Augustine had presented his argument against the Pelagians with great force. The issue for him was the utterly gratuitous character of grace. Any connection between the divine conferral of grace and human distinctions in merit would have the effect of making the former dependent on the latter. Grace would be a reward. Such an arrangement was totally unacceptable to Augustine. Instead, he argued that God had created human nature as good; yet in Adam all participated in sin and, as a result, deserve damnation.[4] The grace of God, however, rescues some from their just deserts and bestows on them eternal life. In describing the character of this bestowal, Augustine ruled out all possibilities that might diminish its utterly gratuitous nature: Any suggestion of fate, fortune, or especially merit he excluded.[5] He argued that the reason why the grace necessary for salvation is given to some and not to others remains hidden in the divine wisdom. The effect is that there is no correlation between God's generosity and any pattern of human life. In fact, the relation of grace to meritorious life became the focus of Augustine's argument.

He insisted that God is in no way unjust toward those who are allowed to be damned for their sin in Adam, as well as for any other sins that they have accumulated as individuals in their lifetime. Their hearts are hardened not by any divine activity but simply by divine inactivity, that is, by God's not being merciful to them. In contrast, without regard to human differences but on the basis of an inscrutable decision, God chooses to be merciful to others.[6] On these latter, God freely confers grace so that they might have faith and in faith pray, in faith be drawn to Christ, and in faith perform good works. The sole basis for faith and its outworking is grace. No room remains for merit antecedent to the divine mercy.[7] Augustine did not wish to exclude all merit, however, for he insisted that eternal life is the reward for the faithful life of the believer. Nevertheless, as this faithful life is the result of God's gracious indwelling, its achievement consists of grace rewarding grace.[8]

It was this declaration of the sovereignty of grace, written in opposition to any Pelagian views to the contrary, that Florus found and sent to his fellow monks at Hadrumetum. There the letter, composed almost a decade earlier,

---

[4]Augustine, *Ep.* 194.4,5,23,27,29,30. All English translation of quotations from the correspondence of Augustine will be taken from *Saint Augustine: Letters*, vols. 4 and 5, trans. Sister Wilfrid Parsons, The Fathers of the Church 30, 32 (Washington DC: Catholic University of America Press, 1955, 1956).

[5]*Ep.* 194.5,6.

[6]*Ep.* 194.12,22,27.

[7]*Ep.* 194.9,10,12,16,18.

[8]*Ep.* 194.18,19,21.

aroused considerable dismay and even triggered a new problem distinct from the Pelagian controversy.[9] Actually the Pelagian position bore considerable resemblance, at least on first glance, to the monastic understanding of the Christian life. Pelagius himself was a serious ascetic Christian dissatisfied with the laxity of the church in Rome and seeking to cleanse and renew it. His intent was that all its members should live under the disciplines of Christian perfection as an elite who, in their striving for obedience, were cut off from the corruption and entanglements of the world.[10] Human responsibility was thus emphasized and excuses eliminated. Despite the initial similarity to the teachings of Christian monasticism, there were important differences. Pelagius stressed human responsibility much more to the denigration of grace than, apparently, did the North African monks. The latter also insisted upon divine aid in a much more immediate fashion than did Pelagius.

It may be said, of course, that Augustine, with his pastoral concern as bishop for the realities of the lives of his laity, was actually battling Pelagius for an inclusive church cognizant of ordinary Christian life.[11] Furthermore, it may be said that Augustine as a monk and as the founder and overseer of his own monastic community at the cathedral at Hippo Regius was certainly mindful of the goals and requirements of monastic life. Yet despite this dual sensitivity Augustine may still have been an inadequate spokesman for either laity or monks.

---

[9]This letter, which had been written nine years earlier was apparently the first news that these African monks had had of a bitter controversy that had racked the western church, particularly in Africa and Italy, and had caused turmoil in the East. The entire affair had lasted from around 411 until the official condemnation of the Pelagians by Pope Zosimus in 418. See Mary Alphonsine Lesousky, *The De Dono Perseverantiae of Saint Augustine* (Washington DC: Catholic University of America Press, 1956) 2.

This delay in awareness indicates the apparent isolation of the monastic community even from the ecclesiastical world. Burning doctrinal issues might remain largely unmarked by the monks. As greatly as Augustine was revered in the African church and even among the monks at Hadrumetum themselves, his anti-Pelagian treatises were missing from the library of this monastery, as were the decisions of the African councils of 411, 416, 418 that pertained to the Pelagian controversy. Brown, *Augustine of Hippo*, 399. See *Ep.* 215.2.

Such isolation is perhaps revelatory of the patterns of communication that existed in the ancient world. News traveled slowly and erratically, depending upon networks of personal association and personal correspondence, and did not easily or quickly reach those who were outside such networks. The isolation might also indicate that monastic life and its institutions were not yet fully woven into the texture of North African ecclesiastical polity but were a new phenomenon still on the fringes of that church.

[10]Peter Brown, "Pelagius and His Supporters: Aims and Environment," *Religion and Society in the Age of Saint Augustine* (London: Faber and Faber, 1972) 194.

[11]Brown, "Pelagius and His Supporters," 203-205.

With regard to the laity, it seems clear that Augustine, because of his overwhelming conviction of human incapacity that has resulted from the fall of Adam, had far more tolerance for the weakness of his fellow Christians than did Pelagius. His position was an attempt to be both realistic about the possibilities for Christian life among the vast majority of church members and patient with their slow, stumbling growth in grace. Any sort of Christian elitism was made impossible by the recognition of a person's utter incapacity for the good apart from grace. Nevertheless, as his remedy to human depravity was a divine sovereignty that seemed to call into question all human agency, the Augustinian position was never to be completely accepted in the church. In other words, the bishop of Hippo may have been an adequate spokesman for the average believer in his insistence on an inclusive church militant but hardly in his equal insistence on an exclusive church triumphant. The criterion for membership in the latter was, of course, hidden in God.[12]

With regard to the monks, Augustine the priest and bishop was a man who gradually came to abandon the optimism of his own early days as a Christian.[13] That initial period following his conversion, spent first in Cassiciacum and, following his baptism, in Thagaste, had been a time of withdrawal and contemplation. His responsibilities toward others had been limited to leading a small community of friends and family, all of like mind, in their growing understanding of the Christian life. In such favorable circumstances, buoyed by the enthusiasm of recent conversion and influenced by the study of Neoplatonism, he had optimistically envisioned the development of the Christian life as a matter of straightforward progress.

Even while he was still at Thagaste, however, his study of Paul led him to call into question the ability of the individual to overcome ingrained habits and dispositions in order to effect personal change for the better.[14] After his ordination at Hippo Regius an even more intensive study of Paul, especially of Romans (chaps. 7–9), led him to the conviction that the transition from simply recognizing the good to actually willing the good does not lie within human power. Recognition comes by means of the law, but the good will can only be the gift of grace. Ensnared in its own evil habits and motivations, the self lacks the

---

[12]The terms "church militant" and "church triumphant," although anachronistic, are appropriate to this context because of the imagery evoked of the church on earth struggling for the victory that the church in eternal beatitude enjoys.

[13]See Brown, *Augustine of Hippo*, 146-57, for the classic account of this change in his attitude.

[14]In *De musica* 6.5.14 and 6.11.33 Augustine displayed his struggles with Romans 7:22-25; see William S. Babcock, "Augustine's Interpretation of Romans (A.D. 394–396)," *Augustinian Studies* 10 (1979): 58; J. Patout Burns, "The Interpretation of Romans in the Pelagian Controversy," *Augustinian Studies* 10 (1979): 43-54.

capacity to pursue that which it knows to be good. Grace alone can effect the transition from knowing to willing and doing.[15] Victory thus always belongs to God and not to human striving. There can be no occasion for Christian elitism.[16] Moreover, the experiences and responsibilities attendant upon his ordination and subsequent elevation to the episcopacy further eroded Augustine's prior confidence. Reflection upon his own incapacity and the incapacity of the very ordinary Christians entrusted to his care called into question any ideal of unimpeded progress. The complexity of his Christian experience, a life in which secular and ecclesiastical worlds inevitably mingled and in which study and meditation combined with vigorous pastoral activity, led him to insights and conclusions quite alien to those of the members of a secluded monastery.

It was those conclusions of the aging bishop, conclusions on grace found in the letter to Sixtus and still to be fully developed, that so disturbed the monks at Hadrumetum. The assumptions on which their very existence was based had been challenged. In brief, Augustine's insistence on grace as undercutting any pretensions to merit called into question the monks' striving to grow into perfection, to achieve union with God. The monks, with their highly intentional, disciplined lives, perceived that if the process of a person's salvation, from beginning to fulfillment, is entirely and solely dependent on grace, and if the rationale of that grace is finally inscrutable, then all grounds for striving to live in conformity to God, for striving to order oneself and one's love to God, appear to be undercut.[17]

Clearly, Augustine's anti-Pelagian views on grace created consternation at Hadrumetum. What is not clear is the way that the monks first construed the problem. The reason for our lack of clarity is twofold. First, what we have available to us are not the questions posed by the monks themselves but the responses of others whose advice was sought. Second, in contrast to the fully developed monastic theology of South Gaul, evident, for example, in the works

---

[15]For a careful study of this development in Augustine's thought, see Babcock, "Augustine's Interpretation of Romans," 55-61.

[16]William S. Babcock, "Augustine and Tyconius: A Study in the Later Appropriation of Paul," *Studia Patristica* 18 (Oxford: Pergamon Press, 1982): 1209-12. See Robert A. Markus, *The End of Ancient Christianity* (Cambridge: Cambridge University Press, 1990) 67-83. Markus has provided a very helpful examination of the distinction between the traditional monastic goal of individual perfection through ascetic discipline and the Augustinian idea of community for both monastery and congregation. Augustine did not allow for the possibility of a spiritual elite. George Lawless, *Augustine of Hippo and His Monastic Rule* (Oxford: Clarendon Press, 1991, repr. 1991) 160-61, pointed to the provision for a "method" or "school" in Gallic monasticism that was absent from Augustine's monastic ideal. See Adolar Zumkeller, *Augustine's Ideal of the Religious Life*, trans. Edmund Colledge (New York: Fordham University Press, 1986) 103-44.

[17]*Ep.* 214.1,2; 215.1,7,8.

of John Cassian, the monastic theology of North Africa is either no longer accessible to us or, more likely, was never explicitly developed.[18] As a result, the questions that arose at Hadrumetum are not directly available. It is evident, however, that the problem was not simply a continuation of the Pelagian controversy, for the monks at Hadrumetum were not so much attempting to controvert Augustine's views on grace as to understand the implications of these views for the monastic life.

The actual course of events is available to us, at least in outline. Florus, upon finding the letter of Augustine to Sixtus, sent a copy of it to Hadrumetum by another monk Felix, while Florus went on to Carthage.[19] Upon his return to Hadrumetum Florus informed the abbot Valentinus that considerable disagreement had arisen among the monks with regard to the letter. The abbot himself was unaware of the disturbance, for neither had Felix shown the book to him nor had the argument that had arisen among the monks been reported.[20] Valentinus expressed no doubts as to Augustine's authorship of the letter and even approved its contents, although some of his monks raised challenges on both counts.[21]

Convinced that the problem was that inexperienced monks were misunderstanding Augustine's teaching, Valentinus sought assistance from Evodius of Uzalis in the interpretation of the letter.[22] Evodius's response was hardly helpful. He briefly stated his understanding that Adam has a free will which, because of his misuse of it, had suffered severe debilitation. The affliction affected not only the first man but all his offspring as well. Christ has been sent as a doctor to cure corruption, and his aid is necessary for the will to be restored to its pristine state. For the bulk of the letter, however, Evodius insisted that all things that happen come about by the judgment of God, which is hidden but never unjust.

---

[18]Georges Folliet, "Aux origines de l'ascétisme et du cénobitisme africain," *Saint Martin et son temps* (Rome: Herder, 1961) 25-44.

[19]*Ep.* 216.2. See also Jean Chéné, Introduction, *Aux moines d'Adrumète et de Provence*, Oeuvres de Saint Augustin 24 (Desclée de Brouwer, 1962) 41-45; and Lesousky, 4-5.

[20]*Ep.* 216.2-3.

[21]*Ep.* 216.1.

[22]*Ep.* 216.3. Valentinus mentioned that he had also sought the guidance of a priest named Sabinus. The identity of Sabinus and his written response, if there was one, have been lost to us. Valentinus simply said that Sabinus read the book with "clear explanations. But not even thus was their wounded soul healed." See Lesousky, 6, n. 23. For the relationship of Evodius to Augustine, see D. G. Morin, "Lettre inédite de l'évêque Evodius aux moines d'Adrumète sur la question de la grace," *Revue Bénédictine* 13 (1896): 481. For Morin's final version of the letter, see D. G. Morin, "Lettres inédites de S. Augustin et du prêtre Januarien dans l'affaire des moines d'Adrumète," *Revue Bénédictine* 18 (1901): 253-56.

One should pray for understanding, should not raise contentious questions, and should piously study the works of the teachers and councils of the church.[23]

At some time during this disturbance Valentinus also sought the advice of a neighboring priest, Januarius.[24] The letter that Januarius wrote in reply was notable for at least two related reasons. First, it indicated that he had adopted without exception the views of Augustine on human capacity and divine grace.[25] Second, his attitude showed remarkable correspondence to that of Evodius with regard to teachings of the church which as yet exceeded the grasp of a Christian's understanding. Both aspects of the letter provide us with a glimpse of the character of the African church.

Concerning Januarius's agreement with Augustine, the letter indicated that its author had studied, understood, and accepted his fellow North African's position in the Pelagian controversy. The similarity of his letter to the one that Augustine had written to Sixtus was considerable. Januarius insisted that in Adam all deserve the punishment of damnation, and from that "damned mass" not one is separated except through the grace of the redeemer, for after the first sin free will is adequate only for further sin. Human nature, marred by original sin, is restored only by grace at the election of God. The divine activity in election is both just and merciful. Those not elected receive the punishment due to them because of their sin, and the elect receive salvation through the mercy of God and not by any merit of their own. Good works, at their beginning and completion, are the gift of God. The penitence by which one is converted, the faith in which one who is justified lives, the capacity of the person to be ruled by God, and thus the good fruits of the Christian's life are all the gift of grace.[26]

---

[23]*Epistula Evodii Episcopi ad Abbatem Valentinum Adrumetinum*, Oeuvres de Saint Augustin 24:46-53.

[24]The date of this letter is unclear. That Valentinus did not mention in his letter to Augustine (*Ep.* 216) that he had sought guidance from even a third source is, as Chéné pointed out, an argument for dating the letter of Januarius after that of Valentinus to Augustine and thus also after Augustine's treatise *De gratia et libero arbitrio*. Chéné also noted that an argument for an earlier date would be that the letter appears to have been written while the dissension at Hadrumetum was still full-blown, whereas the reception of Augustine's first treatise seems to have eased the tension at the monastery (Chéné, 214). For the latter reason I have chosen to include the letter at this point in the discussion, although, like Lesousky, 6-7n.23, I have no suggestion as to why Valentinus did not mention the correspondence in his letter to Augustine. For Morin's comments on the letter as well as his publication of the text itself, see D. G. Morin, "Lettres inédites de S. Augustin et du prêtre Januarien dans l'affaire des moines d'Adrumète," *Revue Bénédictine* 18 (1901): 241-53.

[25]See Chéné, 213.

[26]*Incipit Epistula Sancti Ianuariani*, Oeuvres de Saint Augustin 24:228-45. Januarius confronted the difficulty that 1 Timothy 2:4 poses. This passage, stating that God "desires all men to be saved and to come to the knowledge of the truth," will be cited repeatedly

Januarius's close adherence to Augustine's teaching was consistent with his conviction as to the appropriate response to difficult doctrines of the church. Like Evodius, he argued for humble acceptance of that which one cannot yet grasp. Understanding comes by belief in Scripture and by humble obedience that enables belief rather than by reason and disputation. It is the gift of God to one who accepts the writings of the fathers and doctors of the church and engages in patient and trustful study.[27]

Januarius was obviously a careful student of Augustine's anti-Pelagian writings and an understanding recipient and propagator of his intellectual mentor's teaching on grace. What his letter may have contributed toward settling the confusion at Hadrumetum is not known. Yet, as already indicated, his deferential attitude both to Augustine and to the tradition of the church provides us with two significant clues as to the character of the North African church,[28] as do the somewhat similar attitudes of Evodius and Valentinus.

First, there was an obvious deference expressed toward Augustine. The submission of his fellow North African churchmen to his teaching appears especially striking when one realizes that it was not simply Januarius, an obscure priest, and Valentinus, the abbot of a humble monastery, but also Evodius, a bishop, a long-time friend and colleague, who deferred to this man. Their behavior is not entirely surprising, however.

---

throughout the course of the controversy. As presumably clear testimony to the divine will for universal salvation, the verses were employed as a challenge to the Augustinian view of limited election. Januarius's response is important for indicating the direction of defense that would be consistently taken against this universalistic view.

In line with Augustine he gave examples in which Paul, presumed by everyone throughout this debate to have been the author of 1 Timothy, uses the pronoun "all" at times literally and at times in a less inclusive sense. For example, Januarius appealed to 1 Corinthians 15:21-22 in which Paul said both that "in Adam all die," this "all" being literal, and "in Christ shall all be made alive," this "all" referring only to all who will be saved by grace. From these variations in usage Januarius argued that the latter interpretation is the appropriate reading of the troublesome verse (Chéné, 236-39).

This argument of Januarius that Paul used "all" in different ways at different times was not farfetched in light of the common rejection of the notion of universal salvation in the church. The problem for Januarius and thus also for Augustine was not that of having to argue against universal salvation as a reality, for no one accepted it as such, but to argue against the notion that God wills universal salvation, a notion that was commonly held in the church.

[27]Chéné, 240-43.

[28]Morin stated that this letter allows us to see the extent to which Augustine's teaching on predestination and grace had met a friendly reception in the African Church. See Morin, "Lettres inédites de S. Augustin et du prêtre Januarien dans l'affaire des moines d'Adrumète," 245.

When the disturbance arose at Hadrumetum, Augustine was already in his seventies. For more than forty years he had served as the bishop of Hippo Regius, a port city second only to Carthage in its prestige among African cities. As the author of such treasures as the *Confessiones*, the *De trinitate*, and the *De civitate Dei*, and as the undisputed leader of the Catholics in their victories against both the Donatists and the Pelagians, Augustine was the recognized champion and definer of orthodoxy in Christian North Africa. For a North African churchman to have disputed Augustine at this late date would have been a betrayal of his regional and ecclesiastical loyalties, at least figuratively an act of treason as well as of heresy. By almost any standards the man was a giant, but in a narrow world with all serious challengers long since overcome, the giant's strength was intensified. Such was the position of Augustine near the close of his life.[29]

Yet to acknowledge his formidable stature is not to suggest that his teachings were necessarily accepted without reservation in the African church. About the same time that the dispute arose at Hadrumetum, Augustine wrote a letter to a churchman in Carthage named Vitalis who did not entirely accept the bishop's anti-Pelagian views on grace.[30] Our little information about Vitalis comes solely from Augustine's letter, and even the occasion for that letter is not totally clear. Augustine's familiarity with the Carthaginian's position suggests that Vitalis himself may have initiated the correspondence with a letter outlining his own views. In contrast to the Pelagians, the Carthaginian acknowledged that the faithful life of a Christian is the work of grace; however, he insisted that faith itself is not of grace but of the free will. The beginning of faith is a matter of human decision rather than of divine preparation. Augustine vehemently rejected the argument, for if human initiative precedes grace, then grace is no longer gratuitous but a reward given to merit.[31] Significantly, this insistence that the origin of faith lies in human agency was the very issue that would become the crux of the controversy in southern Gaul. We hear no more of Vitalis. Whether or not he was convinced by Augustine's letter, there is no evidence that he attempted to arouse or organize any opposition. To the contrary, the fact that the two men were in communication indicates the existence of some measure of trust or good will.

Yet whatever the case with Vitalis, the apparently unquestioning acquiescence of so many others to Augustine's position helps to explain why what came to be called the Semi-Pelagian controversy began more in the spirit of inquiry

---

[29]It is noteworthy that the chief controversies of Augustine's last years were with non-Africans: Julian of Eclanum of Italy and the Semi-Pelagians in Gaul. The disturbance at Hadrumetum hardly ranked as a controversy.

[30]*Ep.* 217; Lesousky, 3, 10, 55-56.

[31]*Ep.* 217.1,29.

than of acrimony. In its earliest stage, i.e., at least so long as the dispute remained localized in Africa, it had every appearance of being an amicable disagreement, a courteous attempt to reach an understanding of the teaching of
Augustine and thus of the church in North Africa.

A second indicator of the character of the North African church was the
deference that Januarius expressed toward tradition. The attitude that he, like
Evodius, revealed was that what has been settled is settled, and what has not
been settled is to be reverentially left alone. Such deference toward tradition was
to continue throughout the controversy. The problem, however, would be the
identification of what actually had been settled and of the particular tradition by
which it had been settled. Because of the lack of clarity on these points, there did
exist considerable room for disagreement, with all participants not so reverential
as were these Africans on matters that had not yet been resolved.

Significantly, it was Augustine himself who furnished a refreshing contrast
to the humble, unquestioning submission that others, such as Evodius and
Januarius, had encouraged. The abbot Valentinus, after he had exhausted other
avenues for a satisfactory resolution of the confusion, allowed two of his monks,
Cresconius and Felix, to travel to Hippo Regius to receive guidance from the
bishop himself as to the implications for the monastic life of the letter to Sixtus.
Valentinus, however, did not send an accompanying letter to Augustine.[32] Such
an action, he feared, might convey the impression that he was sympathetic to the
controversialists.[33]

Unlike Evodius and Januarius, Augustine encouraged discussion of the issue
which he frankly acknowledged to be "so very difficult and intelligible to few."[34]
From Cresconius and Felix he received a description of the two opposing
positions that were being taken at Hadrumetum, and he responded with a letter
to Valentinus in which he indicated that his desire to send more explanatory
materials concerning the Pelagian controversy had been frustrated by the
eagerness of the two monks to return to Hadrumetum in time for Easter.[35]
Augustine requested that the one who was being accused of being the source of
turmoil, presumably Florus, might be sent to him, for Augustine thought that
either the man misunderstood the letter to Sixtus or was himself being
misunderstood by those to whom he was attempting to explain it.[36]

It is only now in this letter from Augustine to Valentinus that we are
provided with an account of the issues involved in the controversy. According

---

[32]*Ep.* 214.1,5.
[33]*Ep.* 216.1.
[34]*Ep.* 214.6
[35]*Ep.* 214.5
[36]*Ep.* 214.6.

to his interpretation of the events, the disputants were divided rather neatly. Some understood grace and free will as contradictory, so that in their espousal of grace they denied free will. As a corollary, they also denied that each will be judged by God on the basis of works. Others, in contrast, saw grace and free will as complementary, so that the latter is assisted by the former toward good. As a corollary, they affirmed a final judgment according to works in which those works performed by a free will assisted by grace will be counted as good. Augustine took his stand with the second group.[37] He thereby affirmed the necessary, complex complementarity of grace and free will as well as the significance of works within the context of final judgment and divine justice.[38]

Before Cresconius and Felix were able to return to Valentinus with this letter, another Felix joined them at Hippo, and together the three of them spent Easter with Augustine, who had detained them for further instruction.[39] During this time Augustine wrote a second letter[40] to be carried to Valentinus along with the first. The presentation of the issues in this second letter indicated that the controversy was by no means so clear-cut as the first letter had suggested. The account of the third monk had provided a more complex description of the situation.

In the second letter Augustine warned against the error of the "new Pelagian heretics," i.e., against the error that grace is a reward for merit. The pejorative reference to his questioners not only gave definition to their position but also labeled it as automatically unacceptable. Augustine also warned against the contrary error that judgment is not given according to works.[41] When both of these letters are considered together, it seems clear that Augustine perceived three errors: relying on free will so that the necessity of grace is denied; relying on grace in such a way that the effects of free will for good are denied; relying on grace in such a way that the responsibility for evils resulting from free will is denied. In rejecting these errors, Augustine was arguing in favor of three concepts found together in a difficult tension: the necessity and priority of grace, the freedom of the human will, and a divine judgment that is righteous.

---

[37]*Ep.* 214.1

[38]Although Augustine has presented his perception of the issues that had arisen at Hadrumetum, it is to be noted that we know little about monasticism in North Africa or about what theology, if any, was associated with it. In contrast, Cassian's case, which will be presented in chapter 3, allows us to see a fully developed monastic theology.

[39]*Ep.* 215.1 From the letter from Valentinus (*Ep.* 216.2) it becomes apparent that it was this second Felix who had carried the letter copied by Florus from Uzalis to Hadrumetum and had now arrived in Hippo somewhat later than his two fellow monks. Lesousky, 7n.25, argued that it was at the arrival of this second Felix that Augustine realized the monks' need for further instructions; thus he detained them.

[40]*Ep.* 215.

[41]*Ep.* 215.1.

In this second letter to Valentinus Augustine revealed his considerable concern for the monks at Hadrumetum. He was keenly sympathetic to this community, which was so deeply troubled by the complexity of questions that had arisen that three of its number had journeyed to Hippo for understanding. Besides the two letters, Augustine was also sending a treatise written explicitly in response to the situation at Hadrumetum, i.e., the *De gratia et libero arbitrio*. He informed Valentinus that he was sending both that treatise and various other documents as well. The preponderance of these additional documents, each presented as an authoritative expression of the church's opposition to Pelagianism, was notably African: letters to Pope Innocent, one from the council of Carthage of 416, a second from the council of Numidia of 416, and a third from five African bishops; the pope's response to the letters; a letter from Augustine to Pope Zosimus, with regard to the African Council, and Zosimus's "answer which was sent to all the bishops of the world"; as well as a later paper prepared by a plenary council from all Africa, against the Pelagian error.[42] Augustine further informed Valentinus that the three monks had read with him all of these documents as well as the *De dominica oratione* of Cyprian, the highly esteemed martyr-bishop of Carthage (d. 258). This treatise Valentinus already possessed. Furthermore, Augustine had explained to the men the letter to Sixtus that had aroused their concern in the first place.[43] This substantiation of his own views by means of documentation from authoritative persons and councils is clear evidence of Augustine's own concern with the matter of authority and tradition.

In the conscientiousness of the bishop of Hippo we catch a glimpse of a dual purpose. First, he was painstaking in his efforts to show that his position was in agreement with that of his fellow Africans and that the African position was in accord with the mind of the whole church. Moreover, he tried to demonstrate that there was nothing novel about this position, as it was in line with that of a revered African father of the third century. In other words, he attempted to wrap the entire weight of the tradition around his views (and it is noteworthy that Cyprian's treatise was presented as the touchstone of that tradition). The success of his attempt would encounter a severe challenge later in southern Gaul.

Second, Augustine was deeply appreciative of the anxiety of the monks and obviously accepted it as his responsibility to see that they had a clear understanding of the position of the church. One implication of his attitude is that Augustine assumed that the disputed teaching, rightly understood, in no way undercut the monastic life. The questionable nature of this assumption would become

---

[42]*Ep.* 215.2. For an account of these councils and documents see Gerald Bonner, *St. Augustine of Hippo* (Philadelphia: Westminster Press, 1963) 339-46.

[43]*Ep.* 215.2,3.

increasingly apparent as the controversy developed, both in Africa and later in Gaul.

An equally important implication is that Augustine apparently felt that belief in a doctrine should be a matter of inquiry and understanding as well as of humble submission to the authority of one's superiors or to the authority of the tradition. At the very beginning of the controversy, therefore, we find two types of reactions, even among bishops, to the notion of the authority of the church's tradition. Evodius has counseled unquestioning acceptance of that within the tradition which is not readily understood, and Augustine has actively encouraged investigation and discussion directed toward understanding. The reason for the difference is not clear, as the two men had similar backgrounds including their years together in a quasi-monastic community at Thagaste.[44] Nevertheless, for better or worse, the participants in the controversy largely followed the course of Evodius in appealing to what they understood to be the true tradition. Whereas Augustine could both appeal to authority and encourage inquiry, the others saw these two possibilities as mutually exclusive.

Consistent with the fearless assurance that understanding would promote agreement, Augustine requested that Florus be sent to him. In that way he could deal effectively with any remaining questions or resistance.

De gratia et libero arbitrio

In his *Retractationes* Augustine stated his reason for writing the *De gratia et libero arbitrio*: "because of those persons who, by thinking that free choice is denied when the grace of God is defended, defend free will in such a manner as to deny the grace of God by affirming that it is bestowed according to our merits."[45] It was in response to this view that Augustine in 426/427 wrote the treatise, which was addressed to Valentinus and the monks of Hadrumetum.[46] Augustine's stance, as might be expected, affirmed the necessity of both grace and free will but with far greater emphasis on grace.

Of the three errors that his letters to Hadrumetum had warned against, he specified only one for correction: reliance on the free will to the denigration of

---

[44]Brown, *Augustine of Hippo*, 132-37.

[45]*Retractationes* 2.92. English translations of quotations from the *Retractationes* will be taken from *Saint Augustine: The Retractations*, trans. Sister Mary Inez Bogan, Fathers of the Church 60 (Washington DC: Catholic University of America Press, 1968).

[46]*Saint Augustin: Anti-Pelagian Writings*, trans. and rev. by Benjamin B. Warfield, Nicene and Post-Nicene Fathers f.s. 5 (repr. Grand Rapids: Wm. B. Eerdmans, 1975) 436n.1. A later date would be impossible since this treatise as well as the *De correptione et gratia* were cited in the *Retractationes* published about 427. An earlier date also seems unlikely as the references to these two treatises are the last items in the *Retractationes*.

grace.[47] He mentioned a second, and it would be the starting point of his argument but not its focus. This second error was the reliance on grace to the denigration of the free will. He did not mention the third at all: the reliance on grace to the denigration of responsibility for evil resulting from the free will. This last error was to become the subject of the De correptione et gratia. Although Augustine had identified three errors in his letters to Valentinus, one of them, the denigration of grace, was of far greater consequence to him than the others.

The treatise began with the assertion of the freedom of the will, and it is important to note that of the four treatises that Augustine wrote in this controversy, this first one has the greatest emphasis on human responsibility. As the logic of his argument developed throughout these four works, the significance of human agency diminished as the emphasis on the divine agency increased. Correspondingly, the importance of the law and of the complex of free will and last judgment were greatest in this treatise. Their significance was to decrease as the role of grace was enhanced. It is also noteworthy that the more fullly Augustine elaborated his position, the less he cited Scripture and the more he cited other authoritative sources as support for that position. Accordingly, in the De gratia et libero arbitrio, the treatise in which he made his strongest assertions of the commonly accepted view of the free will, he manifested the least interest in documenting his argument with references to any authority other than Scripture.[48]

Citations from Scripture, however, occured in abundance, and Augustine may well have believed that little further documentation was needed. The simple fact that the Scriptures enjoin us to do certain kinds of things and to refrain from doing others served for him as evidence that the Scriptures presuppose the existence of a free will in the human agent and thus effective human agency. The biblical commandments and admonitions to the will would be senseless if there were no free will. Indeed, the goodness of a work resides in its having been done "willingly," and for such a good work one may hope for a reward from God.[49] Thus at the very beginning of the treatise Augustine affirmed the notions of free will, good work, and reward, all of which were basic to the monastic ideal of training in those things that are pleasing to God. The connection between actions and their outcome is firm: Human agency does affect human action, and the resulting action does affect the destiny of the human agent. The issue to be

---

[47]For discussion of the three errors which Augustine had perceived among monks of Hadrumetum, see 13-14 above.

[48]It must be remembered, however, that he had just sent Valentinus a number of authoritative documents and had appealed to Cyprian; thus perhaps he felt it unnecessary to duplicate the effort in the treatise itself.

[49]De gr. et lib. arb. 2.4. All English translations of quotations from Augustine's treatises will be taken from Saint Augustin: Anti-Pelagian Writings.

pursued, therefore, is not whether Augustine accepted such notions but the peculiar way in which he understood them in the light of his overriding emphasis on grace. In fact, this starting point may plausibly be construed as a concession to the monks of Hadrumetum. Augustine's intent was to establish a mutually acceptable base from which he could move to his views on grace.

Immediately he began a subtle refashioning of the complex of the free will succeeding in good works at the admonition of the divine commandments. He argued that all persons are responsible for living according to God's law and will be punished for failure to do so whether or not they have knowledge of the law. The punishment will be less severe, however, for those who lacked any opportunity to learn than for those who willed to be ignorant in the mistaken notion that ignorance could provide them with an excuse.[50]

Augustine has affirmed human responsibility; nevertheless, he has disallowed any suggestion of human autonomy. He did maintain that the will is commanded and the individual is held accountable for fulfilling the commandment. He insisted, however, that it is only as the will is assisted by grace that obedience is possible. Self-reliance is unjustified.[51] Here Augustine gave his argument a slight twist: in order for the injunctions of the law to have any meaning, they must presuppose a free will; yet without the assistance of grace, free will is insufficient for the fulfillment of the law. One must, of course, be willing, but the accomplishment of what one wills must be the gift of grace.[52]

So far Augustine had made no significant departure from the views that one might expect in the monastic milieu. The crucial shift occurred when he insisted that it is not enough simply to attribute the accomplishment of the good will to grace; the good will itself is the gift of grace. Augustine thus colored his initially straightforward complex of free will, good work, and reward, for that very turning to God by which one freely wills the good is itself the gift of grace.[53] The lopsidedness of the relationship between grace and free will has begun to emerge. Both the conversion of the will so that it desires the fulfillment of the commandments and the accomplishment of that will are the work of grace. Without grace one neither wills nor, already willing, accomplishes the fulfillment of the law.[54] The law, without this assistance of grace, can serve only to increase one's desire for what is prohibited.[55]

Evidence is thus already emerging that, within the Augustinian scheme, the determination of one's destiny is passing from the human self to divine interven-

---

[50]*De gr. et lib. arb.* 2.5-3.5.
[51]*De gr. et lib. arb.* 4.6-7.
[52]*De gr. et lib. arb.* 4.7.
[53]*De gr. et lib. arb.* 5.10.
[54]*De gr. et lib. arb.* 5.12.
[55]*De gr. et lib. arb.* 4.8.

tion and that the operation of grace is overriding the reality of human agency. As Augustine depicted the process of human obedience, the contribution of the will is not that of being a partner with grace but of being the focus of the operation of grace; it is free for the good only as it is dominated and directed by grace.

The reason for this lopsided situation was Augustine's conviction of the utter gratuity of grace. Not only can grace not be a gift if it is a reward, but, equally important, there can never be any antecedent merit for grace to reward. The human condition is such that grace can in no way be considered the reward of merit: There simply is no merit to reward prior to the will's having been called, converted, and assisted in obedience. In other words, the prior shape of a person's life has no bearing on the matter at all. Otherwise, grace would not be grace. Once such grace has been given, merits do accumulate, but these are always the result of that grace, never the cause of it. Grace is necessary, therefore, not only to justify the unrighteous but also to assist the one who is already justified to continue in the good.[56]

Grace is dominant, and the degree of the domination would intensify with each step of Augustine's argument. The result was to make increasingly tenuous any connection between human actions and their outcome or between the human agent and that agent's own action. The notion that a person under discipline can shape his or her life to God has become questionable. Furthermore, as a consequence of this difficulty, the matter of reward, an issue central to the monks' discussion, has also become problematic. On the one hand, Augustine has argued that grace is necessary for continuance in the good, in the life of obedience to the law, the life of good works. On the other hand, he was careful to affirm the reality of reward; yet he was able to do so only by introducing another crucial twist. For him, as for the monks, necessary evidence of one's justification is the production of good works. Nevertheless, for Augustine, as one is justified by faith and not by works and as this faith is through grace, then good works are themselves grace. They are the outcome of the operation of grace. God will most certainly reward these works with the grace of eternal life.[57] The difficulty of describing eternal life as a reward, however, is that it is a reward only for what has been given by grace and thus not a reward for human merit. It is grace rewarding grace.[58] The human agent and agency remain in sight only as shaped and directed by the divine operation. Augustine, of course, tried to overcome this awkwardness by maintaining that what grace moves is precisely the human agent in the exercise of his or her own agency. The will is not

---

[56]*De gr. et lib. arb.* 6.13.
[57]*De gr. et lib. arb.* 6.15; 7.17; 7.18; 8.19; 8.20.
[58]*De gr. et lib. arb.* 9.21; cf. John 1:16.

compelled but converted. Nevertheless, one cannot will the good unless God moves or converts the will to the good.

If one result of Augustine's argument was that it raised questions about the reality of the will's freedom, the assurance that Augustine offered is that one may look to works as evidence both of justification and of future beatitude. One is not left in the dark; there is a genuine connection between works and reward, action and outcome. It is, however, a connection founded in grace, a grace that effects the works and then rewards what it effects. Augustine has managed to retain the complex of freedom and last judgment. It was the complex underlying the monastic conception of life, a theological scheme that on the surface, at least, excluded fatalism and chance but which, with its Augustinian coloration, raised the question of a determinism of grace.[59]

The intent of Augustine's argument was to maintain the tension between the human will and grace found in such passages as Philippians 2:12-13: "Work out your own salvation with fear and trembling; for God is at work in you, both to will and to work for his good pleasure." The command to work presupposes the will; the instruction regarding attitude is a caution against boasting; the assertion of divine activity provides the reason that boasting is inadmissible.[60]

If the question arose regarding how one is to work out that salvation or where one may find a trustworthy guide for Christian obedience, I think that Augustine would, without hesitation, have offered the law.[61] In fact, it was in Augustine's depiction of the proper attitude toward and use of the law that he discussed the tension between grace and free will. He argued that although the law gives knowledge of what constitutes sin, knowledge by itself is insufficient for avoidance of sin. Unless grace both prepares the will for good and then effects this good will, the person is incapable of keeping the law. The result is that the unassisted will not only fails to obey the law but fails with full

---

[59]William S. Babcock, "Grace, Freedom and Justice: Augustine and the Christian Tradition," *Perkins Journal* 27 (1973): 1-15. This article includes a very helpful discussion of Augustine's movement in the controversy from a scheme of freedom, merit, and divine justice to another scheme in which these three elements remain but are overshadowed by the prior judgment of God made in eternal predestination. The basis of predestination is utterly independent of human merit. I am indebted to Mr. Babcock for the suggestion of such a scheme and its development, and throughout this study I shall note the usage of and variations of this original scheme by Augustine, his followers, and his opponents.

[60]*De gr. et lib. arb.* 9.21. See also my article, "Augustine's Use of Scriptural Admonitions against Boasting in His Final Arguments on Grace," *Studia Patristica* 27 (Louvain: Peeters Press, 1993) 424-30.

[61]For earlier discussions of the law, see *Prop. ad Rom.* 13-18, 45-46; *Ad Simpl.* 1, q. 1; *De spir. et litt.* 6-9, 13-17, 30-34.

awareness of its wrongdoing; thus by granting knowledge but not obedience, the law, apart from grace, may be said to increase sin.[62]

But what constitutes grace, at least in relation to the fulfillment of the law? Augustine was careful to refute what he considered to be characteristically Pelagian errors on this matter: the equation of the law and of nature with salvific grace and the limitation of the efficacy of grace to the forgiveness of sins. Augustine believed that although the law provides persons with the knowledge of what God enjoins and forbids and although nature provides the rationality necessary for understanding, neither law nor nature provides the will with the power necessary to fulfill the law and thereby attain righteousness. The empowerment of the will for the attainment of righteousness has come through Christ to those who have faith.[63] For such persons not only are former sins forgiven but their will is able to overcome present temptations and avoid future sins. Grace may thus be characterized as that gift of God by which one is made righteous through faith in Christ; it "accomplishes the fulfillment of the law, and the liberation of nature, and the removal of the dominion of sin."[64]

The inevitable question, of course, is why God even bothers to command if the fulfillment of the command is a divine gift anyway.[65] Augustine argued that the purpose of the commandments is to serve the person's growth in faith. The commandments show what is to be done; yet obedience is impossible on one's own, since the will is inadequate to the task. By virtue of the faith already provided, a person seeks in prayer that God might enable fulfillment of the commandments through the strengthening of the will for the good.

The good will is that love of the good, that longing for the good, by which one desires with all one's heart that which the law requires. Such desire in its fullness is itself the law's fulfillment. This desire and this longing, however, are entirely the work of grace:[66] First, grace operates externally preparing the will of the person to desire the good; then grace operates internally on that good will, enlarging it and enabling it to effect the good works that it wills. In brief, grace creates the good will, then cooperates with that which it has created.[67]

---

[62]*De gr. et lib. arb.* 10.22–12.24.

[63]*De gr. et lib. arb.* 8.19–9.21.

[64]*De gr. et lib. arb.* 13.26–14.27.

[65]*De gr. et lib. arb.* 15.31.

[66]*De gr. et lib. arb.* 15.31. See *Ad Simpl.* 1 q. 2 for the discussion in which Augustine first developed the idea that the person cannot control or direct his or her own desire.

[67]*De gr. et lib. arb.* 17.33. For an examination of Augustine's doctrine of the operation of grace as being both external and internal, cf. J. Patout Burns, *The Development of Augustine's Doctrine of Operative Grace* (Paris: Études Augustiniennes, 1980) 166, 175, 181, 185-86. Burns has provided a careful examination of the distinction between predestination to grace, by which one is brought to grace, and predestination to glory,

Augustine has asserted that grace is necessary to make the will good and to assist it in doing good works; yet a question still remains. Obviously, all wills are not changed. What, therefore, is the nature of the relationship of God with those wills that are free only for evil?

Augustine's response had several facets. First, the divine will accomplishes its purpose through human agency regardless of whether the human will remains inclined toward evil or, by grace, is turned to good. Thus an utterly righteous God may achieve the divine purpose by initiating the movement of a will that is already inclined toward evil, since unconverted. The evil that is thereby accomplished is justly punished, even though it is the vehicle finally for accomplishing the divine good. For example, in the case of Pharaoh, God may be said to have hardened Pharaoh's heart. Such was God's judgment or punishment for Pharaoh's already evil will. Furthermore, Pharaoh may be said to have hardened his own heart in that by his evil will he hardened himself against God and thereby incurred the divine judgment. Finally, however, the divine purpose was achieved, for through this hardening God's power was manifested.[68]

Second, whatever the basis of the divine decision to choose some for the operation of grace while leaving others to the punishment they deserve, the rationale is based on no human distinction between persons and is therefore hidden in God. From a human standpoint, the divine justice is completely inexplicable.[69] Third, a judgment is affirmed in which the "recompense" for evil may be either justice or mercy; for good, however, it will always be good, for God is never unjust.[70]

---

according to which some Christians, independent of merit, are given a gift of unfailing perseverance. I have made use of this distinction throughout my argument and am indebted to Mr. Burns for his help in this matter.

[68]De gr. et lib. arb. 20.41; 23.45; cf. Ex. 7:3, 10:1. This interpretation of the case of Pharaoh represents a development in the thinking of Augustine. Years earlier, in De diversis quaestionibus 83, he had spoken of God's making a distinction between those who are to be justified and those who are not. As God cannot be unjust, Augustine located the basis for the distinction in a prior worthiness of the former for salvation and a prior worthiness of the latter for destruction. The one group is seen to have acknowledged God and the other not to have so done. The result for this second group is that "God gave them over to a reprobate mind, to do those things which are not convenient" (Rom 1:28). This darentur in reprobum sensum is what Augustine had earlier meant by God's also hardening of Pharaoh's heart (De div. quaest. 68.5). (See also the interpretation of Pharaoh in Prop. ad Rom. and Exp. ep. ad Rom. inch.) His interpretation in De gr. et lib. arb. represents a significant change, one already apparent in Ad Simpl. Any notion of prior worthiness or unworthiness has been lost. There can be no merit of any kind on the basis of which grace chooses some and does not choose others.

[69]De gr. et lib. arb. 20.41; 23.45.

[70]De gr. et lib. arb. 23.45.

The assertion of a last judgment would appear to accord with the monks' notion of judgment. For the monks, however, the concept of divine judgment assumed the complementary notion of the human will as free to choose either good or evil. God judges human agency and human action; good is rewarded and evil is punished. The outcome of one's action results from the action itself.

In contrast, Augustine argued that the freedom to choose the good is the gift of grace. A will so empowered may then do the good in cooperation with grace, although it will not necessarily persevere in the good. Both grace and human willing are necessary for the accomplishment of the good; neither is sufficient alone. The outcome of the judgment remains firmly connected to human action, but if there is to be a good outcome, the human will must have been converted and assisted by grace.

Augustine had succeeded in maintaining, with some qualification, the monastic complex of free will, merit, and last judgment. Grace is necessary for the will to be freed for the good, but the will so freed must be exercised. The grace that has converted the will requires the cooperation of the will for perseverance in the good. According to Augustine's view, one cannot attribute to oneself the beginning of a good will or attainments in the good: not the former because it is entirely the work of grace; not the latter because these depend upon the assistance of grace. Nevertheless, a good outcome of the final judgment remains subject to human cooperation with grace.

De correptione et gratia

Once Valentinus had received the *De gratia et libero arbitrio* and the accompanying materials, he wrote to Augustine describing the course of events from the beginning of the disturbance at the monastery and expressing his gratitude for the assistance that Augustine had sent by the three monks. It appears from Valentinus's letter that the situation at Hadrumetum had improved, although Valentinus willingly complied with Augustine's request that Florus be allowed to travel to Hippo, and he encouraged any further guidance that Augustine might wish to give those monks who were still somewhat bewildered.[71]

Presumably it was through Florus that Augustine learned that a new problem had arisen at the monastery.[72] One of the monks, probably after reading the *De gratia et libero arbitrio*, had refused to accept rebuke, arguing that as perseverance in the good is dependent solely on grace, correction for failure is inappropriate. Correction, he reasoned, should take the form of prayer directed to God

---

[71]*Ep.* 216.1,2,6.
[72]Lesousky, 9n.32. As has already been suggested on 16-17 above, this new problem was actually among those cited in his letter to Valentinus; see 13-14 above.

rather than of rebuke directed to the offender. As God is the relevant agent, it is God who should be addressed rather than the human agent, who, for all practical purposes, is irrelevant. The question that now had to be answered, therefore, was whether in cases of moral or religious failure there is any point in addressing the human agent at all since the human agent simply does not seem to be the relevant agent in the case. It was in response to this new difficulty that Augustine wrote the *De correptione et gratia*.[73]

As in the *De gratia et libero arbitrio*, in which Augustine had insisted on the reality of free will yet had sharply delimited its meaning in relation to the sovereignty of grace, so in the *De correptione et gratia* Augustine argued for the propriety and value of rebuke but subordinated its purpose and efficacy to an even more thorough interpretation of grace than he had offered in the previous treatise. In other words, his intent was to show that there is still reason to address the human agent even though the primary, perhaps exclusive, agent is God. Accordingly, the import of this treatise lies in its explication of the multifaceted character of grace, for it is only in the context of the work of grace that the function of rebuke can be properly grasped. In this second treatise, Augustine subordinated every element of the salvific process to grace, thereby ensuring its sovereignty. Little question remained about the dependence of human actions upon the divine will.

One of the primary means by which Augustine characterized the operation of grace was a paradigm. Although grace itself is a unity, a point that will be explored later in this discussion,[74] its activity is variegated. The characteristics differ according to the recipient: the angels, Adam, Christ, and all human beings. It is to be noted that Adam and Christ are the only individual cases with which Augustine was concerned. Otherwise he spoke in terms of classes: angels and human beings at various stages of history. This emphasis on classes will be a factor in distinguishing Augustine from later opponents.[75]

For purposes of contrast and comparison, Adam serves as the central figure in the paradigm. The grace that Adam possessed, like that of the angels, was such that if he had willed to remain in the goodness, the "uprightness and free- dom from sin," in which God had created him he would never have been evil.[76] Adam's own will, like that of all succeeding human beings, was adequate only for evil, unless assisted by grace. Yet Adam received that necessary assistance, the grace by which he was "able not to sin," "able not to die," "able not to

---

[73]*De corr. et gr.* 1.1; 2.4–4.6.

[74]See 29-30 below.

[75]John Cassian, esp. in *Collatio* 13, focused on individual cases, such as the thief on the cross. Similarly, Origen, his theological progenitor, had expressed a strong conviction of the interaction of divine grace with each individual soul in its particular situation.

[76]*De corr. et gr.* 10.28; 11.32.

forsake the good."[77] As in the case of the angels, but not in the case of his successors, Adam's choice was whether to remain in it or to forsake it. He "forsook" the grace.[78]

Some of the angels responded to their similar state in the same way. Through exercise of their free will, these angels turned away and were driven out from God. Yet others, also by free will, remained steadfast and were rewarded in the "absolute certainty" that they would never fall.[79] Significantly, such security is unavailable to human beings in this life on earth, a handicap to be considered later in this chapter in terms of perseverance.[80]

Here then were two cases, that of Adam and that of the angels, in which there was a clear connection of the agent, the agent's action, and the outcome of that action, even though grace was obviously a factor in both cases. In fact, the dual fate of the angels served to illustrate that the fault in Adam's case lay not with God but with Adam who had been good, assisted by all necessary grace, but failed to persevere as a result of his own will, which, being free to serve good or evil, chose evil.[81]

Adam had received grace sufficient for him not to sin or to sin. He possessed the grace to remain in the good if he willed to do so, but he did not so will. In contrast, those in Christ receive a "more powerful" grace. Not only do they receive the grace to remain in the good if they so will but also the grace so to will. They are "made to will."[82] Accordingly, their will perseveres in the good until the end. Augustine, of course, acknowledged that those in Christ do sin, but theirs is not a "sin which is unto death."[83] Inadvertant lapses notwithstanding, they have been given a "persevering hold" on the good.[84]

In heaven, however, the saints will receive a grace that exceeds not only that given to Adam but also that given to those in Christ on earth. It is the grace "not to be able to sin," "not to be able to die," "not to be able to forsake the good."[85]

---

[77]*De corr. et gr.* 12.33: *posse non peccare . . . posse non mori . . . bonum posse non deserere.*

[78]*De corr. et gr.* 11.31.

[79]*De corr. et gr.* 10.27–10.28.

[80]See 26-27 below.

[81]*De corr. et gr.* 11.32.

[82]*De corr. et gr.* 11.31: *Haec prima est gratia quae data est primo Adam: sed hac potentior est in secundo Adam. . . . Haec autem tanto major est, ut parum sit homini per illam reparare perditam libertatem, parum sit denique non posse sine illa vel apprehendere bonum, vel permanere in bono si velit, nisi etiam efficiatur ut velit.*

[83]*De corr. et gr.* 12.35: *non tamen ultra serviant peccato quod est ad mortem.*

[84]*De corr. et gr.* 11.32: *perseveranter tenendo.*

[85]*De corr. et gr.* 11.32–12.33: *non posse peccare . . . non posse mori . . . bonum non posse deserere.*

Thus in contrast to Adam, who was free to sin or not to sin, and to those in Christ, who are free not to sin, the saints in heaven will possess the greatest freedom: They will be unable to sin.[86]

Guy de Broglie has pointed out the collective nature of both the sin of those in Adam and the merit of those in Christ. The individualistic element in each is greatly minimized in this treatise. A person never stands before God guilty simply of particular misdeeds, but these very misdeeds attain their sinful reality as connected with the surpassing fault of Adam. The divine judgment is directed at them in this solidarity. Likewise, the merits of the saints are derived from and relative to the overriding merit of Christ. It is only in Christ's merit that the individual's merits attain their full reality.[87]

Thus, as already noted, it is not as individual cases but as classes that human beings are considered by God. Moreover, even Adam and Christ take on the character of being classes themselves, at least with regard to those persons who are members of each. The responsibility for sin and the reception of grace are to be understood, therefore, without regard to human differences but in a collective sense. Such a notion of human solidarity according to membership either in Adam or in Christ is, of course, quite distinct from the monastic encouragement of individual effort.

An immediate problem concerns the identification of those who are in Christ and the related issue of how grace is understood to be operative in their lives. Who are the beneficiaries of this grace? There are two levels on which this question can be answered. The more obvious concerns the individual identification of these persons; yet in order to serve as a check on pride, this information remains hidden in God.[88] In fact, only perseverance to the end gives proof of election. Assurance concerning one's own predestination or that of anyone else who is living is not available.[89] This security of knowing that they will persevere will be available to persons, as it now is available to the angels, only when in heaven they have been given the fullness of grace according to which they cannot sin and therefore cannot fall into pride.[90]

On another level, however, those in Christ can be described as those who have been foreknown and predestinated by God as elect. Whatever their present state—unborn, unregenerate, lapsed—their election is already accomplished and

---

[86]*De corr. et gr.* 11.32: *Quid erit autem liberius libero arbitrio, quando non poterit servire peccato*; cf. 11.29–11.30.

[87]Guy de Broglie, "Pour une meilleure intelligence du *De correptione et gratia*," *Augustinus Magister* 3 (Paris: Études Augustiniennes, 1954): 325-26.

[88]*De corr. et gr.* 13.40.

[89]*De corr. et gr.* 9.21–9.22.

[90]*De corr. et gr.* 13.40.

secure; they cannot be lost to God. They are elected to eternal life,[91] and their "number is fixed."[92]

Implicit here is a sequence in the work of grace. Initially Adam received a good will. Even in its original unsullied condition, however, human nature was not capable of remaining in the good without further divine assistance. Thus Adam was also given the help by which he might persevere in the good if he so willed.[93] Adam, of course, did not remain in the good, and because of his sin succeeding generations became a "mass of perdition." Adam's offspring thus constitute a class of individuals that deserves condemnation. Nevertheless, grace again becomes evident in that some are elected to "differ," to receive mercy and thus eternal life.[94] Human difference, therefore, follows rather than precedes election. The basis of the election lies hidden in grace and is in no way dependent on human merit or upon any human difference that might be construed as merit.[95] Although the rationale for the divine decision is beyond the limits of human understanding, Augustine repeatedly affirmed the righteousness of God, a righteousness both just and merciful, however unjust and arbitrary it may appear.

A further stage of grace can be discerned in conversion, a process that Augustine had dealt with in the previous treatise. Turning to God through believing is itself a gift from God. As evidence for the sufficiency of grace at this stage, Augustine cited Paul's effectual call and his conversion by that call. Both were the work of grace, for Paul's "merits, though great, were yet evil."[96]

If grace effects conversion, it should not be forgotten that it was in contrast to the grace of conversion that the hardening of the heart, as in the case of Pharaoh, proved crucial in the last treatise. Augustine had insisted that this hardening of the heart, by which the call is not effectual, is not a negative activity on God's part but simply the absence of grace. In his opinion, as God is necessarily blameless, the individual is rightly to be held accountable for

---

[91]*De corr. et gr.* 9.20; 9.21; 9.23.

[92]*De corr. et gr.* 13.39: *certus est numerus.*

[93]*De corr. et gr.* 11.32; 12.34: *Tunc ergo dederat homini Deus bonam voluntatem; in illa quippe eum fecerat qui fecerat rectum: dederat adjutorium, sine quo in ea non posset permanere si vellet.*

[94]*De corr. et gr.* 7.12: *ab illa perditionis massa quae facta est per primum Adam, debemus intelligere neminem posse discerni, nisi qui hoc donum habet, quisquis habet, quod gratia Salvatoris accepit.*

[95]*De corr. et gr.* 7.13.

[96]*De gr. et lib arb.* 5.12: *quia merita eius erant magna sed mala.* For a discussion of the gratuitous character of conversion, see Burns, *The Development of Augustine's Doctrine of Operative Grace,* 168, 176, 179, 181, 185.

hardness of heart, although admittedly the person's will, unassisted by grace, is not free to serve the good.[97]

This understanding of God's justice must have appeared problematic to many readers of Augustine. At the very least, this type of reasoning would have opened the door to the difficulty that the De correptione et gratia addressed, i.e., the idea that the appropriate action in the case of one who breaks the commandments is not rebuke but prayer to God for the offender.[98] The agent who is actually involved, it would seem, is the appropriate one to be addressed. A closely related difficulty, which the letter of Januarius had already tried to remedy and the later controversy in South Gaul would repeatedly underscore, was that this view failed to take into account the biblical theme of God's will for universal salvation. Augustine's treatment of the statement, "[God] desires all men to be saved" (1 Tim. 2.4), did not satisfy the questioners. Augustine interpreted "all" to mean the predestinated, since they would include all types of people.[99] This interpretation, of course, is consistent with Augustine's speaking of classes rather than individuals. Both difficulties just noted are, of course, variations on a common theme: If God is the sole agent and if God wills that all be saved, why are not all saved?

The next stage of grace is evident in the gift of perseverance; for perseverance, or continuing to the end in the holiness into which a person is called, is the final test of one's election. Those whom God has ordained to life will not fail in faith; by grace, they "cannot help persevering."[100] There may be lapses, of course, but they are temporary. Faith is assuredly restored.[101] In other words, even negative actions of the elect do not affect their destiny since that destiny is determined from outside themselves. In fact, either God will not allow them to die until their faith has been restored,[102] or God will cause them to die before they lapse.[103]

The case of those who do not have the grace of perseverance is quite different. Even if they have been baptized and have begun to live in obedience and thus to all appearances are to be numbered among the elect, in reality they must finally fail in perseverance. Since they have not been predestined as elect, they lack the necessary grace.[104] The nonelect converts who "have received faith,

---

[97]De gr. et lib. arb. 23.45.
[98]De corr. et gr. 2.4–4.6.
[99]De corr. et gr. 14.44.
[100]De corr. et gr. 12.34.
[101]De corr. et gr. 7.16; 12.35.
[102]De corr. et gr. 9.21.
[103]De corr. et gr. 7.13.
[104]De corr. et gr. 9.20.

which worketh by love, but. . . have not received perseverance to the end"[105] are nevertheless accountable for their failure to continue in the good. As those who have never even heard the gospel will be condemned for their lack of faith, so also those who have heard the gospel and even received faith will be condemned for their failure to persevere in it. They could have persevered if only they had so willed;[106] yet they did not so will. Of course, without the gift of perseverance, a sustained will for the good is not possible; yet the failure of the will is to be condemned.

The final stage in the work of grace is eternal life. In the previous treatise Augustine had called eternal life itself "grace."[107] This is the "life" to which one is elected, and the consummation of that election is that the chosen "reign with Christ."[108] It is in this condition that the saints receive the grace "not to be able to sin," "not to be able to die," and "not to be able to forsake good."[109] Theirs is a grace not only greater than that given to Adam but greater than that which had been given to the saints themselves while they had still been on earth. The opposite of this life they enjoy is the "condemnation" of those who "perish."[110]

To consider the work of grace in terms of an outline of the stages of its operation may create the misconception that each stage refers to a different kind of grace. To the contrary, grace, as described by Augustine, is a unity, although it is not without tension as to the manner of its operation. De Broglie has particularly stressed the unitary character of grace. Contrasting the situations of Adam and of those in Christ, he has argued that among the latter grace adapts itself to the fallen human condition. It leads and utilizes the human will as its instrument. The will of Adam, in contrast, required no such leading. As innocent creatures, he and the angels had the power of willingly doing the good. The point is that Augustine was not speaking of different kinds of grace, one available to Adam and one available to the saints, but of one grace that accommodates itself to the condition of the recipient. This accommodation to the fallen human condition does make it appear as something radically new, however.[111]

Moreover, this same grace has a variety of manifestations as it accommodates itself to the stages of the human will, from the will's preparation to its final

---

[105]*De corr. et gr.* 6.10: *Accepi enim fidem, quae per dilectionem operatur: sed in illa usque in finem perseverantiam non accepi.*

[106]*De corr. et gr.* 7.11.

[107]*De gr. et lib. arb.* 8.20.

[108]*De corr. et gr.* 7.14.

[109]*De corr. et gr.* 12.33: *non posse peccare . . . non posse mori . . . bonum non posse deserere.*

[110]*De corr. et gr.* 7.12.

[111]*De Broglie*, 329, 333-36.

beatitude. This accommodation is not to particular individuals, however, but to the various stages in the restoration of persons to God.

One further source of possible confusion is that Augustine never clearly distinguished grace from the indwelling of the Holy Spirit. The reason may well have been that in speaking of the operation of grace he was referring to the divine operation in the individual and not to some created thing that God imparts to the person. Considered from this perspective, even the original condition of Adam was not utterly natural, in the sense of his will's functioning according to its own capacity, independent of any interior operation of God.

The crux of the matter, so far as the *De correptione et gratia* is concerned, lies with the grace that effects perseverance, and the key to perseverance or the locus of the operation of grace for perseverance is the will. As the paradigm has shown, free will whether for Adam before the fall or for any of his descendants afterwards is, by itself and without the aid of grace, capable of serving evil only. Of course, God has provided the law, which unassisted by grace is able to set forth what should be done and what should be avoided. Nevertheless, this knowledge that the law provides cannot by itself effect the obedience of the will. The simple interaction of the free will and the law can result only in guilt and death. What this knowledge of the law may provide, however, is the recognition that one is incapable of obedience. It is as a result of this awareness that a conversion is effected from self-reliance to reliance upon grace. This very desire for the "help of grace is the beginning of grace."[112] Such a statement should not be understood to mean, however, that the conversion of one's desires, the turning to grace, is an action of the unassisted free will. The situation is quite the reverse: Without the aid of grace the free will can do "absolutely no good thing, whether in thought or will or affection or action."[113] It must be "led by the spirit of God." Blatantly stated, human persons "are acted upon that they may act."[114]

It is this prior action by God that converts the free will from its attachment to evil to its attachment to the good. The will is now free to love the good of which the law has given it knowledge. This description of the transformation of the will by means of grace is in contrast to the monastic understanding of the gradual conversion of the will to God by means of carefully regulated discipline. Moreover, what is still lacking after the Augustinian conversion is the capability to do the good that one knows and loves. This capability is also the gift of grace.[115] The multifaceted action of God, i.e., the giving of knowledge, love, and

---

[112]*De corr. et gr.* 1.2: *desiderare auxilium gratiae, initium gratiae est.*

[113]*De corr. et gr.* 2.3: *Intelligenda est enim gratia Dei per Jesus Christum Dominum nostrum, qua sola homines liberantur a malo, et sine qua nullum prorsus sive cogitando, sive volendo et amando, sive agendo faciunt bonum.*

[114]*De corr. et gr.* 2.4: *si filii Dei sunt, spiritu Dei se agi. . . . Aguntur enim ut agant.*

[115]*De corr. et gr.* 2.3.

ability so that one actually does the good that one loves, is the being "acted upon that they might act."

This subordination of the human will and action to grace calls into question the degree to which human actions are genuinely human because, although enacted by the human agent, they are enacted by that agent only as the agent is acted upon by God. There is no sense in which the actions are self-initiated. Furthermore, the human reaction to the divine action has the appearance in Augustine of being somewhat mechanical. Whatever God wills is accomplished, for the divine will to give salvation is a will which no human will resists.[116] God "causes . . . the will."[117] Suggestions of an automaton seem to arise at this point.[118] Yet such inferences may be inappropriate in the context of the Augustinian understanding of the freedom of the will. This freedom is not a neutral position from which one may choose either the bad or the good. Instead, it is a condition in which one, without the aid of grace, is free to will only the bad and, with the aid of grace, is free to will only the good. As stated earlier, the latter freedom is the greater freedom.[119]

An implication one may draw is that the will as created by God and as fallen has always been free yet never free for the good without the aid of grace. The need for grace is thus not the result of the fall but of creation itself. Human persons would thus seem to have been created for a certain sort of relationship with God. After Adam's fall the will simply requires a greater assistance of grace. It now needs not only a deliverer for its weakened condition but also increased support against the external evils of the world and against the internal evil of flesh warring with spirit. Adam experienced neither kind of evil in his condition of external and internal peace.[120]

There are several indications here that Augustine was seeking to protect himself against the charge of fatalism. First, he allowed for at least some measure of creaturely initiative. Although in the supralapsarian condition of Adam and the angels grace was necessary for them to remain in the good, the freedom of their wills was such that they were able to initiate good actions, if they so willed. Similarly, those persons whose wills have been converted to the

---

[116]*De corr. et gr.* 14.43.

[117]*De corr. et gr.* 11.32: *Fit quippe in nobis per hanc Dei gratiam in bono recipiendo et perseveranter tenendo, non solum posse quod volumus, verum etiam velle quod possumus; 12.38: qui eis non solum dat adjutorium quale primo homini dedit, sine quo non possint perseverare si velint; sed in eis etiam, operatur et velle.*

[118]See John M. Rist, "Augustine on Free Will and Predestination," *Augustine: A Collection of Critical Essays*, ed. R. A. Markus (Garden City NY: Doubleday, 1972) 218-52. Rist concluded that the human agent is a "puppet," according to Augustine's account.

[119]*De corr. et gr.* 11.32; 12.35.

[120]*De corr. et gr.* 11.29; 12.35.

good but who have not been elected to salvation have been given the freedom to choose the good but not the grace to persevere in that good. Thus to Adam and the angels before the fall and to the nonelect converted following the fall, grace would appear to have given the capacity to choose the good without also giving the assistance by which they will necessarily make such a choice. Of course, without that additional assistance, all, except a portion of the angels, fail to remain in the good. Nevertheless, in each of these instances the initiative can be said to belong to the creature.

In other ways as well Augustine sought to deflect the charge of fatalism. He described the situation of the recipient of grace as one of freedom. He was also careful not to speak of grace as if it were a force overwhelming its object. Instead, he presented grace as the operation of the spirit of God that transforms the attraction of the will so that at every point the will freely loves what it loves. Nevertheless, it must be noted that with reference to the elect there is no allowance for self-initiated desiring, willing, or doing the good.[121] Augustine had not entirely resolved the question of fatalism. In fact, that question was to become even more pronounced in the two subsequent treatises, *De praedestinatione sanctorum* and *De dono perseverantiae*, that Augustine sent to South Gaul. In these he further developed the logic of sovereign grace. Even in the *De correptione et gratia*, however, the tenuous character of the relationship between human actions and a salvific outcome is evident. In order to respond to the monks' inquiry concerning rebuke, Augustine had felt it necessary to provide a prolonged examination of the operation of grace, for it is only in terms of divine grace that the purpose of human rebuke can be ascertained.

According to the scheme that Augustine described, the beginning of the good will and the continuance in it are both the gifts of grace. The capacity to will the good, to effect the good works that one wills, and to persevere in this good willing and doing are all the outworking of grace.[122] Human action for the good can be understood, therefore, only with reference to prior and continuing divine activity. Such being the case, it is only in the context of grace operating on the will for its conversion and perseverance that rebuke can prove effective. The purpose of rebuke is repentance, either so that the unconverted, if among the elect, might receive the "will of regeneration," or so that one who, although "already regenerate," has lapsed may return from an evil attachment to the good.[123]

---

[121]This point seems to be Rist's main argument; see n. 118 above.

[122]*De corr. et gr.* 12.38.

[123]*De corr. et gr.* 6.9: *Corripiatur ergo origo damnabilis, ut ex dolore correptionis voluntas regenerationis oriatur: si tamen qui corripitur filius est promissionis. . . . Si autem jam regeneratus et justificatus in malam vitam sua voluntate relabitur. . . . si correptione compunctus salubriter ingemit, et ad similia bona opera vel etiam meliora revertitur, nempe hic apertissime utilitas correptionis apparet.*

In defending the practice of rebuke, Augustine was arguing against those who would exalt grace at the expense of all human responsibility. His argument, however, did not reinstate human responsibility so much as set up rebuke as an instrument of the outworking of God's infallible knowledge.

The efficacy of rebuke for repentance, according to Augustine, depends on the grace of God.[124] For rebuke to serve as an instrument of mercy, the one rebuked must be among the elect. For the nonelect, rebuke serves only as punishment, as an instrument of justice.[125] Furthermore, rebuke, similar to the law, informs the person of the evil to be avoided. Through the failure of the nonelect to respond rightly, guilt is thereby compounded and final punishment further justified.[126] Presumably in the case of the nonelect the rebuke might lead to a repentance that is temporary, but such repentance does not result in final perseverance. Rebuke can also serve to separate the "diseased," both elect and nonelect, from the healthy elect so that the "contagion" may not spread.[127] For the elect rebuke is an expression of grace. Even such a severe measure as excommunication can lead these to repentance and thus healing. God is, therefore, a cooperating partner in the rebuke.[128]

The difficulty for the one administering the rebuke, of course, is that such a person has no way of knowing whether the recipient is among the elect and thus able to be benefitted. Regardless, the rebuke must be made for the sake of those who will benefit and at the expense of those who will not.[129] Augustine was to use a similar line of reasoning in his last two treatises to justify exhortation and preaching.[130] It may be noted at this point, however, that preaching to a non-Christian possesses much the same character as rebuking a Christian sinner. Preaching and the administration of the sacraments are essential to the conversion process; however, they are efficacious only if God operates on the person in such a way as to move the individual to conversion.

The question which gave rise to this treatise, i.e., why one should address oneself to the human agent if the real agent is God, exposes the dubious role of human agency in Augustine's scheme. Significantly, he did not answer the question either by saying that the human agent is the real agent or that the human agent is also a real agent. Instead, he said that even though God is the real agent,

---

[124]*De corr. et gr.* 4.9

[125]*De corr. et gr.* 9.25.

[126]*De corr. et gr.* 7.11; 13.42–14.43.

[127]*De corr. et gr.* 13.42; 15.46: *Pastoralis tamen necessitas habet, ne per plures serpant dira contagia, separare ab ovibus sanis morbidam.*

[128]*De corr. et gr.* 9.25; 15.46.

[129]*De corr. et gr.* 15.49.

[130]See 65-57 below.

there is still reason to address the human agent. The reason for such an address is that rebuke is an instrument of divine agency, even though what the divine agent is effecting may not be what the person who administers the rebuke intends.

The explanation in the *De correptione et gratia* of the function of rebuke has clearly illustrated the difficulty, given Augustine's understanding of grace, of establishing a connection between human actions and a salvific outcome. The Christian is obliged to rebuke the erring neighbor, but that action must be performed without any assurance of its effect. It is not simply a matter of every human interaction being somewhat unpredictable. The problem is far more complex. It is instead the case that divine action, based in an inscrutable divine will and operating in patterns that are entirely its own, determines the function and result of human agency.

At the conclusion of the treatise an unresolved tension remained. On the one hand, the paradigm has provided instances, the cases of Adam and angels, in which the agent-action-outcome link remains firm while at the same time grace plays a necessary role. These instances show that, for Augustine, action for the good always required the assistance of grace. On the other hand, instances of the operation of grace on all human persons since Adam tend to attenuate the link of agent-action-outcome. With regard to conversion (coming to love the good), perseverance (continuing to love the good), and rebuke, the assistance seems almost to break the linkage. Of course, the converted who do begin to love the good but are nonelect eventually fall away by their own will. The elect, however, continue in their love of the good, although they can, and at times do, falter in that love and thereby sin. Their ultimate perseverance is guaranteed not by an inability to sin but by God's protecting them from sin through such means as the felicitous timing of their death, the prevention of temptation, or the employment of rebuke.[131]

Rebuke itself has a highly abstract character because it is the behind-the-scenes divine direction that actually determines the action, its purpose (either really to restore or really to condemn), and its outcome. However, the defiant hardening of the nonelect and the remorseful repentance of the elect are, in fact, responses of the human agent to the rebuke.

The case of Pharaoh illustrates the point. God controlled the actions that Pharaoh chose to perform and suited them to the divine governance of the universe, although Pharaoh himself was responsible for his evil will that had made such choices. In contrast, in the case of saints who have received the gift of perseverance, God controls both their actions and their willing.

---

[131]*De corr. et gr.* 8.18-19.

Thus Augustine, despite de Broglie's insistence on the unity of grace, is left with an unreconciled tension between an operation of grace that does and an operation of grace that does not preserve the agent-action-outcome link. Stated in another way, despite the assistance of grace, God is not the agent of the good angels' choice to remain obedient or of the bad angels' choice to disobey. Nor is God the agent of Adam's choice to remain in grace, as long as that choice lasted, or of Adam's choice to disobey. In the case of the offspring of Adam, however, God is the agent of the human agent's desire for the good and of the human agent's perseverance in the good. It would seem that the logic of grace overshadows, in varying degrees, all human agency for the good since Adam.

Needless to say, not everyone was in agreement with Augustine's conclusions. We hear no more of the disturbance at Hadrumetum. Perhaps the bishop had satisfied these questioners, but such was not to be the case elsewhere. Specifically, those monks in South Gaul, who regarded Augustine with less awe than did their North African counterparts, found his teachings a challenge to their striving for Christian perfection. It was in South Gaul that what had begun as an amicable misunderstanding came to assume the character of a heated debate.

Chapter 2

South Gaul:
The Emergence of Controversy

Introduction

With the reception of the *De correptione et gratia* at Hadrumetum, the first stage of what finally became a century-long conflict came to an end. With the reception of this same treatise in southern Gaul, an entirely new phase began, the dynamics of which were markedly different.

For one thing, by the early fifth century North Africa was characterized by a growing provincialism, whereas Gaul, particularly in the south, was experiencing an infusion of ideas and renewed vitality, especially from the Roman East. Both regions had ties to the government and to the church in Italy, but prior to this time upwardly mobile North Africans had often migrated to Italy for career advancement, as had Augustine himself, or traveled regularly between Africa and Italy, as had Augustine's patron, Romanianus. After Alaric's sack of Rome in 410, however, the flow of population was reversed. North Africa became at least a temporary refuge for Italians seeking to escape the turmoil of Italy in the wake of the barbarian invasions, and the North Africans themselves tended to remain in their native region. The Africa in which the controversy at Hadrumetum had arisen was a world grown ever more narrow, primarily because of the uncontrollable circumstances of the external world and perhaps also because of local temperament reinforced by geographical isolation.[1]

In contrast, Gaul was increasingly becoming a center for education and for the preservation of the Roman cultural heritage.[2] Moreover, in southern Gaul a form of monasticism was developing which, although distinctively Gallic, was receptive to the influence of its counterparts in Greece and Egypt.[3] The disruption

---

[1] See Brown, *Augustine of Hippo*, 21, 143-45.

[2] Salvian, *De gubernatione Dei* 4.30; Friedrich Prinz, *Frühes Mönchtum im Frankenreich* (Munich and Vienna, 1965) 47-58; Raymond Van dam, *Leadership and Community in Late Antique Gaul* (Berkeley: University of California Press, 1985) 151; N. K. Chadwick, *Poetry and Letters in Early Christian Gaul* (London: Bowes & Bowes, 1955) 21-23.

[3] Jacques Fontaine, "L'ascétisme chrétien dans la littérature gallo-romaine d'Hilaire

and dislocation caused by the barbarian invasions in the West contributed to the growth both of the area and of Gallic monasticism. Among the displaced persons who moved into Provence were many who sought to pursue a religious vocation in their new home.[4]

Second, although the Bishop of Hippo was well respected outside his native Africa, he hardly commanded the same unquestioned authority in matters of doctrine in this Gallic world with its own bishops and own peculiar openness to intellectual ferment as found, for example, at the monastery of Lérins.[5] Augustine did have devoted followers in the area, but such persons regularly had to defend their loyalty and their logic against thoughtful, probing, and sometimes caustic attacks.

Gallic resistance to the African bishop's authority was not merely a function of his being an outsider. The problem was more complex. Even within the confines of the Gallic church itself the locus of authority was subject to question. For example, the account of Martin of Tours by Sulpicius Severus was punctuated by the author's vituperative attacks against the bishops of Gaul. Although Martin himself was a bishop, the *Vita* and the *Dialogi* suggest that

---

à Cassien," *La Gallia romana* (Academia Nazionale dei Lincei: Problemi attuali di scienza e di cultura; Rome, 1973) 87-115. Fontaine has argued for the existence of an early form of Christian asceticism in Gaul that predated Martin of Tours and through the influence of Hilary of Poitiers significantly shaped Martin himself and the expression of monasticism attributed to him. This asceticism drew upon the work of Tertullian and Cyprian in North Africa, particularly their concern for consecrated virginity and preparation for martyrdom. It was also influenced by contact with the East, especially the desert fathers and Athanasius's *Vita Antonii*. Nevertheless, it was sufficiently regional in character to resonate with the sensibilities of the Gallo-Roman aristocracy. According to Fontaine, this Gallic monasticism survived the invasions of 406 and fed into the more specifically eastern monastic model imported most prominently by John Cassian. The reciprocal influence of the two forms resulted in a thoroughly elaborated, distinctively Gallic monasticism that Cassian himself did much to develop. See also Philip Rousseau, *Ascetics, Authority, and the Church in the Age of Jerome and Cassian* (Oxford: Oxford University Press, 1978) 83-87.

[4]Fontaine, "L'ascétisme chrétien," 89, 106; Patrick J. Geary, *Before France and Germany: The Creation and Transformation of the Merovingian World* (Oxford: Oxford University Press, 1988) 144; N. K. Chadwick, 142-46.

[5]Ralph W. Mathisen, *Ecclesiastical Factionalism and Religious Controversy in Fifth-Century Gaul* (Washington DC: Catholic University of America Press, 1989) 123-24. P. Courcelle, "Noveaux aspects de la culture lérinienne," *Révue des études latines* 46 (1968): 379-409. Pierre Riché, *Education and Culture in the Barbarian West from the Sixth through the Eighth Century*, trans. John J. Contreni (Columbia: University of South Carolina Press, 1976) 101-105, pointed out that Lérins was primarily "a center of asceticism" and not a "theological school," but he also acknowledged the intellectual training that some of the more famous Lérinian monks had before they arrived there. Such training suggests an intellectual independence.

consecration to the episcopal office was by itself an insufficient recommendation for authority. Specifically, Martin's voluntary poverty, the self-chosen similarity of his life to that of a Gallic peasant, was set in invidious contrast with the ostentation to be found in the lives of other Gallic bishops, who retained the accouterments of the local Roman aristocracy from which they had come.[6]

Although Sulpicius portrayed the holiness of Martin as a challenge to sheer episcopal authority, the fact of Martin's own position as a bishop suggests that the conflict may not have been so clear-cut as the biography indicated. As Wallace-Hadrill has demonstrated, Sulpicius's portrait of Martin actually provided an ideal of renunciation that was highly attractive to many Gallic aristocrats. They were aroused to become bishops according to the standard set by Martin. In fact, the conflict posed in the *Vita Martini* between Martin and the Gallic bishops may have actually been a conflict between two types of Gallic bishops, that Wallace-Hadrill has designated as "conservative" and "radical or reforming." Both groups were drawn from the local aristocracy and both had an ascetic strain, but what distinguished them was a difference in emphasis. Whereas the self-identity of the conservative bishops derived from a combination of episcopacy and local status, the self-identity of the radical bishops derived from a combination of episcopacy and personal sanctity. The former saw themselves as exercising their aristocratic responsibilities for the conservation of Gallo-Roman ideals and for the protection of the masses through their positions of authority in the church. The latter saw themselves as an ascetic elite. They sought perfection through a monastic renunciation which, however, was not so extreme as to preclude their acceptance of episcopal responsibility. For them Martin, who combined in himself both the episcopacy and monastic asceticism, would have served as an ideal. The fact that he was an outsider who had been born in Pannonia and reared in Italy would have posed less of a threat to them than to their more conservative counterparts for whom episcopacy and local status defined the ideal.[7] Regardless of how the conflict described by Sulpicius is to be

---

[6]*VMart.* 9.2, 4-7; 10.1-2; *Dial.* 1.2.3; 1.21.3-4; 1.24.3; 1(2).1.2; 2(3).11-13; Geary, 140-43. For a discussion of the pattern of authority that Sulpicius presented in the figure of Martin, see Rousseau, *Ascetics, Authority, and the Church,* 143-65.

[7]*VMart.* 2.1-8. J. M. Wallace-Hadrill, *The Frankish Church* (Oxford: Clarendon Press, 1983) 4-6. For a careful discussion of the importance of the holy man's status as a stranger, see Peter Brown, "The Rise and Function of the Holy Man in Late Antiquity," "Town, Village, and Holy Man: The Case of Syria," *Society and the Holy in Late Antiquity* (Berkeley: University of California Press, 1982) 103-52, 153-65. See also Van Dam, 122-24. Van Dam placed the rise of the outsider Martin to a position of ecclesiastical authority in the context of the rise of other outsiders to power in the secular world. For example, the Pannonian soldier Valentinian had not only become emperor but also clearly preferred the military aristocracy and the provincial aristocracy, particularly

interpreted, there was more conflict between monastic asceticism and the episcopacy in Gaul than existed between these same two institutions in North Africa.

A third factor affecting this new phase of the controversy was that as
monastic asceticism posed a challenge to traditional ecclesiastical authority in
Gaul, it was itself severely challenged by the teaching of Augustine. Like their
African counterparts at Hadrumetum, Gallic ascetics found their pursuit of
perfection undercut by the Augustinian understanding of a gratuitous election that
is in no way based on merit. Yet in contrast to the African monks, these Gallic
ascetics, both in the episcopacy and in the monastery, fought back. They
developed their own telling arguments against this Augustinian teaching.

The greater vigor of their response must be attributed to the strength that the
monastic movement had attained by this time in Gaul. As Fontaine has pointed
out, the character and staying power of Western monasticism cannot be understood apart from the intense, yet conflicting, reactions that it engendered within
the Western aristocracy. There was not only the virulent antagonism of some
members of the nobility, who perceived in monastic renunciation of society a
repudiation of traditional Roman values and aristocratic privilege, but also the
wholehearted acceptance of other nobles who found in monastic withdrawal a
correspondence to ancient classical ideals, particularly the ideal of philosophic
retirement. This strong combination of repulsion and attraction among the most
prominent members of society could not have been without effect. Negatively,
monasticism was forced to clarify its purposes, curb its excesses, and order the
behavior of its adherents. Positively, it was enriched by the intellectual vigor of
an educated aristocracy and refined by their inbred temperance and urbanity. The
result was the development of a form of monasticism that increasingly attracted
the elite of Western society.[8]

It was here, in southern Gaul, therefore, that what has come to be known as
the Semi-Pelagian controversy was fully engaged. The term "Semi-Pelagian" is
generally conceded to be a misnomer, as the persons so designated rejected
Pelagianism. They have also been labeled anti-Augustinians; yet that designation
is inappropriate as well. In fact, these persons accepted Augustine's arguments
against the Pelagian heresy. They, too, insisted on the necessity of grace.[9] It was
only as Augustine carried his arguments to their logical, predestinarian extreme
that Gallic opposition arose. As monks striving to please God and thereby attain

---

of Gaul, to the old Roman senatorial aristocracy.

[8]Jacques Fontaine, "L'aristocratie occidentale devant le monachisme aux IVème et Vème
siècles," *Rivista d'Istoria e Letteratura di Storia Religiosa* 15 (1979): 28-53.

[9]For the origin of the name, see M. Jacquin, "A quelle date apparaît le term 'semi-
pélagien'?" *Revue des sciences philosophiques et théologiques* 1 (1907): 506-508. For a
discussion of the term, see Adolf Harnack, *History of Dogma* 5, 3d ed., trans. Neil
Buchanan (New York: Russell and Russell, 1958) 245n.3.

eternal reward for their efforts, they assumed a reliable connection between human actions and the salvific outcome of these actions. The *De correptione et gratia* challenged this connection and, in fact, their whole way of life. Thus the Gallic opposition arose only at the point of monastic insistence upon the genuineness and relevance of human agency in the process of salvation.

As we examine the conflict as it emerged in South Gaul, it will become clear that this was not a dispute within a common framework but a clash between two quite different ways of conceiving restoration to God: the Augustinian and the monastic. The latter, so far as one can tell, had not yet received sufficient theological development in North Africa to constitute a genuine alternative. In South Gaul the differences between the two frameworks were more distinct, at least initially. As the dispute progressed, each side came, to a certain extent, to speak the language of the other and thereby once again blur the difference. This convergence was simply one of terminology, however, and not of views, but the growing similarities of vocabulary tended to obscure the dissimilarities of function for common words and images in the two groups. Convergence of terminology thus tended to obscure the degree to which the two radically different frameworks were in conflict and not just opposing positions within a common frame. Nevertheless, the clearest indication of the difference will be the difficulty of transposing Cassian's views into Augustine's language or vice versa. However, before an examination of Cassian can be made, Augustine's final position must be considered, i.e., his defense against the opposition as that opposition was reported to him by Prosper and Hilary.

Epistula ad Rufinum

The first indication in South Gaul of what was to become known as the Semi-Pelagian controversy was a letter written by Prosper Tiro of Aquitaine to a certain Rufinus. Recognized as the chief defender and interpreter of Augustine in southern Gaul, Prosper was a layman who was involved much of his life in the religious milieu of Marseilles.[10] It was in this role as the authoritative Augustinian spokesman that he composed the letter to Rufinus. Although neither the exact date of the letter nor the identity of this Rufinus has been determined,

---

[10]There is little biographical information available on Prosper. See Gennadius, *De viris illustribus* 85 (PL 58.1099-1120); D. M. Cappuyns, "Le premier représentant de l'Augustinisme médiéval, Prosper d'Aquitaine," *Recherches de théologie ancienne et médiévale* 1 (1929): 310; G. Morin, "Saint Prosper de Reggio," in *Revue Bénédictine* 12 (1895): 241-57; L. Valentin, *Saint Prosper d'Aquitaine: Étude sur la littérature latine ecclésiastique au cinquième siècle en Gaule* (Paris: Alphonse Picard, 1900) 140-51.

it is reasonable to surmise that the letter was written about 427[11] to someone who, trusting Prosper, had sought his guidance regarding the troubling criticisms of Augustine that were already circulating in the area.[12]

In the letter Prosper sought to respond frankly to what were the two most significant current criticisms of Augustine:[13] first, that he taught fatalism disguised as grace, and second, that he divided "the human race into two different substances and natures" as did the pagans and the Manichaeans.[14] Both accusations indicate that, in the estimate of some, Augustine's teaching cast doubt on the significance of human agency and severed the connection between a person's actions and that person's ultimate destiny. Prosper insisted that, to the contrary, Augustine had actually refuted both fatalism and Manichaeism. In fact, for Prosper the significant issue was not human action at all but God's action. As he saw the matter, the problem was that Augustine's opponents refused to accept his thoroughgoing understanding of God's grace, for to do so would inevitably lead to their having to acknowledge that the number of those who have been predestined by God is "fixed."[15] The sovereignty of grace, i.e., the all-determining character of the divine will, was thus a fundamental point.

These criticisms appear to have represented attempts to force Augustine's views into the familiar molds of fatalism and Manichaeism so that his teaching would be vulnerable to the same objections to which these unacceptable doctrines were liable. Prosper sought to deflect this tactic. He did so by insisting that the issue was really one of grace. He pointed out that in contrast to the error of fatalism, Augustine had argued that all things are subject to God's gracious decree. In contrast to the Manichaean error of two substances, Augustine had taught that as offspring of Adam, all persons are created from "the flesh of that first man." In the sin of Adam all have sinned. The only hope for this one fallen nature lies in its recreation, according to the image of God, through the agency of grace.[16]

---

[11]Lesousky, 12-13n.6. Prosper mentioned that the disorder at Hadrumetum, referred to by Valentinus in *Ep.* 216 (426-27), had been resolved; yet he himself had apparently not seen *De corr. et gr.*, of which he would speak in *Ep.* 225.2 (ca. 429).

[12]P. De Letter, "Introduction," *Prosper of Aquitaine: Defense of St. Augustine,* trans. P. De Letter, Ancient Christian Writers (Westminster MD: Newman, 1963) 4. De Letter has proposed that Rufinus was "a friend of Prosper who heard about the rumors spread against Augustine." Regardless, the character of the letter indicates that Prosper was responding to an inquiry and that he perceived the inquirer to be an ally. English translations of quotations from Prosper's *Epistula ad Rufinum* will be taken from de Letter.

[13]Lesousky, 13-14, noted that these criticisms appear to have been unwritten, since Prosper dares the opposition to write them (*Ep. ad Ruf.* 3,18).

[14]*Ep. ad Ruf.* 3,18.

[15]*Ep. ad Ruf.* 11,18.

[16]*Ep. ad Ruf.* 18.

As he sought to hold the doctrine of the sovereignty of grace, Prosper was also making the case for the frailty of the human condition. He argued that Augustine's opponents had erred in their optimism with regard to human capacity and in the resultant limitations that they placed on the necessity of grace. After the fall, Prosper insisted, the will is still free, yet only for its own damnation. All deserve condemnation. It is only by the gracious decision of God that some are elected to a new beginning so that their wills are free to desire and to do the good and to persevere in it.[17] The will is incapable of preceding or meriting grace. Grace must precede and then assist at every step of the process. At this point in Prosper's argument it becomes evident that the real issue for him was the gratuity of grace. Human depravity and divine sovereignty were essential but secondary elements of his argument.

Prosper's argument that Augustine taught a gracious divine decree, a decree that elects some to redemption from that one fallen nature in which all participate, effectively cleared the African bishop of the charge of Manichaeism. Whether he actually met the charge that Augustine's understanding of grace was a disguised fatalism is not so readily apparent. He did, however, make the crucial point that a thoroughgoing understanding of the sovereignty of grace, such as Augustine held, when combined with the notion that not all are finally saved, a notion that was shared by all parties, leads inevitably to the idea that it is God, not the human agent at all, who determines who is to receive eternal beatitude. In this letter to Rufinus, Prosper's Augustinianism was utterly consistent and confident, perhaps more so than it would ever be again.

Two observations are appropriate. First, neither the charge of fatalism nor that of Manichaeism had arisen against Augustine at Hadrumetum. The fact that Prosper found it necessary to defend Augustine against such accusations indicates that the opposition was employing a tactic that the bishop of Hippo had himself employed against his monastic challengers in North Africa. Augustine had pejoratively labeled them Pelagians. He had thereby defined the challengers' position with a label that both colored their stance and made it automatically unacceptable. In South Gaul his own accusers attempted the same ploy against him.

Secondly, Prosper's reaction to the labels was to try to show why they were inaccurate, why divine agency is neither fatalism nor Manichaeism. What he avoided was a defense of human agency. Perhaps he felt that such a defense would have been inconsistent with the Augustinian understanding of nature and grace.

---

[17]*Ep. ad Ruf.* 13,15,17.

Two Appeals to Augustine

If Prosper's letter to Rufinus ever became known to Augustine's critics at Marseilles, it did not satisfy them. Some of them, in deference to Augustine, planned to turn to the African bishop himself for clarification. They assumed that they did not understand his teaching.[18] Among these, according to Prosper, was Hilary, bishop of Arles, who held Augustine in esteem and had, at least initially, considered writing the bishop of Hippo for counsel.[19] Before any such contact was made, however, a copy of the *De correptione et gratia* reached the monks at the monastery of St. Victor at Marseilles. This treatise, which apparently had calmed the storm at Hadrumetum, intensified it in southern Gaul. The fundamental differences between their own position and that of Augustine now became inescapably clear to the Gallic monks.

The effect of the treatise on Prosper was quite different. Although he remained convinced of the validity of Augustine's views, he was far less confident than he had been earlier of his own ability to be the interpreter and defender of these views.[20] Thus Prosper and an ally named Hilary decided to write to Augustine, not only to make him aware of the situation but also to seek his guidance. This Hilary has so far escaped identification. However, on the basis of his letter, a few points can be made with assurance: he was a layman, now living in Marseilles, who had had previous contact with Augustine and was friendly toward the latter's position.[21]

It is notable that not only were Prosper and Hilary laymen but, with the possible exception of Vitalis of Carthage,[22] theirs were the only voices to be heard throughout this dispute that were neither clerical nor monastic. Perhaps not

---

[18]*Ep.* 225.2.7.

[19]*Ep.* 225.9. Prosper stressed that on every other aspect of Augustine's teaching, Hilary was in agreement. The identity of this bishop is in dispute. For reasons given on 93-98 below, I have chosen to follow the reading of "Hilary." For a constrasting point of view, see E. Griffe, *La Gaule chrétienne à l'epoque romaine* 2 (Paris: Letouzey and Ané, 1966) 240-41. Griffe stated the better reading was not Hilarius but Helladius or Elladius, the predecessor of Honoratus. For further discussion, see *The Western Fathers*, trans. and ed. F. R. Hoare (New York: Sheed and Ward, 1980) 271n.2. Also, note Owen Chadwick, "'Euladius' of Arles," *Journal of Theological Studies* 46 (1945): 200-205; cf. Owen Chadwick, *John Cassian*, 2d ed. (Cambridge: Cambridge University Press, 1968) 128. O. Chadwick indicated that Hilary, Bishop of Arles, was not the bishop to whom Prosper referred.

[20]*Ep.* 225.2,9.

[21]*Ep.* 225.9, 10. Regarding the identity of Hilary, see Mathisen, 124n.31; Lesousky 15n.15.

[22]See 12, above.

too much should be made of a connection between their lay status and their alliance with Augustine, but it is not unreasonable to suppose that they may have found in the Semi-Pelagian position a spiritual elitism impossible of attainment for anyone except monks. By contrast, the elitism offered in the Augustinian scheme, based as it was in divine graciousness rather than in human sanctity, may have offered a hope for all kinds of persons regardless of religious vocation or personal sanctity. One might speculate, therefore, that the limitations of their status led them to have more confidence in divine graciousness than in their own possibilities for achievement.

In any case, as laymen, Prosper and Hilary did turn to Augustine for both his authority and his wisdom. The matter of authority was significant to them not only because Augustine was renowned, at least in the Western church, as a teacher, but also because his rank of bishop held its own status. Significantly, among his opponents was one who had also recently attained the episcopal office, presumably Hilary, bishop of Arles.[23] Moreover, the exceptional virtue of certain ones among the detractors lent additional force to their argument.[24] Prosper was well aware that many would keep their silence and others would give their assent, simply in deference to the rank and sanctity of these opponents.[25] Nevertheless, Prosper's own continuing stature in the controversy testified to the status, however exceptional, that a layman might hold.

The difficulty was not merely one of position, whether monastic or episcopal, within the Gallic church. Although a bishop, simply by virtue of his position, had authority as a teacher, Prosper respected the present occupant of the see of Arles as theologically knowledgeable,[26] and he understandably believed that Augustine could explain his own work far more convincingly to his episcopal counterpart than he himself could.

The two letters, one from Prosper and the other from Hilary, complemented each other. They agreed on the issues involved in the dispute but at times varied in the emphasis that they attached to them. The situation as presented by the two men was as follows.

On several points both the Augustinians and their opponents agreed: all have sinned in Adam; grace is essential for salvation; baptism is the necessary rite for regeneration. Disagreement, however, focused on two interrelated areas: the universality of the offer of salvation and the role of merit. The Gallic opponents insisted that the offer of the reconciliation effected in Christ is for everyone so

---

[23]Ep. 225.7. See discussion above, n.19.
[24]Ep. 225.2,9.
[25]Ep. 225.7.
[26]Ep. 225.9.

that whoever responds may be saved.[27] Through the grace of creation, which no one can merit, God has given each person a free will and a rational nature so that all persons are capable of knowing good and evil and are equally capable of choosing either. Grace assists a person who has chosen the good to regeneration in Christ through baptism.[28] Although baptism is necessary for salvation, God has called all to baptism through natural law, written law, or preaching. Thus the onus is on the individual, and anyone who refuses is without excuse.[29] There is no divine injustice.

As the offer of salvation is universal, the difference between the saved and the lost lies with the human agent, not with a divine decision. The difference between human beings is thus crucial. In contrast, for Augustine such a distinction was necessarily irrelevant, for if this distinction were relevant, an unavoidable implication would be that grace is given for merit. To achieve the notion of the utter gratuity of grace, Augustine had lost the notions of the universal will for salvation, of distributive justice, and of human agency in the restoration of the person to God. His reported opponents had gained all these but at the cost of qualifying the gratuity of grace.

Their gains were not without complication. Their insistence on the universal will for salvation was imperiled by the obvious facts that some die at birth without baptism and others never hear the gospel at all. With regard to these cases, the opponents proposed the notion that God foreknows what human merit would have been if opportunity had been given for longer life or for hearing the gospel, and God thus rewards in accord with the divine foreknowledge. Infants die with or without having received baptism on the basis of God's foreknowledge of the life they would have lived had they not died in infancy. Similarly, the explanation for the gospel never having been preached to entire nations lies in divine foreknowledge that the preaching would have been rejected.[30] Foreknowledge, therefore, serves to settle difficult cases; but, unlike Augustinian election, it does not settle everything. Human agency, even if only as foreknown, is still necessary.

The problem raised by Augustine's detractors had different emphases, depending on whether Prosper or Hilary were reporting it; but for both of these men the central issue was the same: the logic of grace. The crux of the matter,

---

[27] *Ep.* 225.3.
[28] *Ep.* 225.4.
[29] *Ep.* 225.4. J. Chéné, "Le semipélagianisme du midi de la Gaule d'après les lettres de Prosper d'Aquitaine et d'Hilare à saint Augustin," *Recherches de science religieuse* 43 (1955): 322-41, has suggested that Prosper has distinguished between two groups of monks at St. Victor. In the first group were those who opposed Augustine's understanding of predestination. The second group (described in 225.4) were the true Semi-Pelagians.
[30] *Ep.* 225.5.

in Prosper's view, was gratuitous predestination. Characterizing the opponents' resistance in much the same way as he had in his letter to Rufinus, he stated that an acknowledgment by Augustine's opponents that grace precedes and enables merit, thus that grace is sovereign, would necessarily entail the admission that justification is determined by an absolute and hidden decree of God, the basis of which resides solely in the divine will.[31] These critics of Augustine found such an acknowledgment utterly unacceptable.

Instead, they insisted that the beginning of salvation or the *ortus bonae voluntatis* is dependent on the use a person makes of the natural capacity of the free will. As they saw the matter, such an unbalanced emphasis as Augustine placed on grace would totally undercut human effort by severing any connection between human action and human destiny, for progress in perfection and the attainment of salvation would depend entirely upon grace and be detached from any human striving.[32]

It is not surprising, therefore, that the criticisms leveled at Augustine were related to this very issue. Once again, the implications of the notion that God, not the human being, is the relevant agent, had proved troubling. Prosper wrote that the adversaries were convinced that Augustine's teaching negated any reason for exhortation. If God's decree is to be accomplished regardless of human effort, why, they asked, should the unbeliever convert or the Christian strive to improve?[33] Neither the conversion nor the striving has any effect on the outcome that has been determined by God, although the conversion or the striving may display the outworking of the divine determination.

The problem perceived by the Gallic monks with regard to exhortation within the Augustinian logic of grace was very much the same as that detected by the monks at Hadrumetum concerning rebuke. One may ask what reason there is to exhort or to rebuke another if that other's fate is already determined by God. More basically, the question pertains to the identity of the relevant agent: who, in fact, shapes a person's life and action? In southern Gaul, at least, Augustine's *De correptione et gratia* had not put that issue to rest.

Prosper's analysis of the opposition to Augustine was confirmed by Hilary, but the latter pointed to another area of contention, one also related to the logic of grace: the opponents' rejection of gratuitous perseverance. Hilary specifically referred to the contrast that Augustine had made in the *De correptione et gratia* regarding the grace given to Adam, that given to fallen humanity, and that given to the elect. He reported the opposition's contention that, first, if Adam, before

---

[31]*Ep.* 225.6.
[32]*Ep.* 225.6. J. Chéné, "Que signifiaient 'initium fidei' et 'affectus credulitatis' pour les semipélagiens?" *Recherches de science religieuse* 35 (1948): 566-88.
[33]*Ep.* 225.3,6.

the fall, received grace by which he might have persevered in the good if he had willed to do so, and second, if fallen humanity receives either no grace by which persons may will the good or only the grace by which they may begin to will it but not persevere in it, and third, if the saints receive grace by which they cannot fail to persevere, then the admonitions of preaching would have been useful only to Adam and to the small number predestined for salvation. For the remainder of humanity, such warning and appeals are pointless. Once again the problem of rebuke has arisen.

In contrast, the opponents recognized that in Adam the grace without which he could not persevere aided a healthy will, whereas in the remainder of humanity with its severely weakened will, grace both restores believers who have fallen and assists them in perseverance.[34] Quite simply, Augustine's detractors rejected a perseverance that "cannot be won by prayer or lost by obstinacy,"[35] a perseverance that makes human striving in the religious life irrelevant. It was on the basis of a different understanding of perseverance, Hilary said, that they denied the teaching of a "fixed number of elect and reprobate."[36] Thus, as Prosper had pointed out twice before, critics rejected Augustine's teaching of an absolute decree of sovereign grace because such a decree robs human effort of any purpose.

A second matter of contention that both Prosper and Hilary reported was the charge that Augustine's teaching was novel. Prosper referred to the assertion of the opposition that it was they, not Augustine, who were consistent with the fathers of the church.[37] Here the issue of tradition and authority only adumbrated in North Africa came to the fore.

The matter of novelty was an important issue. For a doctrine to be acceptable it had at best to appear to be in conformity with that which had been taught by authoritative predecessors in the faith, particularly those church fathers held in esteem locally. In the *De correptione et gratia* and an accompanying letter Augustine had cited Cyprian to substantiate his case,[38] thereby appealing in particular to the North African tradition when he addressed the monks at Hadrumetum. With these monks, however, the issue had not been so significant, as Augustine himself was an adequate authority. In South Gaul, which was separated from North Africa by geography and local tradition, the memory of Cyprian and the present stature of Augustine carried far less weight. In this

---

[34]*Ep.* 226.6.

[35]*Ep.* 226.4. As the examination of the writings of John Cassian in chapter 3 will demonstrate, prayer and obstinacy were central areas of concern in the monastic life.

[36]*Ep.* 226.7.

[37]*Ep.* 225.3.

[38]*De corr. et grat.* 7.12, with a citation of Cyprian, *Testimonia* 3.4; *Ep.* 215.3, with a reference to Cyprian's *De dominica oratione*.

locale an issue that would be significant for the remainder of the controversy had surfaced: the provision of appropriate credentials, specifically, a convincing tradition, to support one's point of view.

Hilary pursued the troublesome question of novelty somewhat differently. He, too, said that in Marseilles and elsewhere in Gaul Augustine's teaching on grace was regarded as "new."[39] Moreover, his letter implied that this teaching was not simply new to the tradition but also new to Augustine. Hilary referred to earlier works of the African bishop that served his opponents as ammunition against his present position.[40] The ticklish issue, of course, was whether or not the early Augustine had been in line with the tradition of the church when he left this difficult question of grace undefined, as the church fathers had left it undefined,[41] or in his suggestion that Christ had preached to those who would believe,[42] or in his allowance that in divine foreknowledge God chooses on the basis of future faith, although not of future works.[43]

Tactfully confronting Augustine with the difficulty of this problem, Hilary asked for a copy of the *Retractationes*, as soon as they should be published, that he might defend the older and wiser Augustine against those who would prefer the misunderstandings of the African bishop's young manhood.[44] Yet he also let Augustine know, in effect, that it would be of little use for the latter to argue further unless he could cite some authority whom the opposition could neither ignore nor deny.[45]

With the reception of these two friendly yet troubled letters, Augustine faced the problem of further clarifying and defending his understanding of the interaction of grace and human nature. In contrast to the dispute at Hadrumetum where explanation was sufficient to calm a friendly misunderstanding, the dispute in southern Gaul was becoming increasingly polarized. With every new insight and clarification Augustine's teaching came under growing suspicion. It was in such an atmosphere that in 429 he wrote his last two treatises, *De praedestinatione sanctorum* and *De dono perseverantiae*.[46]

---

[39]*Ep.* 226.2: *Novum et inutile esse praedicationi.*

[40]*Ep.* 226.3. Examples include references to Augustine's letter to Porphyry, *Ep.* 103, and *Prop. ad Rom.* 62. *Ep.* 226.8 makes reference to *De lib. arb.* 3.23.66-68.

[41]*Ep.* 226.8.

[42]*Ep.* 226.3.

[43]*Ep.* 226.3.

[44]*Ep.* 226.10. The *Retractationes* did, in fact, address this issue. See *Retr.* 1.8.2; 1.22.3,4; 2.27.1.

[45]*Ep.* 226.9.

[46]P. De Letter, "Introduction," *Prosper of Aquitaine: Defense of St. Augustine,* 6. De Letter states that originally the two treatises were a "double tract, later known as two separate books."

It should be noted that in late 429 or early 430, after having written to Rufinus and to Augustine but before having received a reply from Augustine, Prosper wrote the *Carmen de ingratis*. This poem of approximately one thousand lines located the position of the Semi-Pelagians in relation to that of the Pelagians and that of Augustine and harshly reiterated the arguments that Prosper had made in the two letters already examined, but without contributing to the development of his argument.[47]

De praedestinatione sanctorum

In the *De praedestinatione sanctorum* and *the De dono perseverantiae* Augustine constructed an argument designed to overcome the objections reported to him in the letters of Prosper and Hilary. These objections centered on two issues: the logic of grace and the novelty of his teaching on grace. The problem of the logic of grace, as described in the correspondence, had two basic foci: the matter of gratuitous predestination with its attendant question of the *ortus bonae voluntatis* to which the *De praedestinatione sanctorum* responded and the matter of gratuitous perseverance with its attendant question of the value of exhortation and preaching to which the *De dono perseverantiae* responded. The second issue, that of the novelty of Augustine's teaching on grace, also had two foci: the conformity of Augustine's teaching to the tradition of the church and the secondary matter of the conformity of Augustine's present teaching to his own previous teaching. The issue of novelty he dealt with in both of the treatises.

The double argument of the *De praedestinatione sanctorum* was a direct response to the letters of Prosper and Hilary. Its dominant theme was that faith even in its beginning is a gift dependent on a predestination, the rationale of which is hidden in God. The secondary theme, interwoven throughout the treatise, was Augustine's defense against the charge of novelty.

With regard to the matter of novelty, particularly the consistency of his own teaching on the source of faith, Augustine admitted that earlier in his life he had thought and written, as in his *Expositio quarundam propositionum ex epistula ad Romanos*,[48] which Hilary had cited, that faith is not a divine gift but is attributable to human agency rather than to prior grace. Such faith, he had

---

[47]*Carmen de ingratis S. Prosperi Aquitani*, trans., intro., and commentary by Charles T. Huegelmeyer (Washington DC: Catholic University of America Press, 1962) 11-12. See also D. M. Cappuyns, "Le premier représentant de l'augustinisme médiéval, Prosper d'Aquitaine," *Recherches de théologie ancienne et médiévale* 1 (1929): 316-17; Georges de Plinval, "Prosper d'Aquitaine interprète de saint Augustin," *Recherches augustiniennes* 1 (1958): 345-46; E. Amann, "Semi-pélagiens," *Dictionnaire de théologie catholique* 14/2 (1941) 1816-17.

[48]*De praed. sanct.* 3.7; citing *Prop ad Rom.* 60, 62, and *Retr.* 1.22.2-4; see *Ep.* 226.3.

believed, then became the means for the reception of the divine gifts that enable a righteous life. He also acknowledged that he had formerly taught that election is based on divine foreknowledge concerning those who would believe by their own agency rather than on the foreknowledge of what God would do for them. In other words, election depends upon foreknowledge of the "merit of faith" rather than of grace. Augustine now refuted as inadequate his earlier teaching that human agency produces faith.[49] According to his reconsidered opinion, even the faith by which one seeks and wins the other gifts of God is a divine gift; otherwise the foundation for salvation would be human merit rather than divine grace. Faith would be the human difference which would explain why some are saved and some are not. Not insignificantly, Augustine pointed out that it was as a result of reading Cyprian that he had become aware of the inadequacy of his own position, for Cyprian, citing 1 Corinthians 4:7, had taught "that we must boast in nothing, since nothing is our own."[50]

The importance of the reference to Cyprian was, of course, that the citation was intended to lend credence to Augustine's defense against the charge of novelty. For him to say that he had been led to his present opinion by the writing of an authoritative leader in the North African church, a bishop and a martyr, was to say that the tradition itself had corrected his understanding and had thereby been the source of his reformed view. This tactic of appealing to the writings of Cyprian was not new to Augustine. Throughout the Donatist controversy, the Catholic bishop of Hippo Regius had regularly cited the writings of Cyprian as authorization for his own position.[51] Of course, as Cyprian was the common property of all North African churchmen, Augustine's Donatist opponents had used the same stratagem against him. In the Pelagian controversy, Augustine again cited Cyprian as a reference for his arguments, but with considerably less frequency, as this latter controversy was hardly provincial,

---

[49]*De praed. sanct.* 3.7. He had already rejected that earlier view in *Ad Simpl.* 1 qu. 2.

[50]*De praed sanct.* 3.7: *In nullo gloriandum, quando nostrum nihil sit.* Augustine was citing Cyprian, *Testimonia, ad Quirinum* 3.4. Cyprian had used 1 Corinthians 4:7 as a proof text for the precept "that we must boast in nothing, since nothing is our own." [ET is from Ante-Nicene Fathers, 5:528]. Nevertheless, he had not developed his interpretation in the sense that Augustine pursued, although such an interpretation would not have been inconsistent with his argument. In *Retr.* 2.27, Augustine insisted that in the *Ad Simplicianum* he had set out to defend the freedom of the human will but was led by God to realize total human dependence on grace.

[51]Augustine's treatise *De baptismo,* for example, is replete with references to Cyprian and his writings. Only a few items will be noted here for illustrative purposes: *De bapt.* 2.2, Cyprian, *Ep.* 71; *De bapt.* 2.13, Cyprian, *Ep.* 71; *De bapt.* 2.18, Cyprian, *Ep.* 73.2; *De bapt.* 3.17, Cyprian, *Ep.* 73.3; *De bapt.* 4.1, Cyprian, *Ep.* 73.10, 11; *De bapt.* 4.2, Cyprian, *Ep.* 11.1.

whereas the authority of the martyr-bishop tended to be.[52] Nevertheless, these citations, although limited in number, do show Augustine mobilizing Cyprian in support of his anti-Pelagian view of grace. Finally, Augustine had sent a copy of Cyprian's *De dominica oratione* to Hadrumetum. Reference to Cyprian had become standard practice for Augustine.

If Augustine acknowledged that his earlier position had been corrected by the tradition itself, he also chided his opponents for the manner in which they had read his works. Had they been sufficiently diligent, they would have realized that around 396 at the beginning of his episcopate he had taken the position with which his writings were consistent even now. At that time he had written two books to Simplician, a priest in Milan who was later to become bishop of that city. There in explanation of Romans 9:10-29 he had reached what he believed to be an inescapable conclusion: the sovereignty of grace over the human will. It was, moreover, a conclusion that agreed with 1 Corinthians 4:7 and, of course, with Cyprian.[53]

Hilary had warned, however, that Augustine's opponents held a contrary interpretation of 1 Corinthians 4:7: "For who sees anything different in you? What have you that you did not receive? If then you received it, why do you boast as if it were not a gift?" The opponents rejected the suggestion that the passage referred to faith, for they insisted that our nature, although now corrupted, has not lost its power to believe. That power could be exercised without the prior aid of grace and, presumably, in Christians it was so exercised. The opponents were convinced "that they have some beginning of will . . . by which they may obtain or receive [grace]."[54] Similarly, with reference to the statement "Believe, and you shall be saved" Hilary had reported that these same persons contended that a person does possess the capacity to believe, as commanded. Should the person do so, God will bestow salvation, as promised. The human activity of believing has served as the occasion for the divine bestowal of salvation, although human agency lacks the power to attain salvation.[55] These critics of Augustine acknowledged the dominance of divine

---

[52]Augustine's most numerous references to Cyprian in the anti-Pelagian writings are to be found in the treatise, *Contra duas epistulas Pelagianorum*. Examples include *C. duas ep. Pel.* 4.8.21, Cypr. *De opere et eleemosynis* 1,22; 4.8.22, Cypr. *De mortalitate* 2 and *De bono patientiae* 11; 4.8.23, Cypr. *Ep.* 54(64).2,4,5; 4.9.25, Cypr. *De dominica oratione* 12,14,16,17,18,26; 4.9.25, Cypr. *Testimonia* 3.4; 4.9.25, Cypr. *De bono patientiae* 3; 4.10.27, Cypr. *De opera et eleemosynis* 3; 4.10.27, Cypr. *De mortalite* 4,5; 4.10.27, Cypr. *De dominica oratione* 12,22; 4.10.27, Cypr. *Testimonia* 3.54.

[53]*De praed. sanct.* 4.8. It is to be noted that there is no mention of Cyprian in *Ad Simplicianum*.

[54]*Ep.* 226.4; cf. *Ep.* 225.4.

[55]*Ep.* 226.2.

grace, but they did so in such a way as to maintain the reality and purposefulness of human agency. They insisted that the shape of a person's life correlates with the person's destiny, as, Augustine acknowledged, he himself had once taught.

The shift in his views, Augustine pointed out, was evident in a statement in his *Confessiones* that had been unacceptable to Pelagius and presumably was unacceptable to his present opponents as well: "command what you will but then grant what you command."[56] Yet whereas when writing the *Confessiones* he perhaps had had in mind only the requirement for perseverance in the Christian life, he now insisted that the possibility of beginning that life was also a divine gift. Both the fulfillment of the requirement to believe and the giving of the reward of salvation are the gifts of God.[57]

Despite these strong affirmations of the sovereignty of grace, Augustine did not abandon his determination to maintain the significance of the human contribution. And, in fact, he did maintain human agency in two senses. In arguing that faith is a gift that entails the preparation of the will that it might believe, he was also acknowledging that it is the will that believes.[58] Moreover, the will that believes does not do so against its own willing. The human agent is a genuine, uncoerced participant in the salvific process. Augustine was undoubtedly striving to maintain a double agency, one that is divine and the other human.

Nevertheless, the human agent is not the primary or initiating agent, for the will is moved by God in such a way that it believes. The *ortus bonae voluntatis* is not of human agency. Augustine described the preparation of the will as the instruction of the will by God. Such instruction is never rejected, he asserted, because the very preparation itself changes the heart, removing its hardness, so that the person hears, learns, and comes to the Son. There are no exceptions to this rule or to its corollary that all who do not come to the Son have not been taught by the Father.[59]

To counter the objections that John 6:45 ("They shall all be taught by God") might seem to provide, Augustine suggested that God does teach all to come to Christ but only in the restricted sense that "none comes in any other way."[60] This interpretation, however, was probably as unsatisfactory to his opponents as had been Augustine's treatment of 1 Timothy 2:4 in the *De correptione et gratia*, for

---

[56]*Conf.* 10.29.40; 10.31.45; 10.37.60; paraphrased in *De praed. sanct.* 11.22 and cited in *De don. pers.* 20.53. The English translation is taken from the *Confessions*, trans. R. S. Pine-Coffin (Baltimore: Penguin, 1961). For a discussion of Pelagius's reaction to this passage, see Rees, *Pelagius: A Reluctant Heretic*, 1n.2.

[57]*De praed. sanct.* 11.22.

[58]*De praed. sanct.* 3.7, citing *Retr.* 1.22.2-4; *De praed. sanct.* 5.10.

[59]*De praed. sanct.* 8.13.

[60]*De praed. sanct.* 8.14.

in both instances he rejected the straightforward, universalistic reading of the word "all" in favor of a more restricted interpretation. In effect, in each of these cases he made the Scripture subservient to his doctrine of predestination with its notion of a limited divine will for salvation. Perhaps as an acknowledgment of the difficulty of his exegesis, Augustine offered the only justification that he found available to explain why God does not teach all: the existence of the vessels of wrath serves to underscore the divine graciousness toward the vessels of mercy.[61] Augustine was allowing Romans 9 to override other parts of Scripture, and in the process portrayed human action in such a way that it took on the character of unreality under the determination of predestining grace.

He portrayed the Christian life from beginning to end as the gift of grace. One effect was that the agency of the Christian appears real only in terms of receptivity and not in terms of contribution, with the self incapable of initiating its own will or action. Stated differently, the extent of human agency in the case of a Christian is that of being a vessel created, chosen, transformed, and employed by grace, a vessel whose character is determined by its content. The merit and reward scheme remains, but as in the *De correptione et gratia* grace is rewarding grace on the basis of a predestination made from all eternity. In a scheme from which human agency, in the sense of self-initiated willing or doing, has been drained away, the notions of merit and reward have become unreal.

The problem of the unreality of human agency has become increasingly evident as Augustine has developed the primary theme of the treatise: the *ortus bonae voluntatis* is a gift dependent on an inscrutable divine predestination to grace. Problematic or not, Augustine insisted that this understanding of human agency was not new, and he sought to demonstrate that his claim that grace prepares the way for faith did, in fact, conform with the tradition. He thus used the secondary theme of the treatise, his rebuttal of the charge of novelty, to substantiate his primary contention.

He made three points. First, he referred to Cyprian's *De dominica oratione* as evidence that believers pray for unbelievers that the latter might be granted the gift of faith. Such a petition would be nonsensical if the unbelievers already possessed a faith that preceded grace.[62] According to this argument, the petition presupposes that the proper agent for enacting faith is God, not the human being.

Second, Augustine defended his own earlier treatise against Porphyry entitled *De tempore Christianae religionis*. In that work he had stated "that Christ willed to appear to men, and that His doctrine should be preached among them, at that time when He knew, and at that place where He knew, that there were some who would believe on Him." This statement, of course, could be construed to mean

---

[61]*De praed. sanct.* 8.14.
[62]*De praed. sanct.* 8.15.

that foreknowledge of belief, i.e., of merit, occasioned grace, but Augustine insisted that he had not intended such an interpretation. He pointed out that when making this statement he had been responding to the question of why Christ had come so late in history, and he had felt no need to pursue the further question of the source of faith for those who did believe, "that is, whether God only foreknew them, or also predestinated them." The meaning of his original statement was not that Christ had appeared and had the gospel preached among those he knew would believe of their own agency, but among those he knew had been elected before all creation.[63] On two fronts, therefore, Augustine attempted to demonstrate the traditional character of his stance: his doctrine was not novel, for it accorded with the tradition of the church as confirmed by its correspondence to Cyprian; his doctrine was not novel, for it was simply an elaboration of what was latent in his own earlier teaching.

Augustine sought to score a third point against the charge of novelty by referring to the silence of the tradition on particular issues. The fathers of the church, he said, did not address questions that no one was raising during their lifetimes. If, therefore, he was now teaching a doctrine that could not be specifically located in the writings of his predecessors, the reason was not that he was contradicting them but that he was addressing questions which only lately had arisen.[64]

The defense against novelty had been made, at least for the time being. Further defense of gratuitous predestination was still necessary. Augustine employed two examples to reinforce his argument: the instance of those who die in infancy and that of Christ. These two cases, the former rare and the latter unique, he made paradigmatic for all cases: as election settles the extraordinary cases, so it settles all others as well. For those who die in infancy, the reception of baptism prior to death automatically means salvation, as they will not live to commit actual sin. Despite the fact that they will die free of actual sin, their salvation can hardly be construed as a matter of reward, for they will also not live long enough to accumulate merit. Instead, their salvation, effected through baptism, must be attributed to grace, for whether or not such an infant is baptized depends upon whether mercy or judgment prevails for that child. If mercy prevails, it is necessarily the gift of grace; if judgment, it is simply payment of the debt all have incurred in Adam.[65] The fact that before death some infants receive baptism and thereby salvation results from the fact that for them divine mercy has prevailed.

With respect to the case of such infants Augustine's opponents had argued that the reception of baptism is based not on grace but on God's foreknowledge

---

[63]*De praed. sanct.* 9.17; 9.18.
[64]*De praed. sanct.* 14.27.
[65]*De praed. sanct.* 12.23; 12.24; 14.29.

of what their merit would have been had they lived. Augustine refuted this claim on two counts.

First, he asserted that his opponents' position, like the Pelagian teaching, undermined the relation between baptism and original sin. The Pelagians had understood baptism to be a watershed in the adult's life. It functioned to remit actual sins accumulated up to that point as well as to restore the health of human nature, weakened in Adam. To the extent that the Pelagians held a doctrine of original sin, it might be said to refer to the "habit of sin," socially reinforced, that enslaves the individual but does not involve any inherited sinful bias or culpability. Each person, they believed, is born good. With such a restricted understanding of original sin, the Pelagians had no satisfactory explanation for the church's practice of the baptism of infants.[66]

Augustine charged that these new opponents weakened the relation between baptism and original sin. If, as they said, God grants or denies baptism to infants just before their death on the basis of foreknowledge of the quality of the life they would have lived, then the divine decision regarding these infants rests on merit (although future merit never to be actualized). Such an understanding of baptism, he argued, robs grace of its gratuity. Furthermore, by referring baptism exclusively to future (unreal) merit and demerit, it fails to take into account a prior (original) sin that requires remission.[67]

The criticism was not totally justified. From Prosper's and Hilary's letters Augustine had learned that his opponents in Gaul were far closer to his own position than to that of Pelagius in their understanding both of original sin and of the need for grace, although their conception of the fall and its consequences was not nearly so thoroughgoing as was Augustine's. Nevertheless, Augustine's charge was not without justification. The opponents' argument did bypass the doctrine of baptism for the remission of original sin. For them inherited culpability had little import. Moreover, by their subordination of the grace of baptism to merit, they had undercut the gratuitous character of the divine decision to save.

For both Augustine and his opponents the interpretation given to the awkward cases of those dying in infancy proved crucial. For the latter divine foreknowledge provided the explanation for the awkward cases. In this way, human merit retained its significance. In contrast, Augustine made the awkward cases a model for the interpretation of all cases. The gratuity of predestination stood.

Second, Augustine countered his opponents' argument for foreknowledge with a reference to Cyprian's treatise *De mortalitate*. Cyprian had made use of

---

[66]G. W. H. Lampe, "Sin, Salvation, and Grace," *A History of Christian Doctrine*, ed. Hubert Cunliffe-Jones and Benjamin Drewery (Philadelphia: Fortress Press, 1978) 160-61. See also Rees, 13.

[67]*De praed. sanct.* 12.23; 12.24; 13.25.

the passage "He was taken away lest wickedness should alter his understanding" (Wisdom 4:11).[68] As Hilary had pointed out, the opponents rejected the authority of the book of Wisdom: they did not consider it canonical. Augustine responded that it was the tradition of the church to read from Wisdom. Its authority had long been accepted.[69] The importance to Augustine of the reference to Wisdom was that, according to Cyprian's interpretation of the passage, an early death benefits the believer, for it removes the person from the possibility of sinning. Early death would hold no advantage for the believer, Augustine inferred, if God judges on the basis of life as it would have been lived rather than as it is lived.[70] Once again Augustine pressed the point: it is grace, not foreknowledge, that effects salvation. The reference to Cyprian simply corroborated the argument that Augustine had made with regard to those dying in infancy.

Augustine now turned to his second example of gratuitous predestination: the case of Christ. As the infants had no prior merits by which they deserved baptism, neither did the humanity of Christ have any prior merit by which it deserved to be assumed by the Word of God. Not having had any existence before its union with the Word, his humanity had had no opportunity for meriting the special honor bestowed upon it.[71]

By grace alone, based in the predestination of God, Christ was born of the Spirit and the Virgin, free from all sin. Augustine's argument was that this same pattern holds true for the rebirth of the Christian through water and Spirit in baptism by which sin is forgiven. As Christ was predestinated, the members of his body are predestinated in him.[72]

Of course, it might be pointed out that a crucial difference between the case of Christ and that of other persons is that others do have an existence before the gift of grace in baptism. However, according to Augustine's scheme, prebaptismal existence lacks the charity necessary for willing and doing the good. Only at baptism do the offspring of Adam receive the grace requisite for the attainment of merit. The case for gratuitous predestination still stands.

Moreover, as the example of Christ demonstrates that the predestinating judgment precedes not only human merit but also human existence, one can infer that the divine decision to save takes place, in the case of those who will receive salvific grace, even before the person's existence. Human agency is entirely irrelevant to the determination of human destiny.

---

[68]*De praed. sanct.* 14.26, citing Cyprian, *De mortalitate* 23.
[69]*De praed. sanct.* 14.27; 14.28.
[70]*De praed. sanct.* 14.26; 14.28.
[71]*De praed. sanct.* 12.23; 15.30.
[72]*De praed. sanct.* 15.31.

On the basis of the rare case of those dying in infancy and the paradigmatic case of Christ, Augustine sought to demonstrate the necessity of gratuitous predestination. As merit, either actual or foreknown, is inapplicable for these cases, he argued that it is inapplicable for all cases. This employment of extraordinary instances as the standard for interpreting ordinary ones effectively severed any connection between salvation and human agency.

In order further to secure predestination from all talk of merit, Augustine located it prior to the foundation of the world. Dependent only on divine foreknowledge of divine action, election is effected in the life of the individual by a divine calling through which God accomplishes what God has predestined. The one so called is, without fail, justified and finally glorified for all eternity. God elected the person in order to make the person righteous, and indeed, the person is made to believe and made to be holy. The grounds for the election thus lie entirely within God, not at all in the person.[73] It is important to remember, however, that for Augustine, the person really is made righteous, really is brought to will and to do the good. This fact, presumably, is what justifies Augustine in retaining the merit and reward scheme: there is genuine human willing and doing, and to these God responds favorably. The problem is that the human willing and doing are in no sense enacted by the human agent alone but only by human agency as formed, controlled, and directed by God.

The inexorable logic of Augustine's position allowed no possibility for the beginning of faith to be within human capacity; it must be the gift of God. "[God] chose us, not because we believed, but that we might believe, lest we should be said first to have chosen Him."[74] There is no possibility of self-initiated human believing.

Concerning the two themes with which discussion of this treatise began, a brief evaluation can be made. Augustine has demonstrated that if the logic of the sovereignty of grace is developed consistently, then not only does perseverance in faith require the assistance of grace, as his opponents acknowledged, but the very beginning of faith must be the work of grace. The next logical step, and the one which he took in the final treatise, would be to say that even perseverance is the gift of grace, not simply the work of the person assisted by grace. The problem that becomes increasingly apparent, therefore, is that of the reality of the merit and reward scheme as human action seems ever more unreal. There is, to be sure, genuine human merit that God rewards. The problem is just that it is difficult to tell in what sense the human willing and doing can truly be ascribed

---

[73]*De praed. sanct.* 17.34-18.36. Augustine's argument reflects such biblical texts as Ephesians 1:3 and John 15:16.

[74]*De praed. sanct.* 19.38.

to the human agent as his or her own willing and doing. The divine agent is always molding that good will and effecting that good action.

As to the second theme, that of the conformity of Augustine's teaching to the tradition and thus implicitly the authority of his teaching on grace, it is apparent that his heavy reliance on Cyprian was an attempt to demonstrate the congruence of his views with the accepted teaching of the church. What is not apparent, however, is to what degree Cyprian, the martyr bishop of Carthage whose memory was highly revered in the African church, carried weight outside Africa, particularly among those Gallic monks who had been molded by the fathers of the Eastern church. The importance of this question would be underscored by the final treatise of Augustine.

De dono perseverantiae

The companion piece to the *De praedestinatione sanctorum* was the treatise the *De dono perseverantiae*. Apparently Augustine wrote them both at the same time and sent them together, perhaps even as a single work, to Prosper and Hilary. The theme of the former was that of gratuitous predestination. Augustine's intent in it was to demonstrate that the beginning of faith is from God. The theme of the latter was gratuitous perseverance, and here Augustine's intent was to demonstrate that perseverance in faith until death is also the gift of grace. Throughout both treatises runs the appeal to tradition as the guarantee for Augustine's teaching on grace. Furthermore, as the function of rebuke proved to be a derivative issue in Augustine's exposition of the logic of grace in the *De correptione et gratia*, so now, in the *De dono perseverantiae*, the function of exhortation and preaching became a similarly troubling question. In fact, the problem of the unreality of human agency became inescapable with Augustine's new and stark denial of a person's ability to exercise control or direction of that person's own thoughts. As we shall see, this denial struck sharply at the traditions and discipline of the monastic life, particularly as understood and taught by Cassian.

Augustine forthrightly stated the primary theme of the treatise in the first chapter: perseverance in Christ until the end of this life is the gift of God. Whether or not one has actually received this gift, however, cannot be determined until death because the only certain test is that one is still faithful at the time of death.[75] The secondary theme emerged soon afterward. Augustine provided credentials for his views on grace, credentials that embraced non-African as well as African traditions and authorities.

---

[75]*De don. pers.* 1.1.

This secondary theme served as a vehicle for developing the case for a gratuitous gift of perseverance. Augustine called to his defense the witness of the church on grace. That witness had already been employed against Pelagius, and he now offered it in summary form. (1) As all merit is the gift of grace, grace is not bestowed on the basis of merit. (2) Everyone, while in the earthly body, sins. (3) All, at birth, are liable for the sin of Adam and can be excused only through regeneration.[76]

As the African bishop was quick to note, long before the error of the Pelagians arose, Cyprian had written the *De dominica oratione*, which substantiated the first two points just noted. Specifically, Augustine argued that as perseverance is a merit, Cyprian had demonstrated it to be the gift of God. Using the martyr bishop's treatise as his guide, Augustine discussed each petition of the Lord's Prayer. All of them except the fifth, "Forgive us our debts, as we also have forgiven our debtors,"[77] he found to be a request for perseverance. Even this petition, however, might serve as an argument against the Pelagians, for the latter had said that the righteous can be without sin in this life. Thus as Augustine construed Cyprian's interpretation, the petition was in accord with the second point of the Catholic church as made above, as the other petitions were in accord with the first.[78]

The sixth petition, "Lead us not into temptation, but deliver us from evil,"[79] provided an occasion for response to Hilary's statement that "these brethren will not have this perseverance so preached that it cannot be obtained by prayer or lost by obstinacy."[80] Augustine was willing to affirm at this point that perseverance can be "obtained by prayer," although his affirmation was not so straightforward as it may at first appear to have been.

The key lay in his definition of perseverance. According to Augustine, Christ taught the saints that they are to pray for this gift from God, as the petitions of the prayer indicate. Furthermore in the sixth petition, in asking God that they may not be led into temptation, they are asking that they be "not led into the temptation of contumacy." If God grants the petition, then they will not be so

---

[76]*De don. pers.* 2.4.

[77]Mt. 6:12.

[78]*De don. pers.* 2.4-5.9. Augustine presented Cyprian's position fairly with regard to the second point, i.e., as a denial of the possibility of sinlessness; see Cyprian, *De dominica oratione* 22. With regard to the first point, also, he seems to have fairly interpreted Cyprian, i.e., that perseverance is a gift of God. What is not so clear is that Cyprian thought of perseverance as a merit and all merit as the gift of grace. Cyprian did not carry his argument to that conclusion, and it is not evident from the treatise that he would have. Thus, if Augustine was not actually misreading Cyprian, he was at best bending Cyprian's treatise in a direction it did not take itself.

[79]Mt. 6:13.

[80]*Ep.* 226.4, cited by Augustine in *De don. pers.* 6.10.

led, for nothing happens without God's doing or allowing. Perseverance is thus secured, for one who is not led into temptation does not turn from God. Up to this point the opposition would probably have agreed; nevertheless, Augustine had not yet fully addressed either of their reservations: whether or not perseverance is actually gained by prayer and whether or not it is lost by obstinacy. At issue was the nature of perseverance itself. Augustine insisted that perseverance cannot be subject to the conditions of winning or losing. As he had explained in the first chapter of the treatise, perseverance is perseverance to the end. This gift is not the sort that one may have for a time and then lose. Unless one actually has this gift, one will not persevere to the end; on the other hand, if one does have this gift, one will necessarily persevere to the end. After death, of course, the gift cannot be lost.[81]

To underscore his contention that perseverance is a gift, Augustine employed the paradigm that he had developed in the *De correptione et gratia*. In the angels and the first man the free will was adequate not to depart from God. Since the fall, it is only by grace that a person may both approach God and persevere.[82] This work of grace is the predestination of Christ and thus of those who are in Christ, for as Christ is so predestined that he will not depart from God, the members of his body are thereby made secure in their perseverance.[83] As validation of his teaching, Augustine pointed to the church's practice of praying for perseverance, particularly its regular use of the petitions for perseverance in the Lord's Prayer.[84] He claimed, therefore, to be teaching not only what the fathers of the church had taught but also what the people of the church had always practiced.

Yet there was a problem in Augustine's use of the practice of prayer to demonstrate that perseverance is a gift. The very fact that it is a gift given without regard to human merit by divine determination only shows that whether one prays for it or not has no effect on whether one receives it. Augustine's very appeal to prayer put the point of prayer in doubt. Moreover, by indicating the disjunction of prayer from the reception of perseverance, his argument revealed the disjunction of human action from its intended salvific outcome.

The teaching that perseverance is a gift, undeserved by human merit, provoked persistent questions about the justice, perhaps even about the wisdom, of God. Augustine's basic premise for answering all such questions was that there is never any unrighteousness in God. Beyond this premise, however, his answers could hardly be expected to have satisfied those monks seeking to live in such a way as to bring themselves into conformity with God and God's will.

---

[81]*De don. pers.* 5.9-7.13.
[82]*De don. pers.* 7.13.
[83]*De don. pers.* 7.14.
[84]*De don. pers.* 7.15.

For example, in Augustine's view, by righteous judgment some receive the deserved perdition from which others are rescued by grace. The fate of the former serves to underscore the divine generosity toward the latter so that they might appreciate the gift.[85] Yet even if it is granted that this arrangement is necessary for displaying the grace of God, why some are punished more or less than others remains an unanswerable question.[86] The lives of the particular persons condemned or saved make no difference in the divine determination of who will receive the requisite grace.

A further problem arises from the fact that there are some who appear for a while to be among the believers yet do not persevere to the end. Augustine argued that the reason that some who are not elect live for a while among the elect and give the appearance of perseverance before they finally fall away is that such an arrangement serves as a check on pride. It functions as a safeguard against the feeling of security. In other words, the fact that some do fall away serves as a reminder that the possession of the gift of perseverance can never be assumed. Prior to death there is no assurance that God has conferred this grace. The failure of some provides a reminder of the human frailty of all.[87] If their falling away does have the effect of benefitting others, that result does not diminish the fact that genuine failure has taken place. Their success in doing the good, even for a while, indicates that they had received the grace enabling them so to act; the failure to persevere in the good was of their own choosing.

The frailty of human existence and of the human will, exposed in the case of those who fall away, was conspicuously evident to Augustine in the limited control that the self possesses even over its own thoughts. To substantiate this point, Augustine referred to Ambrose's treatise *De fuga saeculi*. Ambrose had written that it is impossible for one to rid oneself of the thoughts and desires of this earth. It is precisely while attempting to direct the mind toward God that one's attention is distracted and overcome by contrary images. Accordingly, Augustine averred, divine aid is essential if one is to entertain the kinds of thoughts that give rise to and support faith.[88]

Augustine may have deduced somewhat more from Ambrose's comments than the latter had intended. Certainly Ambrose affirmed the necessity of the assistance of grace; yet he also indicated that he believed that the self can make

---

[85]*De don. pers.* 8.16.

[86]*De don. pers.* 8.18.

[87]*De don. pers.* 8.19.

[88]*De don. pers.* 8.19-20, citing Ambrose, *De fuga saeculi* 1.1. Previously, in his battle against Pelagianism, Augustine had taught that persons have no control over thoughts entering their mind, but the will is capable of entertaining or rejecting these thoughts (*De spir. et litt.* 34.60) and that grace is necessary for the thinking of good thoughts (*De gr. Chr.* 25.26 and *C. duas ep. Pel.* 8.18).

a positive contribution to the direction of its own thoughts. For example, the flight from the world is in itself a movement of the attention from the entanglements of the world to the pursuit of God.[89] At the very least, it may be said that Augustine placed less emphasis on this positive aspect than Ambrose had done. Nevertheless, by selectively reading Ambrose Augustine was beginning to construct a tradition for his own views by downplaying a part of the very tradition to which he appealed. As we shall see in the next chapter, John Cassian in his guidance to monks on controlling their thoughts, while acknowledging inevitable limitations, emphasized the positive role of submission to discipline in the avoidance of distraction.[90]

The reference to Ambrose here and in later parts of the treatise was significant. As bishop of Milan from 374 to 397, Ambrose had been Augustine's mentor or at least a highly influential, if somewhat remote, figure in the younger man's conversion and baptism.[91] By illustrating his conformity to the tradition of which the bishop of Milan had been a distinguished leader, Augustine was asserting the validity of his own credentials. At the same time, he was extending the Augustinian "tradition" to non-African sources. In contrast to the references to Cyprian, the references to Ambrose would establish his connection to the wider Western church, for Ambrose had been well respected in Italy and South Gaul as well as in Africa. Moreover, he had enjoyed a broader education than had Augustine, an education in Greek as well as Latin, which provided him with access to the philosophy and theology of the East. Through Ambrose, therefore, Augustine could at least appear to be indirectly linked to the East. Cyprian was primarily a provincial hero; Ambrose definitely was not.[92]

Even more to the point, Ambrose had had a special relation to the churches of South Gaul. In the later years of the fourth century when disputes had arisen between ecclesiastical jurisdictions in that area, it was not uncommon practice for the disputants to turn to a third party for a resolution. The churches of South

---

[89]*De fuga saeculi* 1.2; 1.3; 1.4; 2.5.

[90]Augustine's downplaying of human capacity in the control of thoughts was at odds with much of monastic striving, particularly as it was influenced by the desert fathers of the East. The review of John Cassian's work in chapter 3 will offer a glimpse of the nature of Augustine's challenge to monastic life.

[91]*Conf.* 5.13.23; 5.14.24; 6.1.1–6.4.6; 9.5.13; 9.7.15; Brown, *Augustine of Hippo*, 81-87, 124-25.

[92]W. H. C. Frend, *Martyrdom and Persecution in the Early Church: A Study of a Conflict From the Maccabees to Donatus,* (Oxford: Basil Blackwell, 1965; repr. Grand Rapids MI: Baker Book House, 1981) 418-20. Cyprian's sphere of influence extended over the Christian church in North Africa but was not entirely limited to this area. Spanish congregations in León and Mérida appealed to him in the Novatianist controversy, and in this instance as well as others he was in conflict with the bishop of Rome.

Gaul had appealed to Ambrose on such occasions. The practice came to an end only when, in 404, Pope Innocent I ruled that the resolution of intraprovincial disputes must be sought from Rome.[93] In citing Ambrose, Augustine was buttressing his case with one whose authority was formidable.

Furthermore, Augustine demonstrated his conformity to tradition not simply by showing his position as continuous with one of its more prestigious figures but also by showing it as discontinuous with what stood outside the tradition. In reply to Hilary's statement that some of Augustine's earlier works on free will were being cited against what he was teaching now,[94] Augustine replied that in those earlier works he was writing against a different set of problems. His arguments had been directed against the Manichees who believed that there are "two coeternal, confounded substances of good and evil," denied original sin and the responsibility of the free will for evil, and accordingly, rejected the Old Testament and much of the New that affirms original sin. His previous tactic had been to allow that human ignorance and difficulty might be either punishments or aspects of that single human nature with which all are born. Either possibility would serve to refute the Manichees, the first by affirming human responsibility and the second by affirming only one human nature from Adam. For purposes of argumentation against the Manichees, Augustine had allowed for both alternatives. The Pelagian threat had not existed at that time, however. As the Pelagians had opted for the second possibility, and thereby denied original sin, Augustine, in his *Retractationes*, had found it necessary to eliminate that option and take his stand with the first, that is, that ignorance and difficulty are punishment for original sin.[95]

Augustine's explanation of his stand against the Manichees corresponded with the explanation given by Prosper in the letter to Rufinus. The issue was grace. God is to be praised for delivering some from the just condemnation that all deserve. Whatever problem Augustine may have had with the notion of human agency and with the connection between human action and human destiny, it was not the Manichaean problem of two natures. Augustine effectively placed himself within the Catholic tradition by refusing to be identified with what was outside it.

He admitted that because of the nature of the argument against the Manichees many questions that were now being raised had at that time been left unresolved. Citing his *Retractationes*, he pointed out that he had subsequently elaborated these earlier statements to correspond with his present position. Augustine was seeking to demonstrate that his recent teaching was, if not latent

---

[93]Griffe, *La Gaule chrétienne à l'époque romaine*, 1:351-52.
[94]*De don. pers.* 11.26, citing *Ep.* 226.8.
[95]*De don. pers.* 11.26–12.29.

in the earlier writings, at least not inconsistent with them. He also made the point that even if his position had changed somewhat over the years, surely he was not to be begrudged growth and development in understanding.[96]

Although Augustine could effectively dissociate himself from the accusation of Manichaeism, another accusation proved more difficult to refute. His critics had charged that his doctrine of grace made exhortation pointless. This issue was similar to the one that he had dealt with in the *De correptione et gratia*: If all is dependent on God's prior judgment, for what reason would one preach or exhort or rebuke? How can the teaching of such a doctrine cause anything except despair, for does it not undercut and oppose human effort and action? Augustine responded that both the doctrine of predestination and the practice of exhortation are found in Scripture and in tradition. Paul taught predestination, and Paul exhorted obedience.[97] Christ taught predestination when he spoke of Tyre and Sidon; yet he commanded belief for the beginning of faith as well as prayer for its continuance.[98] Cyprian, who taught predestination by such words as "We must boast in nothing since nothing is our own," also preached obedience.[99] Ambrose, while teaching that the will is prepared by God, urged obedience to God's commands.[100] Finally, Gregory of Nazianzus spoke of both belief and confession as being the gifts of God.[101] By this last reference Augustine was tying his teaching to an undisputed authority of the Eastern church, one whose credentials were impeccable. He had shrewdly linked the Augustinian "tradition" to the East.[102]

Apart from grounding the doctrines of predestination and perseverance in Scripture and tradition, his argument for preaching them was twofold. First, Augustine argued that even his opponents preached that other qualities of the Christian's life, such as modesty, continence, patience, and wisdom, are the gifts of God, yet they urged their hearers to strive for these qualities. If such preaching does not produce despair or impede exhortation in the case of these gifts, why

---

[96]*De don. pers.* 11.26; 11.27; 12.30; citing *Ep.* 226.8.

[97]*De don. pers.* 14.34.

[98]*De don. pers.* 14.35.

[99]*De don. pers.* 14.36, citing Cyprian, *Testimonia* 3.4.

[100]*De don. pers.*, 19.48; 19.49, citing Ambrose, *Expositio evangelii secundum Lucam*, Prologue and 7.27.

[101]*De don. pers.* 19.49, citing Gregory of Nazianzus, *Orat.* 41.8 *in Pentecosten*.

[102]The list of predecessors to whom Augustine felt he could appeal in support of his doctrine of predestination was brief and the references scanty, but the authority of the men was indisputable and the geographical diversity conveniently widespread. Nevertheless, the paucity of citations gives the impression that whether or not Augustine was rightly interpreting Paul, he was grasping for straws with regard to the tradition. The charge of novelty for his position, a charge that Prosper and Hilary had both reported, he had hardly disproved.

should it, he asked, do so with regard to the beginning and continuance of faith?[103]

Second, if perseverance is God's gift and is to be prayed for, then not to exhort to prayer those persons who are able to hear obediently is to risk the emergence of their pride.[104] One preaches and exhorts for the benefit of those who have been given "ears to hear"[105] so that they might recognize their situation, their total dependence on God, and then live as is appropriate to that recognition. Those who have "ears to hear" cannot be harmed by such preaching, for the gift of "ears" is the same as the "gift of obeying." If they are able to hear, they will obey, and in order to obey they need to be told what obedience requires. Predestination must be preached that one gives glory not to oneself but to the Lord.[106]

It should be noted that once again Augustine established no direct connection between the action of preaching and the outcome of belief. What must intervene in order for preaching to eventuate in belief is the gift of "ears to hear," a gift that neither the preacher nor the listener can supply. The relationship between the human activity of preaching and the human response of belief can be realized only if and when divine action establishes such a relationship.

Nevertheless, human actions do possess significance. As the elect are capable of sin, preaching has the effect of recalling them from sin and of encouraging them in continued obedience. Preaching is one of those external means, similar to rebuke, that, when addressed to those who have received the internal gift of "ears to hear," produces the willing and promotes the actions that constitute perseverance in the good. Thus preaching as an instrument for effecting perseverance is a human action of undeniable relevance to the salvific process. The divine gift of "ears" requires human agency for its fruitful employment, although the primary agent does remain the divine one.

In describing the way such preaching is to be carried out, Augustine's interest was explicitly pastoral. Here I think it becomes evident why Augustine believed that on a practical level his teachings would not lead to fatalism. The argument that he provided against the charge of fatalism is, in fact, more persuasive than the one that Prosper had given in his letter to Rufinus. Prosper had simply said that the divine decrees, to which all things are subject, and fatalism are not the same thing. In contrast, Augustine focused on the attitude of the individual. Preaching should encourage the believer. To be sure, pride and sloth should be undermined, but the preacher should encourage the believer to "lay

---

[103]*De don. pers.* 17.43–17.45.
[104]*De don. pers.* 16.39.
[105]Luke 8:8; Baruch 2:31.
[106]*De don. pers.* 14.37; 20.51.

hold of the most wholesome discipline" and so to run that "you may know your-selves to be foreknown as those who should run lawfully."[107] A sermon should urge its hearers to hope and to pray for perseverance and to see even this ability of hoping and praying as gifts from God. Such evidence of divine favor should even foster trust that they themselves have been elected.[108] Clearly, Augustine believed that the external instrumentality of preaching could effect in those who had been given the necessary internal grace those dispositions that lead to the good decisions and actions that constitute perseverance. Although he may not have met the charge of fatalism in an entirely satisfactory fashion, he was able to indicate why the attitude of the believer need not be fatalistic.

Finally, Augustine's defense against the charge of novelty was the practice of the church. From the beginning the church has prayed that "unbelievers might believe" and that "believers might persevere." If, he argued, the church makes these requests to God for the beginning and continuance in the faith, yet believes that both are within human capacity, then the practice of the church is a mockery. To the contrary, even the prayer, the "seeking, asking, knocking," are the gift of God through the work of the Spirit.[109] Yet, as already noted, Augustine's own appeal to the church's practice of prayer as justification for his case had put the point of prayer in doubt.[110] If the divine action is unrelated to human merit or request, then the purpose of making that request is called into question. Augustine's argument has cast doubt on the practice of the church.

Conclusion

With the writing of the *De praedestinatione sanctorum* and *De dono perse-verantiae* in 429, Augustine's contribution to the controversy ended. He died soon afterward, in August 430. But the repercussions of the two treatises sent to Hadrumetum and of the two subsequent ones sent to South Gaul had only just begun.

The basic problem had not been resolved but only aggravated by the extreme conclusions to which Augustine had carried the logic of grace. As the Augustini-an scheme developed, the connection between human actions and their outcome in eternity diminished, for at every point grace exercised sovereignty over the self, its desiring, its meritorious activity, and its reward. Human agency appeared to be other than genuinely human as the reward of grace was given to the operation of grace within and through the human vessel.

---

[107]*De don. pers.* 22.57; 22.59.
[108]*De don. pers.* 22.62.
[109]*De don. pers.* 23.63–23.65.
[110]See 61 above.

As Babcock has pointed out, the original scheme of freedom, merit, and last judgment, which was a basic presupposition of the monastic life and of the Eastern church fathers, had undergone a transformation through the course of these four treatises, beginning with the *De gratia et libero arbitrio* and concluding with the *De dono perseverantiae*. An initial revision of that scheme in the *De correptione et gratia* presented grace not only as prior to merit but ultimately as rewarding itself. By the conclusion of the fourth treatise the outline of the revised scheme had become even clearer. Although the last judgment stayed in place, the determination of the final outcome was now located in the prior judgment of God made before the foundations of the world. It was this judgment, the rationale and outworking of which remain hidden in God, to which Augustine's detractors objected. The revised scheme of predestinating grace, freedom, merit, and last judgment was so weighted in its first element that the last three elements, which had been the original three, had ceased to have any reality.[111]

The problem with the revised scheme was that the prior judgment gratuitously elects those who will be given the grace of a will free to choose the good, the grace of perseverance by which they earn merit, and at the last judgment the grace of reward for their merit. Those not elected are free to choose only the evil. If they do appear to attain the good, they are unable to persevere in it, and they are finally judged on the basis of the only kind of merit that they are capable of accruing: evil merit. The original complex of freedom, merit, and last judgment has been maintained but greatly diminished by the overriding emphasis on gratuitous election. Yet it was on the foundation of these original three elements that the monastic life, and, perhaps many would say, the common understanding of the Christian life had been built.

Augustine had developed the logic of grace to its extreme conclusions. He had not abandoned the concepts of free will and human agency, but their meaning had been transformed as both notions became instruments for expressing the outworking of grace. One indicator of this situation was the ambivalent status of exhortation, preaching, and rebuke. Their employment in no way served to guarantee the existence of a free will, as had the biblical precepts to which Augustine had referred in the *De gratia et libero arbitrio*. The inexorable logic of the sovereignty of grace had left diminished the role of the human person. The prescriptive summons to the will made by the law and to a far lesser extent by rebuke, exhortation, and preaching had been overshadowed, if not replaced, by a description of the work of grace upon the will.

Such an emphasis on grace to the denigration of human agency could hardly have been acceptable to participants in the monastic enterprise whose entire lives were governed by the struggle for salvation. Those who worked to train their

---

[111]Babcock, "Grace, Freedom and Justice," 14-15.

wills toward God would understandably have resisted the notion that not only their wills but also their thoughts lay outside their control. These monks never doubted the need for grace, but it was an assisting, cooperating, responding grace rather than a sovereign grace. It was the claim of these monks, as expressed in the writings of John Cassian, that must be considered next.

The attendant problem of the novelty of the Augustinian position remained unresolved as well. The predominantly Eastern tradition that the Gallic monks considered authoritative was not the same tradition to which Augustine had generally appealed; certainly it was not reconcilable with the one that he had attempted to construct. Yet however justifiable the charge of novelty may have been in the early years of the debate, two very practical obstacles emerged to deflect its continued cogency: regional loyalty and the passage of time. The Gallic monks, as we shall see, appealed to an Eastern, Greek tradition in the Latin West at a time in which loyalties and horizons were becoming increasingly local; furthermore, the passage of time would lessen the novelty of the newly constructed Augustinian tradition and robe it with a status of its own.

Chapter 3

Semi-Pelagianism:
The Monastic Tradition of John Cassian

Introduction

The first clear alternative to the Augustinian position on human agency and divine grace came from John Cassian, the abbot of St. Victor, a monastery at Marseilles. Of course, the monks at Hadrumetum may have also represented an alternative position, but even if so, their views are available to us in only shadowy form. Although we cannot assume that it was Cassian's intent to rebut Augustine, it is in his work that we find the first well-developed alternative to the Augustinian logic of grace.

The origins of this alternative are not immediately obvious. Augustinianism was the creation of one man. The tradition to which the bishop of Hippo appealed was primarily one that he himself had constructed. In contrast, the forces that shaped Cassian and the Semi-Pelagian opposition are somewhat less apparent. Augustine was undoubtedly a product of the West. Cassian, on the other hand, had received his monastic training primarily in the Egyptian desert where he had been the recipient of peculiarly Eastern influences. The initial task of this chapter will be to identity those forces that were formative in Cassian's own development as well as in the development of the type of monasticism that emerged and flourished in southern Gaul in the fifth century. It is within the context of those forces that Cassian's two great works, the *Institutiones* and the *Collationes* must be understood, and it is within this context that the opposition to Augustine would gradually take shape.

Specifically, it is from Origen and the Origenist tradition that Cassian's spiritual lineage derived. This heritage is evident at the conclusion of *Collatio* 13 where Cassian offered the double assertion that "God works all things in us and yet everything can be ascribed to free will."[1] It is not an exaggeration to suggest that the challenge that he posed for the Augustinians was precisely in his

---

[1] John Cassian, *Collatio* 13.18. All English translations of quotations from the works of Vincent of Lérins and John Cassian will be taken from *Sulpitius Severus, Vincent of Lérins, and John Cassian*, Nicene and Post-Nicene Fathers, s.s. 11 (repr. Grand Rapids: Eerdmans, 1978).

determined struggle to maintain both of these apparently contradictory assertions. Fallen humanity's utter dependence on grace and the full responsibility of the free will were both necessary to his understanding of the struggle for perfection.

Human dependence on grace meant for Cassian that at every stage of the process of salvation grace must be operative; however, the freedom of the human will meant that grace must function in such a way as not to deprive the will of its freedom to choose. The operation of grace as conceived by Cassian, therefore, is highly variegated. God interacts with the multitude of individual persons in the multitude of ways necessary to assist them toward salvation while at the same time preserving their freedom. The notion of grace as variegated was important to Cassian's position, for it served to protect the self-initiating character of the human will. Accordingly, Cassian believed that in the case of some persons, grace will assist the will that already desires the good, whereas in the case of others, grace will arouse the will to good when it is not so inclined. The beginning of faith may have its source in the human agent, although it will not always have its source there.

A genuine interaction transpires, therefore, between divine initiative and human initiative. Cassian has maintained both the integrity of the human free will and the divine will for universal salvation. The monastic pursuit of perfection that he envisioned presupposed both elements. The result was an unresolved, but apparently necessary, tension.

That same tension had existed in Origen's works. Origen had insisted on the preponderance of grace and, at the same time, maintained human self-initiative. The result was a doctrine of grace as self-initiated divine action, portrayed in both healing and teaching images, interacting with self-initiated human action, consisting of thinking and willing as well as doing.[2] This Origenist view of the divine and human interaction proved to be of immense importance for certain strains of monasticism. It was fundamental to the ascetical theology of Evagrius Ponticus, "the leading Greek theorist of the monastic life,"[3] and in the *Institutiones* and *Collationes* Cassian drew upon this Origenist-Evagrian notion of divine and human interaction. In particular, his description of this interaction in *Collatio* 13 provided a clear alternative to Augustine's thinking on the matter. In these works Cassian acknowledged the necessity of grace in the ascetical life. Nevertheless, monastic experience had convinced him of the significance of self-initiated human action. The purpose of monastic discipline, as presented by Cassian, was the attainment of a limited but genuine control over the self, its thoughts and dispositions as well as its actions. The necessity and the integrity of both divine agency and human agency had to be maintained.

---

[2]See 80, below.
[3]Chadwick, *John Cassian*, 25.

It was not that Cassian was directly dependent upon Origen. Indeed, he knew Origen chiefly as interpreted by Evagrius Ponticus, whose own thought had been doubly formed by the Origenist theological tradition and by the experience of asceticism in the Egyptian desert. Thus Cassian was himself the heir of this double tradition. As such, he was the one in whom the monasticism whose muted voice we have heard in reports of questions at Hadrumetum and in reports to Augustine concerning opposition in Gaul at last spoke in its own right, drawing on its own tradition.

Emergence of Gallic Monasticism

The monasticism of North Africa, so far as can be told, did not make use of this Eastern ascetic tradition, although it did presumably hold the common monastic goal of conformity of the self to God. In contrast, the monasticism in South Gaul drew on and was shaped by the highly developed Eastern monastic tradition and accordingly was, to all appearances, more sophisticated both in its conception and formulation of the monastic life itself and in its monastic theology. During the mid-fourth century the Arian controversy had occasioned considerable traffic between the East and West. The two exiles of Athanasius to the West, and specifically his travels through Gaul during the second exile, had brought news of Eastern ascetic practice to the area. Eusebius of Vercelli, in particular, developed a form of cenobitic life along the lines Athanasius would have known in Egypt. This connection is important, for Eusebius was known to Hilary of Poitiers, the spiritual mentor of Martin of Tours. Through Eusebius and perhaps through his own exile in the East, Hilary would have had some familiarity with Eastern monasticism. Thus it is not unreasonable to assume that Martin, the celebrated father of monasticism in Gaul, came under the influence, however indirect, of the desert fathers.[4] Furthermore, Martin's biography, *Vita Martini*, by Sulpicius Severus, clearly bears the imprint of Athanasius's *Vita Antonii*, the biography of the most renowned of the early Egyptian desert fathers. Thus certainly Gallic monasticism, as affected by the *Vita Martini* and perhaps even by Martin himself, was heir to the Eastern monastic tradition.[5]

---

[4]Jacques Fontaine, "L'ascétisme chrétien dans la littérature gallo-romaine d'Hilaire à Cassien," 93-96; Clare Stancliffe, *St. Martin and His Hagiographer* (Oxford: Clarendon Press, 1983) 24, 29. The sequence of the formation of Eusebius's monastic community and of his own exile in the East is subject to some debate; cf. P. Rousseau, *Ascetics, Authority, and the Church*, 87n.29.

[5]An expression of monasticism in the West other than that prescribed by Martin can be seen in such men as Paulinus of Nola (353/4–431), a contemporary of Martin, and Salvian (ca. 400–ca. 480) whose life spanned the fifth century. Both of these men were well-educated members of the Gallic aristocracy. Both chose, along with their wives, to re-

For our purposes a more pertinent example of Eastern influence on Gallic monasticism was Honoratus, the founder of the monastery at Lérins that bears his name and later the bishop of Arles.[6] Hilary, his biographer and successor at Arles, stated that Honoratus and his brother Venantius went to Greece under the

---

nounce their property and live as celibates, withdrawing from the entanglements of society. Although influential in their own right, such men are not to be considered founders of any Western monastic tradition. Instead, they are merely examples of prominent individuals who made a decision for a life of Christian asceticism. For an examination of the diverse reactions of the Western aristocracy to asceticism, see J. Fontaine, "L'aristocratie occidentale devant le monachisme aux IVème et Vème siècles, *Rivista d'Istoria e Letteratura di Storia Religiosa* 15 (1979) 28-53. Stancliffe, *St. Martin and His Hagiographer*, 26-29. For Paulinus, see Brown, *Cult of the Saints*, 53-55; W. H. C. Frend, "Paulinus of Nola and the Last Century of the Western Empire," *Journal of Roman Studies* 59 (1969): 1-11; Joseph T. Lienhard S.J., *Paulinus of Nola and Early Western Monasticism* (Cologne-Bonn: Peter Hanstein, 1977); Aline Rouselle-Esteve, "Deux examples d'evangelisation en Gaule à la fin du IVe siècle: Paulin de Nole et Sulpice Sévère," *Béziers et le Biterrois* (Montpellier, 1971) 91-98. For Salvian, see Eva M. Sanford, "Introduction," *On the Government of God by Salvian* (New York: Columbia University Press, 1930) 3-14; James J. O'Donnell, "Salvian and Augustine," *Augustinian Studies* 14 (1983): 25-34.

[6]Griffe, 3: 332. Although there was a community of monks who grouped themselves around Martin at Ligugé and Marmoutier, this earliest recorded monasticism in Gaul does not seem to have been highly organized or disciplined during Martin's life or to have continued after his death (see Griffe, 3:143). Nor was such formlessness unique to the life of Martin's followers. By the close of the fourth century, hundreds of monks lived in the Gallic cities. Their lives generally unregulated, the monks were identified only by their withdrawal from the world and their asceticism. Such monasteries as were formed, however, did not tend to be of lengthy duration (see Griffe 1:372).

By the beginning of the fifth century there seem to have been large numbers of solitary ascetic figures throughout Gaul (see Griffe, 3:330). N. K. Chadwick, 143-44, has argued that with the heavy immigration into southern Provence from the north and west as a direct result of the turmoil and dislocations caused by the barbarian invasions and with the ranks of monks swelling rapidly during these years as at least an indirect result of the troubled times, monasticism of necessity had to develop into more organized patterns designed to accommodate large numbers of people. Around the beginning of the fifth century, cenobitic monasticism began in South Provence with the first extensive organization of community life near the mouth of the Rhone and on the islands farther south. See also Chadwick, *John Cassian*, 33-36.

J. Fontaine, "L'ascétisme chrétien dans la littérature gallo-romaine d'Hilaire à Cassien," 94-96, has provided a somewhat different view of the situation. He argued that the form of monasticism that developed around Martin had antecedents specifically in the work of Hilary of Poitiers, became widespread and continued beyond the disruption of the barbarian invasion of 406 and even influenced the work of Cassian. Even if Fontaine is correct, it would still be the case that the definitive systematization of Gallic monasticism came only with John Cassian.

supervision of an anchorite, Caprasius (ca. 380),[7] presumably to receive some form of monastic training.[8] In Greece Venantius died. Although it is not clear whether Honoratus travelled farther east or even how long his travels lasted, Honoratus and Caprasius did eventually return to Gaul where Honoratus founded a monastery on the smaller of the two Lérinian islands,[9] perhaps with the encouragement of Leontius, bishop of Fréjus.[10]

Little is known of the monasticism originally practiced at Lérins. It was basically cenobitic, but there were cells for at least the oldest monks so that the eremitic ideal was not entirely lost. Eucherius of Lyons, who entered this community during its early years under Honoratus, made reference in the *De laude eremi* to the presence of "holy old men in separate cells who introduced the

---

[7]*Sermo Sancti Hilarii de Vita Sancti Honorati* 9.1; 10.3; 12.1; 15.1, trans. Marie-Denise Valentin, Sources chrétiennes 235 (Paris: Éditions du Cerf, 1977). For an English translation of the *Vita* see "A Discourse on the Life of St. Honoratus, Bishop of Arles," trans. and ed. F. H. Hoare, *The Western Fathers*, 245-80. Maurice Jourjon, "Honorat d'Arles," *Dictionnaire de spiritualité ascétique et mystique* (1969) 7:717-18.

For a discussion of the evidence for Honoratus's place of birth, see Adalbert de Vogüé, "Sur la patrie d'Honorat de Lérins, évêque d'Arles," *Revue Bénédictine* 88 (1978): 290-91.

[8]The *Vita* employs several expressions indicative of Honoratus's monastic purpose in making the journey, e.g., *Exeuntes de terra sua et de domo et de cognatione sua, exemplo pares, vere Abrahae filii* (12.1; cf. Gen. 12:1; Jn 8:39; Lk. 19:9) and *quem e patria heremi desideria provocaverant, hunc in heremum huic urbi propinquam Christus invitat* 2 (15.1). For the use of biblical images such as these to refer to the monastic life, see Jacques Biarne, "La Bible dans la vie monastique," *Le monde latin antique et la Bible*, eds. J. Fontaine and C. Pietri, Bible de Tous les Temps 2 (Paris: Beauchesne, 1985) 409-29. See also Antoine Guillaumont, "La conception du désert chez les moines d'Egypte," *Revue de l'histoire des religions* 188 (1975): 3-21.

The reason for the choice of Greece as his destination is a subject of dispute. Nora Chadwick, 149, suggested that as Basil, a formative figure in the development of Eastern monasticism and the bishop of Caesarea, had studied in Athens, Honoratus may have been seeking to do the same. Another related possibility is that he may have wanted to train in some community that was governed by Basil's *Regulae*. Quite in contrast, Griffe, 3:332, suggested that surely Honoratus had wanted to go further east, especially to Egypt; Adalbert de Vogüé, *Les règles des saints pères*, 1, Sources chrétiennes 297 (Paris: Les Éditions du Cerf, 1982) 22, argued that we have no way of knowing whether Honoratus traveled beyond Greece to Egypt either before or after the death of Venantius.

[9]*Vita* 14.1, 15.1–16.1. For a discussion of the chronology of these events, see Valentin, 20-22.

[10]Hoare, 159n.3; Valentin, 109n.2.

fathers of Egypt to us Gauls."[11] A rule, perhaps provided by Honoratus himself, further indicated the influence of the Eastern monastic tradition.[12]

To some extent, therefore, this tradition shaped the way of life practiced at Lérins and consequently those who were under its tutelage. Notably, it was St. Honoratus that, for over a century, trained the outstanding Gallic bishops and intellectuals.[13] Among this list were several of importance in our study: Hilary of Arles, who has already been mentioned in chapter 2 as an objector to some of the more extreme Augustinian doctrines on grace;[14] Faustus of Riez, and Vincent, the author of the *Commonitorium*, both men distinguished among the Semi-Pelagians; and Caesarius of Arles, a later but leading Augustinian. Discussion of the relevant works of Faustus, Vincent, and Caesarius will be provided in the chapters that follow.

John Cassian, therefore, was neither the only person nor the first person to transmit Eastern monasticism to the West. He did, however, establish at St. Victor at Marseilles a well-ordered community informed by the experienced pattern of the East as adapted to the constraints of the West.[15] In this role he became the principal and most effective communicator of the Origenist monastic tradition to the West.

The circumstances that placed him in this role are not entirely clear. Early in the fifth century there seems to have been a group of monks living in Marseilles who in all probability maintained ties with Proclus, the bishop of the city. Although there is some uncertainty surrounding the actual founding of the

---

[11]Eucherius of Lyons, *De laude eremi* 42: *Haec [insula] nunc habet sanctos senes illos qui divisis cellulis Egyptios patres Galliis nostris intulerunt.* See also *Vita Honorati* 22.1; *Encyclopedia of the Early Church* 1:295.

[12]For a discussion of the likelihood of Honoratus as author of the *Règle des quatre pères* and of the evidence of Eastern sources for the rule, see de Vogüé, *Les règles des saints pères*, 1, 10-11, 22-26, 125-55. Griffe, 3:334-35. As evidence for the Eastern influence on St. Honoratus, Griffe argued that the purpose of Cassian's having dedicated *Pars Secunda* of the *Collationes* to Honoratus was to enhance the authority of the latter's teaching. Presumably it was because of Honoratus's Eastern leanings that Cassian wished to call attention to his teaching. Furthermore, Griffe noted that Sidonius Apollinaris had referred in *Ep.* 8.14.2 to the bishop Antiolus. Sidonius related that this man, having lived at Lérins, attempted to imitate "the archimandrites of Memphis and of Palestine." The implication was that it was at Lérins that he was instructed in such Eastern models.

[13]Mathisen, 76-85; A. C. Cooper-Marsdin, *The History of the Islands of the Lérins* (Cambridge: Cambridge University Press, 1913) 42-46.

[14]See 44-45 above.

[15]Chadwick, *John Cassian*, 36. For another study of Cassian's sources and his role as a transmitter and interpreter of particular strands of Eastern monasticism to the West, see Hans-Oskar Weber, *Die Stellung des Johannes Cassianus zur ausserpachomianischen Mönchstradition: eine Quellenuntersuchung*, Beiträge zur Geschichte des alten Mönchtums und des Benediktinerordens 24 (Münster/Westfalen: Verlag Aschendorff, 1961).

monastery, the advent of Cassian in the city sometime between 415 and 417 probably provided the occasion for Proclus to initiate the formation of St. Victor.[16]

For the task of directing a monastery, Cassian was peculiarly well prepared. In Bethelehem and in Egypt he had had extensive personal experience of Eastern monasticism, both with regard to its patterns of discipline and its characteristic ways of formulating and transmitting its tradition, i.e., through the sayings of the fathers. Although Cassian's cenobitic experience was primarily in Bethlehem, it did serve as a basis for his own formative work in Gallic cenobitism years later.[17] In Egypt he had encountered a well-developed eremitism,[18] and in the communities of the Delta and the desert of Scete, he had taken the opportunity to participate in the ascetic custom of having conferences with the fathers. These conferences were subsequently reported in the *Collationes*,[19] which will be discussed later in this chapter. Furthermore, here he had found an asceticism grounded in the Christian Platonism of Alexandria, notably that of such men as Clement and Origen.[20] In fact, the Origenist-Evagrian ascetical theology had

---

[16]Griffe, 3:342-43. For the sequence of events in Cassian's life in the years between his departure from the Egyptian desert in 400 and his arrival in Marseilles, see Griffe, "Cassien a-t-il été pêtre d'Antioche?" *Bulletin de littérature ecclésiastique* 55 (1954): 240-44. Griffe was relying on H.-I. Marrou, "Jean Cassien à Marseille," *Revue du Moyen Age Latin* 1 (1945): 5-26. Fontaine has suggested that a disciple and successor of Martin, the abbot of Marmoutier, Bishop Heros of Arles, was the occasion for Cassian's coming to Gaul. Heros was deposed, along with Lazarus, the bishop of Aix, by Zosimus, the bishop of Rome, in 412. The two men went to Palestine, and Fontaine found reason to believe that one of these men may have been connected with Cassian's move to Marseilles, although there is no record that Heros returned to Provence. Griffe, it should be noted, attributed Cassian's move to Lazarus. Regardless, Fontaine, "L'ascétisme chrétien," 107, has located in Heros, perhaps through Lazarus, a friendly connection between Martin and Cassian and thus between the respective forms of monasticism attributed to each. See also H.-I. Marrou, "Le fondateur de Saint Victor de Marseille: Jean Cassien," *Provence Historique* 16 (1966): 297-99. E. Pichery, "Introduction," *Conférences* 1:21-28.

Cassian actually founded two monasteries in Marseilles, one for men and another for women. See Michel Olphe-Galliard, "Cassien," *Dictionnaire de spiritualité ascétique et mystique* 2:217.

[17]Chadwick, *John Cassian*, 11-13; Jean Cassien, *Conférences* 1-7, E. Pichery, trans., Sources chrétiennes 42 (Paris: Les éditions du Cerf, 1955) 9-13.

[18]Chadwick, *John Cassian*, 22-23; Derwas J. Chitty, *The Desert a City* (Crestwood NJ: St. Vladimir's Seminary, 1966) 35, 46. Hugh G. Evelyn White, *The Monasteries of the Wâdi 'n Natrûn*, 2: *The History of the Monasteries of Nitria and of Scetis* (New York, 1932) 11.

[19]Chadwick, *John Cassian*, 14-15, 18-22.

[20]Chadwick, *John Cassian*, 25; Pichery, 1:58-63; Courcelle, *Late Latin Writers and Their Greek Sources*, 227-31. Jean-Claude Guy, S.J., *Jean Cassien* (Paris: P. Lethielleux, 1961) 21-22.

strongly influenced Cassian, and evidence indicates that he had even been involved to some extent in the so-called Origenist controversy.[21]

With such a background Cassian, far more than Honoratus, represented the psychological and theological sophistication of Eastern monasticism. Even if St. Victor did not produce the string of theological writers that Lérins did, Cassian himself became a dominant voice on the Western monastic and even theological scene. His works were recommended reading in the *Regula* of St. Benedict[22] and in the *Institutiones* of Cassiodorus, although in the latter case there was due warning about his views on the freedom of the will.[23]

It was in his development of a Latin formulation of the Eastern, Origenist monastic tradition that we find the basis for what would become Semi-Pelagianism. Cassian's work offers us the greatest access to the context, outlook, and perspective from which the Gallic opposition to Augustine on grace and human agency arose and out of which it was expressed.[24]

The Ascetical Theology of Origen and Evagrius

The monasticism of which Honoratus and John Cassian were representative had its roots in the Christian East. In fact, the monasteries of St. Honoratus and St. Victor may be considered to have been the windows through which the Eastern monastic tradition became visible to South Gaul. Cassian was particularly important for having formulated in the *Institutiones* and *Collationes* a lucid, orderly account of monastic theory and method as gleaned from the experience of the desert fathers.

---

[21]Chadwick, *John Cassian*, 25-30; Griffe, "Cassien a-t-il été prêtre d'Antioche?" 55, 240-41. For an examination of the Origenist controversy, see Elizabeth A. Clark, *The Origenist Controversy* (Princeton: Princeton University Press, 1992). An incident recorded in the *Collationes* (10.1-5) indicates something of Cassian's involvement in the controversy and the alignment of his views with those of Evagrius on the anthropomorphite question. For a list of persons whose work influenced Cassian, see Michel Olphe-Galliard, "Cassien," *Dictionnaire de spiritualité ascétique et mystique* 2:223-25.

[22]Benedict, *Regula* 73.

[23]Cassiodorus, *Institutiones* 1.29.2.

[24]One thing that can be seen in the entire Massilian milieu, although particularly at Lérins, is the open, even heated, discussion of contemporary religious questions by bishops, monks, and laity. Doctrinal issues that were still awaiting resolution were open to the debate of all. Such an atmosphere stood in sharp contrast to the situation in North Africa where the authority of Augustine lessened, if it did not squelch, creative exchange among others in the church. Strangely enough, the weight of a long-standing monastic tradition that emphasized submission did not hamper debate, whereas the presence of an authority, forceful enough to construct his own tradition, did.

The Greek monks in Egypt had developed a carefully considered ascetical theology rooted in the Christian Platonism of third-century Alexandria.[25] As the fourth century drew to a close, the influence of Origen pervaded the Hellenized monasticism of the desert.[26] Thus it is necessary to consider Origen's contribution and influence. His importance for us has to do with two matters: his understanding of the interaction of grace and free will and his elaboration of an ascetical theology.

In contrast to the pervasive determinism of the age[27] and perhaps even more precisely in response to Gnostic determinism,[28] Origen presented what he believed to be the commonly held faith of the church, the "rule of faith."[29] He stated that every rational soul has a free will, is not compelled by any necessity and, by the righteous judgment of God, will be rewarded or punished on the basis of its freely chosen actions.[30] Not God, not fate, not anyone else but we ourselves determine whether we fulfill our proper task, which is to live a good life.[31] The Christian doctrine of the righteous judgment of God "assumes that [Christians] acknowledge that deeds worthy of praise or blame lie within our own power."[32] Thus Origen's theology set forth a scheme of free will, divine judgment, and reward or punishment and invested it with the authority of "apostolic teaching."

---

[25]Clark, 57; Chitty, 53; Jon F. Dechow, *Dogma and Mysticism in Early Christianity: Epiphanius of Cyprus and the Legacy of Origen*, Patristic Monograph Series 13 (Macon: Mercer University Press, 1988) 149, 171; Chadwick, *John Cassian*, 24-30. The monks of the Egyptian desert were not all of one mind. One of the more notable divisions, not confined to the desert, existed between the Coptic and the Greek monks. The antagonism had its roots in nationalism, in varying theological perspectives, and, generally speaking, in divergent levels of sophistication. Cassian, himself a foreigner and an Evagrian, attributed the anthropomorphic views held by most of the monks to their "simplicity" (*Coll.* 10.2).

[26]Dechow, 149-81; Clark, 22; Chadwick, *John Cassian*, 25, 82-83.

[27]E. R. Dodds, *Pagan and Christian in an Age of Anxiety* (New York: W. H. Norton, 1970) 1-36.

[28]Peter J. Gorday, "*Paulus Origenianus*: The Economic Interpretation of Paul in Origen and Gregory of Nyssa," *Paul and the Legacies of Paul*, ed. William S. Babcock (Dallas: Southern Methodist University Press, 1990) 141-63. See also Clark, 194-96.

[29]Origen, *De princ., Praef.* 2. All English translations of quotations from *De princ.* will be taken from Origen, *On First Principles*, trans. G. W. Butterworth (Gloucester MA: Peter Smith, 1973). For a helpful discussion of Origen's teaching on free will, see Joseph Wilson Trigg, *Origen: The Bible and Philosophy in the Third-Century Church* (Atlanta: John Knox Press, 1983) 115-20.

[30]*De princ., Praef.* 5.

[31]*De princ.* 3.1.6.

[32]*De princ.* 3.1.1.

Origen was able to summon numerous citations from Scripture to support his emphasis on human moral responsibility,[33] but he also acknowledged passages where Scripture appears to contradict his argument, notably in the case of God's hardening of Pharaoh's heart,[34] and in Paul's apparent denials of free will and assertions that all is finally in the hands of God.[35] With regard to these difficult passages, Origen insisted that Scripture was not denying the validity of human agency. Instead, it was affirming the complexity of the interaction of divine grace and human agency. It was witnessing to the reality that although grace is indispensable for salvation, its operation is manifold, never compelling its object but always fitted to the receptive capacity of the person to whom it comes.[36] God alone has complete knowledge of all the individual souls and of the means most suitable for their care and oversight.[37] Origen employed medical and pedagogical imagery to reinforce the notion of the individualized divine care of souls. God adapts the method of teaching or healing to the particular case.[38] Origen also used navigational imagery to indicate that although human efforts are necessary, the "greater part" of human perfection is dependent upon factors which, like the wind and weather, are subject to divine, not to human, direction.[39] The emphasis both on human responsibility and on the variegated operation of grace would become important notions for Cassian, as well.

Among the heirs of the tradition stemming primarily from Origen were many monastic communities of the fourth and fifth centuries.[40] These communities, built around the notion of training in the Christian life, were the beneficiaries not only of Origen's understanding of the interaction of grace and the free will but also of his second contribution: the elaboration of an ascetical theology. Owen Chadwick has pointed out that in Origen's homilies can be found that probing of the psychology of the soul from which he derived the principles of a Christian asceticism. "In his homilies appeared the first inquiry into the origins of sins in the heart; into the nature of virtue; into temptation, and the struggle of the soul with demons; into the value of temptations in the training of the soul; into fasting and prayer and meditation upon Scripture."[41]

---

[33]Mi. 6:8; Dt. 30:15, 19; Is. 1:19, 20; Ps 81:13, 14; Mt. 5.39, 22, 28; 7:24, 26; 25:34-35, 41; Rom 2:4-10.

[34]Ex. 4:21; 7:3; 9:12; 10:1, 20, 27; 11:10, 14.4.

[35]Rom. 9:16, 18-21; Phil. 2:13.

[36]Benjamin Drewery, *Origen and the Doctrine of Grace* (London: Epworth Press, 1960) 15-16, 86.

[37]*De princ.* 3.1.14.

[38]*De princ.* 3.1.15-17.

[39]*De princ.* 3.1.19.

[40]Babcock, "Grace, Freedom and Justice," 10.

[41]Chadwick, *John Cassian*, 83. For an example of Origen's teaching regarding the ascent of the soul through stages, see *Homily 27 on Numbers*. English translation in *Origen:*

Origen's *De oratione* serves as an example of the careful study that he devoted to the nurture of the soul. In this work he offered elaborate guidance in the discipline of prayer and attended to the maturation of the soul through this discipline.[42] He provided elementary instruction with regard to preparation of the disposition, posture, locations, directions, and subjects for prayer,[43] and acknowledged the reality of evil powers that beset the soul.[44] Simply the condition of being in the state of prayer was, for Origen, the advantage of prayer. In that condition the mind is undistracted, and the person is dedicated to God and better equipped to have union with God.[45]

The results of Origen's exploration of the soul's struggle for perfection, interpreted in terms of his own Neoplatonism and presupposing his Christian conviction of free will and divine judgment, became an invaluable guide for sophisticated ascetics of the late fourth century.[46] In fact, in the late fourth and early fifth centuries there was an Origenist revival within monachism. This widespread popularity of Origen should not disguise the fact, however, that there were many strains within asceticism. By this time Origenism was itself hardly monolithic.[47] This point is important for locating the place of John Cassian within the ranks of Christian asceticism.

Among those who participated in varying degrees in the ascetic movement of the late fourth and early fifth centuries were such prominent Westerners as Jerome, Rufinus, and Pelagius. With ties to the East, each not only felt the influence of the revival of Origenism but even contributed to the transmission of that revival to the West.[48] Yet although Cassian was acquainted to some degree with

---

An Exhortation to Martyrdom . . . Homily 27 on Numbers, trans. and intro. by Rowan A. Greer, Classics of Western Spirituality (New York: Paulist Press, 1979) 245-69.

[42]Origen, *De oratione* 2.4; 23.1; 27.4; *Alexandrian Christianity*, trans. John Ernest Leonard Oulton and Henry Chadwick (Philadephia: Westminster, 1954) 199-200.

[43]*De orat*. 31.1-3, 4-7; 32; 33.1-6.

[44]*De orat*. 25.2; 26.5; 30.1-3.

[45]*De orat*. 8.2; 9.2; 10.2.

[46]In the Origenist controversy that erupted at the conclusion of the fourth century, it would seem to have been the case that it was the more sophisticated ascetics who, influenced by Evagrian Origenism, opposed what they believed to be the anthropomorphic theology of other, less sophisticated monks. See Socrates, *Historia Ecclesiastica* 6.7.

[47]Clark, 6-7, 85-158, made this point forcefully.

[48]For an excellent examination of the social networks involved in the Origenist controversy, see Clark, 11-42. For other discussions of Jerome's connections with Origen, Rufinus, and Pelagius, see Jean Steinmann, *Saint Jerome*, trans. Ronald Matthews (London: Geoffrey Chapman, 1959) 98-100, 162-63, 185-90, 232, 279, 331-42; Ferdinand Cavallera, *Saint Jérôme* (Louvain: "Spicilegium Sacrum Lovaniense" Bureaux, 1992) 1:230-32, 324-27; 2:126-27, 134-35; Paul Antin, *Essai sur Saint Jérôme* (Paris: Letouzey and Ané, 1951) 95-102, 164-71, 176-81, 206-207; Maurice Testard, *Saint Jérôme* (Paris:

their work,[49] it was not through such sources as these but through an Eastern ascetic that he was to come under the influence of Origen. Appropriate to Cassian's own interests, his connection with Origen came through Evagrius Ponticus (345–399), the leader of a monastic community in Nitria and the first to systematize monastic spirituality.[50]

Société d'édition "Les belles lettres," 1969) 26-29, 59-74, 75-77; Rees, 4-17. For an examination of Rufinus's relation to Origenism, see Clark, 159-93. For Pelagius's connection with Origen's work through the translations of Rufinus and the continuities between the Origenist controversy and the Pelagian controversy, see Clark, 187, 194-244.

[49]In the *Institutiones, Praef.* 5 Cassian states as one reason for his hesitancy in writing that *quod super hac re viri et vita nobiles et sermone scientiaque praeclari multa iam opuscula desudarunt, sanctum Basilium et Hieronymum dico aliosque nonnullos. Quorum anterior sciscitantibus fratribus super diversis institutis vel quaestionibus non solum facundo, verum etiam divinarum scripturarum testimoniis copioso sermone respondit, alius vero non solum suo elucubratos ingenio edidit libros, verum etiam graeca lingua digestos in latinum vertit eloquium.* Although there seems to be no evidence that Cassian had contact with Jerome in Bethlehem, he obviously was familiar with at least some of Jerome's monastic writing.

The possibility that he was also familiar with Rufinus is somewhat less obvious. Léon Christiani, *Jean Cassien* (Éditions de Fontenelle, 1946) 1: 244, 260, argued that the *alioque nonnullos* to whom Cassian referred would likely have included Rufinus. Christiani, 2:128, also suggested that it was from Rufinus (*Historia Monachorum* 1) that Cassian derived the distinction between two forms of pride (*Inst.* 12.2). J. Gribomont, *Histoire du texte des ascétiques de saint Basile* (Louvain: Publications Universitaires, 1953) stated that the work of Basil to which Cassian referred would have been a Latin version of Basil's questions, probably translated by Rufinus. Chadwick, *John Cassian*, 61-63, argued much the same. Elsewhere in the *De incarnatione* Cassian explicitly evoked the authority of Jerome (7.26) and Rufinus (7.27).

As will become apparent later in this chapter in the examination of Cassian's teaching on grace, he not only knew but also rejected Pelagius's teaching. Chadwick, *John Cassian*, 32n.4, suggested the possibility that Cassian may have even met Pelagius during his stay in Rome. In the *De incarn.* 1.2-5; 5.2; 6.14; 7.21, Cassian drew comparisons between the teaching of Pelagius and that of Nestorius. In 1.2-5 and 7.21 he referred specifically to Leporius as one in whom the two heresies had been combined. Leporius, a Gallic monk who had gone to southern Gaul, presumably as a refugee, *ex maxima Belgarum urbe*, had advocated Pelagianism in combination with the teaching that Jesus was born a man and later exalted to divine status by virtue of his merit. Having been admonished by Cassian and expelled by Proclus and Cillenius, another Gallic bishop, he went to Africa, where, under Augustine's instruction, he made a recantation. See Mathisen, 126-27; Gibson, Nicene and Post-Nicene Fathers, s.s. 11:552-53; Aug., *Ep.* 219.1.

[50]John Eudes Bamberger, Introduction to *The Praktikos and Chapters on Prayer* (Kalamazoo: Cistercian Publications, 1981) xlii, xlix-l. All quotations from the *Practicus* and the *De oratione* will be taken from this translation. For discussions of the attribution to Evagrius of the *De oratione*, which has generally been considered the work of Nilus, see Bamberger, xxxii, and Chadwick, *John Cassian*, 90. For a warning against any neat identification of the Origenism of Evagrius Ponticus with the teaching of Origen himself, see Henri Crouzel, *Origen: The Life and Thought of the First Great Theologian*, trans.

Cassian drew from Evagrius in a variety of ways, with regard both to overall scheme and to specific detail. Evagrius employed a distinction that Origen had made between the active and the contemplative life; yet contrary to Origen's description of these two modes of ascetic behavior as overlapping each other in the monk's development, Evagrius described them as being successive: the contemplative form follows the active form.[51] Cassian followed Evagrius in establishing a distinction between the successive stages of ascesis and contemplation, although for him the distinction was not so clear-cut. For Cassian continuing ascesis was needed in the life of contemplation. Nevertheless, as Evagrius described the active life in the *Practicus* and the contemplative life in the *De oratione,* Cassian's division of subject matter in the *Institutiones* and the *Collationes* fundamentally conformed with this pattern.

Furthermore, as Evagrius had described the ascetic life as "the spiritual method for cleansing the affective part of the soul,"[52] he had organized the *Practikos* around the discussion of the evil or passionate thoughts, the *logismoi,* a scheme inherited from Origen[53] that would eventually form the core of Cassian's discussion of the active life. Evagrius carefully distinguished eight categories of

---

A. S. Worrall (San Francisco: Harper & Row, 1989) 168, 175-76; see also A. Guillaumont, *Les Kephalaia Gnōstica d'Evagre le Pontique et l'histoire de l'origénisme chez les Grecs et chez les Syriens* (Paris: Les Éditions du Cerf, 1962) 40-43. For a discussion of the anthropology of Evagrius, see Michael O'Laughlin, "The Anthropology of Evagrius Ponticus and Its Sources," *Origen of Alexandria: His World and His Legacy*, eds. Charles Kannengiesser and William L. Petersen (Notre Dame: University of Notre Dame Press, 1988) 357-73.

For Jerome's belated awareness of Evagrian theology and its importance in the Origenist controversy, see Clark, 7, 114, 121-51. For Rufinus's considerable acquaintance with Evagrius and his teaching, see Clark, 7-8, 188-93.

[51]Crouzel, 100-101. See J. Lemaitre, R. Roques, M. Viller, "Contemplation: Contemplation chez les orientaux chrétiens," *Dictionnaire de spiritualité* 2/2:1775-86. Chadwick, *John Cassian,* 88. See Rowan A. Greer, *Broken Lights and Mended Lives* (University Park: Pennsylvania State University Press, 1986) 62-65, 112, 179-82, for a discussion of Evagrius's and Cassian's modification of Origen's and the Cappadocians' scheme for the Christian life from three stages to two. For an equation of the process of the development of the soul with the three books of Solomon, see *The Prologue to the Commentary on the Song of Songs*, in *Origen*, trans. Greer, 231-36; for a discussion of Origen's understanding of the interpenetration of the moral sense of Scripture with its mystical sense and of asceticism with mysticism, see Bouyer, 1:269-99; for Evagrius's distinction between practice and contemplation, see Bouyer, 1:384.

[52]*Practicus* 78. For a discussion of the ascetic and theological factors that contributed to Evagrius's concern for thoughts, see Clark, 75-79.

[53]Irénée Hausherr, "L'origine de la théorie orientale des huit péchés capitaux," *Orientalia Christiana* 86 (1933): 164-75. For a discussion of the evolution of this teaching through the Middle Ages, see Aimé Solignac, "Péchés capitaux," *Dictionnaire de spiritualité* 12/1 (1984) 853-62.

such thoughts: gluttony, impurity, avarice, sadness, anger, acedia, vainglory, and pride. He first described the characteristics of the members of each category,[54] and then suggested remedies for each kind of evil.[55] Depending upon the particular kind of evil to be overcome, Evagrius recommended such strategies as readings, prayers, vigils, hunger, toil, solitude, and almsgiving. Each of these, if properly employed, could contribute to the mastery of one's thoughts.[56]

Evagrius stressed the importance of identifying the source of a particular thought, since he believed that it is the thoughts that provide the demons with a means of access to a monk. In fact, Antoine and Claire Guillamont have said that "the ascetic life is essentially a combat with the demons."[57] Accordingly, Evagrius offered meticulous instructions for studying the character of these assaults so that the monk might overcome them.[58] Victory in the ascetic battle with the demons consists in the attainment of *apatheia*, a condition in which the mind is undisturbed and free from distractions.[59] This condition, which Evagrius described as "the health of the soul,"[60] is the immediate goal of ascesis.[61] It, in turn, gives rise to *agape*, a precondition for contemplation.[62] Evagrius understood *agape* to be natural to the soul that has been freed from distractions and passion. This understanding differed radically from Augustine's view that charity is the infused presence of the Holy Spirit.

Cassian identified purity of heart with charity and designated it as the initial goal of the monk, the purpose of all ascetic efforts.[63] Generally following Evagrius, he correlated evil thoughts with the passions in such a way that to

---

[54]*Practicus* 6-14.

[55]*Practicus* 15-39.

[56]*Practicus* 15.

[57]A. and C. Guillaumont, *Traité pratique ou le moine*, 1:94; cf. Clark, 77, on good *logismoi*.

[58]Among the repeated references to the connection between the demons and the passionate thoughts and to strategies for overcoming the demons, see especially *Practicus* 36, 39, 43-51, 54, 80. See also the discussion by Clark, 82-83, and Bernard McGinn, *The Foundation of Mysticism* (New York: Crossroad, 1991) 1:147-49.

[59]*Practicus* 64-65, 67, 69. Evagrius recognized an imperfect as well as a perfect form of *apatheia* (cf. *Practicus* 60). For a discussion of Evagrius's use of *apatheia*, see A. and C. Guillaumont, 1:98-112. Henri Crouzel, 7, 52, argued that Origen preferred the term *metriopatheia* to *apatheia*. Evagrius's use of the term *apatheia*, he suggested, indicates dependence upon Clement, who used the term *apatheia* frequently, rather than upon Origen, who rarely employed it.

[60]*Practicus* 56.

[61]Bamberger, lxxxiii.

[62]*Epistula ad Anatolium*, trans. Bamberger, 14; *Practicus* 81. For a discussion of the relationship of this letter to the *Practicus*, see A. and C. Guillaumont, *Traité pratique*, Sources chrétiennes 170 (1971) 1:383-86.

[63]*Inst.* 4.43; *Coll.* 1.4-7.

overcome these thoughts was also to overcome the passions.[64] As the passions were eradicated and the virtues inculcated, the heart was thereby purified and love perfected. The heart, in other words, was being prepared for enjoyment of the kingdom of God, the ultimate goal of the monk.[65]

The painstaking instruction regarding thoughts was indicative of an assumption that both Evagrius and Cassian held. They believed that monks can exercise at least some control over their thoughts and that they bear responsibility for them. Human efforts are necessary, perhaps even determinative, in this struggle.

Although Cassian would provide a far more extensive discussion of the significance of divine agency and the character of grace than had Evagrius, Evagrius's influence on Cassian was apparent even with regard to this matter. Evagrius expressed a deep sense of reliance upon God in the ascetic struggle. He taught that reunion with God[66] requires divine assistance. For example, he advised that once a monk has attained *apatheia*, humility must be fostered by the remembrance of past sins and by the recognition that it is through the mercy of Christ that the present condition has been achieved.[67] Similarly, placing one's hope in God is the means for overcoming the demon of *acedia*.[68] Progress against all types of demons, he taught, requires both human attentiveness and divine grace.[69] Even the monk's cowl serves as a symbol of the love and protection of God. As such, it is a defense against pride and an encouragement to humility.[70] For those who progress beyond ascesis to contemplation, Evagrius offered the reminder that prayer itself is the gift of grace.[71] Thus although Evagrius's interest was ascetic discipline and its corresponding psychology, his recognition of dependence upon God as integral to that discipline and psychology makes it impossible to classify him according to any neat categorization. He made no choice between grace and human free will but ascribed to both the success of the religious life. As a result, he simply cannot be appropriately measured by Augustinian categories. The same may be said of Cassian.

The *Practicus* concluded with a list of "Sayings of Holy Monks." The first of these sayings admonished monks to attend to the ways of their predecessors

---

[64]He presented the *octo principalia vitia* of *Inst.* 5.1 and the *passiones* of 5.2 as equivalents. For Cassian's discussion of these faults and their remedies, see *Inst.* 5-12.

[65]*Coll.* 1.4-7, 11-13.

[66]For a discussion of the cosmology of Evagrius, see Bamberger, lxxi-lxxix, and McGinn, 144-57.

[67]*Practicus* 33.

[68]*Practicus* 27.

[69]*Practicus* 43.

[70]*Epistula ad Anatolium.*

[71]*De oratione* 58, 69, 74.

and to follow the example of those who had been righteous.[72] In including this admonition Evagrius was advancing the principle (faithfully followed by Cassian) that the wisdom of one's predecessors, carefully distilled through their own monastic experience, is the authoritative guide for the pursuit of perfection. Presumably Evagrius understood his own elaboration of a theology of the ascetic life as a faithful representation of this distilled wisdom.[73]

Ascesis did not encompass the monastic endeavor in its entirety, however. For Evagrius, fruitful ascesis led to contemplation,[74] a state described in the *De oratione*. This successive pattern, although with significant modification, one also finds in Cassian. The *De oratione* began with instructions on practical means for clearing the mind for prayer and for understanding the kinds of obstacles to prayer that regularly occur in the spiritual life. Evagrius was concerned not only about evil thoughts but even about the monk's preoccupation with pure thoughts. Such a condition was itself distraction from prayer and caused distance from God.[75] Instead, prayer was "the rejection of concepts."[76] It was "a continual intercourse of the spirit with God" without the necessity of an intermediary.[77]

The *De oratione* described the progression of the self in terms of a search for virtues. The process was that of ascesis leading to *apatheia* and *agape*, as described in the *Practicus*. It was undertaken in order to reach "the inner meanings of what is created." One was to seek these inner meanings "for the sake of attaining to the Lord who has created them." The state of prayer was the condition most conducive to the experience of the revelation of God.[78] Evagrius was describing a multistage process: ascesis, through which one systematically eradicates evil thoughts and their attendant passions and replaces them with the corresponding virtues; *apatheia*, an ordered state of mind, which is the fruition of effective *ascesis*; *agape*, the by-product of *apatheia* and the sine qua non for a two-stage contemplation: knowledge of the creation, corporeal and incorporeal, through contemplation, which may but does not necessarily result from *agape*; knowledge of the Trinity through contemplation, which may but does not

---

[72]*Practicus* 91. For the relationship of the "Sayings" to the *Practicus*, see *Traité pratique* 1:118-20.

[73]*Traité pratique* 1:121, 383.

[74]Even in Evagrius, the distinction may not be absolute. McGinn, 1:151, "The necessity for the continuing operation of *apatheia*, either perfect or imperfect, for any kind of *thēoria* is one of the many ways by which the abba shows the interdependence of the practical and contemplative lives."

[75]*De oratione* 55.

[76]*De oratione* 70, 68, 117, 120, 153.

[77]*De oratione* 3.

[78]*De oratione* 51.

necessarily result from knowledge of the creation.[79] Elsewhere, Evagrius spoke of the process in terms of three stages:

> The goal of *praktikē* is to purify the intellect and to render it impassible; that of the *physikē* is to reveal the truth hidden in all beings; but to remove the intellect from all material things and to turn it toward the First Cause is a gift of *theologikē*.[80]

The interrelationship of knowledge, contemplation, and prayer is such that it is not clear that they are separable. "Spiritual prayer is nourishment for the intelligence."[81] "Knowledge. . . . is a fellow worker with prayer, acting to awaken the power of thought to contemplate the divine knowledge."[82] In fact, Evagrius equated the higher form of contemplation or knowledge with "pure prayer," for in such prayer the mind is empty of all except the infinite, incorporeal God.[83]

Although Cassian's description of the movement toward the ultimate goal of the kingdom of God would not entirely correspond with Evagrius's description of the movement toward reunion with God, the similarities between their descriptions were pronounced. For both men growth was conceived as a type of progression in which mastery of one level is a precondition for advancement to the next. For the pupil as for the teacher, progression is through a series of stages toward a final pure contemplation of God. Finally, although Evagrius did not emphasize cenobitic life as Cassian was later to do, he clearly presupposed the discipline of monasticism as the context for advancement in the life of perfection, the locus for the interaction of divine grace and the human will.

Neither Evagrius nor the Egyptian monsticism of his day construed human striving and divine grace as mutually exclusive. The same held true for Cassian. The tradition to which Cassian was heir did, however, provide a sophisticated understanding of the ascetic life and its psychology as leading to love and knowledge of God. It was a tradition of practical religious discipline and of ascetical theology. The challenge that Cassian faced in the West was the double one of interpreting this sophisticated tradition to persons who had, at best, limited familiarity with it, and to do so at a time and place in which long-cherished

---

[79]*Practicus* 1-3, 55, 57. See Chadwick, *John Cassian,* 89-90; McGinn, 1: 151. For a discussion of five degrees of contemplation, the highest being the contemplation of the Trinity, a condition that is entirely the gift of grace, see Lemaitre, Roques, Viller, "Contemplation: Contemplation chez les orientaux chrétiens," *Dictionnaire de spiritualité* 2/2 (1953) 1775-86.

[80]*Gnosticus* 49, translated by McGinn, 1:149.

[81]*De oratione* 101.

[82]*De oratione* 86.

[83]*De oratione* 2, 3, 60, 66.

convictions about the value of human agency had been called into question by Augustine's teaching on grace.

Although John Cassian was influenced by others, notably Origen, Jerome, Basil, and John Chrysostom, Evagrius was the crucial figure in the formation of his understanding of the pursuit of perfection.[84] Certainly, it was through his association with Evagrius rather than with such Western figures as Jerome or Pelagius that he took his place in the Origenist tradition.

De coenobiorum institutis

It was approximately two decades after leaving the Egyptian desert that Cassian wrote the *Institutiones* and the *Collationes*. He wrote the former at the request of Castor, Bishop of Apta Julia, north of Marseilles, some time between 419 and 425, probably around 424.[85] According to Cassian, Castor wished instruction concerning the customs of Egyptian and Palestinian monasticism. The bishop was establishing a monastery in an area where there was none, and he sought to benefit from the wisdom of the more experienced Eastern monks as it had been accommodated to the West in the practice of the founder of St. Victor. With hesitation Cassian agreed, defining his task as that of writing to new monks concerning how they might reach perfection. His guide was to be the instruction and example of the elders of the monasteries of Egypt and Palestine dating from apostolic times and continuing into the present. In fact, Cassian saw the authority for the Eastern monastic teaching and practice to be derived at least in part from its presumed continuity with apostolic times.[86] Where these customs might be too difficult because of differences in climate or habits, he would seek to moderate

---

[84]Chadwick, *John Cassian,* 92. A frequently cited study examining this dependence is D. Salvatore Marsili, *Giovanni Cassiano ed Evagrio Pontico: Dottrina sulla carità e contemplazione,* Studia Anselmiana 5 (Rome: Herder, 1936) 87-149.

[85]Most estimates for the writing of the *Institutiones* fall within the range of 419–426. See Jean-Claude Guy, "Introduction," *Institutions cénobitiques,* 11; M. Olphe-Galliard, "Cassien," *Dictionnaire de spiritualité* 2/1 (1937) 217; Edgar C. S. Gibson, "Prolegomena," Works of John Cassian, Nicene and Post-Nicene Fathers, s.s. 11:189. Chadwick, *John Cassian,* 39. Because of the dates proposed below for the *Collationes* and because of the seemingly close connection between the two works, I would argue that the *Institutiones* were written no more than a year or so prior to the *Collationes,* thus probably about 424.

[86]Regarding Cassian's claim of apostolic origin of monasticism, see A. de Vogüé, "Monachisme et église dans la pensée de Cassien," *Théologie de la vie monastique: Études sur la Tradition patristique* (Paris: Aubier, 1961) 213-40; Peter Munz, "John Cassian," *Journal of Ecclesiastical History* 11 (1960): 2-3. For origins of the designation of "monachos" for a specific type of figure in society, see E. A. Judge, "The Earliest Use of the Word 'Monachos' for Monk," *Jahrbuch für Antike und Christentum* 20 (1977): 72-89.

them by using, instead, the example of the monasteries of Pontus and Mesopotamia.[87]

From the very beginning of the *Institutiones* Cassian was concerned with the practical means to be employed in the struggle for perfection. Of the twelve books that constitute this work, he devoted the first four books to a description of the customs of cenobitic life and the last eight to the struggle against the eight basic sins of which Evagrius had warned. The purpose of the *Institutiones*, therefore, was to supply guidance for the active life, i.e., the life of the ascetic who is struggling to reach the higher life of contemplation. In contrast, the *Collationes* pertained to the life of contemplation itself, although they provided direction for the conduct of the active life as well. In principle, then, Cassian was following the Evagrian division of lower, active life, and higher, contemplative life; yet in actuality the division was not so clear-cut for him.[88] He must have found a complete separation unworkable.

Cassian presented the cenobium as the most favorable context for the active life.[89] The carefully regulated context provided training in perfection for a person's will and actions. Through the cenobitic disciplines the monk might progress in his goal of pleasing God; a divine reward could be expected as the outcome for his carefully disciplined efforts.

Fundamental to this discipline was an emphasis on obedience to authority and mortification of the self. One was to pray according to established custom, be obedient to all, and submit to the rules of the elders. Those monks who had reached a position of some seniority were to guide others in accordance with that pattern of life that they themselves had learned through the discipline of obedience.[90]

What was at stake was the subjection of the will, a prerequisite for perfection. The primary intent of instruction was to train the monks to overcome their own wishes,[91] to abdicate reliance on their own judgment.[92] The totality of this submission is starkly apparent in Cassian's instructions. Any disturbing thoughts were to be disclosed to a senior, "and in forming a judgment about

---

[87]Cassian, *Inst., Praef.* 9.

[88]Chadwick, *John Cassian*, 88; Philip Rousseau, "Cassian, Contemplation and the Coenobitic Life," *Journal of Ecclesiastical History* 26 (1975): 113-26. Rousseau, 126, suggested that the "*Institutes* . . . provided a framework of organisation and discipline, within which the spiritual (and contemplative) ideals of the *Conferences* would have the freedom to develop in practice."

[89]J. Rippinger, "The Concept of Obedience in the Monastic Writings of Basil and Cassian," *Studia monastica* 19 (1977): 11.

[90]*Inst.* 2.3; Rippinger, 8-13.

[91]*Inst.* 4.8.

[92]*Inst.* 4.9.

them, [the junior monks were] not to trust anything to their own discretion, but to take it on trust that that is good or bad which is considered and pronounced so by examination of the senior."[93] Furthermore, the monks were to be "quick to fulfill without any discussion all those things ordered by him [a superior] as if they were commanded by God from heaven."[94] The command of the superior was to be considered on a par with the divine law, for these two alone provided the criteria for judging what was beneficial for a monk's development.[95]

For Cassian the subjection of the will was accomplished by means of cenobitic discipline. The authority to which the monk owed such submission was not clearly delimited[96] but was described in a variety of ways, all of which had to do with the tradition of the elders.[97] This tradition was presumed to have derived from Scripture and the earliest days of the church, but fundamentally it was that body of practical wisdom that had developed from the experience of monks struggling against their own sinfulness in an attempt to achieve evangelical perfection. The tradition itself was the authority. The authority of the elders was derivative as they, having themselves been molded by the tradition, attempted to interpret it for the training of others who are also engaged in the pursuit of perfection.[98] Significantly, the tradition as interpreted by the elders had not only the authority of training and discipline but also of precept and command.

At least two assumptions need to be noted. First, the subjection of the will was understood to be accomplished by the efforts of the monks themselves, although under the guidance and direction of the elders. Cassian had nothing but disdain for those who tried to live the monastic life entirely on their own or outside the established lines of tradition. The subjection was accomplished, therefore, by an individual's own efforts yet within a social system that had not only been designed and directed precisely to help a person toward that end but one that also drew upon a tested tradition of guidance in this matter. It was not a case of purely individual efforts. Second, because the judgment of the superior

---

[93]*Inst.* 4.9.

[94]*Inst.* 4.10.

[95]*Inst.* 4.41.

[96]Rippinger, 13.

[97]Cassian employed a cluster of words: *disciplina, regula, institutum, praeceptum, mandatum, canonicus, imperare.* The term *lex Dei* is used, but by far the stress is on the cluster of terms. See also *Coll.* 18.3-4. For forms of authority within a monastery, see Adelbert de Vogüé, *"Sub Regula vel Abbate*: The Theological Significance of the Ancient Monastic Rules" in *Rule and Life: An Interdisciplinary Symposium*, ed. M. Basil Pennington (Spencer MA: Cistercian Publications, 1971) 21-64.

[98]Michel Olphe-Galliard, "Cassien," *Dictionnaire de spiritualité* 2 (1937) 245-46.

was assumed to be an expression of divine direction, adherence to it was believed to be efficacious for salvation.

What we find here are echoes of the Eastern, Origenist tradition. For example, reminiscent of Evagrius, Cassian described the entire process of growth through ascesis as consisting in a succession of stages, the necessary mastery of each one leading to ascent to the next level. In order, they were "the fear of the Lord,"[99] "compunction," "renunciation . . . of all possessions," "humility," "mortification of desires," eradication of faults, growth of virtues, "purity of heart," and "perfection of apostolic love."[100] The movement was from fear to love through a process of transformation of the self. Basic to this scheme was a notion inherited from Christian Platonism that the human heart cannot be empty or, stated differently, that the soul must at any point in time be turned toward the good or away from the good; neutrality is not possible. The heart will always be filled with or motivated by good or by evil. If either is removed, the other will inevitably take its place.[101]

Cassian's understanding of the developmental process entailed what Owen Chadwick has described as the "successive view of free will and grace," a view to be found in some form throughout all the writings of Eastern asceticism.[102] The process is successive in that at each stage of ascent, as sin is progressively undercut, the operation of grace is extended. The obvious transition occured in the progress from the extirpation of faults to the increase of virtues. As sins are removed, virtues take their place. As grace can operate in unimpeded fashion only after the passions have been removed, the reason for the urgency of the ascetic effort becomes apparent, as does also the danger of pride,[103] a hazard of which Cassian showed himself to be well aware in his treatment of the "eight principal faults."[104]

---

[99] Ps. 111:10.

[100] *Inst.* 4.43.

[101] The notion of the necessary movement of the soul had been developed extensively toward the end of the fourth century by Gregory of Nyssa, who, like Evagrius, also stood in the Eastern, Origenist tradition. Gregory had held that, as created beings, persons are always undergoing change of one of two sorts. The inferior change is of a cyclic type such as is found in nature and involves no progress. Its opposite, however, is the perpetual, and unlimited growth in the good. See Jean Daniélou, "Introduction," *From Glory to Glory*, trans. and ed. Herbert Musurillo (New York: Charles Scribner's Sons, 1961) 47-53. Daniélou cited *Oratio catechetica magna* 21, *De vita Moysis, Oratio Funebris de Placilla, De perfectione.* On the absence of any neutral stability for the soul, see Olphe-Galliard, "Cassien," 2:242-43.

[102] Chadwick, *John Cassian,* 110-11.

[103] Chadwick, *John Cassian,* 111.

[104] *Inst.* 5.1, 12.

Cassian, following the classification established by Evagrius with only a slight change in ordering, treated these faults as areas for combat. Accordingly, he made abundant use of the language of war, with its battles, skirmishes, conquests, and defeats. As expressions of the unreformed self, these faults betrayed the need for the discipline of submission by which the self was to be reformed unto God. The life of the monk, as conceived by Cassian, was one of struggle between flesh and spirit, between self-will and submission, between the faults and their corresponding virtues. The soul itself was the battlefield; the enemy, internal.[105]

Important for our purposes is the fact that although the battle was to be waged within the soul, Cassian assumed that the proper environment for the soul's warfare was the cenobium. There the soul would undergo the discipline of submission. Cenobitic monasticism provided for the struggling self the training, the context of authority, and the communal structure in which and, equally important, by which the transformation of the will was effected.

Cassian, of course, recognized the necessity of grace in the self's struggle for perfection; yet because he was writing the *Institutiones* for inexperienced ascetics who were just entering the battle, he employed terminology that would serve as a spur to human effort. The monks were to consider themselves soldiers of Christ. It was their task to win victory over the enemies of Christ within themselves and by so doing to eradicate their faults in order that virtues might flourish. The freedom of the will and the responsibility of the individual for salvation were inescapable messages. The problem was that, as one progressed in the battle, the likelihood increased that pride would emerge, marring every accomplishment by fostering the notion that spiritual achievements were entirely of one's own doing. Cassian's check against such pride was the virtue of humility born of the knowledge of the necessity of grace.

What Cassian presented in the *Institutiones* was a description of the struggle for perfection as properly located in the communal and regulatory context of the cenobium. The advantage of such a context was that it was specifically designed for inculcating the hard lesson of submission. Through the process of subjection of the will to the wisdom of one's betters, the monk accomplished the transformation of self leading to reunion with God.

Stated differently, the cenobium was that context most favorably suited to a type of human action that had been found to result in divine blessing. Cassian had maintained the connection between action and outcome, for, according to the pattern of life he presented, what the monk did had genuine importance for the monk's destiny, a destiny that had not been determined from all eternity by God's election or nonelection. Cassian had upheld the necessity of grace, but it

---

[105]*Inst.* 5.18, 19.

was a grace that the monk would seek out of an awareness of need, a grace that was given in response to that need. Growing recognition of such dependence was simply part and parcel of an ever-increasing subjection and conformity of the self to God.

Collationes

As Cassian intended the *Institutiones* to serve as instruction in the cenobitic life, so the purpose of the *Collationes* was to provide guidance in the eremitic. The *Collationes* themselves were ostensibly the reports of a series of conversations that Cassian and his companion Germanus had had with the anchorites in the desert of Scete.[106] The custom of the *collatio* was a practice based on the conviction that the desert fathers were a peculiar repository of wisdom to whom those training in asceticism might turn for guidance. Certainly Cassian and his companion Germanus had attended such extended discourses during the years which they spent in lower Egypt.[107] By reporting these conversations and thereby conveying the wisdom of the desert, Cassian was giving definition to and appealing to a tradition utterly different from the one that Augustine had defined and to which he had appealed. It was a tradition based on the transmission of the spoken words of the elders, directed to particular persons asking guidance, and conveying the wisdom acquired through accumulated experience in the religious life. It is a tradition of guidance in the religious life rather than a tradition of authoritative theological definition.

Approximately a quarter of a century intervened between Cassian's experience among the desert fathers and his report of his conversations with them in twenty-four *collationes*. The question of authenticity is inevitable. Owen Chadwick discussed the matter at length. He argued that the *Collationes* were not simply reports of the discourses with twenty-four Egyptian abbots (or fifteen, as several abbots are credited with two or three *collationes*). Cassian himself acknowledged that he was adapting Egyptian monasticism to the exigencies of the West. Nevertheless, as one who regularly emphasized the need for fidelity to tradition and to the practices that have proved efficacious through experience, Chadwick suggested, Cassian must have rooted the *Collationes* in the teaching of the monastic giants of Egypt, particularly the Greek monks.[108]

Cassian wrote the twenty-four *Collationes* in three parts (*Coll.* 1-10, 11-17, 18-24), each with its own preface, probably between 425 and 427. He had

---

[106]*Praef. Pars. Prima Coll.*
[107]Chadwick, *John Cassian*, 14.
[108]Chadwick, *John Cassian*, 18-22; see also Hans-Oskar Weber, *Die Stellung des Johannes Cassianus zur ausserpachomianischen Mönchstradition.*

written the *Institutiones* at the request of Bishop Castor, but in the preface to the first group of *collationes*, Cassian stated that Castor had died.[109] Accordingly, he dedicated this group to Leontius, perhaps the Leontius who was the bishop of Fréjus,[110] and to Helladius, who was to become a bishop by the time that the preface to the second group had been written.[111]

He dedicated the second group to the *fratres* Honoratus and Eucherius. He referred to one of these as the abbot of a large cenobium;[112] thus this set of *collationes* must have been written while Honoratus was abbot of Lérins and before he succeeded Patroclus as bishop of Arles in late 426. The first two groups of *collationes*, therefore, would have been completed before the end of 426. It was not until 434 that Eucherius became the bishop of Lyons;[113] thus that date is not helpful, although the episcopal position helps to point out the significance of the persons to whom Cassian dedicated the work. He dedicated the third group to the *fratres* Jovinianus, Minervius, Leontius, and Theodore, who, it might be noted, in 432 succeeded Leontius as bishop of Fréjus.[114] The preface mentioned Honoratus as a bishop;[115] thus this set of *collationes* would have been completed between Honoratus's accession in late 426 and his death, probably early in 429. Because of the close relation among the three groups of *collationes* it seems reasonable that the third group was composed soon after the first two, thus probably in 427.

This choice of dates requires defense. It does coincide with the traditional chronology given for the bishops of Arles from 426-30. According to this chronology, Patroclus was succeeded in late 426 by Honoratus, who served for approximately two years until his death in early 429, when he was succeeded by Hilary. Because Honoratus was referred to in the preface to the second group of *collationes* as an abbot and in the preface to the third group as a bishop, the preface to the second group would have had to have been written sometime prior to Honoratus's elevation to the episcopacy at the end of 426, and the preface to the third group would have had to have been written sometime after that date. Moreover, Prosper's letter to Augustine informing him of the considerable resistance to his views (*Ep.* 225), especially as they were expressed in the *De correptione et gratia* (427/428), identified Hilary as the bishop of Arles; thus Prosper's letter would not have been written prior to early 429, when Hilary became bishop of Arles.

---

[109]*Praef. Pars Prima Coll.*
[110]Pichery, 2:99n.1; Chadwick, *John Cassian*, 38.
[111]*Coll.* 1, *praef.* See *Coll.* 11, *praef.*; Edgar C. S. Gibson, 11:293nn.2, 3.
[112]*Coll.* 11, *praef.*
[113]N. K. Chadwick, 224.
[114]N. K. Chadwick, 142, 148, 224.
[115]*Coll.* 18, *praef.*

At least two difficulties arise from this chronology. First, if the date of the second group was no later than 426, *Collatio* 13, which is generally considered to have been an expression of the very resistance that Prosper's letter had described, would have been written before the composition of *De correptione et gratia* and thus before the outbreak of controversy reported in Prosper's letter. Second, Prosper's letter, written over two years later, gave no indication of the existence of *Collatio* 13.

Approximately half a century ago Owen Chadwick proposed an attractive alternative chronology that avoided the difficulties entailed in the traditional dating. The manuscript tradition for Prosper's letter contained an alternative reading of the name of the bishop of Arles. Rather than the usual "Hilarium," one manuscript referred to "'elladium." Similarly, in one ancient list of the bishops of Arles, the name "Euladii" stood between "Patruli" and "Honorati." Chadwick equated "'elladium" with "Euladii" and proposed that the reference in Prosper's letter was not to the Hilary who succeeded Honoratus as bishop of Arles but to a certain Euladius, who would have served briefly between the episcopacy of Patroclus and that of Honoratus. According to this revised chronology, early in 427 during the episcopacy of Euladius the *De correptione et gratia* would have arrived in Gaul. Both Prosper's letter to Augustine describing the controversy that it had provoked and *Collatio* 13, Cassian's contribution to that controversy, would have followed sometime during the episcopacy of Euladius and before the elevation of Honoratus in late 427 or early 428.[116]

Chadwick's proposal has considerable appeal. It located the composition of *Collatio* 13 squarely within the context of the controversy and in such close temporal proximity to Prosper's letter as to explain Prosper's apparent unawareness of this crucial work, which he would later criticize in detail in the *Contra collatorem*. The proposal has its critics, however. Cappuyns has argued that the list of bishops on which Chadwick relied contained the names of many who were bishops elsewhere than in Arles. He suggested that the Euladius named in the list was the same Helladius designated in the preface to the first group of *collationes* as a *frater* and in the preface to the second as an *episcopus*. Where this Helladius served as bishop is unknown, but Cappuyns argued that he would have been an episcopal collegue of Honoratus and not his predecessor at Arles. This line of reasoning, of course, suggested an early date, probably 426, for the second set of *collationes*. Cappuyns dated the composition of the third set in the same year. He noted that the preface to the second set contained a reference to another collection of seven *collationes*, presumably *Collationes* 18-24; thus the second and third sets must have been written about the same time. As external evidence

---

[116]Chadwick, "Euladius of Arles," *Journal of Theological Studies* 46 (1945): 200-205.

of the compressed and early time frame within which Cassian composed the *collationes* Cappuyns pointed to Prosper's knowledge of *multae collationes* in his letter to Rufinus, which Cappuyns dated about 426-27.[117]

Recently, Robert Markus has argued in favor of the traditional dating in contrast to Chadwick's alternative. Markus has challenged the assumption that *Collatio* 13 was a response to Augustine's predestinarian teaching and thus something of an anomaly among the other *collationes*. Instead, he has suggested that it was of a piece with the other members of the second group, especially *Collatio* 12, and that, to the extent that it was a controversial piece at all, it was an attack on Pelagian views, which would seem to have had enough continuing support in Gaul to have necessitated condemnation in 425.[118] Markus did not completely dissociate *Collatio* 13 from early Gallic uneasiness over Augustine's predestinarian teaching. To the contrary, he argued that Cassian would have been aware that the anti-Pelagian arguments that he offered in *Collatio* 13 differed significantly from Augustine's anti-Pelagianism. This divergence could have been an expression of the Gallic misgivings that Prosper, in his letter to Augustine, spoke of as having preceded the arrival of *De correptione et gratia*.[119]

Chadwick's argument depended, first, on a list of Arlesian bishops, the reliability of which Cappuyns has questioned, and, second, on the assumption, challenged by Markus, that *Collatio* 13 was written in the context of a strong antipredestinarian reaction that followed the arrival of the *De correptione et gratia* in southern Gaul. An argument for the traditional dating, although immune from these criticisms, must, nevertheless, take into account the fact that Prosper's letter reporting the strong Gallic antipredestinarian sentiment to Augustine made no explicit mention of *Collatio* 13, which within a few years Prosper would consider to be worthy of a point-by-point rebuttal. Although there is, at present, no completely satisfactory solution to this difficulty, Markus has suggested an attractive possibility: that *Collatio* 13, although not written in the heat of controversy, came to be considered as part of the antipredestinarian attack once such a controversy did arise.[120]

---

[117]M. Cappuyns, "Cassien," *Dictionnaire d'histoire et de géographie ecclésistique* (1949) 11:1331. See also Pichery, 2:99n.1; Prosper, *Ep. ad Ruf.* 4. Regarding the list of bishops to which Chadwick and Cappuyns referred, see L. Duchesne, *Fastes épiscopaux* 1 (Paris: Thorin & Fils, 1894) 243-46.

[118]Robert Markus, *The End of Ancient Christianity* (Cambridge: Cambridge University Press, 1991) 177-78. Markus referred to *Constitutiones Sirmondianae* 6; *Codex Theodosianus* 16.5.62, 63, 64.

[119]Markus, 178; cf. *Ep.* 225.2.

[120]Markus, 178-79; Markus, "The Legacy of Pelagius: Orthodoxy, Heresy and Conciliation," *The Making of Orthodoxy*, ed. R. D. Williams (Cambridge: Cambridge University Press, 1989) 214-34.

In view of these arguments, it now seems possible to suggest the following sequence of events, in accord with the traditional dating. In 426 Cassian composed *Collatio* 13, his discussion of the operation of grace, as an integral element of his instructions for monks and as a companion piece to *Collatio* 12, his discussion of chastity. The unmistakably anti-Pelagian tone of the *collatio* suggests that he found it necessary to warn monks against views that had been rejected by the church in Rome and North Africa but were still supported by some in Gaul. The equally unmistakable antipredestinarian tone suggests an awareness of elements of Augustine's anti-Pelagianism, also known in Gaul, that he likewise found to be inimical to the monastic endeavor.

Furthermore, it seems probable that Prosper, writing to Rufinus in 426 or 427, had this *collatio* in mind when he spoke of opposition to Augustine's predestinarian views; however, the assured tone of this letter indicates that he was confident of the power of Augustine's arguments to prevail over any opposition. Between the composition of this letter and of his letter to Augustine in 429, Prosper's confidence was shaken by the negative reaction of highly respected persons, particularly the bishop of Arles, to the *De correptione et gratia*. His specific mention of Hilary but not of Cassian may suggest that as a layman Prosper had less concern for the reaction of the abbot of a monastery than for the reaction of a prominent bishop. If so, it also may have been the case that those with whom Prosper was in conversation shared this bias.

Moreover, although the criticisms that Prosper reported to Augustine were similar to those found in *Collatio* 13, there is no reason to believe that these criticisms were peculiar to Cassian or that they had been expressed in their most virulent form by Cassian. In fact, Prosper did not seem to have found it necessary to respond specifically to Cassian until about 432, i.e., about the time that other clearly anti-Augustinian works were being published.[121]

Finally, Markus has suggested that the predestinarian debate that so concerned Prosper during these years was not, in fact, widespread.[122] That the number of persons actually involved may have been limited would not necessarily indicate that Prosper's alarm was unjustified. The dedications of the *Institutiones* and particularly the *Collationes* create the impression that Cassian had an impressive network of prominent allies during this period. Presumably, many, if not all, of these individuals would have been sympathetic to his antipredestinarian views.[123] The dismay that Prosper and Hilary expressed over the

---

[121]*Prosper of Aquitaine: Defense of St. Augustine*, ed. P. De Letter, 8.

[122]Robert Markus, "The Legacy of Pelagius," 117-18, and *The End of Ancient Christianity*, 178-79.

[123]If the Leontius of these dedications were, in fact, the Leontius of Fréjus, then he was among the bishops whom Pope Celestine, at the request of Prosper and Hilary,

formidable character of Augustine's critics would seem to have been well founded.

Like the *Institutiones*, however, the *Collationes*, with the possible exception of *Collatio* 13, were not written as a response to Augustine's predestinarian teaching. Because Prosper and others after him did come to consider *Collatio* 13 as a specifically anti-Augustinian statement, we shall examine it separately. On the whole, however, the *Collationes* should be viewed as a supplement to or a continuation of Cassian's description in the *Institutiones* of the monk's struggle for perfection.

As such, they also employed the imagery of a military engagement found in the *Institutiones*. This continuing emphasis on struggle may seem somewhat surprising since the *Collationes* are describing the life of contemplation. Yet the use of military imagery was necessitated by Cassian's conviction that the soul never attains a state of utter stability and uninterrupted contemplation. Immutability belongs to God alone. The soul is always changing, either increasing in the good or regressing into evil.[124] As stated earlier, the soul must be inhabited by either virtue or vice. With the extirpation of the latter, the former takes its place, but if the virtues diminish, the vices will increase. This situation of instability creates a pressure on the monk for constant vigilance. As the repeated questions of Germanus about achieving constancy would indicate, the problem of instability was of great concern, particularly with regard to the difficulty of controlling one's thoughts.[125] In fact, one could almost say that it was the central psychological concern of the *Collationes*. Cassian presented the battle as unending, for even in the higher life of the anchorite change would not always be for the better. The active life had to continue, if perhaps in a more subtle form, interwoven throughout the fabric of the contemplative life.

Because the notion of struggle remained fundamental, even in the description of the life of contemplation, it is a useful key for explicating the *Collationes* as a whole. Three aspects of the religious struggle bear examination: first, the interaction of grace and free will in the struggle; second, the goal of the struggle; third, the means, particularly that of submission, by which one attains this goal.

As to the first of these elements of struggle, the interaction of grace and the free will, Cassian asserted that "the beginning of our salvation" derives from the "call" and "inspiration" of the Lord and that its "completion of perfection and

---

reprimanded in a letter stating that they were not controlling their presbyters' expressions of doctrine. Clearly, Leontius's allegiance would have been with Cassian rather than with the Augustinians. N. K. Chadwick, 148-49, 224.

[124]*Coll.* 6.14. For a discussion of Cassian's teaching on the eradication of sin, see Peter Munz, "John Cassian," *Journal of Ecclesiastical History* 11 (1960): 1-22.

[125]Examples of Germanus's questions on achieving constancy include *Coll.* 1.12, 16; 6.13; 7.7, 9, 14; 9.7; 10.12, 13.

purity" is the gift of divine "guidance" and "illumination";[126] yet between initiation and accomplishment lie divinely given "opportunities" for obedience to that original call.[127] The responsibility for obedience falls on the individual, but continual exertion toward perfection still requires the Lord's "cooperation" and the divine "directing" of the human will.[128] It would thus appear to be that case the the free will operates within a framework created and permeated by grace. (As an aside, it should be noted that in *Collatio* 13 Cassian allowed for the possibility that the human good will may precede the work of grace.[129])

Within this framework the will must move through a series of stages. One advances from fear to hope to love or from the condition of a slave to that of a hireling to that of a son. Stated differently, three virtues comprise salvation: faith that controls faults through "servile" fear of death and punishment, a somewhat "mercenary" hope that forsakes earthly pleasures in anticipation of reward in heaven, filial love that does the good entirely out of the love of goodness.[130] These virtues are ascending in value, and by the time that one has attained to the love of the good for its own sake, conflict, with its attendant dangers of defeat or wounding, has ceased, at least to the extent that stability in the soul is possible in this life.[131] The final stage is again fear but of a different sort from the servile fear with which one begins. This ultimate fear is the outcome and perfection of love, for it is the fear of offending the beloved, God.[132]

On the one hand, advancement through these stages to the perfection of love is given to those who rely not on their own capacities but on the grace of God;[133] yet on the other hand, the "grades of perfection" that these three virtues embody make clear that, as persons vary in their "virtue, purpose, or fervor," the level of individual attainment varies as well.[134] Both grace and human effort are essential to the process.

Cassian has made a careful distinction between the work of grace and the work of the free will. It is the gift of grace that the will should be good and that the will and its actions should be perfected. Between the beginning and fulfillment, however, the responsibility lies with the human agent, for it is within the power of the person's good will, again assisted by grace, to strive for salvation. This exercise of human responsibility becomes the locus of divine

---

[126]*Coll.* 3.10.
[127]*Coll.* 3.12.
[128]*Coll.* 3.12.
[129]See 111-12 below.
[130]*Coll.* 11.6,7,9.
[131]*Coll.* 11.7,8.
[132]*Coll.* 11.13.
[133]*Coll.* 11.9.
[134]*Coll.* 11.12.

reward and punishment.[135] The genuineness of the responsibility must be underscored. Evil has the power of "inciting" us but not of "forcing" us; otherwise it would be unavoidable. The will can freely accept or reject the allurements of evil; furthermore, grace provides ready assistance in the battle.[136]

The language of conflict permeates even Cassian's discussion of human nature itself. A continuing struggle exists within the person between the flesh, evil desires, and the spirit, spiritual desires. (The former desires are not necessarily evil per se but evil in that they are inferior to and distract from the spiritual desires.) Cassian argued that as this struggle has existed in every descendant of Adam, it must be considered a part of human nature, "implanted in us" for our good. The opposition between flesh and spirit is a struggle for obedience to God and has the beneficial effect of "prevent[ing] you from doing what you would."[137]

The free will is located between these two conflicting sets of desires, committed to neither preference entirely. In fact, it would be "lukewarm" were it not for the struggle going on around it. Although the will is "somewhat worthy of blame" in its attraction to carnal desires, its intermediate position serves as a source of equilibrium between the excesses of flesh and of the spirit. If the resulting tension is maintained, the spirit serves to check preoccupation with carnal comforts and pleasures, and the flesh serves to check spiritual zeal that would neglect bodily necessities. Together these operations effect the progress of the soul to a further plane in which "we should do what we would not."[138] Thus the free will, even in its fallen condition, is not totally unable to will the good but is in itself the locus of the God-given conflict which, if faithfully sustained, becomes the means for progress toward purity of heart.

In this description of the human condition the role of grace does not receive prominence. Instead, the emphasis falls on vigilance, unceasing struggle, in the attainment of salvation. It must not be forgotten, however, that the very existence of the conflict is itself the work of grace, although its maintenance is the work of the will. The "valuable discord" that God introduced into human nature after the fall creates the necessary condition for a salvific humility, in contrast to the destructive pride that a unity of flesh and spirit had engendered in the original human condition. That grace operates through the creation of a humbling conflict within the will reinforces Cassian's notion of the validity of monastic striving and thus of human agency itself.

---

[135]*Coll.* 3.19.
[136]*Coll.* 7.8.
[137]*Coll.* 4.7; Gal. 5:17.
[138]*Coll.* 4.9,11,12.

The necessary interaction of grace and human effort is peculiarly evident in Cassian's discussion of prayer. Prayer and its preparation are inseparable.

> The aim of every monk and the perfection of his heart tends to continual and unbroken perseverance in prayer, and, as far as it is allowed to human frailty, strives to acquire an immovable tranquility of mind and a perpetual purity, for the sake of which we seek unweariedly and constantly to practice all bodily labors as well as contrition of spirit. And there is between these two a sort of reciprocal and inseparable union. . . . For lasting and continual calmness in prayer . . . cannot be secured or consummated without them, so neither can those virtues which lay its foundations be fully gained without persistence in it.[139]

If this quotation sounds like a paean to human efforts, it must be remembered that Cassian understood the effort to be inspired, assisted, and consummated by grace. Furthermore, the formula that the monk was continually to recite was a prayer for deliverance amidst adversity and for protection from pride in prosperity: "Be pleased, O God, to deliver me! O Lord, make haste to help me."[140] The true poverty of the monk lay in the repeated request for divine aid made in the knowledge "that every single moment his life and substance depends on Divine assistance."[141]

Cassian's emphasis on prayer was important not only for the relationship that it manifested between grace and free will, the first element of the monk's struggle, but also for its bearing on the second aspect that we have noted, that is, the immediate goal of the struggle: purity of heart which is also called charity. What Cassian's monk was finally seeking was, of course, the kingdom of God, but this proximate goal of purity of heart was needed to provide the monk with a sure day-to-day signpost toward that kingdom. Purity of heart, then, served as the standard according to which monastic struggling and striving were to be regulated and all acts of discipline and edification were to be judged.[142] It was the condition or intermediate goal that must be satisfied if one were to engage in the contemplation of the divine, the principal task of a monk.[143]

At least two aspects of this proximate goal, as depicted by Cassian, are significant for us. First, as thoughts serve as the avenue by which vices gain entrance to the soul, the eradication of sinful thoughts, such as pride, anger, and lust, is the precondition for purity of heart. All the struggles and self-examination

---

[139]*Coll.* 9.2.
[140]*Coll.* 10.10; Ps. 70:1.
[141]*Coll.* 10.11.
[142]*Coll.* 1.4-5,7.
[143]*Coll.* 1.8.

that precede and accompany the contemplative life aim for this goal.[144] Second, discipline of thoughts must include not only the removal of sinful thoughts but an "abiding" of the attention on the good, "righteousness and peace and joy." This persistence in the good is the means by which the kingdom of God is established in the soul.[145]

By calling attention to the need to school one's thoughts, Cassian was claiming that persons possess some measure of control over the emergence of thoughts as well as total responsibility for whether they accept the thoughts or banish them from their mind. He argued that if a person did not have some degree of control in the matter, "there would not remain any free will . . . nor would efforts for our improvement be in our power."[146] Scriptural admonitions of accountability for thoughts imply just such capacity.[147] Responsibility for one's own thoughts was a crucial element in Cassian's argument for human agency.

The matter was of such significance that Cassian recommended a methodology for its accomplishment. By examining one's thoughts in accordance with criteria that Cassian provided, it would be possible to determine both their origin (whether they were of God, of the devil, or of the self) and their value.[148] Those thoughts that do not promote progress toward purity of heart are to be eliminated. By keeping the mind occupied with Scripture, one could exercise at least partial control over the emergence of thoughts, for through deliberate attention to the good, less opportunity is given to its opposite.[149]

Although the mind is always in action, through daily practice in concentration on the good, Cassian believed that it could attain a degree of fixity on the good and not be at the mercy of evil or distracting thoughts.[150] He was convinced that such control could be learned through training and practice; it was within human capacity. Nevertheless, as noted above, that very training and practice entailed appeals to God for aid; "Be pleased, O God, to deliver me! O Lord, make haste to help me."[151]

Cassian would seem to have derived his optimism on this matter from Evagrius. Although Evagrius had clearly recognized the difficulties involved in stabilizing the thoughts, as his own classification of evil thoughts and careful instruction for their regulation would indicate,[152] that same classification and

---

[144]*Coll.* 7.17, 24; 8.19.
[145]*Coll.* 1.13.
[146]*Coll.* 1.17.
[147]*Coll.* 7.4; Mt. 9:4, Isa. 66:18, Rom. 2:15-16.
[148]*Coll.* 1.19-22.
[149]*Coll.* 1.17,18,22.
[150]*Coll.* 7.5.
[151]*Coll.* 10.10; Ps. 70.1. See above, n. 140.
[152]See *Practicus* 6-39.

optimism were equally indicative of his conviction that progress in this very bothersome problem was possible.

For Cassian, the key for evaluating one's thoughts and actions and finally for attaining purity of heart was discretion. He portrayed discretion as the gift of grace but a gift given only to the humble. It came to one who submitted to the authority of the elders and the tradition.[153] Cassian advised that a monk should subject everything to the examination of the elders and accept their judgment, for this judgment was itself the outcome both of the elders' own submission to tradition and of their righteous lives. Novelty and self-reliance were to be shunned.[154] Discretion, therefore, consisted of a judgment formed and informed by the traditions of the elders and applied wisely to the religious life. Here the tradition and authority to which Cassian appealed and his ideal of the religious life converged. The attainment of the monk's goal, purity of heart, lay in what was received, whether from obedience to authority or through grace. Cassian's argument took into account both free will and grace. Significantly, he set the exercise of the former within the context of disciplined submission. "The Lord does not show the way of perfection to anyone who having the opportunity of learning despises the teaching and training of the elders."[155]

In fact, that the elder's command was to be considered a command from God reinforced the notion that the judgment of an elder or "more experienced" monk was to be trusted more than one's own.[156] Practically speaking, it might not be the case that the other person was always wiser, but the monk would gain strength through "putting up with" the neighbor.[157] What was to be avoided was obstinate persistence in one's own judgments.[158] The point was to subdue one's own will in order to bring it into conformity with God and God's will.

Clearly, the inescapable fact of the religious life as Cassian described it was submission. Through the subjection of one's will to God by means of obedience to the intermediate authority of elders, of tradition, and of Scripture, the will was to be transformed and purity of heart attained. Thus, the struggle for submission of the will or humility will be the third and last element of the monk's life to be considered in this discussion of the *Collationes*.

An example may illustrate the importance that Cassian attached to submission. He classified monks into four groups according to type of governance. Cenobites were those who shared a common life under the direction of

---

[153]*Coll.* 2.1,2,10.
[154]*Coll.* 2.10,11.
[155]*Coll.* 2.15.
[156]*Coll.* 2.15; 16.11; cf. *Inst.* 4.10.
[157]*Coll.* 16.23.
[158]*Coll.* 2.10; 17.23,24.

one elder. Anchorites were those who, having completed their cenobitic training and having attained perfection, presumably through internalization of this discipline, lived in the desert apart from the community.[159] Sarabaites Cassian characterized as persons who sought the honor given to monks but refused to accept the discipline of the cenobium or the rule of elders. They lived as they pleased, often with comrades, pursuing economic security.[160] A final group consisted of persons who, living alone as anchorites, appeared virtuous but actually were unable to accept the discipline of cenobitic life.[161] Cassian judged the last two groups to be fruitless and disreputable from lack of humility. With regard to the first two groups, although initially in the *Collationes* he gave pride of place to the anchorites, by the conclusion of the work it was the cenobites to whom he gave prominence. The cenobium came to represent for Cassian the arena most conducive to the pursuit of that form of perfection that he believed to be possible in this life, particularly as it entailed the attainment of humility through obedience.[162]

Humility, he believed, was not simply the sine qua non for purity of heart but also the essential foundation for any progress in perfection toward purity of heart.[163] Humility derived from trusting the teaching and practice of the elders rather than one's own judgment,[164] from withstanding the salutary struggles with temptation,[165] and from recognizing not only that one's enemies are internal but also that one must overcome these internal foes if the kingdom of God is to be firmly established within the heart.[166]

Yet as strongly as Cassian stressed the importance of humility, his message was somewhat ambiguous. He presented humility both as the gift of grace and as the achievement of one who strives through the abnegation of the will; thus, oddly enough, the attainment of humility could be a source of pride.

Moreover, he conceived the interaction of humility with grace to be highly complex. Cassian considered divine forgiveness of sins, which involves both grace and penitence, as a precondition for purity of heart. In penitence one "somehow . . . stays the right hand of the Avenger even against His will."[167]

---

[159]*Coll.* 18.4.
[160]*Coll.* 18.4.7.
[161]*Coll.* 18.8.
[162]Cf. *Coll.* 18.6 and 19.2-3, 5-6. Recently, Robert Markus has pointed out how Cassian's own thinking shifted during the writing of the *Collationes*, such that by their conclusion the "superiority [of the solitary life] is subtly but radically undermined." See *The End of Ancient Christianity*, 182.
[163]*Coll.* 9.3.
[164]*Coll.* 18.3.
[165]*Coll.* 18.13.
[166]*Coll.* 18.16.
[167]*Coll.* 20.4.

Thus penitence, which is itself based in humility, removes the obstacles to grace and earns the "reward of pardon."[168] Cassian even listed various "fruits of penitence by which we can succeed in expiating our sins," and he suggested that if one method is not possible for a penitent then another should be tried. He also reminded that grace is necessary for expiation but that it is the person's responsibility to strive. Grace will assist human efforts.[169]

In effect, one punished oneself now in order not to be punished later by the divine judgment. As a result, one's present action, so far as it is conformed to the divine standard, which will eventually be enforced at the last judgment, does affect one's destiny.

Yet the monk's major preoccupation was finally not the negative goal of avoiding pain but the positive goal of attaining the reward of an undistracted enjoyment of God. This positive goal, Cassian recognized, was inherently humbling, for the continuous contemplation of God is simply not an innate possibility for creatures, who by their very nature are mutable. It is only "by participation of their Creator and by grace," and not through natural means that the creature can attain "eternity and immutability."[170] The attainment of the highest good, the sustained contemplation of God, is possible only by means of a transformation of human nature such that it participates in the attributes of the divine. The fullness of that participation Cassian believed to be available only in beatitude. Even then the goodness and immutability of the Creator will remain incomparable.[171]

In this life, however diligently one may strive, earthly thoughts intervene. Those who strive are inevitably confronted with the humbling fact that there exists a "law of sin" in their "members" that resists the "law of their mind" or the "law of God" in which they take delight.[172] This law of sin is the inheritance of the offspring of Adam, who as a result of the fall can attain the vision of God, partake of the bread of heaven, only by extreme exertion[173] and grace.[174] That law of sin continually diverts the attention to lesser thoughts.[175] This failing leads not to damnation but to dissatisfaction and unhappiness in those who are yearning for uninterrupted contemplation.[176] Their mutable condition, which prevents the total subordination of the self, specifically the thoughts, to the contemplation of

---

[168]*Coll.* 20.7.
[169]*Coll.* 20.8.
[170]*Coll.* 23.3.
[171]*Coll.* 23.3,5.
[172]*Coll.* 23.11; Rom. 7:22-23.
[173]*Coll.* 23.11.
[174]*Coll.* 23.15.
[175]*Coll.* 23.13.
[176]*Coll.* 23.15.

God, humbles them. Cassian's monk, therefore, was consigned to a life not only of striving but also of reliance on grace for both forgiveness and improvement.

All the efforts at subjection of the will were ultimately directed to this submission of the self in the contemplation of God. Achievement of this goal would come only through grace, but grace was given in greatest measure, in this life at least, to those who strove.

The *Collationes* aimed to describe that life which seeks purity of heart or continuous contemplation of God. The means by which purity of heart was to be pursued and approached, if not fully attained, in this life was the subjection of the self, the will. Such subjection was the result of the interaction of grace and human effort, an effort that was always constituted by a struggle. That struggle was central to the monk's life. It was the discipline that at all times had to be undergone so long as one remained in the state of mutability.

Because of the critical importance of this struggle, Cassian understandably placed great stress upon it. Such an emphasis was entirely appropriate for the instruction of monks whose very lives were consumed in the struggle and who needed guidance in their efforts. On the other hand, the attention that Cassian directed toward human effort may convey the impression that he understood the struggle to be an entirely human effort that merits the reward of grace. Cassian did not so envision the matter, however. Of course, he did believe that human striving for the good does have its outcome in the recompense of grace, but for him the very struggle was itself a divine and human interaction. There could be no such struggle without the assistance of grace; in fact, it was underwritten by grace. What Cassian could never allow, however, was that grace controlled the struggle.

Augustine and Cassian

Although Cassian did not write the *Institutiones* and *Collationes* in response to Augustine, he has traditionally been considered one of the most significant critics of Augustine's predestinarian teaching. Moreover, these two works had a formative influence on the development of Lérinian monasticism, from which emerged some of the most telling challenges to that same teaching. Thus it is appropriate that we note the more significant differences between the understanding of grace and human agency presented in those treatises of Augustine that we have examined and the understanding of grace and human agency presented in the *Institutiones* and *Collationes* of Cassian. As noted above, we will consider *Collatio* 13 separately.

Perhaps the most obvious differences between these two understandings of grace and human agency pertained to context. Cassian's writing assumed the highly controlled and disciplined environment of a cenobium, which he believed provided the optimum conditions for the interaction of grace and human striving.

Augustine, in contrast, appears not to have thought in terms of such a specifically defined and regulated communal context, except perhaps in terms of a congregation with its ill-defined and constantly violated social boundaries. Such an amorphous setting could hardly be trusted as a reliable instrument of divine direction. For him the locus for the operation of grace was far more narrowly construed as simply the human heart.

As the contexts differed so did the membership of each. Cassian was instructing monks in the life of contemplation, its preparation and pursuit. In other words, he was addressing that elite group of Christians who had committed their lives to the pursuit of perfection.[177] In contrast, the object of Augustine's concern was the wide spectrum of Catholics, few of whom belonged to any spiritual elite but all of whom required the pastoral oversight of the church. Broadly stated, in relation to monks the question that Cassian addressed was how perseverance in prayer is possible; in relation to all Catholic Christians the question that Augustine addressed was how perseverance even in the faith itself is possible. The former question had to do with a psychological possibility, the condition of unceasing and stable prayer. The latter question had to do with a logical possibility, the condition of finally being among the saved; direct psychological implications were reserved only for the moment of a person's death. This difference in the membership of their respective social contexts must assuredly have affected the character of their questions and their answers.

The difference in polemical contexts would have colored their statements, as well. Augustine, particularly in the letter to Sixtus (*Ep.* 194), had been responding to the perceived Pelagian assertion that the will can attain perfection with divine guidance and exhortation. Cassian gave no evidence that he had ever considered such a possibility seriously. Augustine thus found it necessary to take a defensive position on a question that Cassian felt no need to address at all.

A cluster of issues surrounding the human will was a second area in which the teaching of the two men diverged significantly. First, Cassian understood the subjection of the will to be the key to the achievement not only of purity of heart but finally of the kingdom of God. The trustworthy means for the attainment of purity of heart was obedience, in particular, obedience to the ascetic tradition, as expressed in the highly regulated life of the cenobium and, more specifically, in the judgments of the superior.

Augustine, in contrast, possessed no such sense of assurance as to the effect of human guidance. For Augustine, human correction or rebuke always functioned under the prior determination of an inscrutable divine will; it could not be.

---

[177]Although Cassian was addressing a Christian elite, he did take account of various kinds and various levels of prayer, some of which belong to the lowest orders of the religious life, e.g., *Coll.* 9.8-18.

consistently depended upon as an efficacious medium for salvation. Moreover, although Augustine would have agreed with Cassian in the identification of pride or self-will as the fundamental sin, he emphasized the efficacy of love, the gift of the Holy Spirit, rather than of obedience in the battle against pride.[178] In fact, preoccupied with perseverance in the good rather than with purity of heart, Augustine stressed the need not for the subjection of the will but for the complete transformation of the will so that it might delight in the good. Thus whereas Cassian described with painstaking care a sequence of stages for the progression of the will in virtue and, toward that end, offered elaborate guidance for the regulation of thoughts, Augustine, in the works that provoked and sustained the controversy, provided no such scheme or guidance. Until transformed by grace, the Augustinian will is incapable of the good. The limited control that people have over their own thoughts he employed as evidence of human frailty and of the necessity of grace.[179]

Second, as the two men presented contrasting versions of the goal and consequently of the type of change that the will must undergo if it is to attain that goal, they also differed in their assessments of the respective roles to be assigned to human agency and to grace in the accomplishment of a changed will. Admittedly, they were in accord over the necessity of grace, and they even utilized some of the same passages from Scripture to establish that point.[180] Similarly, they agreed that it is to God rather than to oneself that one must look for salvation.

Yet in arguing that one's confidence is to be located in God and not in one's own capacities and efforts, Cassian was indicating only that the monk is not self-sufficient for the accomplishment of perfection. Even his assertions that faith is

---

[178]Adolar Zumkeller, *Augustine's Ideal of the Religious Life*, trans. Edmund Colledge (New York: Fordham University Press, 1986) 164-65. Markus, *The End of Ancient Christianity*, 162-63. George Lawless, *Augustine of Hippo and His Monastic Rule*, 81, 117. Lawless provides a translation of the text for males and for females. See 7.1, 2, 4 of both versions.

[179]See 62 above.

[180]Cassian's references to these passages include the following: 1 Cor. 4:7 *Inst.* 12.10, *Coll.* 3.16; 1 Cor 15:10 *Inst.* 12.9. (also in *Coll.* 13.13); Phil. 2:13 *Inst.* 12.9 (also in *Coll.* 13.9, 12); Jn. 15:5 *Inst.* 12.9; Ps. 127:1, 2 *Inst.* 12.9 (also in *Coll.* 13.10); Rom. 9:16 *Inst.* 12.9, *Coll.* 4.5 (also in *Coll.* 13.9). The Augustinian references to these passages include the following: 1 Cor. 4:7 *De gr. et lib. arb.* 6.15, *De corr. et gr.* 3.5, 6.10, 7.12, 9.21, *De praed. sanct.* 3.7, 4.8, *De don. pers.* 17.43; 1 Cor. 15:10 *De gr. et lib. arb.* 5.12; Phil. 2:13 *De gr. et lib. arb.* 9.21, 16.32, 17.33, *De corr. et gr.* 2.4, 9.24, *De praed. sanct.* 12.37, *De don. pers.* 13.33, 14.34; Jn. 15:5 *De gr. et lib. arb.* 7.13, 9.20, *De corr. et gr.* 1.2, 12.34; Ps. 127:1,2 *De praed. sanct.* 7.12; Rom. 9:16 *De gr. et lib. arb.* 7.16, *De don. pers.* 11.25.

the gift of God[181] and that grace is necessary for the performance of the very ascetic acts that aim for perfection in no way diminished for him the importance of human striving.[182] In fact, Cassian could assert that human actions, such as prayer, can even elicit the bestowal of grace.[183] God is ready to give that which is sought if the good will of the person provides the occasion.[184] Augustine, of course, would have agreed that grace is given in response to prayer, but he would also have insisted that the very desire and capacity to pray is itself the gift of grace.

According to Cassian, what is needed from God for the human will is direction. In contrast to Augustine, Cassian perceived the condition of the will not as enslaved to sin, free only for evil, but as "more readily inclined to vice either through want of knowledge of what is good, or through the delights of passion." The will requires divine assistance as it struggles between the desires of the flesh and those of the spirit in order to ensure that any stumbling and mis-steps do not lead to utter destruction.[185] Cassian recommended praying that God "turn" the will to virtue,[186] but this turning consists not in grace determining the direction of the will but in grace creating conditions favorable to the will's making its own determination for the good. As already noted, the "valuable dis-cord" within which the will operates, as conducive to humility, is itself the gift of grace.

Augustine could, of course, speak in the language of warfare and battles;[187] yet the character of the conflict that he described differed from that envisioned by Cassian. For Augustine the ostensible combatants were the heirs of Adam unprotected by the benefits that had originally surrounded their progenitor. If victory were to be won, it must be the achievement not of Adam's incapacitated offspring but of grace. If there were to be victory against evil, the actual com-batant must be grace itself working through the human agent.[188] The conflict for Augustine was not a matter of the self struggling for its reformation by means of cenobitic discipline but of grace accomplishing that reformation by means of its operation within the person. Augustine was assigning to grace both what Cassian assigned to grace as well as what Cassian assigned to the disciplinary and communal context. Cassian's monk stood in need of grace from beginning

---

[181]*Coll.* 3.16.
[182]*Inst.* 12.11,14,15,16.
[183]*Inst.* 12.13.
[184]*Inst.* 12.14.
[185]*Coll.* 3.12.
[186]*Coll.* 3.12.
[187]*De. corr. et gr.* 11.29, citing Rom. 7:23; *De gr. et lib. arb.* 7.16, citing 2 Tim. 4:7.
[188]*De corr. et gr.* 11.29; *De gr. et lib. arb.* 7.16.

to end of the process of salvation, but it was a grace that called, inspired, and assisted. The person was to function as a partner, a viable agent, rather than as a vessel shaped by its contents.

Collatio 13: *De protectione Dei*

Midway through the *Collationes*, situated between a discussion of the attainment of chastity and a discourse on spiritual knowledge, stands *Collatio* 13, *De protectione Dei*. At least from the fourth decade of the fifth century, it has been viewed in some quarters as the definitive statement of the Gallic monastic alternative to Augustine's predestinarian views. About 432 Prosper of Aquitaine, in his role as defender of the deceased Augustine, considered it to be a sufficiently dangerous challenge to merit a lengthy, almost point-by-point response. Almost two centuries later Cassiodorus was referring to this same work when he warned his own monastic community against Cassian's somewhat suspicious views on free will.[189]

As indicated above in the discussion of dating of the second group of *collationes* of which this one is a part, this *collatio* appears to be integrally related to that which immediately precedes it as well as to the *Institutiones* and *Collationes* as a whole and need not be considered primarily as a controversial piece. On the other hand, it does seem probable that Cassian was aware of Augustine's predestinarian views and that he himself was giving voice to a tradition that stood in tension with those views. It also seems likely that he deliberately used this *collatio* to underscore that tension. Whatever Cassian's intent, however, the importance of *Collatio* 13 for our purposes is that in a single unified argument, it applied the wisdom of the elders and the Origenism of Evagrius to the relation of grace and free will and to the connection between human action and its outcome. Because Prosper would soon come to see this *collatio* as a dangerous attack on the final outworking of Augustine's teaching on grace, we shall examine it specifically in relation to that teaching.

Cassian began the *collatio* by stating that "the exertions of the worker can do nothing without God's aid" but also that

> the initiative not only of our actions but also of good thoughts comes from God, who inspires us with a good will to begin with, and supplies us with the opportunity of carrying out what we rightly desire: for "every good endowment and every perfect gift is from above, coming down from the Father of lights," who both begins what is good, and continues it and completes it in us.[190]

---

[189]*Institutiones divinarum litterarum* 29.2.
[190]*Coll.* 13.3; Jas. 1:17.

Cassian has unequivocally stated the case for the necessity of grace from beginning to end of the process of salvation. He reinforced his point by examples from the monastic life, showing that without divine assistance, nothing that pertains to salvation lies within the frail capacity of the human being. Capacity and opportunity both are dependent upon grace.[191]

Had Cassian stopped here, the Augustinians would not have had grounds for argument. Undoubtedly, the man was thoroughly anti-Pelagian in his stress on both the necessity of grace and the internal character of its work. It would even have been possible to infer from his statements that grace is sovereign and its rationale unaccountable. Yet Cassian quickly moved to exclude such a possibility. He sought to balance his assertion of the necessity of grace with corresponding affirmations both of the divine will for universal salvation and also of the significance of human will and effort.

Citing 1 Timothy 2:4, he accepted at face value that God wills the salvation of all and concluded that any who perish do so "against the will of God." In this regard Cassian was not an elitist. He had no elite of the elect. He believed that when God finds a beginning of good will in the heart, a beginning which either grace or human effort has engendered, God nurtures it toward salvation.[192] In responding to this passage later, Prosper was willing to give Cassian the benefit of the doubt by suggesting that it was sufficiently ambiguous for Cassian to have meant that grace preceded the human effort for good.[193] However, when Cassian further specified that the beginning of the good will could have its source either in divine grace or in human effort alone,[194] he and the Augustinians parted ways.[195]

Cassian appears here to have deviated from statements elsewhere in the *Collationes*[196] that the beginning and perfection of the good will are the work of grace and that the context for human striving is within the framework provided by grace. It is reasonable to assume that this apparent shift in his position arose from his awareness of Augustine's predestinarian teaching and his own consequent need to present human agency in such a way that it not be overridden

---

[191]*Coll.* 13.6.

[192]*Coll.* 13.8.

[193]Prosper, *Contra collatorem* 2.3.

[194]*Coll.* 13.9.

[195]*Contra collatorem* 2.4.

[196]The primary references that stress that the beginning and the end of the process are the work of grace are from *Collatio* 3, thus from the first group of *collationes*. See, for example, *Coll.* 3.4,5,10-12, esp. 3.10,16,19. Presumably this material was written before the *De correptione et gratia* reached southern Gaul, thus before the emergence of the controversy.

or controlled by grace. Nor was Cassian necessarily being inconsistent. His previous assertions that the beginning of the good will is a gift of grace were clearly not references to predestination or election but to the divine will for universal salvation. This gift of grace he believed to be available to all. As such, it is as much a precondition for monastic striving as is self-initiated human action.

Cassian's intent was to maintain both grace and the freedom of the human will. He argued that the will at times might initiate its own movement toward salvation but that it is incapable of attaining its goal without the assistance of grace. Through the grace of creation, human nature is in certain instances enabled to take the first step on its own without the assistance of preparatory grace,[197] an assistance the Augustinians believed to be essential. Cassian acknowledged that the will has been injured by the fall, but he believed that it might still freely choose the good, although not achieve it, without grace. The fall did not deprive Adam of the knowledge of good that he already had but engendered in him a knowledge of evil that he had previously lacked.[198]

Cassian wanted to maintain the necessary interaction of grace and the free will in a way that upheld the dominance of grace without diminishing the genuineness of the will's freedom. Thus he stated that to achieve the divine purpose of salvation grace assists the will already desiring the good and arouses the will toward good when it has not been so inclined.[199] In effect, Cassian refused to make the choice that Augustine had tried to force: either grace or free will. More accurately, he refused to accept free choice, as understood on Augustine's terms, only as initiated and directed by God and that ultimately on the basis of divine election.

Instead, through a variety of scriptural examples Cassian, reminiscent of Origen, argued for the manifold character of grace.[200] Grace is always far greater than anyone's deserving, but even such deserving implies human effort;[201] grace provides protection that prevents a person from being overcome in temptation but does not protect that person from being tempted at all, for it is through the struggle that one grows;[202] grace may be given in proportion to the capacity of the recipient's faith, a faith which may itself be either the gift of God or may

---

[197]*Coll.* 13.9,12.
[198]*Coll.* 13.12.
[199]*Coll.* 13.11.
[200]Cassian contrasted such passages as Isa. 1:19 and Rom. 9:16; Rom. 2:6 and Phil. 2:13, Eph. 2:8, 9; Ezek. 18:31 and Ezek. 1:19, 20; Prov. 4:23 and Phil. 4:7; Mt. 11:28 and Jn. 6:44; 1 Cor. 9:24 and Jn. 3:27. See *Coll.* 13.9,10,11.
[201]*Coll.* 13.13.
[202]*Coll.*13.14.

have its origin in the person;[203] or grace may exceed the recipient's faith.[204] Finally, because God wills the salvation of all, grace operates on the human will in a variety of ways, assisting and inspiring those who already desire the good, forcing others who resist, calling and drawing those who are ignorant.[205] Perhaps one can say that for Cassian the varieties of grace meant the various ways that God interacts with various individuals, whereas for Augustine the varieties of grace meant the various forms of grace appropriate to the various stages of the human condition.

In the last analysis, for Cassian, both the divine will for the salvation of all and the freedom of the human will must be affirmed such that at every stage in the process of salvation grace is operative. Yet that affirmation of the operation of grace must not in any way deprive the will of its freedom to choose.[206]

Ironically, as Owen Chadwick has pointed out, Cassian used one of Augustine's favorite quotations against the African bishop. Augustine had cited "O depth of the riches and wisdom and knowledge of God! How unsearchable are his judgments and how inscrutable his ways! For who has known the mind of the Lord?" His point had been to argue that the human mind could not question the divine decrees of predestination. In contrast, Cassian employed the same citation as evidence that finally the human mind cannot fathom the divine work of salvation. The problem was not to be solved by appealing to the notion of predestination.[207] Such an interpretation calls to mind Origen's statement, noted earlier, that God alone has knowledge adequate to the superintendence of the innumerable souls for their salvation.[208]

Several points may be noted. Cassian never entered the discussion of predestination and the divine decrees; however, his insistence on the divine will for universal salvation precluded his acceptance of such notions. Moreover, although he was Augustinian in his affirmation of the necessity and superabundance of grace, he refused to go the full distance in affirming the sovereignty of grace. Such an affirmation would have been a denial of the freedom of the human will as Cassian envisioned such freedom.

In fact, his understanding of the operation of grace was similar to the view that Origen had held. Origen had shown particular sensitivity to the variety of ways in which the working of grace variously adapts to the particular state of the person to whom it comes. Such an assessment of grace and human capacity was

---

[203]*Coll.* 13.15.
[204]*Coll.* 13.16; Rom. 11:33-34.
[205]*Coll.* 13.17.
[206]*Coll.* 13.18.
[207]Chadwick, *John Cassian*, 125-26; *Coll.* 13.17; Rom. 11:33-34.
[208]*De princ.* 3.1.14, cited above, n. 37.

far more sophisticated than that which Pelagius had offered. The latter had viewed the work of grace as external to the human person. Its operation occurred through such agencies as the teaching and example of Christ. This interpretation of grace had, of course, accorded with Pelagius's view of sin as being equally external to human nature. Pelagius, however, had not attributed particular gravity to the human predicament or particular complexity to the divine efforts necessary for salvation.

In a different way, one might say that Augustine's depiction of the operation of grace also lacked the variegated character that Cassian had ascribed to it. It was not the case, of course, that Augustine did not consider the human condition to be in especially grave straits. To the contrary, it was probably because he was so utterly convinced of human incapacity that he insisted upon the necessity for a thoroughgoing remedy. Moreover, unlike Cassian, he did not think that each individual stood in a different condition with regard to the need for divine assistance and thus that grace was variously given according to need. He believed that all offspring of Adam were members of that *massa perdita* from which only the sovereignty of electing grace could separate them. Thus, although the operation of grace was variegated in terms of its operation on the person progressing toward salvation, it was hardly a matter of more or less, for all stood equally in need.

The point of view that Cassian held in maintaining both that all should be ascribed to God and all to free will entailed a portrayal of the work of grace as multifaceted. It is from this position, which clearly emerged from the Origenist-Evagrian-desert tradition and the specifically monastic setting that the question of the *ortus bonae voluntatis* stood out as critical in a way that it never had in the reports of Hilary and Prosper. It became critical as a way of protecting the self-initiating character of the human will; yet as Cassian thought grace works variously with various individuals, he did not need to say that the *ortus bonae voluntatis* always comes from the human side, only that it always can come from the human side. It may come from either side. What makes the *ortus* question the key point of Cassian's critique of Augustine is that it served as Cassian's safeguard for human self-initiation. This self-initiation was fundamental to his view of the monastic life as a genuine interaction of divine initiative and human initiative. Through the training and discipline that the monastic context made available, the self was formed to God.

Cassian's careful examination of the necessity for submission and the struggle entailed in that process of submission at all times presupposed the value of human agency and finally had to take exception to the Augustinian theology of grace. He took exception by affirming, first, that salvation must be open to all, as there is no elite of the saved, and, second, that it is the human agent who enacts the religious life, although always and everywhere assisted by the divine grace to which the agent must constantly appeal for aid.

Conclusion

A general observation can now be made on Augustine's and Cassian's respective positions on the interaction of divine grace and the human free will. What we have found are two different accounts of the turning of the will to God.

For Augustine the key was the moment in which the will comes to delight in the good. This transition takes place by grace alone because the will cannot force itself to delight in that in which it does not take delight. In this sense the will is not free. Three elements clearly have shaped Augustine's account: a predestination that assures that grace is not given for merit; the radical effects of the fall that account for the will's inability to force itself to delight in that in which it clearly ought to delight; perseverance that maintains a continuing delight in the good.

For Cassian the key was the progress of the will from fear of God to love of God by monastic discipline. Again, three elements can be seen to have shaped his account: the universal will for salvation as God offers aid to all involved in the struggle; self-initiating human agency that is presupposed by the disciplines of the struggle; the longing for stability as undeviating devotion to God.

These two accounts, which differed in emphases and formative elements, also diverged in another crucial way. What Augustine located at the moment of transition, i.e., delight in the good, Cassian located at the end of a long and arduous process, i.e., true delight in, undiluted love for, God. For the former, love for God, which was the gift of the Holy Spirit, was the precondition of the Christian life. For the latter, love for God, which was the attainment of disciplined struggle, was the culmination of the monastic life. This critical difference in schemes illuminated the problem between Augustine and Cassian. In effect, they spoke out of such utterly different frameworks that it was actually quite difficult for them to speak about the same thing. Cassian could look Pelagian on some points and Augustinian on others. He was, however, neither of the two but a third thing altogether. That peculiarity was what kept the early Gallic skepticism toward Augustine's predestinarian teaching from leading merely to a rerun of the Pelagian controversy. Yet it was Cassian's apparent proximity, at times to the Pelagians and at times to the Augustinians, that has made it so difficult to give him and the monastic theology that he represented their independent due.

Augustine and Cassian had now had their say, however. Augustine died in 430. With the completion of the *Collationes*, probably in 428 or 429, Cassian seems to have had no further involvement in the debate. His own death came only a few years afterward in 435. Yet even before his death the nature of the argumentation changed significantly. Caricature replaced courtesy, and cautious appeal to authority took the place of a creative exploration of ideas. As positions solidified, the controversialists became far more preoccupied with defining and defending an authoritative tradition than with elaborating a resonant theology of grace.

Chapter 4

Prosper of Aquitaine:
South Gallic Augustinianism

Introduction

After the great contributions of Augustine and John Cassian, the writings of Prosper become the means for tracing the immediate course of the Semi-Pelagian controversy in Gaul. The *Contra Collatorem*, Prosper's rebuttal of *Collatio* 13, served as the one direct Augustinian response to Cassian. It was this somewhat unjust attack by Prosper that finally gained general acceptance as the definitive critique of Cassian's views on grace.

The rebuttal was preceded and followed by a succession of three pamphlets that Prosper had prepared. These pamphlets enable us to see the debate in its less considered form as an exchange of charge and countercharge. The first pamphlet was a respectful but thoroughly Augustinian response to questioners who were perplexed, perhaps even distressed, by a number of passages from the *De praedestinatione sanctorum* and the *De dono perseverantiae*. The last two pamphlets consisted of Prosper's vituperative attacks upon objections that had been raised against Augustinian teaching on grace. The objections themselves were caricatures of the African bishop's position. For the moment, constructive debate had ended.

A new stage in the controversy can be seen in the publication of the *Auctoritates*. This document consisted of a compilation of ecclesiastical pronouncements from the Pelagian controversy, references to liturgical practice, and a commentary by Prosper. The *Auctoritates*, therefore, represented a shift in the methodology of the debate. A carefully arranged list of official citations, all of which reinforced the Augustinian position, replaced harsh attack, as Prosper presented this position through the location and citation of authoritative tradition. One might infer from this document that Prosper's views had softened. Because the more difficult Augustinian points were original to Augustine, they could not be substantiated by citations from other authoritative ecclesiastical figures. Consequently, these teachings had to be left unsaid.

This more conciliatory approach continued in the *De vocatione omnium gentium*, in which Prosper attempted to find a satisfactory Augustinian resolution to the thorny issue of the divine will for universal salvation. Nevertheless, although the tone was mediating, the conclusion was not. The rancor had subsided, but even in this, Prosper's last contribution to the debate, no solution was in sight.

Pro Augustino responsiones ad excerpta Genuensium

With the death of Augustine in 430 Prosper became the recognized interpreter of the African bishop and the chief spokesman for the Augustinians in Gaul. Soon afterward two priests from Genoa, Camille and Theodore, troubled by a number of passages from the *De praedestinatione sanctorum* and the *De dono perseverantiae*, sent Prosper a list of excerpts with a request for his explanation.[1]

The burden of the extracts had to do with the logic of grace as it had been developed by Augustine to its extreme predestinarian conclusions. Although any questions that the priests might have had are not available to us, it can be surmised from the list of excerpts that their apprehensions had to do with a doctrine in which the sovereignty of grace appears to undercut the significance of human agency. The request of the priests indicates that the misgivings about Augustine's doctrine that were arising outside the monastic context were closely related to the concern for human agency that we have found in Cassian.

Prosper's reply to these extracts reveals, as his letter to Rufinus did earlier, an Augustinian thoroughly convinced of his position. He grouped the first three extracts as all referring to the same issue: the development of Augustine's understanding of grace from the period of his earlier writing before his episcopate to the time of his final treatises. Prosper charged that Augustine's critics were denying the thoroughgoing character of Adam's fall: They preferred the view of the young Augustine, that election is based on divine foreknowledge of faith engendered by the human agent, to the teaching of his maturity, that faith itself is the gift of God. In fact, Prosper argued, it was faith that Adam had first lost, and in the absence of faith, all other good was forfeited as well. As all Adam's progeny also suffered the full extent of his loss, they, too, in their corrupted nature, are wanting faith and must receive it as a divine gift.[2]

Prosper's responses to the remainder of the extracts grew out of his wholehearted acceptance of the twin teachings that the fall thoroughly incapacitated human nature and that election, whether to grace or to glory, is based

---

[1]P. De Letter, Introduction, *Prosper of Aquitaine: Defense of St. Augustine*, trans. P. De Letter (Westminster MD: Newman, 1963) 7. Most of the English translations of quotations from the *Contra collatorem*, *Pro Augustino responsiones ad excerpta Genuensium*, *Pro Augustino responsiones ad capitula objectionum Vincentianarum* and *Auctoritates* will be taken from de Letter. I have offered a fresh reading where it seemed better suited to the Latin text.

[2]Prosper, *Pro Augustino responsiones ad excerpta Genuensium* 1-3.

entirely on grace. Initially, he focused on those questions surrounding predestination to grace. An issue to be resolved was the identity of the one who initiates the action of the will. According to Prosper, persons believe or disbelieve of their own volition; yet it is the work of grace that the free will of one person can and does believe and the work of divine justice that the free will of another remains incapable of belief.[3]

For the sake of preserving the sheer gratuity of grace, Prosper contended, in effect, that there is a certain disjunction between the person and the action in which the person engages. Grace must intervene in order to make possible the action. The action does not emerge from the person's own self-direction but comes about only by the intervention of an outside agency, divine grace. Apparently, Prosper felt that this disjunction is required if certain forms of prayer are to make sense. Specifically, he argued that faith in its beginning and completion is always the gift of God but is bestowed only on some. Otherwise, it would be the case that prayers of intercession that unbelievers may have faith and prayers of thanksgiving for the believers that they do have faith are all pointless.[4] Such prayers presuppose that God is the agent from whom one must request that unbelievers come to faith and to whom one owes thanks when they do.

Further issues that the extracts raised he answered in much the same way. Assertion after assertion served to underscore Prosper's seemingly unshakable conviction of divine sovereignty and human depravity. Adam and all his descendants are deserving of damnation; thus there is no occasion for complaint that some are justly damned. The reason that others are saved remains hidden in God. As a result, their election is not a matter of desert but of grace.[5] The accomplishment of evil lies within human capacity: The person is entirely responsible. Yet not only is the exercise of this capacity subject to the governance of God, but its effect is controlled by God to serve the divine purposes.[6]

Near the conclusion Prosper began to speak more explicitly about the gift of perseverance and predestination to glory. He argued that in predestination God has foreknown those to whom the gifts of grace would be given that they should believe and that they should never be lost to Christ; thus predestination to both grace and glory is a matter of foreknowledge of divine gifts rather than a matter of human merit. Those who are not foreknown as recipients of grace are by divine decree not delivered from damnation.[7] Finally, Prosper responded to the objection that preaching about predestination will effect despair among the faith-

---

[3] *Resp. Gen.* 4.
[4] *Resp. Gen.* 5.
[5] *Resp. Gen.* 6.
[6] *Resp. Gen.* 7.
[7] *Resp. Gen.* 8.

ful and undermine their efforts for the good. The issue for Prosper was not whether the doctrine was to be preached in the church but the manner in which it was to be preached. He argued that the doctrine should be presented in such a way that it engenders hope, encourages striving, and elicits prayers for perseverance in the grace that has already been received.[8]

It might be noted that of the ten excerpts about which the Genoese raised questions, seven were taken from the *De praedestinatione sanctorum*, and, of these, five concerned the *origin of faith*.[9] Of the last two excerpts, which were drawn from the *De dono perseverantiae*, only the final one dealing with the preaching of predestination to the church was chiefly concerned with the grace of perseverance. It would appear, therefore, that the major issue troubling the Genoese priests and thus the issue to which Prosper addressed himself was Augustine's doctrine of predestination to grace.

The thoroughly convinced Augustinian had presented his opinion. Nothing more was heard from the Genoese priests. Whether or not Prosper's response had allayed their apprehensions, the opposition in Gaul was of sufficient strength that Prosper and Hilary now felt it necessary to go to Rome to seek the support of Pope Celestine.[10] The pope responded with *Epistula 21 ad episcopos Gallorum*.

It is noteworthy that it was to the pope that Prosper and Hilary appealed. When an authoritative judge was deemed necessary in this conflict that was basically between North African and South Gallic doctrine, anyone with loyalties to either of these regions could hardly be trusted as impartial. Thus in accord with his growing stature within the Western church, the bishop of Rome was invoked for an official statement.[11]

---

[8]*Resp. Gen.* 9.

[9]De Letter, *Defense of St. Augustine*, 7.

[10]Cf. Reinhold Seeberg, *The History of Doctrines*, 2 vols., trans. Charles E. Hay (Grand Rapids: Baker, 1977) 1:264-65. It was Pope Celestine who secured the condemnation of Pelagianism at the Council of Ephesus in 431. He had instructed his legates to favor Cyril against Nestorius. See also Chadwick, *John Cassian*, 130-32, 141-43. Celestine's opinion of Nestorius had been informed or at least corroborated by John Cassian, who, at the request of Leo the archdeacon, had written an explanation of Nestorianism. Chadwick has suggested that Cassian was needed not to advise but "to support an already held belief that Nestorius was wrong." Regardless, Cassian in the *De incarnatione* (ca. 430) linked Nestorianism to Pelagianism, condemning both; thus Cassian clearly was a foe of Pelagianism. Significantly, in appealing to Celestine against the Semi-Pelagians, Prosper and Hilary were asking the support of one who was publicly opposed to Pelagianism but publicly indebted to a Semi-Pelagian who had served him as an authority against the Nestorians.

[11]See Wallace-Hadrill, *The Frankish Church*, 110-12, for the mediatorial role that the bishop of Rome played in major disputes, particularly in matters pertaining to orthodoxy.

Far from being definitive, however, the pope's letter was sufficiently vague that it was able to be cited by both sides as evidence for their respective positions. To the advantage of Prosper and Hilary, the letter commended Augustine, encouraged calm, and condemned novelties.[12] This rejection of novelty could also be used in the arsenal of the opposition, however, as could the letter's failure to be specific in its praise of Augustine's works, most notably his final writings. The ambiguity with regard to novelty was important. As the pope had not defined what he meant by either novelty or tradition, the door remained open for further dispute over the formulation of the position of the Western church on the matter of the interaction of grace and human agency. The options were the newly constructed but indigenous Augustinian tradition, the imported but modified Eastern, Origenist tradition, or some combination of the two. With none of these alternatives authoritatively labeled as novelty or tradition, all three remained open.

If the letter had a salutary effect on the Augustinian cause, this impact was not long lasting. With the death of the pope soon afterward in July, 432, the opposition became increasingly active. Among their publications were John Cassian's *Collatio* 13 and pamphlets misrepresenting the implications of Augustine's teaching. Discussion here will be restricted to the development of Prosper's thinking as he continually had to reconsider and defend the teaching of Augustine against such attacks.[13]

Contra collatorem

Probably the most notable of Prosper's writings at this stage was his response to Cassian's thirteenth *collatio, De protectione Dei.* Although written earlier, this *collatio* was not published and available to Prosper until 432.[14] Hardly a scathing attack on Augustine, it affirmed the necessity and complexity of grace but allowed instances in which the beginning of the good will might be of human origin. At issue was whether there exists within the person, prior to the work of grace, any capacity for salvation, any capability for arousing oneself to faith. Cassian had allowed room for this possibility, thereby undercutting the notion of the absolute sovereignty of grace and safeguarding the notion of self-

---

[12]Celestine, *Ep.* 21; Chadwick, *John Cassian,* 131-32; De Letter, *Defense of St. Augustine,* 7-8.

[13]Cappuyns, "Le premier représentant," 321, suggested that Prosper may not have known all of the Semi-Pelagian literature. Regarding the *Praedestinatus,* to which Prosper did not respond, see D. H. von Schubert, *Der sogenannte "Praedestinatus."* Texte und Untersuchungen 24/4 (Leipzig: J. C. Hinrichs, 1903); G. Morin, "Arnobe le Jeune," *Études, textes, découvertes* (Paris: A. Picard, 1913) 315-24; M. Abel, "Le *Praedestinatus* et le pélagianisme," *Recherches de théologie ancienne et médiévale* 35 (1968): 5-25.

[14]De Letter, *Defense of St. Augustine,* 8-9.

initiated willing on the part of the human agent. In other words, Cassian had elaborated a view of divine grace that was alternative to Augustine's in that it preserved in a genuine sense the reality of human agency.

In his rebuttal, *Contra collatorem*, Prosper focused upon the divergence between the understanding of grace held by Augustine and that held by Cassian. In arguing against the latter, he made apparent his own fear of the consequences of such divergence. For Prosper what was at stake was the utterly gratuitous character of grace in both predestination and perseverance. For Cassian the crucial point had been differently identified. For him, the key issue had been whether human agency in the religious realm would be reduced to a mere shadow signifying nothing. In short, there was not even agreement between the two men regarding the identification of the central issue of the controversy. In contrast, a secondary issue for both was fidelity to the tradition of the church. Yet even on that matter there was no agreement. Each man held a different understanding of what constituted the tradition.

Prosper was convinced that it was differing opinions regarding the fall of Adam that had led to the divergence between the Augustinian position and Cassian's position on the operation of grace. Nobody, not even Pelagius himself, had denied the priority of grace, i.e., everybody agreed that by grace human beings are created in the image of God. The locus of the disagreement was the effect of the fall on human capacity for good, i.e., on human nature as the product of the grace of creation. For the Pelagians the effect of the fall had been that it caused in Adam, and in his descendants by the imitation and influence of social custom, a tendency toward sin. Human capacity was weakened and mis-directed by bad habit; yet a person could still break the custom of sin. This break with detrimental habits occurred with difficulty in the case of the early genera-tions when the habits were not so strong. In later generations, after the habit of sin had become entrenched, the break could be effected with the aid of the law or, as habit became binding, with the example and teaching of the Redeemer.[15] The initiative for reform lay with the individual guided by the external aids of either the law or the Redeemer's example. Human nature, the effect of the grace of creation, still remained intact, obscured and forgotten perhaps, but once aroused by external reminders, capable of turning the self to God.

For the Augustinians on the other hand, the effect of the fall on human nature was far more devastating. The grace of creation had to be followed by the grace of recreation before the will could freely seek God. This second expression of grace, still prior to human initiative, worked in the calling, preparation, and

---

[15]G. W. H. Lampe, "Salvation, Sin, and Grace," *A History of Christian Doctrine*, ed. Hubert Cunliffe-Jones and Benjamin Drewery (Philadelphia: Fortress Press, 1980) 158-61.

turning of the will, all of which were the internal work of the Spirit. External aids were inadequate, for fallen human nature itself required transformation.

For Cassian the result of the fall was a human nature badly impaired, incapable of healing itself. The person's situation was not simply that of a traveler who has wandered off the path and needs signposts to get back on, as the Pelagians had suggested; yet neither was it that of one who is so disoriented as to be unable to look for the path or to recognize it as the right one even if it were found, as the Augustinians believed. Instead it is the situation of one who is lost and cannot find the path but still may be capable of desiring and seeking it. Cassian affirmed the necessity of grace; yet he allowed that the effects of creative grace had not been so corrupted by the fall as to destroy all freedom of the will for the good. Prosper's argument against him had to do with this allowance to nature. For Prosper the will must be prepared by God so that even the asking, seeking, and knocking which lead to salvation are themselves the work of grace.[16] In order for grace to be utterly gratuitous, no human good can precede its action.

A brief survey may illustrate the character of Prosper's argument against Cassian on the consequences of the fall. In response to those statements of Cassian that indicated that the beginning of the good will and perseverance in the good are within human capacity, Prosper argued that both are the gift of grace to human incapacity. Cassian had stated that Adam was created with knowledge of the good. At the fall he did not lose this gift but acquired knowledge of evil.[17] Cassian's point was to substantiate his larger case, made from a variety of biblical references, that grace operates in a multitude of ways to accommodate itself to the condition of the particular individual. It assists human agency according to need.[18]

Prosper apparently saw in this brief reference to Adam the key to Cassian's understanding, or rather misunderstanding, of the work of grace. He, too, affirmed that Adam was created good, and following Augustine, he noted the freedom and ability of Adam's will so long as he did not turn from grace. Of course, Adam did turn from grace. By rebelling against God, not only did he perish, but "all perished in him."[19] The result of the fall was that "neither the substance nor the will of human nature was lost," but its virtue, its capacity to achieve eternal incorruption, was forfeited. The natural state for humanity now is its fallen state, a life of "condemnation and punishment" from which the only

---

[16]Prosper, *Contra collatorem* 4.
[17]*C. coll.* 9.2; Cassian, *Coll.* 13.12.
[18]Cassian, *Coll.* 13.13.
[19]*C. coll.* 9.3, citing Ambrose, *In Lucam* 7.15.

escape is regeneration in Christ.[20] As it was the free will from which sin arose, so it is the free will that is now weakened and "blinded." Its present fallen condition is the result of just punishment. The responsibility for the weakened will is human and not divine, and all humanity shares in the guilt.[21] With the will impaired, the "good conscience" has been lost and with it the "knowledge of the good." Freedom to choose evil remains, therefore, within human power, but freedom to choose the good requires the grace of Christ.[22]

Prosper further pursued the problem of nature's capacity or incapacity for good after the fall. Cassian had asserted that every soul has been created with the "seeds" of the virtues.[23] Prosper insisted that these "seeds" were lost by Adam and can be recovered only through Christ. The rational soul remains but is now inhabited by vices unless Christ reinstates the virtues.[24] Unbelievers may exhibit particular virtues; yet because they do not offer these virtues in the service of God, they bring only an earthly, not an eternal, reward.[25] Furthermore, such apparent virtue is, in reality, vice, as the persons are turned from God.[26] Most important, however, the free will has lost its freedom to choose the good. Rather than occupying a neutral position from which it can choose either to delight in grace or not to do so, the will can delight only in wrong unless transformed by grace.[27] In other words, the only field in which human agency can now operate is the field of evil.

Prosper insisted that the case of the Gentiles, who lack the law of Moses but act from the law written in their hearts,[28] is no proof of human capacity to will the good. Cassian, in contrast, had attempted to use the case of the Gentiles as evidence of the health of the human will. According to Prosper, some "remnants" of our nature as created do remain, and this residual good makes rational achievements possible. Otherwise, without any rationality at all, there would be no such thing as human life. Nevertheless, these remnants are inadequate for salvation. In fact, without the gift of charity provided by the Holy Spirit, this residue of our nature is insufficient to perform even a good act of the will. Yet when the will does act for good through the work of the Spirit, the person is

---

[20]*C. coll.* 9.3.
[21]*C. coll.* 9.4.
[22]*C. coll.* 9.5.
[23]*C. coll.* 13.1, citing Cassian, *Coll.* 13.12.
[24]*C. coll.* 13.2.
[25]*C. coll.* 13.3.
[26]*C. coll.* 13.5.
[27]*C. coll.* 13.6.
[28]Cf. Rom. 2:14-16.

genuinely acting out of a knowledge and a desire for the good. Grace has transformed the will.[29]

The case of the Gentiles had been only one element of Cassian's more optimistic view of human nature. He had also used scriptural injunctions as evidence that the hearers are of their own nature able both to know and to do what is good. In reply, Prosper offered a contrary interpretation of the commandments: they provide a twofold form of instruction. By reminding their hearers of what is required, the commandments also remind them of the weakness of human nature incurred by guilt and lead them to turn to grace for what nature cannot offer.[30] In this pedagogical sense, at least, the commandments function as the instrument of grace. They are hardly indicative of human capacity.

Prosper simply could not accept Cassian's positive arguments for human agency, but he was even less amenable to Cassian's more negative appeal. The latter had feared that only evil will be attributed to human nature if "all merits of the saints" are ascribed to God. Here Prosper detected a double error: that there are merits that are not the gift of grace and that grace is not needed for every good work.[31]

As Prosper argued that the condition of the will is such that it cannot make a beginning in good, in other words, that the *ortus bonae voluntatis* must be the work of grace, he similarly insisted that perseverance is not within unassisted human capacity either. Affirming the reality of human effort, Cassian had offered the example of Job as one who had persevered in good despite the nearly overwhelming attacks of the devil. The only assistance that Job had received was that God had allowed the attacks to be no greater than Job's strength.[32] Prosper objected that even the strength by which Job had withstood the attacks had been given to him by God. God had not forsaken Job, but the Holy Spirit had been within him assisting him[33] so that the resistance had actually been the Spirit's rather than Job's. Prosper's aim was to guard against the notion that, if Job were presented as withstanding such difficulties by the strength of his free will alone, then Cassian's readers will think that in their own considerably easier lives their natural free will is adequate for good. Such thinking, he was convinced, was akin to a tenet of the Pelagian heresy, which held that justification merely facilitates the fulfillment of the commandments, and to its corollary that without grace one

---

[29]*C. coll.* 10.1-3; 12.4.
[30]*C. coll.* 11.1.
[31]*C. coll.* 11.2; see De Letter, *Defense of St. Augustine*, 215n.171.
[32]*C. coll.* 14.1, citing Cassian, *Coll.* 13.14.
[33]*C. coll.* 15.2,4.

could fulfill the commandments, although with difficulty.[34] For Prosper both the beginning and the continuance in the faith must be the gifts of grace.

By arguing against statements that Cassian had made concerning human capacity, Prosper attempted to show that Cassian had failed to recognize the devastating consequences of the fall and the resultant need for an utterly gratuitous grace. Prosper's argument against Cassian went further, however. Prosper also faulted Cassian for the apparent ambivalence in his position.

For example, Prosper acknowledged that *Collatio* 13 actually began well. It commenced with Catholic truth: the beginning and completion of good works and good thoughts are from God. Furthermore, the divine gifts serve not to undermine but to "strengthen" the free will. The problem was Cassian's departure from this truth with which he had begun, for, as already noted, Cassian had also tried to maintain the apparently contradictory notion that some turn to God of their own free will, a will not prepared by grace.[35]

For Prosper, Cassian's refusal to take his stand firmly in either the Augustinian camp where it was asserted that the initiative for good always belongs to God or in the Pelagian camp where it was held that this initiative always belongs to the person, resulted in an "unformed third thing" acceptable to neither side. Prosper's perception of Cassian's position was itself an important indication that Cassian should be seen neither as a Semi-Augustinian nor as a Semi-Pelagian but as one who was developing a line of his own. Cassian's apparently ambivalent position had been made possible by his practice of juxtaposing scriptural texts that appear to be mutually contradictory and then suggesting that those referring to divine initiative apply to the situation of some persons and those referring to human initiative apply to the situation of others. The effect, as perceived by Prosper, was a division of humankind: "those whom the grace of God saves, and those whom the law and nature make just."[36] The former are in need of a savior and the latter only of a helper. The problem that Cassian had attempted to surmount, that free will is denied if the beginning and perseverance in good are the work only of grace, Prosper believed to be an unreal dilemma. The reality of which Prosper was convinced was that "divine grace helps by strengthening the human will." As an element of human nature free will is never lost; its "quality and condition are changed" through Christ "who turns our wills away from their evil objects and turns them to willing what is good" so that "they submit to a free servitude and renounce an enslaving freedom."[37]

---

[34]*C. coll.* 15.4, citing Council of Carthage, can. 5.

[35]*C. coll.* 2.2-4.

[36]*C. Coll.* 3.1.

[37]*C. coll.* 18.2,3: *opitulationes divinae gratiae stabilimenta sunt voluntatis humanae.*

The fact that persons are praised in Scripture for particular virtues, for example, Christ's praise of the centurion's faith,[38] did not indicate that these virtues were not divine gifts. Instead, according to Prosper, all virtue is God's gift, and praise is deservedly given to those on whom God has bestowed virtue; otherwise, those to whom it has been given to believe in Christ and to suffer for him[39] have no praise or merit, although Scripture clearly indicates the contrary.[40] (Perhaps here the difficulty of Prosper's scheme first becomes clear: the person is praised merely for being a receptacle, i.e., for something of which the person is not, properly speaking, the agent in his or her own right.)[41] Nevertheless, although such persons as the centurion are rightly praised, to state, as Cassian had, that such praise indicates that their faith is of themselves and not of God is to have merit precede and be the occasion of grace, an arrangement that Cassian had elsewhere denied.[42] Prosper charged that by attempting a synthesis Cassian had trapped himself in his own logic.[43] Prosper's charge, however, fails to convince. Cassian has given us no reason to believe that he was attempting to achieve a synthesis. Instead, his argument in *Collatio* 13 appears to have been the author's attempt to feel his own way in relation to two mutually opposed positions.

In fact, it is not clear that Prosper correctly presented Cassian's position on several matters. For example, he accused Cassian of dividing humankind into two groups with respect to the need for grace. Yet one might simply say that, for Cassian, there are those whom grace brings to salvation in one way and those whom it brings to salvation in another way. No one is saved without grace, but grace always works in one or another pattern of interaction with self-initiating human agency. It was Prosper, not Cassian, who made Cassian a Semi-Pelagian.

Prosper may have also misconstrued Cassian's position regarding the fall of Adam, for not only did Prosper find in the fall of Adam the center of gravity for his own theological position, but he also attempted to criticize Cassian's position

---

... *quod liberum arbitrium naturaliter homini inditum maneat in natura; sed qualitate et conditione mutata per Mediatorem Dei et hominum, hominem Christum Jesum: qui ipsam voluntatem ab eo quod perverse volebat, avertit, et in id quod ei bonum esset velle, convertit; ut delectatione affecta, fide mundata, spe erecta, charitate accensa, liberalem susciperet servitutem et servilem abjiceret libertatem.*

[38]Mt. 8:10.
[39]Phil. 1:29.
[40]*C. coll.* 16.1.
[41]The Platonic and Christian traditions had typically associated praise and blame with freedom of the will. With the limited notion of freedom in his scheme Prosper had difficulty in justifying praise and blame.
[42]*C. coll.* 17, citing Cassian *Coll.* 13.16.
[43]*C. coll.* 17.

as if the same doctrine served as the theological center of gravity for the monk's views as well.[44] Cassian's real interest, however, was that of understanding and interpreting the religious life; the fall did not have a prominent place in *Collatio* 13. Prosper's own preoccupation with the fall led him to present Cassian's position differently from the way in which Cassian had actually presented it. In effect, Prosper might be said to have altered Cassian's position in order to create the view to which he wished to respond. He made his argument for grace by directly attacking Cassian's portrayal of Adam, although the case of Adam had hardly served as the focal point for the monk's teaching on grace. On the other hand, in fairness to Prosper it should be acknowledged that Cassian's relative minimization of the fall and its consequences allowed him to maintain views on the operation of grace and the character of human agency that were necessarily at odds with the heart of Prosper's argument.

Nevertheless, Prosper's interpretation of these views was skewed to an exaggerated degree by his conviction that the presupposition on which they rested, Cassian's understanding of the fall, was fatally flawed. For example, Prosper summarized Cassian's position as holding that Adam and his descendants, and thus human free will, were unharmed by the fall, that all persons are capable, by means of reason, of anticipating grace, and that the virtue granted by nature is healthy and can be practiced by each person without grace assisting.[45] In other words, Prosper made Cassian into what Cassian was not. Furthermore, not only finding in Cassian some seeds of Pelagianism but also being faithful to Augustine's habit of carrying the logic of his position to its extreme conclusion, Prosper assumed the full growth of the seeds and placed his opponent firmly in the camp of heresy.[46] This assumption was ill-founded. As became apparent in the previous chapter, although Cassian's position might be developed to a heretical conclusion, it was not Cassian's nature to carry his argument to its logical extreme. In fact, his opposition to Augustine did not lie in the African's presupposition concerning the fall of all people in Adam or in the necessity of grace for salvation but in the extremes to which Augustine's logic led him. Prosper recognized that Cassian's position could not be reconciled with his own; thus he rejected it. Yet it seems clear that Prosper read into Cassian's opposition more than was actually present.

Ironically, despite Prosper's penchant for finding in *Collatio* 13 more than was actually there, he manifested little, if any, interest in a vital element of the argument that was there: Cassian's emphasis on the divine will for universal

---

[44]See 122-23 above.
[45]*C. coll.* 20; cf. De Letter, *Defense of St. Augustine*, 220-21n.337.
[46]*C. coll.* 21.4.

salvation.[47] The reason can only be surmised. Perhaps it was the case that the doctrine was awkward for an Augustinian or that his strategy was strictly one of offense, i.e., to expose where Cassian had erred in falsely diminishing the role of grace. Regardless, Prosper's insistence on judging Cassian according to Augustinian standards allowed him to ignore, or at least to minimize, elements of the argument that reveal Cassian as operating not as anti-Augustinian but outside an Augustinian framework.

Nevertheless, as unbending as Prosper's position appears here, his silence on two issues may be the first sign of flexibility or change on his part. Prosper mentioned neither predestination nor irresistible grace in the *Contra collatorem*. The reason may merely have been that as Cassian had remained silent on these issues there was no occasion for Prosper to make mention of them. On the other hand, at some point he did become convinced, as he would later indicate in his *Auctoritates*, that the silence of the church on such matters might be the greater part of wisdom, for they were not necessary to Catholic doctrine.[48] Prosper's position may already have begun to soften, if only in his perception of what need not be insisted upon.[49]

Prosper did remain unrelenting, however, in his insistence that the gratuity of grace must not be jeopardized. Cassian had attempted to maintain an apparent contradiction: both self-initiating human agency and unmerited divine grace. The monk had insisted that each element is inadequate alone but that together they comprise the truth. To make his case against Cassian, Prosper did not simply rely upon the authority of his own arguments but appealed to the teaching of the church. By combining the Catholic position with a position that the church had denounced as heretical, Cassian had denigrated the authority of the church and had elevated the status of heresy. Prosper argued this point and then, to reinforce his accusation of heresy, quoted a letter of Pope Innocent to the council of Carthage of 416,[50] referred to the Eastern bishops' requirement that Pelagius deny that grace is a payment to merit,[51] noted the pronouncements of the African councils of Mileve and Carthage in 416,[52] and cited the letter of the Council of

---

[47]Cassian, *Coll.* 13.7.

[48]*Auctoritates* 10; cf. De Letter, *Defense of St. Augustine*, 222n.367.

[49]Cf. D. M. Cappuyns, "Le premier représentant de l'augustinisme médiéval, Prosper d'Aquitaine," *Recherches de théologie ancienne et médiévale* 1 (1929) 322-26; M. Jacquin, "La question de la prédestination aux Ve et VIe siécles," 277-81. See discussion of *Responsiones*, 230-41.

[50]*C. coll.* 5.3; Innocent, *Ep.*29.3; *Ep.* 29.6; see *Auct.* 1,2.

[51]*C. coll.* 5.3; cf. Augustine, *De gest. Pel.* 14.30,33,40.

[52]*C. coll.* 5.3. The correspondence between the councils and Innocent is found in Innocent, *Epp.* 26-31 (*PL* 20.564-97) and in English translation in Augustine, *Epp.* 175-77, 181-83.

Carthage of 418 to Pope Zosimus upholding Innocent's judgment against Celestius and Pelagius,[53] as well as Pope Zosimus's concurrence with the African bishops.[54] Prosper intended this compilation of citations to show that Cassian's apparent attempt at synthesis was contrary to the authoritative tradition and teaching of the church. The monk was opposing tradition, however recent its development. Significantly, the tradition to which Prosper appealed was the one represented by the pronouncements of bishops and council and not the tradition of the elders upon which Cassian had relied.

Prosper also faulted Cassian's method of juxtaposing apparently conflicting examples from Scripture as a misrepresentation of the scriptural tradition regarding grace. Both men agreed that the sudden conversions of Paul and Matthew were illustrations of the operation of grace without human merit or cooperation. In contrast, Cassian had interpreted the cases of Zaccheus and the crucified thief as evidence that, at least in some instances, the human will precedes and seeks grace. Prosper argued that these latter cases do not prove that some achieve conversion by their unassisted free will. Instead, the two sets of examples simply reveal that some respond to God's call whereas others are slower. The wills of Zaccheus and the thief had already been prepared by God so that their conversion was merely the response to the prior, yet hidden, work of grace.[55] This insistence on the hidden operation of grace was essential to Prosper's argument. Cassian had simply described what can be observed; Prosper had to insist on what cannot be observed but must be assumed if grace is to remain gratuitous. In other words, Prosper had insisted upon what is not, at least explicitly, in the scriptural accounts at all.[56]

Both Prosper and Cassian maintained that grace and free will are encompassed in the faith of the church. Cassian, however, understood them to be distinct. They were interacting agencies, each with the power of self-initiation, both of which must be held together in a necessary tension in order to do justice to the complexity of the church's faith. Prosper perceived the faith of the church to be centered on grace, and he provided a long series of scriptural citations in

---

[53] *C. coll.* 5.3; cf. De Letter, *Defense of St. Augustine,* 212, n. 59.

[54] *C. coll.* 5.3; Zosimus, *Ep. tractoria*; cf. *Auct.* 5; Augustine, *Ep.* 190 and *Indiculus Caelestini* 5, 6.

[55] *C. coll.* 7.

[56] In *De gratia Christi* 45.49 Augustine had argued that it was an internal glance or admonition of the Lord rather than an external one that had evoked Peter's repentance in Luke 22.61. The fact that such an internal admonition would have not been observable served as evidence for Augustine that the operation of grace upon the will necessarily precedes repentance despite the fact that in some instances that preparation may occur entirely in secret. Although Prosper made no reference to this interpretation of Peter's repentance, his own reliance on that which cannot be observed but must be assumed was consistent with Augustine's point.

proof of his case, thereby, of course, reinforcing his appeal to authority. He insisted that the effect of grace on the free will is not deprivation of power but empowerment, for the will, without grace, has no power to undertake or accomplish the good. By grace the will is enlivened for the good.[57]

To some extent at least, Prosper and Cassian were operating from two different theological frameworks, with divergent preoccupations. As a result, their arguments and conclusions failed to overlap sufficiently for there to be mutual understanding or even genuine debate. There was enough overlap, however, to create the impression of clear disagreement over shared foci. Consequently, Prosper, presumably through misunderstanding, argued against a Cassian whom he himself had constructed.

The issue between them was not that, judged by Augustinian standards, Cassian had a deficient understanding of grace. Instead, the issue was the nature of the interaction between divine grace and human agency. For Cassian, a monk instructing other monks, the fundamental point was to maintain the connection between human striving for the good and the outcome of that striving in divine reward. He affirmed the necessity of grace but was careful to do so in such a way as not to jeopardize human agency. In contrast, for Prosper the fundamental point was to safeguard the sovereignty of grace. It was not that he spoke of the connection between human action and its outcome as being severed by the operation of grace. That connection simply had little significance in the mind of one preoccupied with grace.

Pro Augustino responsiones ad capitula objectionum Gallorum calumniantium *Pro Augustino responsiones ad capitula objectionum Vincentianarum*

At this point it is appropriate to acknowledge the reasons for the admittedly arguable order in which Prosper's writings of the early 430's are being considered. Although it is probably impossible to establish the precise dates of Prosper's works during these years, evidence of shifts in Prosper's own views suggests a probable sequence. The *Responsiones ad excerpta Genuensium* appear to have been written first. They reveal a Prosper no longer troubled by the questions that he had raised in his letter to Augustine but, to the contrary, thoroughly confident of the answers that the bishop had provided in the *De praedestinatione sanctorum* and the *De dono perseverantiae*. Never again, however, would Prosper appear so content with the whole of Augustine's

---

[57]*C. coll.* 6, 8.

teaching on grace. The *Contra collatorem*, with its evidence of emerging doubts, probably came next. In this work Prosper's failure to provide a counter to Cassian's emphasis on the divine will for universal salvation as well as his silence on the doctrines of predestination and irresistible grace suggest that his confidence in these particular elements of the Augustinian scheme had begun to waver. A further stage in Prosper's thinking can be found in the two sets of *responsiones*, one to the Gauls and one to someone referred to as Vincent. Although in these *responsiones* Prosper would once again strongly defend the doctrines of predestination and of perseverance, his introduction of foreknowledge of demerit as an explanation for God's withholding of the grace of perseverance represented a decisive shift from Augustine.[58]

Whether or not this sequence is correct, the opposition to Augustine's predestinarian teaching provoked a bitter reaction in the years immediately following his death. In particular, two sets of objections caricaturing Augustine's teaching elicited direct counterattacks by Prosper.

The *objectiones Gallorum* consisted of a list of fifteen objectionable conclusions drawn from Augustinian doctrine as interpreted and misrepresented by his opponents. The author is not known, and the text exists only as contained in Prosper's *Pro Augustino responsiones ad capitula objectionum Gallorum calumniantium.*[59] This pamphlet was followed by another containing sixteen objections. Again, the author is not known, although O'Connor has demonstrated that it was not Vincent of Lérins as has often been argued.[60] The text is extant only in Prosper's response, *Pro Augustino responsiones ad capitula objectionum Vincentianarum.* These latter objections were an even greater caricature of Augustine's position than were the *objectiones Gallorum.*[61] As there was much similarity in intent and style, and two pamphlets will be examined together.

It would be desirable to be able to identify the persons responsible for these two sets of objections. In the introduction to his responses to the *objectiones Gallorum*, Prosper did refer to "some people," thereby suggesting more than one author. Considering the title, one can plausibly assume that these persons were

---

[58]For differing views regarding the sequence of these works, see Cappuyns, "Le premier représentant," 317-26; M. Jacquin, "La prédestination aux Ve et VIe siècles," 276-99.

[59]De Letter, *Defense of St. Augustine,* 222-23n.2.

[60]W. O'Connor, "Saint Vincent of Lerins and Saint Augustine," *Doctor Communis* 16 (1963) 141-73. Hugo Koch, *Vincenz von Lérins und Gennadius: ein Beitrag zur Literaturgeschichte des Semipelagianismus,* Texte und Untersuchungen 31/2 (Leipzig: J. C. Hinrichs, 1907) 40-58; É. Amann, "Semi-pélagiens," *Dictionnaire de théologie catholique* 14:1822-24; Jacquin, "La question de la prédestination," 290-93.

[61]De Letter, *Defense of St. Augustine,* 12.

Gallic.[62] On the other hand, in the introduction to the *objectiones Vincentianarum* he also referred to "some people";[63] therefore, even if, as the title suggests, only one person penned the work, Prosper's reference indicates that the opinions were common to a group of objectors.

It does not seem farfetched to suggest that the persons to whom Prosper referred in these responses were South Gallic sympathizers. A few of them, at least, may well have been members of the monastery at Lérins where those who opposed Augustine's predestinarian teaching had close ties. Such an assumption allows the conclusion, not otherwise disproved, that Gallic antipredestinarian sentiment was still localized in and around South Gallic monastic communities. If so, it continued to be monks and their sympathizers who produced the most heated opposition to the African's teaching.

The pamphlets, and thus Prosper's responses, focused on two issues: predestination and the divine will for universal salvation. The objections to the doctrine of predestination were of several kinds, but the fundamental difficulty that each attacked was that the doctrine severed the connection between a person's actions and the outcome of those actions. In his responses Prosper sought to demonstrate the existence of this connection.

Insisting by this time that predestination was a Catholic doctrine, Prosper countered the criticisms of its detractors.[64] To those who would interpret the doctrine as meaning a "fatal necessity" to sin and death, he responded by denying any sort of fatalism and insisting that evil is not to be attributed to God as creator but to the sin of Adam.[65] No one is created for eternal reprobation. The nature in which all are created by God is good, but in the sin of Adam all have sinned and are deserving of reprobation unless remade in Christ.[66] Similarly, no one was created to serve the devil, although anyone who is unredeemed is a "slave of the devil" as just punishment for sin.[67] As God is not responsible for the evil will of the sinful angels, so God is also not responsible for the evil human will. Not only did God not make persons desirous of evil, but, indeed, human beings are always able to receive forgiveness, if God is merciful to them, whereas devils have no possibility of conversion.[68]

---

[62]Prosper, *Pro Augustino responsiones ad capitula objectionum Gallorum calumnianti-um, Praef.*

[63]Prosper, *Pro Augustino responsiones ad capitula objectionum Vincentianarum, Praef.*

[64]*Resp. Gall.* 1.1.

[65]*Resp. Gall.,* 1.1; 2.1.

[66]*Resp. Vinc.* 3.

[67]*Resp. Vinc.* 4.

[68]*Resp. Vinc.* 6.

Augustine's Gallic critics also objected that, according to his scheme, baptism has no efficacy for those who are not predestined. It does not remove their original sin; furthermore, as God extends their lives until they do fall into sin, neither their baptism nor their virtue serves any purpose. Prosper countered that baptism remits both original and actual sins. Those who return to sin after baptism, including those who abuse the gift of a long life by using it as an occasion for postbaptismal sin, are responsible for the eternal penalty that they receive. Prosper insisted that divine foreknowledge of postbaptismal sin was the occasion for God's withholding predestination.[69]

That Prosper could assert the efficacy of baptism in the case of persons not predestinated because of divine foreknowledge of their postbaptismal sins suggests that he, like Augustine, distinguished between predestination to grace, by which a person receives both a good will and the remission of sin in baptism, and predestination to glory by which a person receives the gift of perseverance. The former can be operative even in the absence of the latter. Prosper has deviated from Augustine, however, by qualifying the utterly gratuitous character of the divine operations as they pertain to the gift of perseverance. In the case of predestination to grace, Prosper gave no indication that the *ortus bonae voluntatis* or the remission of sin in baptism is dependent upon anything other than the divine good pleasure. In contrast, he portrayed the lack of the gift of perseverance as a direct result of divine foreknowledge of postbaptismal sin.[70]

Prosper made only erratic use of the appeal to foreknowledge as an explanation of why some who have come to grace are not given perseverance. He did, nevertheless, repeatedly emphasize human responsibility for bad choices. God wills that persons remain in the good and abandons no one who has not already turned away, although, of course, perseverance in the good could have come only through grace.[71] Similarly, the one who turns from God is deprived, by that person's own freely chosen act, of the desire for the good and the ability to accomplish it, including the desire and ability to repent. Thus God is not accountable for the failure to repent, although, in fact, repentance can come only by grace.[72] For Prosper the responsibility for evil deeds lies squarely with the person despite the obvious correlation between the withholding of grace and the inability to do the good. Predestination, he insisted, pertains only to the judgment of sin and to the gift of grace.[73] It does not cause falling, obstruct perseverance,

---

[69]*Resp. Gall.* 1.2; 2.2; 1.3; 2.3.
[70]See also *Resp. Gall.* 1.7; 2.7.
[71]*Resp. Vinc.* 7.
[72]*Resp. Vinc.* 15.
[73]*Resp. Vinc.* 11.

or prevent repentance. Correspondingly, infallible divine foreknowledge of just recompense for merits does not necessitate sin.[74]

It should be noted that Prosper's statements regarding the behavior of persons following baptism referred only to the condition of Christians, individuals who have been liberated from an ill will and really do have a choice between good and evil. These statements do not address the case of those whose condition has never been otherwise than that of enslavement to the sin of Adam. With regard to both conditions Prosper has argued for the same kind of connection as had Augustine between human action and its reward or punishment in eternity. He has departed from Augustine, however, in seeking to establish a connection between foreknown evil action and punishment in this life, i.e., the divine withholding of the gift of perseverance from one whose evil action is so foreknown. Prosper has now allowed that human moral difference is relevant to the determination of those who do not receive grace. In response to the charges that the doctrine of predestination severs the connection between human action and its outcome, Prosper has sought not only to demonstrate the reality of that connection but also to strengthen it. As a result, the Augustinian view has undergone a significant change.

The second set of objections in these pamphlets pertained to the divine will for universal salvation. The specific criticism was that, according to Augustine's teaching, saving grace is not available to all. Such a charge would again involve the accusation that the person does not have control over actions and thus does not effect the result. Accordingly, Prosper attempted a rebuttal, discussing a question that he had left untouched in the *Contra collatorem*. To the assertion that the call to grace is not universal, he answered that all to whom the gospel has been preached are called, although many throughout the world have never heard the preaching.[75] The assertion that "some are called to faith, others to unbelief" is fallacious, for unbelief is the fault not of the call but of the free will of the one who refuses.[76] Nor is free will to be denied by the incorrect notion that predestination leads persons to good or to evil. The free will is always present, although without grace it desires only evil, whereas by the grace of justification a person willingly turns to good and perseveres in it. The will, now good, cooperates with grace.[77] Many, of course, do perish, receiving the damnation they deserve, but God wills the salvation of all.[78]

---

[74] *Resp. Vinc.* 13.
[75] *Resp. Gall.* 1.4; 2.4.
[76] *Resp. Gall.* 1.5; 2.5.
[77] *Resp. Gall.* 1.6; 2.6.
[78] *Resp. Vinc.* 2.

Prosper has maintained the universal salvific will but only in a highly qualified sense. First, for him as for Augustine, the universality of the call simply means that the elect come from throughout the world. Second, although all are addressed, the media vary: preaching of the gospel or law or nature. Presumably these forms are not equally effective. Third, despite the universality of the call, fallen humanity is incapable of receiving it. The faith to recognize and respond must come from God.[79] Finally, Prosper has not entirely rejected the possibility that God even prevents some from hearing the gospel by which they could be saved.[80]

Undoubtedly Prosper believed the divine call for universal salvation is restricted; yet Prosper was quick to emphasize that the responsibility for damnation lies with the human agent, not with God. In response to the objection to the notion that Christ did not die to redeem the whole world, Prosper allowed that the situation can be stated in two ways: Christ took the nature of all humanity and died for the redemption of all; Christ's death was only for those who were to benefit from it. It is not enough that Christ died for all; through baptism, a person must also accept the liberation offered in Christ and then persevere in it.[81]

Prosper insisted that it is utterly wrong to say that God is the cause of sin. Scripture testifies of God's hardening the heart or forsaking;[82] yet by such action God did not cause those so treated to sin but only gave them their just desert, allowing them to continue in their sin.[83] Prosper did concede, however, that God creates some who are foreknown to be reprobate. Arguing that their nature is from God, he rejected the charge that they were not created for eternal life but acknowledged that God uses them to serve the divine purpose.[84] Although Prosper did not pursue this line of thought, it does seem that he is allowing here for the possibility that the decision to withhold predestination to grace is in some way dependent upon foreknowledge that the person would not accept it. If Prosper were indeed making such an allowance, he was departing even further from Augustine for whom predestination to grace and predestination to glory are entirely gratuitous and in no way dependent upon foreknowledge of merit. Moreover, although such an allowance by Prosper would seem to strengthen the tie between human action and its outcome in reward or punishment for the

---

[79]*Resp. Gall.* 1.8; 2.8. For a discussion of Prosper's method for dealing with the question of universality, see Jacquin, "La question de la prédestination," 282-86.

[80]*Resp. Gall.* 1.10; 2.10.

[81]*Resp. Gall.* 1.9; 2.9.

[82]Cf. discussion of the explanation given by Augustine and by Origen with regard to this issue, 22 and 80 above.

[83]*Resp. Gall.* 1.11; 2.11.

[84]*Resp. Gall.* 1.13; 2.13.

person from whom the grace of a free will is withheld, in actuality the tie would be weakened: the only choice freely made between good and evil would be the choice made in Adam.

In response to the criticism that the doctrine of predestination restricts the divine will for salvation, Prosper has tried to make the case that the failure of the human agent, admittedly one doomed in Adam, and not predestination, is the true impediment to universal salvation. However, his efforts to reinforce the connection between human action and reward and punishment have made him a less than faithful interpreter of Augustine's teaching.

In his *Pro Augustino responsiones ad capitula objectionum Gallorum calumniantium* and *Pro Augustino responsiones ad capitula objectionum Vincentianarum* Prosper sought to defend the Augustinian position, once again asserting predestination, now as a tenet of the Catholic faith. Nevertheless, his own position manifested some signs of softening. Specifically, he allowed predestination to be affected by foreknowledge. Rather than predestination arising solely from the hidden judgments of God, the divine decision not to predestine is based in the foreknowledge of a person's future sins and impenitence. The decision to predestine some is still an inscrutable judgment of grace, but the rationale for the decision not to predestine is no longer hidden.

By appealing to the foreknowledge of future sin, Prosper was utilizing the kind of explanation that Augustine had explicitly rejected. The African bishop, in the two treatises that he had sent to southern Gaul, had refused to make anyone's fate dependent on what that person had not done. To do so would be illogical. Perhaps Prosper felt that the explanation that Augustine had provided for the nonpredestination of some was inadequate. Augustine had simply argued that these persons were receiving the punishment that all deserve, for all are already guilty of original sin quite independently of any sins that they might commit in the future. Finally, the decision as to whether one is to be predestined or not lies in the hidden justice of God.

This explanation Prosper may have found to be unsatisfactory in that it had the effect of destroying the connection between the sinful actions of a person and their outcome in punishment. It did so by making the latter not the result of the former but both the effect of an unfathomable decision to withhold grace. In contrast, Prosper's new explanation recreated the connection by making the divine determination of the outcome, i.e., punishment, dependent on foreknowledge of future sinful action.

The result of Prosper's shift from Augustine was significant. Since he explained the nonelection of some by means of divine foreknowledge of their future sin, the implied explanation for the election of others would seem to lie in divine foreknowledge of their future nonsin. Such an implication was, of course, unacceptable, for he consistently maintained that election is utterly gratuitous. The result was that now Prosper's explanation of nonelection was no longer coherent with his explanation of election.

Regarding the question of God's universal will to save, Prosper's position proved to be no more satisfying than that of Augustine. Prosper affirmed that God wills the salvation of all and that Christ died for all; yet qualifications abounded. "All," he argued, refers to an election of all types of people from all parts of the world. The call does not go out to everyone equally but through means of diminishing effectiveness: preaching, the law, or nature. Moreover, none of these means is adequate without the grace of regeneration. All persons, therefore, do not receive the grace to profit by Christ's death. Perhaps it may be said, then, that general but inadequate grace supplements the grace effective for salvation.[85]

It is important to note the literary style that the controversy took in this stage, particularly in the *objectiones* and *responsiones*. The argument on both sides was reduced to caricature and to unjustified vituperative attacks. The time of thoughtful questioning and careful elaboration of definition was supplanted by arguments abbreviated to key words and slogans. As a result, nothing genuinely constructive occurred during the interchange just described, although with regard to foreknowledge Prosper did shift his views in a most extraordinary way.[86]

In the next years, the tone of the argument changed again. Restraint, more than passion, characterized efforts on both sides. By mid-decade, when Cassian died, Prosper was in Rome in the service of Leo, whose own respect for Cassian seems to have tempered Prosper's views.[87] The *De praedestinatione et gratia*, an apparent attempt at mediation, particularly with regard to the issue of grace and free will working together,[88] and the *Hypomnesticon*, which reflected Prosper's

---

[85]Cf. De Letter, *Defense of St. Augustine*, 19-20.

[86]For a contrasting perspective on Prosper's fidelity to Augustine, see G. de Plinval, "Prosper d'Aquitaine interprète de saint Augustin," *Recherches augustiniennes* 1 (1958): 339-55, and Plinval, *Pélage: ses écrits, sa vie et sa réforme* (Lausanne: Librairie Payot, 1943) 369.

[87]It was at the request of the archdeacon Leo that Cassian had written the *De incarnatione*. R. A. Markus, "Chronicle and Theology: Prosper of Aquitaine," *The Inheritance of Historiography*, ed. Christopher Holdsworth and T. P. Wiseman (Exeter: Exeter University, 1986) 31-43.

[88]A. Zumkeller, "Die pseudoaugustinische Schrift 'De praedestinatione et gratia': Inhalt, Überlieferung, Verfasserfrage und Nachwirkung," *Augustinianum* 25 (1985): 539-63.

evolving position, may have originated as this time,[89] as did the *Commonitorium* of Vincent.[90]

Auctoritates

It was in the court of Pope Leo I in the years between 435 and 442 that Prosper prepared the *Praeteritorum episcoporum sedis apostolicae auctoritates de gratia Dei*.[91] The *Auctoritates* consisted of a list of authoritative pronouncements made by Pope Innocent, Pope Zosimus, and the Eighteenth Council of Carthage that had been approved by Pope Zosimus, two references to liturgical practice, as well as a commentary by Prosper.[92] It was Prosper's intent to clarify. By presenting the official teaching of the church, he sought to clear up misunderstanding that he believed to be caused by those who claimed to be Catholics but whose views on grace were continuous with those of the Pelagians.[93] He would settle the matter by appealing to authority.

The first four quotations, all from Pope Zosimus, along with Prosper's comments, described the fall and its results. By free will Adam fell, and in him the capacity for good was lost to all his descendants. Only by grace through baptism in Christ is there forgiveness and regeneration.[94] Thus "goodness" is not of human origin but is the gift of grace,[95] and perseverance in this good is also

---

[89]John Edward Chisholm, *The Pseudo-Augustinian Hypomnesticon against the Pelagians and Celestians* 1 (Fribourg: University Press, 1967); Chisholm, "The Authorship of the Pseudo-Augustinian *Hypomnesticon* against the Pelagians and Celestians," *Studia Patristica* 11, Texte und Untersuchungen 108 (1972) 307-10. Chisholm made a strong case for the authorship of Prosper and a date between 430 and 435. See also Markus, "The Legacy of Pelagius," 219-20.

[90]E. Griffe, "Pro Vincentio Lerinensi," *Bulletin de littérature ecclésiastique* 62 (1961) 26-31.

[91]D. M. Cappuyns, "L'origine des capitula pseudo-célestiniens contre le semipélagianisme," *Revue Bénédictine* 41 (1929): 156-70. The *Auctoritates* were added to the *Ep.* 21 sent by Pope Celestine to the bishops of Gaul (see 120 above). The PL numbers the *capitula* accordingly (PL 50.528-37). De Letter numbers the *capitula* as if the *Auctoritates* were a self-contained work. I have followed the latter system.

[92]De Letter, *Defense of St. Augustine*, 13.

[93]Prosper, *Praeteritorum sedis apostolicae episcoporum auctoritates de gratia Dei, Praef.* As early as his *Epistula ad Rufinum* Prosper had linked the opponents of Augustine's predestinarian teaching with the Pelagians.

[94]*Auct.*, citing Pope Innocent, *Ep.* 29, *In requirendis* 6 to the Council of Carthage of 416.

[95]*Auct.* 2, from the same letter.

dependent on grace.[96] Accordingly, right exercise of the will requires regeneration in Christ.[97]

Next, two quotations from Pope Zosimus, accompanied by the response from the African bishops and by Prosper's commentary, described how the saints must depend upon grace in order to will and to do the good. The free will is to be understood as a coparticipant with grace in any good, although grace is the decisive factor,[98] for both the origin of good in thought and its accomplishment in action are to be referred to God.[99]

Three quotations from the Council of Carthage of 418, along with their interpretation by Prosper, pertained to the work of grace. Grace both forgives sins already committed and assists forgiven persons to refrain from others.[100] This assistance consists not only in providing "knowledge" of one's "duty" through the commandments but also in providing a love of that duty and the ability to perform it.[101] Moreover, without this assistance of grace the free will would be unable to keep the commandments.[102]

Prosper also cited the practice of the church as evidence of the necessity of grace. First, that the church intercedes for the entire world asking that all might be converted and receive salvation demonstrates that such transformations are the work of God's mercy.[103] Second, that baptism is preceded by exorcisms reveals that all must be released from the captivity of sin and transferred to the service of God.[104]

A summary of the church's position, as understood by Prosper, followed. God is the source of all good. Accordingly, grace precedes merit. The will is not overcome but freed. It is transformed to desire and to accomplish the good, and is made a cooperator with grace. Reward is given to merit, but as these merits are the gifts of grace, it is a matter of grace rewarding grace.[105]

Neither Prosper's summary nor the *Auctoritates* taken as a whole anywhere mentioned predestination or the divine will for universal salvation. In fact, Prosper concluded by acknowledging that he had not discussed "the more pro-

---

[96]*Auct.* 3, from the same letter.

[97]*Auct.* 4, citing Pope Innocent, in *Ep.* 30, *Inter caeteras* 3 to the Council of Mileve of 416.

[98]*Auct.* 5, citing Pope Zosimus in *Ep. tractoria* of 418 and the response of the African bishops.

[99]*Auct.* 6, citing same letter from Zosimus.

[100]*Auct.* 7, citing article 3 of the council.

[101]*Auct.* 7, citing article 4 of the council.

[102]*Auct.* 7, citing article 5 of the council.

[103]*Auct.* 8.

[104]*Auct.* 9.

[105]*Auct.* 9.

found and difficult points."[106] Nor had he mentioned Augustine by name, probably because he had already presented what he considered to be the crucial aspects of the Augustinian position. The omission would also serve as a conciliatory measure, since the African's name was so closely associated with those "difficult points." Prosper made clear that the official position of the church regarding grace was contained in this compilation. Other matters that were consistent with these teachings could be accepted, but he did not indicate that he considered such acceptance to be necessary.

With the *Auctoritates* some revision was evident in Prosper's position. He had made a discrimination between the essentials of the church's doctrine of grace and the difficult corollaries that were worthy of but not necessary of acceptance. The move may simply have been a pragmatic one. Prosper could appeal to the authority of popes, councils, and liturgical practice, all supplemented by citations from Scripture, to give unquestionable authority to the broad framework of the Augustinian teachings on grace. Perhaps he felt that it was not necessary to make explicit what any good Augustinian would have believed to be logically implicit in such a framework. For the present, the difficult statements of the master, certain to be bones of contention, could be assumed in silence.

The writing of the *Auctoritates* signaled, too, a temporary shift in the emphasis of the controversy. As the title indicates, the issue of authority had become dominant. For the moment at least, the proper presentation of one's case had become the recitation of the tradition itself, accompanied by judicious commentary. From a carefully arranged list of official citations major points could be scored with minimal elaboration. The proof lay in the official pronouncements themselves. Any extrapolation was presumably a matter of logical, thus safe, inference.

Prosper may have written the *Auctoritates* at least partially in reaction to the formula given in the *Commonitorium* of Vincent of Lérins: *quod ubique, quod semper, quod ab omnibus*. As we shall see in the next chapter, Vincent's work showed that the appeal to tradition could also be used against the Augustinian view. Both sides, it seems, were adopting the same strategy. In doing so, they drastically shifted the style of argumentation in the controversy. Now the emphasis was on a carefully discriminating presentation of those elements within the tradition from which points could be scored. Augustine's initial reliance on argument has been replaced by the force of the appeal to authoritative pronouncement and traditional practice.

The immediate result was that the controversy was compressed into those points for which clear *auctoritates* were available. The search for authorities,

---

[106]*Auct.* 10.

although not taking precedence over the original issue of the connection between action and outcome had begun to determine its shape: one asserted that for which one could supply the authorities and left alone that for which one could not. The result was that the earlier wide range of issues had begun to shrink. In its new reduced form the problem had become that of delimiting the role of divine agency and the role of human agency in the determination of human destiny. This delimitation was to be made on the basis of appropriate authority.

De vocatione omnium gentium

The *De vocatione omnium gentium* was probably Prosper's final contribution to the debate. As such, it represented his concluding response to the ongoing question of the divine will for universal salvation. The circumstances of the writing of the treatise are uncertain. It was obviously the work of an Augustinian in opposition to those who opposed Augustine's predestinarian teaching; yet its mediating quality suggests that it was not composed in the heat of the controversy. It would thus seem to have been written between the stage of the dispute that coincided with Prosper's *Auctoritates* and the next stage that began with the publication in 462 of the *De gratia Dei* by Faustus of Riez.

Although there has been debate since the seventeenth century regarding authorship, Cappuyns has argued convincingly that Prosper wrote the *De vocatione* at mid-century. At that time he was living in Rome in the service of Leo.[107] It may well be that the mediating tone of the work, especially its attention to the divine will for universal salvation, stemmed from Prosper's association with Leo, whose favorable opinion of John Cassian would have been well known to him.[108] Prosper does appear to have been trying to clarify both those areas where

---

[107]M. Cappuyns, "L'auteur du *De vocatione omnium gentium*," *Revue Bénédictine* 39 (1927): 198-226, provided a discussion of the history of the scholarship on the question; Amann, "Semi-pélagiens," 1830-33; Lionello Pelland, *S. Prosperi Aquitani* (Montreal: Studia Collegii Immaculatae Conceptionis, 1936) 144-81. For an opposing point of view, see G. de Plinval, "Prosper d'Aquitaine interprète de saint Augustin," *Recherches augustiniennes* 1 (1958): 351.

Most of the English translations of quotations from the *De vocatione* will be taken from P. De Letter, *St. Prosper of Aquitaine: The Call of All Nations* (Westminster MD: Newman, 1952) 6-7. I have offered a fresh reading where it seemed better suited to the Latin text.

[108]R. A. Markus, "Chronicle and Theology: Prosper of Aquitaine," 36-39. For an examination of Prosper's involvement in the composition and editing of various works of Leo, see N. W. James, "Leo the Great and Prosper of Aquitaine: A Fifth Century Pope and His Adviser," *Journal of Theological Studies* n.s. 44 (1993): 554-84. See above, n. 87. For a different perspective on Prosper's universalism, see Czeslaw Bartnik, "L'universalisme de l'histoire du salut dans le *De vocatione omnium gentium*," *Revue d'histoire ecclésiastique* 68 (1973): 731-58.

flexibility was possible and those areas where it was not, if he were to remain faithful to an Augustinian understanding of grace.

The treatise itself was divided into two books. Both examined the issue of universal salvation, but each from a different perspective. The first book began by calling attention to a fundamental dilemma: as it is undeniable that God wills the salvation of all, why is the divine will not accomplished? If the failure is attributed to the human will, then the efficacy of grace would seem to have been discounted; furthermore, if grace is thus made dependent on merit, then grace is not gift but payment. Such implications appear to rule out the possibility that the human will is the determining factor. If, on the other hand, grace is understood to be a gift necessary for salvation, then why is it not given to all since God wills the salvation of all?[109]

Prosper began his attempt to resolve this dilemma by describing the character of the human will. Whatever its stage of development, and Prosper argued that there are three such stages, the human will seeks what pleases it and rejects what displeases it.[110] As vitiated by the fall, the will in its first stage is "carnal," limited to the attractions of the "bodily senses." The situation of infants illustrates the character of the will at this stage.[111] The second stage, the "natural" will, results from the development of rationality. At this stage, such goods as justice attract the will; yet because God is not recognized as the proper object of desire and the source of all good, pride and downfall result.[112] Everyone is rightly held accountable for this failure of recognition, for at this stage knowledge of God, equivalent to that offered in the law and prophets, is presented in the creation. All nations have access to this gift.[113] Nevertheless, human nature as fallen in Adam, even as it lives amidst these gifts of grace, is incapable of loving properly. The attachments of the will lead it away from God, even though good actions may be performed.[114]

Prosper wished to make clear that the will, at any of its stages, is capable of attractions and choices. As the will of Adam had the capacity to choose good or evil and willingly chose evil, the human will as fallen remains able to choose but not righteously, for the object of its desire is not the goal of pleasing God. Because the will is capable of seeking only what attracts it, and as the fallen will is not attracted to God, it is incapable of seeking God. The only possibility for

---

[109]Prosper, *De vocatione omnium gentium* 1.1.

[110]*De voc.* 1.2.

[111]*De voc.* 1.3: *Sensualis igitur voluntas, quam et carnalem possumus dicere.*

[112]*De voc.* 1.4: *ad animalem surgitur voluntatem; quae . . . supra sensualem motum sese atollere potest.*

[113]*De voc.* 1.5.

[114]*De voc.* 1.6.

redirection of the will lies not in the will itself but in its creator. God must redirect the affections, removing the imperfection acquired not through creation but through the fall.[115] Only as God restores it does the will love properly, living for God.[116] The third stage, therefore, consists in the spiritual will, the will as renewed in righteousness.[117]

This restoration of the will is the interior work of grace that first prepares the will, giving it the desire for God. This desire is truly a gift. If conversion could result simply from reason's reception of doctrine, then grace would be entirely external, and faith would be derived totally from the will. Prosper could accept neither implication of this possibility. First, if grace is merely teaching, then it cannot be distinguished from the law. Law has the character of commanding but not of assisting, and the result is an obedience based in fear rather than in free choice. In contrast, grace transforms the heart, abolishing sin through pardon, creating a new will, and restoring the image of God. The final victory is not yet won, as the old will and new will still battle within the person, but with the interior assistance of God, the new will proves to be stronger. The second implication, that faith is derived entirely from the will, is also unacceptable. Although the free will was not lost in the fall, its good judgment was, and this loss must be restored by the work of grace before the will can desire and choose the good, as was explained above.[118] Thus the work of restoration is a matter of grace restoring to the free will, which the person never loses, its good judgment, its decision for the good.

Prosper's depiction of the interaction of grace and human willing is that of a cooperation necessary for salvation. The result is that, although the dominant role is played by grace, a subordinate but vital role appears to be ascribed to free human agency, namely, the struggle of the new will, the will restored by grace, against the old will for the good.

Nevertheless, a question remains. As grace is the dominant element in the cooperation between grace and the free will, and if God wills the salvation of all, why then are all not saved? Prosper's answer, at least at this point, is faithfully Augustinian and therefore, as in the case of Augustine himself, hardly satisfying. Those who are "the sons of promise," "the spiritual progeny of Abraham," i.e., those who have been foreknown and predestined, are given a "desire for salvation" and, through the interior teaching of the Spirit, a "knowledge of the truth"[119] by which they are changed from error to knowing and willing the truth

---

[115]*De voc.* 1.7.

[116]*De voc.* 1.6,7.

[117]*De voc.* 1.2,7: *spiritalis.*

[118]*De voc.* 1.8.

[119]*De voc.* 1.9. *Qui ad Deum per Deum veniunt, et salvari volentes omnino salvantur: quia ipsum desiderium salutis ex Dei inspiratione concipiunt, et per illuminationem*

and persevering in it. As God's will never fails and as the divine foreknowledge never proves false, this sequence is inexorably carried out. Those who do not believe the gospel are "inexcusable," but they are by their final condition proved not to have been "sons of Abraham" in the first place.[120]

The division of humankind into two groups is a settled and unchangeable reality, according to the Augustinians, and an empirical reality, according to both sides. How then can it be reconciled with the testimony of Scripture that God wills the salvation of all? Prosper treated this question by reference to the conventions of speech. Specifically, Scripture regularly speaks of the part as if it were a whole. Such a figure of speech accounts for the apparently inclusive terminology that is employed with regard to the divine will for salvation.[121]

Yet Prosper recognized that he could not simply brush the problem aside as due only to a figure of speech. He pointed out that the context of the difficult passage, 1 Timothy 2:4, is the apostolic teaching that prayer is to be made for all persons. The resultant universal practice of the church has been to intercede with God for the salvation of all. As a practice of the entire church, such prayer should be acknowledged as the appropriate interpretation of the passage and an accurate reflection of the will of God.[122] Prosper was making a significant distinction: the will of God is that the church should pray for universal salvation but not that all shall be saved. Prosper acknowledged that in the case of some the prayers of the church are not heard. The reason for this omission lies hidden in divine inscrutability.[123] Prosper has made a significant disjunction. The human action is that of prayer for all; yet its outcome, determined by an entirely external agency and with no apparent reference to the human action, is that some are saved and some are not.

That such a division of persons is made the human mind can only recognize; it cannot fathom the divine rationale.[124] To seek a reason in the fates or in the stars for all of the differences among persons is to deny both that God is the author of all and that all share the same nature.[125] To propose merit as the basis of salvation is to leave unexplained the case of later generations receiving the gospel when they deserved it no more than their forbearers[126] or the case of some

---

vocantis in agnitionem veniunt veritatis. Sunt enim filii promissionis, merces fidei, spiritale semen Abrahae . . . praescitum et praeordinatum in vitam aeternam.

[120]*De voc.* 1.9.
[121]*De voc.* 1.9-11.
[122]*De voc.* 1.12.
[123]*De voc.* 1.13.
[124]*De voc.* 1.14.
[125]*De voc.* 1.14.
[126]*De voc.* 1.15.

infants incapable of earning merit who are baptized before death[127] or the case of some who, after blatantly unworthy lives, are baptized immediately before death.[128]

Instead, the divine will is the basis for election, and baptism is the origin of the new life. Merit can only follow grace.[129] The reformation of a person from the "old creation to the new" is from beginning to end the work of grace.[130] The condition of all before regeneration is the same: their nature is fallen and their free will, while able to refuse the good, is unable to desire it. Some are elected to receive the necessary assistance of grace; others are not.[131]

With this description of the interaction of grace and human nature Prosper concluded the first book of the *De vocatione*. He was acutely aware, however, that he had not yet reconciled such a description with the doctrine "according to which we devoutly believe that God wills all to be saved through recognition of the truth."[132] The second book would have to effect this reconciliation.

Prosper began this latter book with three affirmations: God wills the salvation of all; it is by grace rather than by merit that one has knowledge of the truth and salvation; the divine judgments are inscrutable and immune from questioning.[133] Together the three affirmations raised the issue of authority, specifically the authority of Scripture. Prosper set the guideline that no statement in Scripture could be interpreted in such a way that it minimized the difficulty of reconciling grace and universal salvation. On the contrary, Prosper announced that "the more difficult is its understanding the more praiseworthy will be the faith that believes. That assent is indeed very strong whose motive is derived from authority as a sufficient proof of truth, even though the *why* of things remain hidden."[134]

In an attempt to find a way of reconciling, without violating the integrity of, apparently conflicting scriptural claims regarding grace and universal salvation, Prosper began to develop a point to which he had referred in the first book, a point that would become the theme of the second book: the distinction between general and special grace. It should be noted that as Prosper referred here to the variety in grace, he specified that he was speaking not of several distinct types

---

[127]*De voc.* 1.16.
[128]*De voc.* 1.17.
[129]*De voc.* 1.18.
[130]*De voc.* 1.23.
[131]*De voc.* 1.25.
[132]*De voc.* 1.25.
[133]*De voc.* 2.1.
[134]*De voc.* 2.2.

of grace but of one grace that is always present. It has no variation in power or purpose yet is diverse in intensity and results.[135]

In every age and to every nation a general grace has been made available by which all persons might have knowledge of God. This grace has always been accessible in providence and in the works of creation so that all might learn to worship the creator. The result has been that the same benefits that the law and the prophets provided Israel have been made available to every age and nation.[136] Nevertheless, although a general grace is given to all, it is obviously given in different degrees and in differing manifestations at various times and places. To some has been given only the witness of creation, to others the law, prophets, angels, and miracles, and now to all the incarnation.[137] Furthermore, the gifts of grace are granted at different rates to various individuals. To some it is given to attain maturity in grace quickly, whereas to others development is given more slowly, as the gifts of faith, understanding, and charity are imparted to them and made to grow.[138] As subsequent gifts depend on prior ones,[139] the effect is that grace is given to grace. Prosper did not discount human agency entirely, for the possibility of rejecting the gifts of grace remains open.[140] Nevertheless, the dominant factor is grace, and whereas everyone receives grace adequate for knowledge of God, not all receive grace adequate for salvation.[141]

Yet with all these discriminations within grace, Prosper still claimed that Christ died for everyone, since all are sinners,[142] and that God wills the salvation of all.[143] This divine will for universal salvation manifests itself in the general grace, which is enhanced in varying degrees by special expressions of grace. For example, in the latter days, the Gentiles have been called,[144] and Christianity has become widespread.[145] Even if there are nations that have not yet heard the gospel, God has established a time for them to receive it.[146]

From this description one can conclude that Prosper, when he spoke of a divine will for universal salvation, was referring, first, to the gracious will of

---

[135]*De voc.* 2.5.

[136]*De voc.* 2.4.

[137]*De voc.* 2.9.

[138]*De voc.* 2.11; cf. Prosper, *C. coll.* 7; 8.3; 14.2 on the difference between the conversion of Paul and that of the thief.

[139]*De voc.* 2.11.

[140]*De voc.* 2.12.

[141]*De voc.* 2.15.

[142]*De voc.* 2.16.

[143]*De voc.* 2.19.

[144]*De voc.* 2.19.

[145]*De voc.* 2.16.

[146]*De voc.* 2.17.

God manifested in the general grace available to all in the creation. This grace is adequate for recognizing that there is a creator who is to be worshiped. In the second place, Prosper was referring to a final worldwide spread of the gospel by which all nations will hear of Christ. The universality of the divine salvific will has to do with the general availability of the knowledge of the redeemer rather than with God's will for the salvation of specific individuals. The reason for this distinction lies, I think, in the efficacy of what Prosper would call special grace, a grace that is directed toward the salvation of particular individuals. A fundamental assumption for him was that the divine will is not thwarted.[147] If God wills the salvation of a person, that person will be saved. Obviously, many people throughout the past and now in the present have given no evidence of their salvation: they either have not understood or have rejected the knowledge available in the creation; they have never heard or have rejected the gospel. Therefore, it must be assumed that God did not specifically will the salvation of these individuals. Yet God may still be said to have willed their salvation generally in that grace did make available to them, as to everyone, a knowledge of the creator and of appropriate human life.

A difficulty arises, of course, in explaining how such general grace is available to infants dying without baptism, and thus without salvation. Infants obviously are incapable of receiving the knowledge of God given either in the creation or in the gospel, just as they are incapable of performing guilty actions.[148] Prosper approached the problem through analogy. As in mundane matters, children, until they reach the age of reason, are dependent upon and share the condition of those persons who care for them, so must they do so with regard to the reception of grace. Infants receive the general grace that is accessible to all through their parents or those who are responsible for them, and if the latter have rightly used this grace, the infants derive salvation from it.[149]

De Letter, acknowledging the lack of clarity in the argument, has proposed that Prosper was suggesting that if those who have responsibility for an infant make right use of general grace, whereby they have knowledge of God, God will give them the special grace of faith, and they, in turn, will, on the basis of this faith, bring the infant to baptism so that the child receives salvation.[150] There are at least two difficulties, however, with such an interpretation: Prosper did not elsewhere indicate that God gives faith in response to right use of general grace

---

[147]De Letter, *Defense of St. Augustine,* 18-20; *The Call of all Nations,* 15-19.
[148]*De voc.* 2.20,21.
[149]*De voc.* 2.3; cf. 2.4.
[150]De Letter, *The Call of All Nations,* 206n.209.

and, in fact, argued the contrary,[151] and, as Prosper himself acknowledged, some infants of believing parents die unbaptized.

The difficulty of Prosper's argument increased with his discussion of the special grace of election as it applies to children. He pointed to two kinds of cases among infants in which election is given. First, children whose parents are elect also participate in this election even though they may not receive baptism. Second, children who are baptized are elect, although their parents may not be elect, for other adults provide for these children's baptism.[152] The second kind of situation had been discussed by Augustine and is clear enough.[153] The first, however, is somewhat contorted. De Letter has interpreted it to mean that the parents of these children, as they are elect, receive the special grace of faith. In most cases the faith of the parents provides the occasion for the baptism of the child. These children, up to the point of baptism, can be said to participate in election as would any child of elect parents. However, because they die unbaptized, that election is of no salvific value for them.[154]

Prosper's argument for both situations, that of children whose parents are the recipients of general grace and that of children whose parents are the recipients of general and special grace, depended on the analogy he made to secular life: as in mundane matters children share the condition of those who care for them, so do they in regard to grace. By extension of the analogy, it appears that Prosper was also saying that as the condition and behavior of the responsible adult often influences but does not determine the future of the child in secular matters, the same holds true with regard to salvific ones. Baptism, a necessary precondition for salvation, remains the gift of grace. The argument that Prosper was making regarding the access that infants have through their protectors to general and special grace is only as convincing as the analogy. Whatever Prosper's own estimate of it, he did not pursue it further.

Prosper's assumption that baptism is necessary for infants served as proof for the gratuity of salvation. If baptism were not necessary, then infants dying without baptism would be among the elect because of their merit or rather lack of actual demerit. Such a state of affairs would mean both that all are not bound by original sin and that salvation is by merit rather than by grace. The doctrine of the necessity of baptism was thus a protection against both the other erroneous positions.

---

[151]*De voc.* 1.8,9,18.

[152]*De voc.* 2.23.

[153]Augustine, *Ep.* 194.32; *De gr. et lib. arb.* 22.44; *De corr. et gr.* 8.18; cf. De Letter, *The Call of All Nations*, 208, n. 216.

[154]De Letter, *The Call of All Nations*, 207-208.

Having presented his argument that in every age God has made available to all a general grace adequate for teaching that God is to be sought, Prosper turned to an examination of special grace. This grace, not withheld entirely in previous times, he characterized as having now been given more fully, although through a variety of means and not to everyone. The reasons for these variations in its bestowal remain hidden in God.[155]

This special grace operates in conjunction with the human will. Grace first prepares the will, removing its blindness and enabling it to desire and to accept the goods that grace provides. Although the role of grace is dominant, the willing cooperation of the will is essential, for at every stage of the process, from the beginnings of faith through perseverance unto death, both elements are always at work. Prosper's insistence that grace does not supply the willing cooperation of the will underscored the genuineness of the human contribution. Grace influences but does not determine the will's choice for the good. Furthermore, failure is possible through the fault of the will.[156]

In the interaction of grace and the human will, grace first creates both faith and a good will in the person. The gift of faith can be refused, but the will that accepts it does so out of love: the divine love has inspired the human will to love.[157] The possibility exists at any point, however, that the free will may reject grace. Grace assists the unbeliever to attain to faith and the believer to persevere; yet the unbeliever and believer may both refuse. The fault is their own. Even so, absolute steadfastness in the faith is not available in this life, for the will remains at war with itself. Thus the believer must not only struggle but also pray for assistance in perseverance. Significantly, although perseverance is a matter of the cooperation of grace and the will, a cooperation in which grace is dominant, Prosper insisted that the person who remains steadfast receives a reward.[158] Prosper has affirmed merit.

In this description of the interaction of grace and free will Prosper has given somewhat more prominence than had Augustine to the distinct agency of the human person. Although Augustine had taught that the will voluntarily wills the good, he had said that in the case of those chosen for eternal salvation and given perseverance, grace effects the choice of the good. In the case of those who receive the gift of good will but not perseverance, the will is transformed while the possibility and even reality of the choice of evil remains. Admittedly, the differences were not great, but the *De vocatione* did have a different tone than did Augustine's final writings. Prosper was trying to reclaim and reemphasize the

---

[155]*De voc.* 2.25.
[156]*De voc.* 2.26.
[157]*De voc.* 2.27.
[158]*De voc.* 2.28.

genuineness of human participation and decision making. The result was a vision of the Christian life that was similar to that offered by Cassian, but Prosper presented it in such a way that it could be correlated with the Augustinian view of grace.

Perhaps to buttress his allowance to the free will Prosper stated that even with the assistance of special grace, some may turn away into death.[159] This statement has the effect of calling into question any necessary efficacy of special grace and, at the same time, of making room for a distinct human agency. Furthermore, Prosper has divided the elect into two groups. One group consists of those who will not advance or will not be helped by the reception of grace; the other, of those who will persevere.[160] The implication is that the elect are those who have received special grace for faith and have been converted. The division among the elect results from the use made of special grace. If such an interpretation is appropriate, by the time that Prosper wrote the *De vocatione* his definition of election had changed significantly from his earlier years. De Letter has suggested a possible way out of this dilemma. When Prosper later claimed that a "special call has now also reached the whole of humanity," and then went on to say that "from every nation and every condition," people receive the "grace of adoption,"[161] De Letter remarked that this *specialis vocatio* may not be the same thing as the *specialis gratia*, or it may be the special grace that is "given also to those who will not persevere."[162] If this suggestion is correct, then special grace is given in varying measures as Prosper has affirmed,[163] and an inadequate measure is not efficacious for perseverance. Another interpretation that is more consistent with Prosper's teaching elsewhere as well as with Augustine's is that God has now made the good news of the incarnation available to all. To believe, however, is a *specialis vocatio*. Many do believe and become Christians, and, in this sense, are elected for belief. To persevere, however, requires a further gift of grace, one that is not given to all Christians. Those who are given this grace are elected for glory and not simply for faith.

The discriminations within grace that Prosper found it necessary to maintain as he attempted to underscore human agency resulted in a return to the old Augustinian emphasis on the sovereignty of grace. In fact, the concluding chapters of book 2 reasserted this position. Eternal foreknowledge of election in

---

[159]*De voc.* 2.29.

[160]*De voc.* 2.29.

[161]*De voc.* 2.33. *Et licet illa generalis vocatio non quiescat, tamen etiam ista specialis jam universis est facta communis. Ex omni gente, et ex omni conditione adoptantur quotidie millia senum, millia juvenum, millia parvulorum.*

[162]De Letter, *The Call of All Nations*, 216n.305.

[163]*De voc.* 2.25,33.

Christ is the determinant of salvation.[164] Added to his old Augustinianism, however, was a recognition of free will and merit. This recognition was not new in its content but was somewhat surprising in the imagery that it utilized. In metaphors typical of monastic practice, Prosper described the Christian life as a battle and the Christian as a soldier armed with divine weapons that are to be used in the fight.[165] He characterized election as operating not in such a way as to dismay the free will but so that merit could increase through works and effort. God has preordained that "those who accomplish good works may be crowned not only according to the purpose of God but also according to their own merits.[166]

As can be deduced from the previous chapter, such a description exposes the influence that the Semi-Pelagian position, particularly the writings of John Cassian, had on Prosper. The old scheme of free will, merit, and last judgment had been at least partially restored among the Augustinians, but the fundamental chasm that separated them from the Semi-Pelagians still remained. Among the former group this scheme was still overshadowed by the judgment of grace made prior to any human action.

Prosper did not achieve a consistent position in the *De vocatione*. Whatever he may have intended, he sometimes did and sometimes did not affirm a distinct human agency. The spirit of the treatise was obviously conciliatory. It gave great attention to the character of the human will and the contribution that the will makes to a person's ultimate destiny. There is clear evidence of a softening of the Augustinian position, if not a departure from it. Nevertheless, Prosper was finally unable to give up the notion of the sovereignty of grace. The result was an unsuccessful attempt to introduce the Semi-Pelagian emphasis on distinct human agency into an Augustinian logic that necessarily undercut such an emphasis.

Conclusion

In this survey of Prosper's literary contribution to the Semi-Pelagian controversy, we have found evidence of development in his position. That development can be characterized in terms of three stages. Until 432 Prosper parroted Augustine. Predestination firmly joined to an understanding of grace as gratuitous was a necessary element of this strict Augustinian view, along with the notion of a limited divine will to save. This first period covered the time from the letter to Rufinus through the reply to the Genoese. From 432 through 435,

---

[164]*De voc.* 2.33.

[165]*De voc.* 2.35.

[166]*De voc.* 2.36: *qui bona gesserint, non solum secundum propositum Dei, sed etiam secundum sua merita coronentur.* Prosper has dropped the earlier suggestion of nonelection on the basis of foreknowledge of future sin.

the period encompassing his responses both to John Cassian and to the two sets of objections, Prosper weakened the link between predestination and the gratuity of grace by suggesting that nonpredestination to glory is based on foreknowledge of impenitence. He also affirmed a divine will for universal salvation, although only in a highly qualified sense. In the final period, beginning after 435 and including the *Auctoritates* and the *De vocatione*, he gave more attention to the divine will for universal salvation. He also differentiated between the official teachings of the church and those of its doctors, including Augustine, and in so doing broke the connection between the gratuitous character of grace and the doctrine of predestination.[167]

This pattern of development may have involved less evolution than at first appears to be the case. Prosper's difficulties in reconciling the doctrine of a divine will for universal salvation with the doctrine of the gratuity of grace in the *De vocatione* revealed a fundamental problem that thwarted his attempts to mediate these two, perhaps unreconcilable, teachings. In the *De vocatione* he went to great lengths to affirm that God wills to save all. He repeatedly cited as evidence the general grace that is available to everyone. Nevertheless, general grace is not adequate for salvation. Special grace is also necessary, but God gives it efficaciously only to the elect. De Letter has suggested that had Prosper said that special grace was denied to some because these persons would refuse it, then the problem would have been far closer to resolution.[168] Prosper, however, was bound by an Augustinian view of election based on grace and not on merit, and finally this tenet won out over the doctrine of the divine will for universal salvation. Thus Prosper's final effort was not entirely successful because he was never freed from the doctrine of predestination, which, if accepted, seems inevitably to control the argument.

It was not merely Prosper's position, however, that had undergone alteration. The debate itself had changed both in terms of its participants and in terms of its character. On the Augustinian side Prosper had clearly become the spokesman following the death of Augustine. On the Semi-Pelagian side, however, a variety of characters emerged. John Cassian, of course, was the chief figure. Two priests from Genoa, Camille and Theodore, although apparently not opponents of Augustine, were at least sufficiently troubled by his teaching on grace to seek Prosper's interpretation of difficult passages from the African bishop's writing. Explicit opposition, however, came in two pamphlets, probably originating in the environs of Lérins, that caricatured the Augustinian position. Although no clear leader immediately emerged to fill the void created at the death of Cassian,

---

[167]De Letter, *The Call of All Nations,* 10-11; Cappuyns, "Le premier représentant de l'augustinisme médiéval, Prosper d'Aquitaine," 309-37.
[168]De Letter, *The Call of All Nations*, 17.

monks, priests, and perhaps others, were keenly disturbed by the Augustinian position on grace.

The evolution of the debate at this stage involved much more than simply a change in participants. The methods of argumentation also changed. The carefully reasoned and courteous arguments that Augustine and Cassian had presented were replaced at first by Prosper's somewhat unfair attack on Cassian. Later, in the pamphlets and Prosper's responses to them, there were misrepresentations by each side of the position of the other. The debate had degenerated into sloganeering, and neither argument was appreciably clarified or refined. With the *Auctoritates* the character of the debate changed once again, with the citation of authoritative sources replacing strident argumentation. The establishment of a tradition was becoming an important means for advancing one's case. One side effect, however, was that the issues to be debated were limited to those for which authorities could be found. One further shift in methodology can be seen in the *De vocatione* in which Prosper attempted, however unsuccessfully, to mediate the two opposing views.

This attempt at mediation could not have been convincing to either side, however. On the one hand, Prosper suggested that human agency is not itself supplied and directed by grace, but on the other hand, he insisted upon the sovereignty of grace. At the conclusion of this stage of the debate, therefore, no acceptable resolution had been found for the opposing arguments. The respective roles of divine grace and human agency in determining human destiny had yet to be satisfactorily defined.

As a footnote to this discussion of Prosper's efforts in defense of Augustine, it should be noted that perhaps his most significant contribution to the Semi-Pelagian controversy arose not from the explicitly interpretive pieces that we have considered but from a collection of almost four hundred passages from Augustine's works that Prosper not only selected but also edited. Lacking any reference to predestination and drawn from a range of sources, the *Liber sententiarum* would provide crucial elements of the language by which the controversy was to be resolved in 529 at the Council of Orange.[169]

---

[169]Rudolf Lorenz, "Der Augustinismus Prospers von Aquitanien," *Zeitschrift für Kirchengeschichte* 73 (1962): 217-52; Cappuyns, "Le premier reprèsentant de l'augustinisme médiéval, Prosper d'Aquitaine," 334-37.

Chapter 5

The Diffusion of the Debate

Introduction

With the death of John Cassian in 435 and Prosper's subsequent move to Rome, the first phase of the Semi-Pelagian controversy in southern Gaul came to an end. It was not that the dispute had been resolved to anyone's satisfaction or that either party had prevailed, but the character of the controversy underwent a transformation. There were several reasons for this changed condition.

First, the principals in the dispute changed. On the Semi-Pelagian side, no one immediately filled the void left by Cassian's death. It was not until almost half a century later that Faustus of Riez began to emerge as the primary antipredestinarian voice. Among the Augustinians themselves Prosper remained the spokesman, but his *De vocatione omnium gentium*, written in Rome and not until about 450, had a mediating tone that had been lacking in his earlier works composed in the heat of battle. Furthermore, after his death, around 463, no obvious successor arose until Fulgentius of Ruspe, early in the next century.

Second, as the conditions surrounding the change of principals indicate, the controversy itself had subsided. The dissipation of intensity was primarily due to temporal reasons but also to geographical ones. From the arrival of the *De correptione et gratia* in Gaul in 427/28 to the publication of Prosper's *Contra collatorem* and the two sets of *responsiones*, between 432 and 434, the dispute was at its highest pitch. In contrast, the major publications thereafter by Prosper (450), Faustus (474/5),[1] and Fulgentius (523) encompassed more than three-fourths of a century, with considerable lapses of time between them. Furthermore, although in the past Augustine's aid had been summoned from Africa and Pope Celestine's from Rome, the argumentation had been centered in South Gaul. In the later stage, the major disputants themselves were scattered: Prosper in Rome, Faustus in South Gaul, and Fulgentius in North Africa. Thus, although the same geographical areas were still involved, the debate was no longer concentrated in any one of them. It was, instead, diffused throughout them all.

---

[1]Gustave Weigel, *Faustus of Riez*, (Philadelphia: Dolphin, 1938) 108-109. Weigel provided an extensive discussion of the problem of dating Faustus's *De gratia Dei*. See also Thomas A. Smith, *De gratia* (Notre Dame: Univ. of Notre Dame Press, 1990) 56-59.

Third, the changed character of the Western empire had become increasingly difficult to ignore. Or, if it were ostensibly ignored, it nevertheless took its toll on the church, the population, and inevitably the debate itself. Problems of physical and cultural survival against the barbarians, decreasing literacy, the Arian threat, and the disappearance of the Western empire all affected the lives of the participants in this controversy. If nothing else, the attention and energy of the church were distracted from a doctrinal dispute which few understood and no one had been able to resolve.[2]

One feature of the changed social conditions that was especially pertinent to the Semi-Pelagian controversy was the role of the church as an instrument of stability and of social continuity. With the withdrawal and disintegration of Roman rule, the church, particularly through its bishops, became the primary institution for the maintenance of order.[3] As the case of Faustus and later that of Caesarius will demonstrate, bishops not only negotiated with barbarian chieftains but also made provision for the poor and dispossessed.

The church also served a somewhat ambiguous role as the continuator and preserver of classical culture. On the one hand, bishops, such as Faustus and Fulgentius, who had been educated in the classical tradition, were able to make use of that training in their service to the church. Both of these men, of course, employed their literary skills in the Semi-Pelagian debate itself, and Faustus, a skilled orator, also became a celebrated preacher.[4] On the other hand, the church tended to view a fundamentally pagan education with some suspicion. Monasteries, of course, were educational institutions of a sort. Yet although they might provide rudimentary instruction, they were designed to train those whose goal it was to remove themselves from the surrounding culture, not those who wished to be grounded in it. It was sacred texts and works on asceticism that were most highly valued. St. Honoratus at Lérins, which was known for its vigorous

---

[2]For surveys of conditions at this time see Herwig Wolfram, *History of the Goths*, 2nd ed., trans. Thomas J. Dunlap (Berkeley: University of California Press, 1988) 117-246; E. A. Thompson, *Romans and Barbarians: The Decline of Western Europe* (Madison: University of Wisconsin Press, 1982) 23-57; Patrick J. Geary, *Before France and Germany: The Creation and Transformation of the Merovingian World* (Oxford: Oxford University Press, 1988) 3-76; J. M. Wallace-Hadrill, *The Barbarian West: The Early Middle Ages* (New York: Harper & Row, 1962) 21-42; Walter Goffart, *Barbarians and Romans A.D. 418–584* (Princeton: Princeton University Press, 1980) 3-39, 103-26.
[3]T. A. Smith, 21-29; Wolfram, 193-202; Geary, 69-73; R. A. Markus, *Christianity and the Roman World* (London: Thames and Hudson, 1974) 141-61; L. Musset, *The Germanic Invasions: The Making of Europe A.D. 400–600*, trans. E. and C. James (University Park: Pennsylvania State University Press, 1975) 125-34.
[4]William G. Rusch, *The Later Latin Fathers* (London: Duckworth, 1977) 180; Weigel, 76-77; G.-G. Lapeyre, *Saint Fulgence de Ruspe: un évêque catholique africain sous la domination vandale* (Paris: P. Lethielleux, 1929) 91-95.

theological discussion, especially its notable contribution to the Semi-Pelagian debate, does seem to have been a center for the preservation of classical culture. Its monks had access to translations of Greek texts, but neither in this nor in other Gallic monasteries does the Greek language seem to have been taught.[5]

Inevitably, the transformation of social conditions and the changes in leadership affected the character of the controversy. The purpose of this chapter will be to examine the course of this new phase of the debate.

The Continuing Controversy

Although the monastery at Lérins has been regularly identified as a bastion of Semi-Pelagianism, it is important to note that Faustus, the Lérinian figure best known for having advocated a Semi-Pelagian point of view, became associated with the controversy only after he had left the monastery. It was as bishop of Riez that he wrote the *De gratia*.[6] The participation of another monk from Lérins, Vincent, remains the subject of dispute.[7]

Vincent has generally been identified as the author of the *Commonitorium*, which was written under the pseudonym Peregrinus in 434 but was attributed to Vincent of Lérins by Gennadius of Marseilles in *De scriptoribus ecclesiasticis* around 495. Little is known about Vincent, but he seems to have been a Gaul who had held secular employment before entering the monastery.[8]

Vincent wrote the *Commonitorium* prior to Prosper's *Auctoritates*. Both works displayed what was to become a dominant feature of the later stages of the controversy: a concern for the identification and rejection of novelty. Although the *Commonitorium* has regularly been classified as a Semi-Pelagian, even anti-Augustinian, document, the case is not clear-cut. Vincent's title indicates a broad purpose: *Commonitorium primum Peregrini pro Catholicae fidei antiquitate et universitate adversus prophanas omnium haereticorum novitates.* As commoni-

---

[5]P. Courcelle, "Nouveaux aspects de la culture lérinienne," *Revue des études latines* 46 (1968): 379-409; P. Courcelle, *Late Latin Writers and Their Greek Sources*, trans. Harry E. Wedeck (Cambridge MA: Harvard University Press, 1969) 235, 261-62. Courcelle spoke of a renewal of interest in Greek culture, specifically Neoplatonism, in the last third of the fifth century; Neoplatonic asceticism was also known in Latin through Cassian. For a different point of view, see Pierre Riché, *Education and Culture in the Barbarian West*, trans. John J. Contreni (Columbia SC: University of South Carolina Press, 1976) 100-104. See also Prinz, 452-61.

[6]Riché, 103-104; T. A. Smith, 55-59.

[7]William O'Connor, "Saint Vincent of Lérins and Saint Augustine," 123-257, traced the history of interpretation of Vincent's work.

[8]C. A. Heurtley, Introduction, *Commonitory of Vincent of Lérins*, Nicene and Post-Nicene Fathers, s.s., 11:127. All English translations of quotations from the *Commonitorium* will be taken from Heurtley. See Weigel, 49-50n.77.

torium means "a letter of instructions" or "a means of reminding,"[9] Vincent's intent was to provide a set of guidelines by which doctrine might be tested and the purity of the Catholic faith might be maintained. The test consisted of an appeal to the common memory of the church. The foundation of that memory lies in Scripture, which Vincent understood to be the origin of all right doctrine and the final criterion for orthodoxy. Nevertheless, as Scripture is subject to a variety of interpretations, these interpretations must be validated by a further test, the tradition of the church.[10] Here Vincent offered his famous rule: "we hold that faith which has been believed everywhere, always, by all" (*quod ubique, quod semper, quod ab omnibus*). He amplified:

> This rule we shall observe if we follow universality, antiquity, consent. We shall follow universality if we confess that one faith to be true, which the whole church throughout the world confesses; antiquity, if we in no wise depart from these interpretations which it is manifest were notoriously held by our holy ancestors and fathers; consent, in like manner, if in antiquity itself we adhere to the consentient definitions and determinations of all, or at least of almost all priests and doctors.[11]

These guidelines in themselves are hardly sufficient to justify numbering Vincent among the Semi-Pelagians. Other evidence, however, indicates that one novelty against which the guidelines were directed was a particular form of predestinarian teaching on grace.[12] Vincent did not mention Augustine by name, but he assailed a distorted version of Augustine's teaching that an otherwise unidentified group or sect was propagating.[13] As reported by Vincent, the group taught that there is peculiar grace that is available to a select number. These persons, without making any effort of their own, i.e., without asking, seeking, or knocking, are so protected by this special grace that it is impossible for them to fall.[14] The fact that the adherents of this novel doctrine employed wrongly interpreted citations from Scripture compounded the problem.[15]

---

[9]Charlton T. Lewis and Charles Short, *A Latin Dictionary* (Oxford: Clarendon Press, 1975) 382.

[10]Vincent, *Commonitorium primum Peregrini pro Catholicae fidei antiquitate et universitate adversus prophanas omnium haereticorum novitates* 2, 29.

[11]*Comm.* 2.

[12]E. Griffe, "Pro Vincentio Lerinensi," *Bulletin de littérature ecclésiastique* 62 (1961) 26-71, argued that Nestorius was the true object of Vincent's attack.

[13]He seemed to suggest that there was a group or sect that held a distorted version of Augustine's teaching. See *Comm.* 26; Amann, "Semi-pélagiens," *Dictionnaire de théologie catholique* 14/2:1819-22; Markus, "The Legacy of Pelagius," 220; O'Connor, 205-206.

[14]*Comm.* 26.

[15]*Comm.* 26.

Vincent was probably keenly aware that the position that he was attacking was a distorted version of Augustine's predestinarian teaching. Nevertheless, the language that he employed in speaking even of this skewed Augustinianism corresponded closely to the language that Prosper had used when writing to Augustine to tell him of the charges made against him by the Massilians.[16] Three references are significant. First, Prosper had presented a criticism made by the opposition: To teach that there is a divine decree which precedes the human will has the effect of stifling human effort. Second, he had reported their own teaching that the grace of creation enables persons to seek, ask, and knock. Through their natural capacities persons can attain to the grace of regeneration in Christ. Finally, Prosper had warned that, although Augustine had used countless citations from Scripture as proof of his argument, his opponents countered these with *vetustas*, antiquity.[17] Augustine himself, in responding to Prosper in the *De dono perseverantiae*, had employed similar language when he argued against the error of his Gallic opponents: The seeking, asking, and knocking are a divine gift; grace precedes all merits.[18] The vocabulary of *petendo, quaerendo, pulsando* highlights an area of contention that was crucial to all.

To the extent that the *Commonitorium* was directed against even a distorted form of Augustine's teaching on grace, its point was to judge it according to the tests that Vincent provided. The doctrine could be supported by the first test, Scripture, but only if Scripture were interpreted in a novel way; thus the doctrine could be demonstrated to be fallacious according to Vincent's second test, which by requiring fidelity to the tradition eliminated novelty. To reinforce his point, Vincent quoted from the letter that Pope Celestine had written, at the request of Prosper and Hilary, to the Gallic bishops: "Let novelty cease to assail antiquity."[19] As noted in chapter 4, the letter was ambiguous and was capable of being employed by both sides in the debate. In this instance Vincent quoted it, presumably somewhat ironically, against the novelty of distorted Augustinianism.

From the *Commonitorium* it probably is not possible to determine Vincent's views on what Augustine actually did teach.[20] Yet even in arguing against skewed Augustinianism, Vincent was rejecting any predestinarian fatalism and any elitism of grace that would sever the connection between purposeful striving

---

[16]Heurtley, app. 2, 158.

[17]Prosper, *Ep.* 225.3,4.

[18]Augustine, *De don. pers.* 64.

[19]*Comm.* 33, citing Celestine, *Ep.* 21 *ad episcopos Gallorum*; cf. Heurtley, app. 3, 159.

[20]O'Connor, "Saint Vincent of Lérins and Saint Augustine," 123-257, has argued that Vincent held Augustine in high esteem. See also Markus, "The Legacy of Pelagius," 219-20. Jules Lebreton, "Saint Vincent de Lérins et saint Augustin," *Recherches de science religieuse* 20 (1940): 368-69.

for perfection and divine reward. A doctrine of an apparently arbitrary election was unacceptable to him.

The formula of *quod ubique, quod semper, quod ab omnibus* that Vincent provided the church, although important in ecclesiastical history, was hardly crucial to the development of the Semi-Pelagian controversy. It did call attention once more, however, to the problem with which Augustine and his followers had been plagued from the start: the apparent discontinuity of their position with the tradition of the church. Appeals to Scripture were inadequate, for Scripture could be variously interpreted. A doctrine also needed to have authoritative standing in the tradition, a tradition that was accepted by all as binding. Of course, that authoritative tradition might itself be variously understood. Although the *Commonitorium* was not simply an antipredestinarian work, it certainly could have been used to support that position.

Vincent's overarching intent had been the establishment of a standard by which the normative belief of the church might be secured and aberration rejected. This desire for the clear identification of tradition was hardly peculiar to him. As already noted, in the *Auctoritates* Prosper's aim was the compilation of authoritative statements of the church's faith concerning the interaction of grace and human nature. The *Auctoritates*, of course, followed the *Commonitorium* and may have been something of a response to the challenge laid down by the latter. This emphasis on the establishing and securing of a tradition was to have noticeable effect on the subsequent character of the controversy. As each side attempted to define the tradition in a way favorable to its own interests, the result was the generation of competing traditions. As we will see, Faustus, although a Semi-Pelagian, was engaged in the task of threading in and around the competing definitions. He was not seeking to mediate but to find a middle ground.

The effort to secure an approved tradition was not confined to the Semi-Pelagian controversy. Manifestations of this phenomenon can be located among highly diverse figures over a prolonged period of time. For example, near the beginning of his collection of sermons, Caesarius of Arles presented the trinitarian faith of the church. The statement is entitled "The Beginning of the Catholic Faith of St. Athanasius, Bishop."[21] Although Caesarius was instrumental in the resolution of the Semi-Pelagian dispute, in this instance at least, his appeal to tradition was unrelated to the controversy. His intent was to establish himself as orthodox and to define the authoritative tradition for those who must preach. The instrument that he used to accomplish his task was, with only minimal changes in the wording, what is known as the Athanasian Creed or *Quicunque*.[22]

---

[21]Caesarius, *Serm.* 3, *Incipit Fides Catholica Sancti Athanasii Episcopi.*

[22]J. N. D. Kelly, *The Athanasian Creed* (New York and Evanston: Harper & Row, 1964) 35-37.

Kelly has dated the composition of this creed as "sometime between 440 and the high noon of Caesarius's activity." Although its actual author has not been identified, "there is every probability that the creed was composed in his [Caesarius's] milieu, and quite possibly at his instigation."[23]

The importance of trinitarian creedal formulations during the fifth through the seventh centuries is, in fact, further evidence of the zeal in the West to secure an authoritative tradition. For example, the collection of sermons of Columbanus ca. 543–615), a missionary from Ireland to Gaul, also began with an explication of the trinitarian faith of the church.[24]

As another illustration of the attempt to guarantee a tradition, one might point to Cassiodorus, who, late in the sixth century, encouraged that monks be instructed in the work of Cassian. At the same time, however, he warned that Cassian had erred in his understanding of the freedom of the will. Prosper's warning of Cassian's failing was accepted by Cassiodorus, and presumably by others, as authoritative.[25] Cassiodorus had also worked to cleanse Pelagius's commentary on the Pauline epistles of its heresy.[26] A kind of censorship had thus begun in the continuing effort to define a normative tradition.

To return to discussion of the controversy itself, probably around 450 in Italy an obviously antipredestinarian piece, *Praedestinatus*, was written. It thus approximated in time Prosper's final, mediating work, the *De vocatione omnium gentium*, but was itself anything but mediating. It appears to have been in line with the objections to which Prosper had earlier responded in that it misrepresented the Augustinian position, caricaturing both the teaching and its consequences. For example, it presented the elect as the recipients of salvation, even in some cases against their will, and the nonelect as damned by an eternal decree despite their earnest efforts to gain beatitude. The circumstances surrounding the production and reception of *Praedestinatus* are not known,[27] but its very existence does

---

[23]Kelly, 123.

[24]Columbanus, *Instructio I, Sancti Columbani Opera,* ed. G. S. M. Walker, Scriptores Latini Hiberniae, 2 (The Dublin Institute for Advanced Studies, 1970) 60-67.

[25]Cassiodorus, *Inst.* 1.29.2.

[26]James J. O'Donnell, *Cassiodorus* (Berkeley: University of California Press, 1979) 218, 232-33. In the late sixth century Cassiodorus worked to remove heretical ideas from the writings collected for the Vivarium. He began revision of the commentary on the epistles that had been written by Pelagius. Although transmitted to him as the work of Gelasius, he recognized its Pelagian character (*Inst.* 1.8.1). His work on the commentary was confined to Romans, but the enterprise was continued by his monks after his death. See Cassiodorus Senator, *Divine Letters* 1.8.1, *An Introduction to Divine and Human Readings,* trans. Leslie Webber Jones, p. 90.

[27]D. H. von Schubert, *Der sogenannte "Praedestinatus";* G. Morin, "Arnobe le Jeune," 315-24; M. Abel, "Le *Praedestinatus* et le pélagianisme," 5-25.

show the vitriolic extreme that the debate reached in the mid-fifth century, even outside of Gaul. The issue was neither resolved nor forgotten.

Whoever the author of the *Praedestinatus* may have been, by far the most outstanding spokesman for the Semi-Pelagian cause following John Cassian was Faustus. The man's origin has been subject to some speculation. He was probably from Britain, and immigrated with his family to Roman Gaul, perhaps Riez, while he was still quite young. Weigel speculated that he was born around 403-404 and was educated in rhetoric and philosophy. When he was about twenty years old, he entered St. Honoratus.[28] In 433 Faustus succeeded Maximus, the abbot of Lérins, who had become bishop of Riez. About 457 he succeeded him again, this time as bishop. It was in 434, soon after Faustus became abbot, that Vincent, one of the monks at Lérins, wrote the *Commonitorium*.[29] Sidonius Apollinaris generously extolled Faustus in poetry and correspondence. The Faustus he presented remained an ascetic even after becoming a bishop. He often made austere retreats and at times returned to Lérins where he continued to serve the monks. The picture that we receive is of a man deeply marked by that monastic tradition and monastic theology of which Cassian was the spokesman and at the same time a continuator of the Gallic line of monk-bishop. In his public role as bishop he worked to relieve the results of social disintegration caused by the barbarian invasions and the breakdown in the Roman system. He was exemplary in his ability to organize the resources of the church to benefit the poor, the sick, and the traveler. Finally, Sidonius portrayed him as an excellent preacher, one remarkable in his oratorical skills and learning.[30] It was probably these last capacities that contributed to his employment in both ecclesiastical and secular diplomacy. In 462/3 the council of Arles sent him to Pope Hilary to speak on behalf of issues affecting the Gallic church, and in 474 he served as a negotiator, along with several other bishops, in the siege of Auvergne by Euric,

---

[28]Weigel, 11-15, 22; N. K. Chadwick, "Intellectual Contacts Between Britain and Gaul in the Fifth Century" and "Note on Faustus and Riocatus," in *Studies in Early British History* (Cambridge: Cambridge University Press, 1959) 224-27, 254-63.

[29]Weigel, 20, 54, 57, 74-75. Weigel suggested that the *Commonitorium*, although written by Vincent, reflected the conversations of the monks of Lérins and that Faustus surely would have contributed to these conversations.

[30]For Sidonius's view of Faustus, see, e.g., Sidonius Apollinaris, *Carmen eucharisticum ad Faustum Reiensem episcopum; Ep.* 9.3; 9.9. Pierre de Labriolle, *Histoire de la littérature latine chrétienne*, 3d ed. [rev. et aug. by G. Bardy], 2 (Paris: Société d'édition "Les belles-lettres," 1947) 654-55. N. K. Chadwick, *Poetry and Letters in Early Christian Gaul*, 193-96; cf. Weigel, 76-79, 82. Griffe, "Nouveau plaidoyer pour Fauste de Riez," *Bulletin de littérature ecclésiastique* 74 (1973): 187-92. For an assessment of the compassion exercised by the church, especially through its bishops, see R. P. C. Hanson, "The Reaction of the Church to the Collapse of the Western Roman Empire in the Fifth Century," *Vigiliae Christianae* 26 (1972): 283-85.

the leader of the Visigoths. Faustus was banished from his see, probably in 476/7 when Euric gained control of all Provence. His lengthy exile, which was spent in an unidentified monastery, in all likelihood ended at the death of Euric in 485. He returned to Riez and died sometime between 490 and 500.[31]

The impression that this picture generates is of a man whose life spanned the fifth century and illuminated the character of the age. Educated in a classical tradition somewhat diminished but still vigorous, trained in the growing monastic movement which was beginning to stabilize and mature in Gaul, elevated to the episcopacy where he both maintained his ascetic discipline and functioned as an effective public figure expanding the role of the church in the crises of the day, Faustus was thoroughly a man of his own era, more specifically, an exemplar of its best features. As such he was highly esteemed during his life. Apparently it was only after his death that several of his teachings became an occasion for dismay. One peculiar view, espoused in a short tract and again in correspondence, was that as only God is spirit, the soul must be material.[32] The theological stance with which we are concerned, however, was his Semi-Pelagianism, in which he expressed the opinion generally held by his contemporaries in Gaul.

His views in this regard were best developed in the *De gratia*, a work dedicated to Leontius, the bishop of Arles, and written in late 474 or early 475. This writing was to serve as an explanation of the teaching on grace and predestination of the Council of Arles in 473 and the Council of Lyons in 474. The former council had dealt with the strongly predestinarian position of Lucidus, a presbyter in Faustus's diocese.[33] Before the council met, Faustus had attempted unsuccessfully to convince Lucidus to change his views, even sending him a letter with a series of anathemas to which Lucidus was to subscribe.[34] Subsequently he had been an active participant when the Council of Arles condemned the teaching of Lucidus and sent him a somewhat different list of anathemas that he was to sign.

The letter of submission that Lucidus sent in reply to the bishops denounced elements of Pelagianism as well as predestinationism. The anathemas it contained were presumably those which the bishops themselves had sent to Lucidus. If we

---

[31]For correspondence related to these events, see, e.g., Sidonius *Ep.* 7.7; Faustus, *Ep.* 6, 9. See also Wolfram, 199-200; Wiegel, 113-19; N. K. Chadwick, *Poetry and Letters in Early Christian Gaul*, 198.

[32]Faustus, *De spiritu sancto, Ep.* 3; see T. A. Smith, 56, n. 92.

[33]Cf. C. Munier, *Concilia Galliae* A. 314-A. 506, *CCSL* 148.159-61, and Griffe, *La gaule chrétienne*, 2:289 for other dates for these councils.

[34]Faustus, *Ep.* 1; Munier, *CCSL* 148.159. See T. A. Smith, 56-59, for a discussion of the origin of the letter and sequence of events surrounding the councils. For an analysis of Faustus's understanding of Lucidus's views and the relation of Lucidus's views to those of Augustine, see Marianne Djuth, "Faustus of Riez: *Initium bonae voluntatis,*" *Augustinian Studies* 21 (1990): 35-53.

can assume that Lucidus was not an entirely isolated figure but that his views were representative of a type of Gallic Augustinianism, then the antipredestinarian anathemas may reveal the character of this extreme form of Augustinianism. Among the rejected teachings were the following: the operation of grace apart from human effort, the loss of free will as a consequence of the fall, limited atonement, damnation effected by the divine will and foreknowledge, baptism as inefficacious in the case of some, predestination to damnation.[35] At issue in these anathemas was the integrity of human agency. The council required that divine will and action should in no way be construed as undercutting the necessary contribution of the human agent in the determination of that agent's destiny. The Council of Arles in 473 was thus rejecting a manifestation of Augustinianism that was in some respects a significant departure from the teachings of both Augustine and Prosper. By anathematizing specific Pelagian teachings, the council attempted to locate the authoritative tradition between the two extremes that it condemned.[36]

In response Lucidus repudiated his former position, and Faustus, at the request of his fellow bishops, wrote a work on grace to explain the position adopted by this council.[37] It appears that Faustus submitted this document to the Council of Lyons but that events between that council and the one of the previous year at Arles made necessary a fuller treatment of the doctrine of grace and predestination. As a result, Faustus composed the *De gratia* which presumably contained the earlier work.

Weigel has speculated that the events that necessitated the elaboration may have been a protest by Augustinians that the position of the Council of Arles had, in effect, anathematized Augustinianism instead of the doctrine of predestination alone. Such an attack on Augustine in general had been unacceptable since Prosper's *Auctoritates*, although the issue of predestination was still open. Faustus's *De gratia* may well have been an attempt to protect himself and these two Gallic councils against such protests.[38] Furthermore, as an explanation of the

---

[35]Faustus, *Ep.* 2; T. A. Smith, 62-65; Weigel, 101-102; John Keble, *The Works of Mr. Richard Hooker*, 2 vols. (New York: D. Appleton and Company, 1845) 2:51. Mathisen, 265, pointed out that Ludicus would not necessarily have held all the views that he was forced to reject.

[36]For an investigation of the complexity of the Lucidus affair, the participants at the Council of Arles, and the various degrees of Pelagian, anti-Pelagian, Augustinian, and anti-Augustinian sentiment represented, see Mathisen, 246-61.

[37]Faustus, *Prologus de gratia*; Weigel, 101-102; Adolph Harnack, *History of Dogma*, 5:252-53.

[38]Weigel, 102-103; for an extended and illuminating examination of the background of the *De gratia*, see T. A. Smith, 21-60. Mathisen, 264-68, emphasized the desire of Faustus and his supporters to condemn Pelagianism more explicitly than had been done by the Council of Arles.

teachings of the councils against both Pelagianism and severe Augustinianism, the treatise was an attempt to locate a middle position between the two unacceptable extremes.

Faustus of Riez: *De gratia*

Faustus stated that his purpose was to chart a middle course between the Pelagian error of asserting human work as adequate in itself for the achievement of salvation and the predestinarian error of asserting divine grace as the single effective element in the salvific process. In contrast to these extreme positions, the true course, Faustus insisted, required the retention of both elements: works and grace. Human efforts and divine assistance are both necessary.[39] In other words, he was continuing Cassian's teaching that all is to be ascribed to grace and all is to be ascribed to free will.

He briefly stated his argument against the Pelagians. Their basic error lay in the assumption that human nature is sufficient by itself to the attainment of salvation. Such an assumption denied both the need of Adam for grace before he fell and the impairment of nature as a consequence of Adam's fall.[40] It was the second element of the denial that was of greater importance to Faustus, for, in effect, it called into question the very concept of original sin. This denigration of the significance of original sin was underscored by the fact that Pelagius had disallowed any connection between Adam's mortality and his sin: Adam would have died regardless of whether or not he had ever sinned, for mortality is intrinsic to human nature as created. By implication, Faustus noted, death would not be attributable to human sin as elicited by the envious entrapment of the devil, nor would it be a matter of punishment. In fact, with original sin denied or at least its significance sorely diminished, there would be no occasion for such punishment, and, in fact, Pelagius denied that infants were bound by sin and thus in need of baptism.

Faustus found a double difficulty arising from this rejection of the concept of original sin. First, if death is an element of human nature as created, then God, as creator, must be held responsible for death. Second, if humankind is not held in the grip of original sin, then there is no need for a redeemer.[41] The crea-

---

[39]Faustus, *De gratia* 1.1. For a helpful summary of this work, see P. Godet, "Fauste de Riez," *Dictionnaire de théologie catholique* 5/2:2101-2105. For a survey of the response to Faustus's teaching on grace, see T. A. Smith, *De gratia*, 1-20. For the historical placement of Faustus's teaching on grace, see Anton Koch, *Der heilige Faustus, Bischof von Riez: Eine dogmengeschichtliche Monographie* (Stuttgart: Roth'sche, 1895) 44-74.

[40]*De gr.* 1.1.

[41]*De gr.* 1.1.

tive and redemptive work of the Trinity has been effectively undercut, a result which Faustus could not accept. In contrast, he affirmed the goodness of human nature as created and thus the goodness of the creator, the reality of original sin, and the consequent need for the grace of redemption. Human effort without the daily gracious assistance of God is not sufficient for salvation.[42]

Faustus argued that the source of original sin lay in Adam's disobedience to the divine law. This disobedience arose from cupidity, the prideful desire for divinity. Immortality and purity were lost; all humankind was subjected both to death and to the corruption of passion.[43] As a result, all persons are born mortal, and all are born through the now sinful, because passionate, process of generation. Adam, Eve, and Christ were the only persons whose creation was not the outcome of passion; thus they were the only ones not born in sin. It is, therefore, through our fleshly generation that original sin is transmitted. Even procreation from baptized parents is subject to the same affliction; thus for each person a second, nonfleshly birth is required by which divine adoption and regeneration are effected. This second birth is brought about by the Spirit in baptism.[44]

By locating the transmission of original sin in the act of procreation, Faustus has made inescapable the proposition that all are born in sin and are in need of the grace of redemption through baptism. No one is immune, not even infants incapable of actual sin. By virtue of our birth in the flesh we all stand in need of grace. Faustus has thus taken up and reiterated one of Augustine's fundamental themes. Pelagianism has been effectively refuted and with it all idea of a human agency effective for the good independent of the assistance of divine grace.

Pelagianism, however, was not the present danger for Faustus. Predestinarianism was, and it was apparently a far more subtle enemy; thus Faustus devoted the bulk of the *De gratia* to his criticism of the view that salvation is effected by grace alone apart from any requirement of works. Human destiny must not be understood as entirely a human achievement, as Pelagianism would lead one to believe, but neither must it be understood as entirely a divine achievement, as predestinarianism would imply. Instead, Faustus sought the middle course between extremes so that human destiny could be seen to depend upon both human and divine agency.

His insistence that salvation is the accomplishment of both grace and works had a negative and a positive aspect. Negatively, it was an argument against the determinism that he believed to be entailed in the notion of predestination by grace. Positively, it was an argument for human responsibility. Stated differently, Faustus in no way denied the necessity of grace, but he located its operation

---

[42]*De gr.* 1.1.
[43]*De gr.* 1.2.
[44]*De gr.* 1.2.

within the old monastic scheme of free will, divine judgment, and reward or punishment. The disciplines of transformation of the will that stood at the heart of the monastic life were thereby safeguarded.

In arguing against determinism, Faustus attacked the predestinarians on their own turf from two basic fronts. First, he utilized scriptural passages dear to his opponents but interpreted them in such a way as to make his own case. Second, he appropriated the doctrine of foreknowledge by defining it in a way suitable to his purposes. Both tactics were general enough to allow for the inclusion of specific assaults with regard to particular issues.

First, in making his case against determinism, Faustus undertook the necessary task of examining passages from Scripture which the Augustinians had seen as evidence of the sovereignty of grace. For example, passages that were interpreted by the Augustinians to mean that all is of grace alone, such as "it depends not upon man's will or exertion, but upon God's mercy,"[45] received a more moderate explanation from Faustus. He characterized their intent as that of curbing the pride of those who relied on human effort alone. These persons attempted justification through the law and did not acknowledge their need for God's help.[46] Faustus's interpretation would hardly have satisfied the Augustinians. The latter acknowledged that one purpose of such passages was to inculcate humility, but they took them as literal statements of the overriding character of the work of grace.

Another scriptural reference important to the Augustinians was the image of the vessels of honor and the vessels of abuse.[47] Augustine had understood the image to be evidence of predestination. In contrast, Faustus interpreted the passage as being indicative of the human capacity to change. He insisted that it is possible for the vessel of abuse, with divine assistance, to become a vessel of honor. One is a vessel of abuse through personal guilt. This guilt appears to be entirely the consequence of actual rather than inherited sin, although Faustus was not explicit on this point. The good that the individual possessed at birth but has subsequently lost is still to be found within the self. What appears necessary, therefore, is not the transformation of the self or of the will by means of grace but the rediscovery of the self or of the good will that has not been destroyed but only forgotten or hidden within the person. Grace contributes to the process of rediscovery, but its contribution is that of assisting human zeal in its self-reformation.[48] Through Christ the desired good is attained.[49] On the other hand, a vessel

---

[45]Rom. 9:16.
[46]*De gr.* 1.9.
[47]Rom. 9:21; 2 Tim. 2:20-21.
[48]*De gr.* 1.11.
[49]*De gr.* 1.9.

of honor is also able, by free choice, to become a vessel of abuse, and it would appear that this capacity to change from one condition to the other remains until death.[50]

Faustus's argument here has several significant aspects. First, he offered both a hope and a warning. The former was given to the despair of a sinner who desires to be converted to the good; the latter, to the false confidence of one who is convinced of possessing salvation. Second, he has given the individual the responsibility for personal salvation or damnation, although he acknowledged that grace must assist in the attainment of the former. He has thus reestablished the link between action and outcome by defining a place for human agency. He has replaced the inscrutability and determinism of the divine decrees by the presumed security of personal autonomy. In other words, in contrast to Augustine who believed that final security and intelligibility reside only in God,[51] Faustus argued that eternal reward and punishment are afforded to human deserts. The outcome of an action is the logical result of that action. Third, he has characterized the sinfulness of the human condition as external to fallen nature, similar to an undesirable garment that can be put on or taken off at will. The Augustinian sense of sin as an enslavement of the will that requires an utter transformation of our internal condition entailed a view of sin as pervasive, internal corruption. The extreme difference between an external, undesirable garment and internal corruption is the difference between something that can be remedied with effort and assistance and something that requires recreation, rebirth. The removal of a garment can be accomplished by the human agent with divine assistance, but rebirth is the work of deity within the human receptacle. The key is that these two views of sinfulness are correlated with two views of human agency and its effectiveness in the moral realm.

The difference just mentioned in the location of security, for the Augustinians and for Faustus, had a particular bearing on how each understood the redemptive work of Christ. For Faustus Christ, as redeemer, assists, repairs, heals the infirmity of nature consequent on sin and brings to perfection the gifts of creation.[52] Augustine had understood the purpose of the death of Christ to be that of cleansing sin and liberating humanity from the dominion of the devil. His Christology does, nevertheless, appear subservient to the divine decrees.[53] On the

---

[50]*De gr.* 1.11.

[51]See Brown, *Augustine of Hippo*, 403-405.

[52]*De gr.* 2.9,12; for an discussion of the relationship of the *gratia creatoris* and the *gratia salvatoris*, see T. A. Smith, 196-202. For the vocabulary of redemption used by Faustus, see Anton Koch, *Der heilige Faustus, Bishof von Riez*, 89-90n.6.

[53]According to Augustine, Christ, by his incarnation, righteous life, and sacrifice of his death, cleansed, healed, freed from captivity, imparted divinity, and overcame death for those who were to be justified (*De trin.* 4.2.4; 4.12.15; 4.13.17); he defeated the devil

other hand, Faustus's notion that Christ came in order to empower human self-reformation is not especially reassuring either. In the latter position, the activity of grace is dependent on the fragility of human decisions, whereas at least in the former position grace is dependent on the sovereignty of a God revealed as love in Christ. However, Faustus's argument does suggest a correlation between Christ's coming and the reestablishment of human agency.

The strength of Faustus's position lay in his insistence that Christ died for all. The universality of the divine will for salvation as expressed in 1 Timothy 2:4 received a far more credible interpretation from him than it had from the Augustinians. If some are not recipients of salvation, it is through their own refusal, for to all who earnestly seek, grace is given.[54] Obstinacy or hardening is a freely chosen response to the kindness and long-suffering of God and is in no way a matter of divine compulsion.[55] A careful division of responsibility must be maintained: It is of God to call and encourage; it is of the human person to be obedient, to follow.[56]

The case of Pharaoh, of course, was the prime example of hardening. Scripture speaks of God as hardening Pharaoh's heart, and Faustus, like Origen, Augustine, and Cassian before him, felt the onus of demonstrating how the example of Pharaoh was congruent with his own argument. Faustus saw the situation as that of Pharaoh's free reaction to divine activity. The fact that the Egyptian ruler made two responses to the two types of divine activity was evidence to Faustus that free human choice was at work.[57] In the face of divine severity, Pharaoh relented and released the Israelites; yet in response to divine graciousness, he rebelled and ordered the people back. Divine mercy, therefore, can be said to have hardened the ruler's heart, but it was indeed mercy and not compulsion. As the decision lay entirely with Pharaoh, so had the blame to be attributed to him as well.[58] As Faustus pointed out, the pity of God evokes emendation among the

---

and liberated Christians from enslavement to guilt (13.12.16; 13.18.23). Although both clusters of benefits of Christ's death are closely related, the former pertains somewhat more closely to the notion of obedient sacrifice and the latter to the notion of ransom in the sense of overcoming the devil. See Eugène Portalié, *A Guide to the Thought of Saint Augustine*, trans. Ralph J. Bastian (London: Burns and Oates, 1960) 161-73; Eugene TeSelle, *Augustine the Theologian* (London: Burns and Oates, 1970) 165-76; Albert Outler, "The Person and Work of Christ," in *A Companion to the Study of St. Augustine*, ed. Roy W. Battenhouse (Grand Rapids: Baker Books, 1979) 359-62.

[54]*De gr.* 1.16.
[55]*De gr.* 1.17.
[56]*De gr.* 1.18.
[57]Ex. 8:15, 9:27.
[58]*De gr.* 2.1.

obedient and hardening among the impenitent.[59] Such an interpretation of the case of Pharaoh was, of course, reminiscent of Origen, who had spoken of the operation of God through Moses as revealing, not causing, the hardening of Pharaoh.[60] Yet Faustus differed from Origen in that for Faustus the divine action was understood not simply to have revealed but also to have evoked the hardening or the softening of the heart. In other words, Faustus spoke of a more direct interaction between the divine agent and the human agent than had Origen.

In Christ's injunctions to pray[61] Faustus found further ammunition against determinism. The Augustinians held not only that salvation was by grace alone but also that grace is available only to those preordained to life. If both of these tenets are maintained, he argued, then the value of prayer becomes problematic. It is unnecessary for those chosen for beatitude and fruitless for those judged for damnation. How then is it to be explained that Christ has commanded prayer?[62]

By exposing this dilemma Faustus also exposed the weakness of a central Augustinian claim: since it is God who is addressed in prayers which request that the unbelievers may come to faith, the implication must be that God is the relevant agent. This claim makes human agency seem impotent and prayers for the unbeliever nonsensical. Furthermore, if the divine decrees are maintained, then the element of just judgment based on human action, including prayer, is lost, for divine judgment is now positioned before our birth rather than following our death.[63]

Successfully or not, Faustus battled determinism, first, by employing standard Semi-Pelagian interpretations of scriptural passages which, differently understood, would appear to undercut his case. But the battle was also carried to a second front, again on Augustinian turf. Faustus reinterpreted the doctrine of divine foreknowledge in such a way as to serve his own argument for the necessity of human agency in the outworking of human destiny. According to Faustus, God wills and assists the pursuit of the good while allowing the evil; in neither case is there any compulsion, but both are foreknown.[64] Specifically, divine foreknowledge pertains to the consequences of human actions: God foreknows that merits will result from good enacted by the human agent, good which is willed but not compelled by God. Merit and divine foreknowledge thus depend upon the character of human action, which may be either good or evil at any given time.[65] According to such an understanding, there is no compulsion in fore-

---

[59]*De gr.* 2.1.
[60]Origen, *De princ.* 3.1.10-11.
[61]Mk. 14:38; Lk. 21:36.
[62]*De gr.* 1.3.
[63]*De gr.* 1.3.
[64]*De gr.* 2.2.
[65]*De gr.* 2.2.

knowledge, but one is left to wonder if the concept has been robbed of its substance. Rather than being absolute and secure, divine foreknowledge is made contingent upon created action.

Faustus further insisted that if foreknowledge has to do with merit, then predestination pertains to reward for merit. The latter operates on the basis of the former, and in this operation it is the righteous judge of the content of the foreknowledge.[66] The human will still retains the freedom and responsibility of the choice whose merits God foreknows and whose reward God predestines.

If there is no necessity in divine foreknowledge and predestination, neither is there any in divine mercy and justice. The Augustinians had said that God showed mercy toward the elect and justice to the rest, and, of course, without God's mercy there could be no salvation. Such an apparently deterministic statement was unacceptable to Faustus, who insisted the Scripture provides repeated instances of the divine mercy and patience toward the obstinate. Their obstinacy, therefore, cannot be attributed to divine neglect, as he felt the Augustinians implied. Instead, with divine mercy available to all, obstinacy is entirely of human contrivance. Moreover, as God is just to the unrighteous, so is God just toward the righteous, rewarding their good work.[67] The outcome of human action is a just divine judgment whether the action be good or evil. The action itself is genuinely human, although no one lacks some measure of that divine mercy necessary for choosing the good.[68] To everyone grace has given the capacity to believe, but whether one believes or not is a function of the will.[69] Furthermore, in utter contrast to Augustine's doctrine of perseverance but fully in keeping with Faustus's emphasis on human freedom,[70] Faustus insisted that the benefit of salvation already conferred can be lost through a later departure from the good.[71] Never is judgment a matter of grace not given by God but always of grace not employed by the human person.

Again invoking a passage dear to the Augustinian argument and clearly aware of its harshest predestinarian interpretation, Faustus spoke of divine foreknowledge as disclosed in the case of Jacob and Esau.[72] He treated the story as

---

[66]*De gr.* 2.3.
[67]*De gr.* 2.4.
[68]*De gr.* 2.4.
[69]*De gr.* 2.5.
[70]*De gr.* 1.12.
[71]*De gr.* 2.5.
[72]*De gr.* 2.6; Rom. 9:9. Whether or not Faustus had actually read Augustine's teaching on this matter, he knew and rejected a predestinarian interpretation of the passage:
  in his verbis hoc vult intellegi gentiliciae persuasionis impietas, quod deus absque
  ullo inter malum et bonum moderatis examine non ordine regentis, sed iure
  dominantis illum affectu dignum reddat, hunc odio, illum recipiat studio, hunc

an allegory. Jacob represented the Gentiles and Esau the Jews. In other words, Jacob represented a people who would be faithful and Esau a people who would be unfaithful. Faustus interpreted this allegory in such a way that divine foreknowledge consists neither in compulsion nor in prejudgment. Instead, foreknowledge is the knowledge of the divine love that is given to faithfulness and of divine hatred given to unfaithfulness.[73] The faithfulness of Jacob is an obedience that involves works of grace,[74] that is, those works required and assisted by grace.[75] Works, therefore, are still required. Nevertheless, the works of the law by which the unfaithful attempt to justify themselves apart from the assistance of grace have been rejected.[76]

Successfully or not, Faustus had tried to refute a scriptural cornerstone of Augustine's teaching by making the concept of foreknowledge operate otherwise than it had operated for Augustine. He had also rejected the notion of an election independent of works. He did not understand grace to be the utterly gratuitous and inscrutable divine will to save at least some of the ungodly but the divine cooperation with human effort. Faustus had maintained the monastic insistence both that human striving is necessary and that the assistance and reward of grace are reliably given to that striving. His emphasis on human agency disallowed a divine determinism.

In arguing against Augustinianism as it posed a threat to the significance of human agency, Faustus's thesis was that salvation is the accomplishment of both grace and works. The negative side of that argument, his attack on determinism, has now been examined, with particular attention given to his utilization of Scripture and of the doctrine of divine foreknowledge. The positive side still remains to be considered: the case for human responsibility. Faustus developed this aspect of his argument by discussing the human condition in terms of its natural capacity, the consequences of the fall, and the redemptive work of Christ.

He affirmed that human nature as created has been impaired by the fall of Adam; however, impairment means weakness, not total incapacity. As evidence, he cited the case of Abel, who pleased God by his sacrifices. As Abel lived before the written law, his knowledge of how to please God must have arisen

---

excludat imperio, et inter duos perditos nulla consideratio laboris, nulla devotionis habeatur, sed unus sine ratione cessantibus officiis adsumatur, alter sine discretione damnetur. Ac sic dum in alterutro nec meriti existit materia nec delicti, aufertur omnino futuri causa iudicii.

Quod si haec rerum tam indigna confusio etiam a sensu humanae mentis aliena est, sollicitius requiramus, quid divinae conveniat apostolo disserente iustitiae.

[73]De gr. 2.6.
[74]De gr. 2.6.
[75]De gr. 2.4.
[76]De gr. 2.6; references to opera legis can be found in De gr. 1.4, 6, 9; 2.6.

from the law within him and from the faith given to him, both the gifts of God at creation.[77] Faith is a gift, yet not in the sense in which Augustine had understood it to be a gift but as Cassian had previously characterized it. For Faustus the capacity for faith is a gift of creation, presumably a natural capacity, which was weakened but not vitiated by the fall; thus it was not necessary that Abel receive the gift a second time, as the Augustinians presumably would have attested, in order for him to act in such a way as to please God. In a somewhat contorted argument, Faustus contended that free will was also given in creation. From Adam we have received that which is of nature, i.e., our sense characteristics that we as human beings hold in common with the animals. From the triune God we have received that which is of grace, the image of God. From this image (impaired in the fall but restored in the incarnation) derives the human capacity to know the good and to distinguish it from evil; our virtues comprise our likeness to God. Thus as God is righteousness, mercy, holiness by divine nature, a person can be just, merciful, and holy, yet not by nature but through having received these attributes by grace.[78]

I understand Faustus to have meant that the image of God and thus the capacity for knowledge of God and for free judgment remained after the fall, although blemished. Attainment of the likeness to God is dependent on the virtues acquired through the free choice of the good.[79] Election follows, not precedes, human decision as the remuneration for choosing the good;[80] a just punishment is given for the free choice of evil.[81] Abel, Enoch, and Noah are examples of those who lived according to the law of nature imprinted on the heart in creation[82] and thereby fulfilled the law of Moses even though it was not yet given.[83] It is by this law of nature, not utterly erased in anyone, that the wicked do make some virtuous judgments.[84] It is to this law of God[85] that faith was joined for salvation in various persons before the coming of Christ.

At all times, however, fulfillment of this law has required the assistance of grace. Moreover, in all its forms, law presupposes and addresses the free will, summoning it to good works. Faustus has succeeded in placing the law, and

---

[77]*De gr.* 2.8.

[78]*De gr.* 2.9.

[79]See Gerhardt B. Ladner, *The Idea of Reform: Its Impact on Christian Thought and Action in the Age of the Fathers* (Cambridge: Harvard University Press, 1959) 83-107, for a discussion of the distinction made in the early church between image and likeness.

[80]*De gr.* 2.9.

[81]*De gr.* 2.9.

[82]*Legem naturae, De gr.* 2.9.

[83]*Legem litterae, lex Moysi, De gr.* 2.9.

[84]*Regulis naturalibus, De gr.* 2.9.

[85]*De gr.* 2.9,10.

thereby the free will, within the context of grace. Such an arrangement Augustine either was never able to achieve or simply did not want.

To those who would argue against Faustus's position, saying that before the coming of Christ the law of nature did not suffice to lead nations to salvation, Faustus responded that nature, just as grace, is of God and thus is good, although he admitted that our nature as repaired in Christ is "repaired into better."[86] As evidence of the goodness of our nature even as fallen, Faustus argued that there are instances throughout our lives when the desires of the good will precede the work of grace. Grace is not needed at every step to precede and prepare the way.[87]

Faustus presumably would have known of Cassian's teaching that in certain instances the *ortus bonae voluntatis* may derive from human effort rather than from grace. Presumably he would also have been familiar with Prosper's somewhat inappropriate criticism that such a possibility creates two classes of Christians: those whose turn to faith is initiated by God and those who initiate their own conversion. In the latter cases nature would not require the preparation of grace.[88] Faustus distanced himself from Cassian on this point by stating that the beginning of the good will, as well as its consumation, lies with God. Calling by God precedes the decision of the will to seek God and thereby to obey the call. Similarly, the reward for an obedient human response is also from God. Obedience itself, however, lies with the person. Of its own power the will is able to respond so that the will's desire for grace precedes that grace.[89] Between the divine call and the divine reward lies a middle point in which obedience precedes grace. Obedience is thus a choice of the free will given in nature.

Faustus avoided setting up two orders of salvation, but the result may have been a greater reliance on human initiative than even Cassian had suggested. For Cassian there were certain exceptional cases in which nature precedes grace. Faustus insisted that grace always precedes nature, but the grace to which Faustus referred was only the grace of the universal call. The will that is called is the natural will, created good. Although fallen, it still retains the capacity to respond in obedience. Following the divine call, the *ortus bonae voluntatis* in all cases, not just in the exceptional ones, lies with the human agent. Faustus's case for human responsibility was far more consistent than Cassian's had been. The necessary operation of grace is, of course, not limited to calling and rewarding, to the beginning and completion of salvation. Throughout the process grace assists the free will in its desire for obedience by granting liberation from sin and

---

[86]*De gr.* 2.10.
[87]*De gr.* 2.10.
[88]Weigel, 58; see 127 above.
[89]*De gr.* 2.10.

by bestowing virtues. Grace is thus indispensable for the accomplishment of the will's free choice.[90]

Faustus placed the emphasis, however, on this free choice, and he further underscored it by his description of God's patience in the human decision-making process. Judgment and redemption are delayed as God waits for the increase of obedience on the part of the good and the increase of evil among the wicked. Both kinds of persons have selected their course out of the freedom of their nature, a nature that knows the good and either pursues or abuses it.[91] This reference to the patience of God with regard to the diverse conditions of human persons accorded with the multi-faceted character of grace that Origen and, to a lesser extent, Cassian had taught. Faustus did not develop the notion as fully as either of his predecessors had, but it is clear that for him the divine agent is respectful of the human will and its activity. God responds mercifully in grace but also reliably in justice.

The overriding concern for Faustus in his explication of the human condition was to safeguard human agency. Against Pelagius he acknowledged the deleterious effects of the fall, but against Augustine he refused to construe those consequences as so thoroughgoing that they made dubious the reality of human agency. Fundamental to his argument for that agency was the notion of freedom.

Faustus understood human freedom to be equivalent to the situation of the person at a crossroads. The individual has been placed in this condition through the divine gift of a free will. Evil seduces the will in one direction, and grace attracts it in the other; yet neither has the power of necessity over the will's decision.[92] This concept of freedom was, of course, considerably different from that which Augustine had held. Augustine conceived true freedom as a product of divine grace which confers the love of good; the greater is the love, the more spontaneous the willing of good and the less the agony of choice of good over evil. In contrast, Faustus believed that divine judgment can justifiably be exercised with respect to human choice only on the basis of a genuine crossroads situation.[93]

That choice is, of course, not made only once. The crossroads imagery and Faustus's interpretation, already noted, of the scriptural image of vessels of honor and vessels of abuse are mutually reinforcing. A person remains under the necessity of decision throughout life. As the will is free to choose either direction, it is also free to change its orientation once chosen and to move in the

---

[90]*De gr.* 2.10; T. A. Smith, 99-100; for a somewhat different interpretation of the relationship of the views of Faustus to those of Cassian, see Djuth, "Faustus of Riez," 46-48.

[91]*De gr.* 2.10.

[92]*De gr.* 1.12.

[93]*De gr.* 1.12.

opposite direction. The more one strives for the good, however, the more one is aided by grace.[94] As is becoming evident, in his characterization of the human condition, Faustus was operating with the twin presuppositions of the freedom of the human will, a freedom that entails responsibility, and the necessity of grace. He described the divine activity as that of creating capability, whereas the human responsibility lies in the use that is made of that capability. In each person God has granted the capacity for rational judgment, a will by which choices may be freely made. If evil is pursued, the responsibility clearly lies with the one who made the decision for evil but could have willed the contrary. If, on the other hand, the good is pursued, the implementation of that freely made choice requires that the assistance of grace be sought. There is not a perfect symmetry here.

The human moral situation is one in which all receive the same opportunity. As a result, a clear cause and effect relationship exists between human decision and divine reward. Nevertheless, the relationship is not perfectly proportionate since grace is required in order to live the form of life that attains reward.

Significantly, the righteousness sought by one who wills the good Faustus referred to as a "general" and not a "personal" gift. He described it as a fountain in the middle of the world, available to all. It is the individual's decision whether or not to drink from the fountain, but for those who refuse to partake, the fault lies not with the gift but with the refusal to receive. Because this righteousness is available to all, it is also justly required from all by the judgment of God.[95] The old monastic scheme of free will, divine judgment, and reward has been staunchly affirmed.

Faustus offered what he considered to be two irrefutable examples of the necessity of human effort. One was from the witness of Scripture and the other from the experience of the church. First, he argued, much as Augustine had done in the *De gratia et libero arbitrio*, that the very presence of divine precepts throughout Scripture is a guarantee of the validity of duties incumbent on the person. Related to this testimony of Scripture, Faustus made two important comments. The first comment was that the blemish of sin is not an inseparable aspect of the human origin and condition but can be removed. This cleansing is promised in Scripture through the precepts to those who strive with grace cooperating. Sinfulness can thus be removed by human effort as assisted by grace. Faustus's idea of the consequences of the fall hardly matched Augustine's sense of enslavement to sin.

The second comment was that if merit and virtue are not the achievement of great human effort but are merely a gift, they lose their value. If reward is

---

[94]*De gr.* 1.12.
[95]*De gr.* 1.9.

given to laziness, then the righteousness of the one who rewards as well as the honor of the recipient are denigrated. Furthermore, if the road to virtue is broad, then Scripture, specifically Matthew 7:14 ("For the gate is narrow and the way is hard, that leads to life, and those who find it are few"), is called into question. The idea of merit as a precious gift of grace had no appeal to this monk.[96]

The second example that Faustus offered as evidence of the necessity of human effort was the operation of the church. By observation one notices that it is through human effort, the work of the priests and saints, of the apostles and martyrs, that the Lord builds up the church. Yet the beginning and end of the church's work, like the beginning and end of the individual's salvation, must be attributed to God.[97]

It is noteworthy that Faustus's reference to the church had to do with the congregation or even the community of all Christians rather than simply with the monastery. It indicates that he was transferring elements of the monastic ideal, such as the necessity of human agency, to a congregational setting. This monk-bishop has thus provided an alternative to the contrast noted earlier between Augustine and Cassian. The African bishop had experienced the congregation as the external setting in which the interaction between grace and human agency might occur. That context, ill-defined and poorly regulated, could not be reliably presumed always to function as the instrumentality of grace. The true context in which grace operates is internal: the human heart. In contrast, the monk Cassian had viewed the external monastic setting as the trustworthy locus for the interaction of grace and human agency. Faustus has maintained the monastic emphasis on the significance of human agency but has transferred its interaction with grace to another external context, the church. As we shall see in the next chapter, it would be to Gallic congregations that Caesarius of Arles, another monk-bishop, would take the message of human agency empowered by grace.

Nevertheless, if one is to operate as Faustus did with the twin presuppositions of the freedom of the human will and the necessity of grace, a problem arises in situations where the former is inoperative. How is one to explain the case of two infants obviously unable to exercise any freedom of judgment, one baptized, the other unbaptized? Here Faustus, like Cassian, refused to abandon the realm of the observable.[98] To introduce the speculative notion of predestination to explain these cases would undercut the presupposition of free will that Faustus, from human experience and from the witness of Scripture, knew to be true. Exceptions should evoke the silence of humility, not a rejection of what is

---

[96]*De gr.* 1.10.
[97]*De gr.* 1.10.
[98]Cf. Chadwick, *John Cassian,* 120, 125-26.

already certain.[99] For Faustus, the hard or unusual cases remained hard or unusual, instead of being made paradigmatic, as they had been for Augustine. Ironically, both Faustus and Augustine located humility in the acceptance of what cannot be understood, but whereas the latter humbled himself before the inscrutability of predestinating grace, the former found the doctrine of predestination itself an expression of human arrogance. For Faustus humility consisted in the acceptance of apparent divine inequity, not in any speculative attempts to explain it.

Another problem arises with regard to the second of Faustus's twin presuppositions: the necessity of grace. The apparent ineffectuality of grace among those who pursue evil after baptism seems to deny any necessary purpose that the grace of baptism serves. That grace could be necessary but ineffectual was a problem not only for Faustus but for the Augustinians as well. Faustus tried to strengthen his own position on this issue by pointing out the weakness of his opponents, but his criticism of their stance is somewhat off target. He presented the Augustinians as saying that the efficacy of baptism for the removal of original sin depends on the faith of the one baptized. If such is the case, Faustus said, first, the objective efficacy of baptism is denied, a point that he rejected, and second, human effort is made a necessary complement to the divine activity, a point that he affirmed.[100]

Faustus's misdirected criticism raises questions about which Augustinians he had in mind. Prosper, for example, had argued, not that original sin is not removed--it is--but that as actual sin continues, without repentance, one is justifiably damned for his evil work following baptism.[101] According to Prosper's and Augustine's scheme, the unrepentant continuance in evil would result, of course, from the fact that one has not been predestined to salvation. Thus to the nonelect grace is given in baptism, a grace sufficient to overcome original sin, but the grace necessary to salvation is withheld.

Even apart from Faustus's criticism, however misdirected, Augustine's concept of the efficacy of grace in baptism for the nonpredestined was unsatisfactory. In fact, a basic problem for the Augustinian position was the failure to resolve the apparent discrepancy between the efficacy of the sacraments and a determination by grace and election. Nevertheless, Faustus did not fault the Augustinians in this regard, but instead he faulted them on the basis of his opinion that they were denying any efficacy at all to baptism apart from faith. The character of his criticism indicated that he was not working with the texts of Augustine himself, at least on this point, but with those of Augustinians,

---

[99]*De gr.* 1.13.
[100]*De gr.* 1.14.
[101]Prosper, *Resp. Gall.* 1.2.

presumably such as Lucidus, whose own views deviated from those that Augustine had held.

Faustus's own resolution to the dilemma was to affirm that although original sin is removed by baptism, the sacrament alone is inadequate for salvation. Good works must be added. Otherwise, idleness rather than diligence will characterize the post-baptismal life of the individual.[102] Such inactivity was unacceptable to one who believed that reward was granted to striving.

Perhaps the case that Faustus was making for the necessity of both human and divine agency can best be seen in the example of the Ninevites that he used. Here all the elements of the process of salvation are demonstrated: As the mercy of God was concealed, the people's faith, desire, and affection for God were tested and proved; with the help of grace the people exercised the longing for God that God had implanted in their hearts. By employing the capacities that were granted in creation and assisted by grace, this people attained salvation before the coming of Christ. Yet although before Christ, salvation was still of grace and not of law.[103]

Cassian had also employed the case of the Ninevites as evidence that changes for the good by the human agent result in a beneficial outcome, for God changes the divine determination so that it accords with human deserts. Cassian and Faustus thus each had a somewhat different point to make; however, for both men the case of the Ninevites served as an example of the importance of human agency. Significantly, Augustine made no reference to the Ninevites in the four treatises we have considered.

The message at the conclusion of the *De gratia* was the same as that at the beginning. The consequences of the fall are not so thoroughgoing that the human person has lost the freedom of the will. The interaction between grace and nature is such that the person has the responsibility for making right choices. Grace is necessary to enable the implementation of those choices. In a rational, comprehensible way good is rewarded and evil punished. The reward for good works is double. Grace assists the one pursuing the good with the attainment of temporary virtues, such as faith, temperance of heart, benevolence, chastity. Grace also recompenses the exercise of these virtues with a final and lasting gift, the inheritance of heaven. Such an arrangement manifests the justice of God; fatalistic decrees would demonstrate divine injustice.[104]

Such an arrangement also gives meaning to reward, for without the option of choosing evil, the choice of good has no merit.[105] The value of the good seems

---

[102]*De gr.* 1.14.
[103]*De gr.* 2.12.
[104]*De gr.* 2.12.
[105]*De gr.* 2.12.

to emerge only in contrast to its opposite.[106] Reminiscent of Cassian and thus consistent with his own experience as a monk, Faustus insisted that life is a struggle, a battlefield in which one must work strenuously for the victory, the attainment of beatitude in eternity.[107]

Throughout the *De gratia* Faustus attempted to chart his own middle course between the two extremes: Pelagianism and the predestinarian elements of Augustinianism. Of necessity, he was compelled to deny the former, as it had been officially rejected by the church. Nevertheless, by employing the argument that what was wrong with Pelagianism was its extreme character, he could make the same case against the predestinarian elements of Augustinianism, asserting that these were the extreme opposite of Pelagianism and thus equally wrong. The outcome of such a tactic was that Faustus was then able to offer his own views as a middle ground between erroneous extremes, and as such, representative of the normative tradition of the church.

This middle ground was quite simply an argument for the necessity of both human agency and divine grace in the achievement of salvation, a necessity in which neither cancels the other. As such, it did uphold the Augustinian emphasis on the necessity of grace.[108] Yet because this argument was primarily against predestinarianism, the burden of Faustus's argument was the maintenance of human agency. Determinism had to be rejected and human freedom and responsibility upheld. The case to be made was that a person's salvation was directly traceable to that person's free will and action as assisted by grace.

Response to Faustus

The councils of Arles and Lyons and the views of Faustus himself came to represent a prevailing south Gallic consensus that generally held for over half a century, until it was officially rejected at the second Council of Orange.[109] In the

---

[106]*De gr.* 2.12.

[107]*De gr.* 2.12.

[108]Smith, 222-27, argued that Faustus upheld Augustine's teaching not only on the necessity of grace but also somewhat less forcefully on the prevenience and gratuity of grace.

[109]Markus, "The Legacy of Pelagius," 221-22; Amann, "Semi-pélagiens," 1838-40; Mathisen, 264-68.

There is some question about whether the works of Faustus were condemned by Pope Gelasius I (492–496) in the *Decretum Gelasianum de libris recipiendis et non recipiendis* (Gelasius, *Quo a septuaginta episcopis libri sacri et authentici ab aprocryphis sunt discreti*). In its present form the decree confirms the writings of Augustine and Prosper but rejects those of Cassian and Faustus. Evidence suggests that the names of Cassian and Faustus were not in the original decree but were added at some later date. Two points might be noted here. When nearly two decades later the African Bishop

meantime, however, some of the severer elements of Augustinianism were not entirely without defenders, as, for example, Avitus of Vienne, who was consecrated bishop about the time of Faustus's death (c. 490). His *De spiritalis historiae gestis* made a strong case for human depravity and incapacity as a result of the fall. The question of the beginning of faith was settled to the denigration of human agency: there could be no movement toward the good prior to the work of grace. This strongly Augustinian work suggests that there was some prominent opposition to Faustus in Gaul. That it was either widespread or organized, however, is not at all clear.[110]

Oddly enough, the dissolution of the prevailing consensus occurred as an episode in the Christological controversy in the East. Certain parties to the latter dispute, influenced by the Monophysites, were suspicious of any emphasis on the human contribution to salvation and, accordingly, disapproved of the Semi-Pelagian position as presented by Faustus.

Specifically, a group of Scythian monks in Constantinople around 519 approached, first, the legate of Pope Hormisdas and, finally, in Rome the pope himself with a statement rejecting both Nestorianism and the notion of the freedom of the will to choose and to effect the good apart from grace. These monks also communicated their views on Christology and on grace to certain North African bishops who had been banished by the Vandals and were living in Sardinia. Included was a condemnation of Pelagius, Caelestius, Julian of Eclanum, and the books of Faustus against predestination.[111] Nestorianism and Pelagianism, of course, had been linked, rightly or wrongly, as early as the Council of Ephe-

---

Possessor questioned Pope Hormisdas about the views of Faustus, the pope indicated no awareness that Faustus had ever been condemned. Furthermore, nearly three decades later the Council of Orange rejected the tenets of Semi-Pelagianism without indicating any awareness of a prior condemnation of the two most significant formulators of these doctrines. It seems improbable that both the pope and the council would have failed to cite such a condemnation had it existed. *Das Decretum Gelasianum de libris recipiendis et non recipiendis*, ed. E. von Dobschütz, 38.4; G. Bardy, "Gélase (Décret de)," *Dictionnaire de la Bible, Supplément* 3:279-90; Weigel, 132-35; Harnack, 5:255.

[110]Avitus, *De spiritalis historiae gestis* 1-3; Daniel J. Nodes, "Avitus of Vienne's Spiritual History and the Semipelagian Controversy," *Vigiliae Christianae* 38 (1984): 185-95. Markus, on the other hand, has raised questions about Avitus's familiarity with Faustus's teaching and his commitment to the predestinarian position. He suggested that Avitus's defense of the need for grace in his letter to the Burgundian king (*Ep.* 4) reflected "a shift towards the unity imposed a decade or two later at Orange." Markus, "The Legacy of Pelagius," 221-22. See also, Amann, "Semi-pélagiens," 1837. G. Bardy, "Les repercussions des controverses théologiques des Ve et VIe siècles dans les églises de Gaule," *Revue d'histoire de l'Église de France* 24 (1938): 33-35.

[111]Fulgentius, *Ep.* 16; É. Amann, "Scythes (Moines)," *Dictionnaire de théologie catholique* 14/2 (1941) 1746-53; Harnack, 5:254-56; Weigel, 121-42; Harnack, 5:254-57.

sus in 431, although it should be remembered that Cassian himself had written against the Nestorian heresy.

The activities of the Scythian monks were not without effect. The African bishops in Sardinia responded to the monks with a letter, written by Fulgentius of Ruspe, that affirmed the sovereignty of grace but was noncommmital on the theopaschite formula that the monks sought. The letter did not mention Faustus.[112] When the African bishop Possessor, who was living in exile in Constantinople, inquired of the pope as to the authority of Faustus,[113] the reply was that, as Faustus had never been a doctor of the church, his private opinions were not a matter of concern; Augustine's teachings on grace, especially those elicited by Prosper and Hilary, were an adequate expression of the church's teaching; the Scythians were judged to be troublemakers. Hormisdas also made reference to a set of *capitula* taken from Augustine's writings that were in the papal archive and could be sent if necessary.[114] When the Scythians became aware of the pope's response to Possessor, they responded that if Augustine were right, Faustus must necessarily have been wrong, as he had been in recognizing the operation of grace as being external only.[115] Once again, they appealed to the African bishops. The chronology is not entirely clear, but two works by Fulgentius, *Epistula* 15 and the *De veritate praedestinationis et gratiae Dei*, written after his return from exile, affirmed a thoroughgoing Augustinianism.[116]

Fulgentius of Ruspe:
De veritate praedestinationis et gratiae Dei

The last notable African defender of Augustinianism was Fulgentius, the bishop of Ruspe. The dates of his life have been set variously at 462-527 or 468-533. As noted above, Fulgentius had the benefit of a classical education, and contrary to its Christian detractors, he apparently found it no hindrance to his own faith.[117] More important, the literary training that his education had provided enabled him, like his counterpart Faustus, to be one of the principal spokesmen

---

[112]Fulgentius, *Ep.* 17; Amann, "Scythes (Moines)," 1750.

[113]Possessor, *Ep. ad Hormisdam, inter ep. Hormisdae.*

[114]Hormisdas, *Ep.* 70.

[115]John Maxentius, *Ad epistolam Hormisdae responsio.*

[116]For the chronology of Fulgentius's works, see J. Fraipont, *Corpus Christianorum SL* 91:5-8; Lapeyre, 327-30.

[117]Lapeyre, 90-95; Riché, 88; Judith Herrin, *The Formation of Christendom* (Princeton: Princeton University Press, 1987). See Ferrandus, *Vita Fulgentii.* For a discussion of the difference between Fulgentius the mythographer and Fulgentius the theologian, see M. L. W. Laistner, "Fulgentius in the Carolingian Age," in *The Intellectual Heritage of the Early Middle Ages*, ed. Chester G. Starr (New York: Octagon Books, 1966) 202-15.

in the Semi-Pelagian debate. Rather than being a hindrance, his education was put to the service of his Augustinian faith.[118]

Fulgentius's contributions to the church followed time spent in the secular world, as administrator of his family's property and in the civil office of procurator.[119] Once he had committed himself to the religious life, Fulgentius lived from then on, in one form or another, as a monk: first on his own estates, then in an African monastery, later as an abbot, and afterwards among a group of African solitaries. After becoming bishop of Ruspe, he continued to live as a monk and in exile built at least one monastery. With such predilections it is not surprising that Fulgentius held Cassian's ascetic works in high regard. Influenced by the *Institutiones* and *Collationes*, he travelled as far as Syracuse before he was finally dissuaded from his attempt to join the fathers of the Egyptian desert. Moreover, as an abbot he recommended these writings to the monks under his care.[120]

About 502 or 507 Fulgentius was elevated to the episcopacy. Soon afterward he and sixty other Catholic bishops were banished to Sardinia. In 510 or 515 he was again in Africa for debate against the Arians, was banished two years later, but in 523 King Hilderic permitted him to return.[121]

From this brief sketch two points of interest can be noted. First, Fulgentius's experience as a monk in Africa was consistent with that of the monastics that we have seen in Gaul. According to Riché, the similarities extended to Italy and Spain as well. As a result, Riché was able to speak of a "Mediterranean monasticism."[122] Second, considered more broadly, Fulgentius's whole life fit the general pattern of the educated, aristocratic, monastic bishop noted earlier. Not only Faustus but also many of the readers of Sulpicius Severus had come from the same mold.[123] However, the similarities should not mislead. The evidence suggests that Fulgentius was not successful in integrating the world of monk and

---

[118]For an examination of the relationship of Fulgentius's aristocratic background, including his educational training, to his significance in the church, see S. T. Stevens, "The Circle of Bishop Fulgentius," *Traditio* 38 (1982): 327-41.

[119]Lapeyre, 95-100; Hans-Joachim Diesner, *Fulgentius von Ruspe als Theologe und Kirchenpolitiker* (Stuttgart: Calwer, 1966) 10-12.

[120]Lapeyre, 100-56; Riché, 109. J.-J. Gavigan, "Vita monastica in Africa desiitne cum invasione Wandalorum?" *Augustinianum* 1 (1961): 19-49, followed Fulgentius's monastic career. Zumkeller noted the probable Augustinian influence on the monks under Fulgentius's care during his exile, 90-92. For Fulgentius's influence on monasticism in his province of Byzaecena, see Diesner, 64.

[121]Lapeyre, 156-76, 323-27.

[122]Riché, 109.

[123]See 38-40 and 162-63 above.

bishop.[124] Moreover, Markus has pointed out that there was no ascetic "takeover" of the church in Africa or in Italy as was the case in Gaul. These two areas lacked the rich monastic culture and the large numbers of aristocratic bishops with ties to monasticism that typified the Gallic church.[125]

Even within the general pattern of aristocratic monk-bishop there were marked contradictions, for Faustus and Fulgentius were on opposite sides of the Semi-Pelagian controversy. In Fulgentius's case, a Mediterranean-trained monk-bishop was the defender of Augustine. One must wonder, therefore, whether geography and provincial loyalty did not still play an important part in theology. An African trained in the teaching of Augustine and loyal to his authority had a different theological orientation than his Gallic counterpart. If Faustus may be said to represent Cassian in the congregation, perhaps Fulgentius could be said to represent Augustine in the monastery. In any case, both men were formed not only by monastic but also by episcopal experience. In encouraging the reading of Cassian, Fulgentius was taking up precisely the same version of Western monasticism in North Africa that had shaped Faustus in South Gaul. The patterns of monasticism and episcopacy that we find in the Mediterranean world at this time were not only broad but contained highly complex gradations.

Fulgentius first emerged as a significant figure in the Semi-Pelagian controversy in response to the furor created around 519 by the Scythian monks over the teaching of Faustus on grace. The monks had sought to link this issue with the Christological controversy. These monks made known their predestinarian and Christological views to the North African bishops exiled in Sardinia. The bishops concurred with the monks' position, at least with regard to grace, and Fulgentius, as one of their number, responded with *Epistula de incarnatione et gratia domini*

---

[124]Markus, *The End of Ancient Christianity*, 202, 214. Markus called attention to D. König's interpretation of the *Vita Fulgentii* 2, in *Amt and Askese: Priesteramt und Mönchtum bei den lateinischen Kirchenvätern in vorbenediktinischer Zeit*, Regulae Benedicti Studia, Supplementa 12 (St. Ottilien: EOS Verlga, 1985) 167-87.

[125]Markus, *The End of Ancient Christianity*, 214. Even Gaul had more than one pattern for its bishops. Along with the aristocratic monk-bishop, there was also the educated, aristocratic, but nonmonastic bishop exemplified in someone such as Sidonius Apollinaris (ca. 432–ca. 487), who, although an activist bishop, seems never to have engaged in the Semi-Pelagian controversy. Sidonius's overriding concern was the preservation of classical culture rather than the preservation of the purity of the faith. Such a contrast as posed by these two patterns gives credibility to the view that the preoccupations of these two types of bishops, although perhaps no longer at odds, were still dissimilar. See Wallace-Hadrill, *The Frankish Church*, 3-5, for the distinction between the "conservative bishop" and the "radical bishop." Cf. Stevens, "The Circle of Bishop Fulgentius," 328, 340-41, for a discussion of the linkage of "aristocratic background, literary activity, and the prominence" in church and state in the case of Fulgentius and the existence of a similar linkage in the case of Gallic bishops, such as Hilary of Arles and Sidonius Apollinaris.

nostri Iesu Christi, an expression of the Augustinian position.[126] Fulgentius wrote, therefore, as Faustus had, i.e., in relation to an attempt to define and secure an authoritative tradition.

The contribution of Fulgentius to the Semi-Pelagian controversy had only begun. At the urging of the Scythian monks, he wrote against Faustus. The *Contra Faustum Gallum* has been lost, but *De veritate praedestinationis et gratiae Dei*, written in 523 after his return to Africa,[127] remained the definitive Augustinian response to Faustus. It was here that Fulgentius's views on grace were most fully and clearly expressed.

Fulgentius wrote the *De veritate praedestinationis et gratiae Dei* to reassert divine sovereignty and human impotence in the process of salvation against those who insisted upon the efficacy of the human will and the possibility of human virtue apart from grace.[128] Faustus, of course, had not held this position. In fact, no one had, not even Pelagius himself. It is not evident, therefore, that Fulgentius was always arguing directly against Faustus, although sharp differences of opinion on specific points are apparent. It is probable, however, that the object of his antipathy was simply Semi-Pelagianism in its most exaggerated form, as, for example, the phenomenon had been reported to Augustine by Prosper and Hilary.

In making the case for divine sovereignty, Fulgentius covered the range of issues which by this time had become characteristic of the debate: the fall of Adam and its consequences for his progeny; predestination, foreknowledge, and the universality of the divine will to save; the operation of grace, particularly with regard to the free will; the functions of the law; the locus of authority. Both sides, in varying degrees, had found it necessary to examine these issues in order to construct their positions. What varied, therefore, was not so much the elements of the argument as the interpretation given to each element. That interpretation was itself determined by whether the emphasis fell on divine grace or human agency. For Faustus the point was to underscore the importance of human agency without undermining the role of grace. In contrast, for Fulgentius the point was

---

[126]*Ep.* 17; the letter is also referred to as *Ep. de incarnatione et gratia Domini nostri Iesu Christi, ad Petrum Diaconum et alios qui ex Oriente in causa fidei Romam missi sunt, Liber unus.* Amann, "Semi-pélagiens," 1837-40; Amann, "Scythes (Moines)," 1746-53. For a discussion of the Christology of Fulgentius as found in this letter, see Bernhard Nisters, *Die Christologie des Hl. Fulgentius von Ruspe* (Münster: Aschendorffsche, 1929) 80-95. While he was in exile and presumably before he wrote *Ep.* 17, Fulgentius also wrote *Ad Monimum, Libri tres*, in response to a friend who was having difficulty understanding Augustine's doctrine of predestination.

[127]De Letter, *The Call of All Nations*, 160n.21, pointed out that although *Contra Faustum* has been lost, Fulgentius's reply to Faustus can be found in *Ep.* 15, *Iohanni et Venerio*, and in *De veritate praedestinationis et gratiae Dei.* Harnack, 5:256-57.

[128]Fulgentius, *De veritate praedestinationis et gratiae Dei* 1.1.1.

to safeguard the role of divine grace, if necessary even to the point of jeopardizing the role of human agency.

In typically Augustinian fashion, Fulgentius considered the fall of Adam to have brought about the present human condition. In that first man, human nature was entirely good, upright in will and untouched by any necessity of death or any enslavement to sin. Through the transgression of the first man, all are now born in original sin and are subject to the punishment of death. Included in this number are children who do not yet have the exercise of their own will.[129] Adam's sin occurred through the exercise of his free will which was able to choose either to sin or not. He chose to sin[130] and thereby lost that freedom.[131] Only Christ, born of the Virgin and the Holy Spirit, was free of original sin and thus able to make atonement both for that inherited condition and also for sins committed voluntarily.[132] This atonement is entirely gratuitous. There is no consideration of accumulated or future merit.[133]

In describing the weakness of the fallen human condition, Fulgentius made it clear that salvation is the work of grace. The Semi-Pelagians, of course, would not have denied the necessity for grace but would have disallowed its sovereignty. In other words, they would have denied both that the human will cannot in any sense will the good except as moved and activated by God and that the sole determinant of who is saved and who is not is God's election, to which no moral differences among human beings are relevant. Fulgentius defended this sovereignty with several arguments. One concerned the doctrine of predestination.

The bishop argued that this teaching had to be maintained if the integrity of the doctrine of God were to be secured. In a forceful attack against the concept of foreknowledge as defined by Faustus, Fulgentius insisted that if God cannot be said to have eternal and unchangeable foreknowledge of all temporal, changeable events and to have eternally and unchangeably ordered all divine actions, then it must be conceded that God is mutable; the divine knowledge and ordering would depend upon the mutability of temporal events.[134] The divine knowledge would thus be subject to increase with the reception of new information and the divine predestination subject to the reordering of God's works of mercy and justice. Such a concession was unacceptable, for Fulgentius held, as did all parties in this dispute, the doctrine of the immutability of God.[135]

---

[129]*De ver.* 1.1.2, 1.2.4.
[130]*De ver.* 1.2.3.
[131]*De ver.* 1.2.4.
[132]*De ver.* 1.2.5, 1.3.6.
[133]*De ver.* 1.3.7.
[134]*De ver.* 3.1.1.
[135]*De ver.* 3.1.1.

By insisting on the immutability of the divine foreknowledge Fulgentius was not claiming that human action is without consequence in determining human destiny. He was insisting that from all eternity God predestined those who are to be called, justified, glorified: their persons, their good works, and their reward.[136] Their number cannot be changed.[137] Similarly, the nonelect, because of their fall in Adam, are predestined to judgment,[138] the justice of which is confirmed by their life of transgressions. In each case, God foreknows not only the individual human life but also the divine judgments, both prior and final, by which it is bracketed. Consistent with the Augustinian position, Fulgentius accepted the concept of predestination as a necessary safeguard of theology, whereas for the Semi-Pelagians, such as Faustus, it was rejected as a devastating attack on anthropology and a threat to divine justice, thus to theology.

This charge that the doctrine of predestination jeopardizes the justice of God would hardly have swayed Fulgentius. Like Augustine, he was able to find in the situation of Jacob and Esau ample evidence of the gratuity of predestination and the justice of nonelection. Jacob was elected before birth, and thus before having achieved merit, by the predestination of God, whereas his twin Esau, conceived by the same act, was not elected. Bearing equally the guilt of original sin, one was mercifully chosen for salvation while the other was justly passed over.[139] From eternity God hated in Esau human wickedness, the condition and consequence of original sin. Accordingly, Esau was punished. From eternity God prepared the grace of justification for Jacob by which Jacob was freed from sin, a good will was begun in him, and its outworking in good works was given.[140] In contrast to Faustus, who had interpreted the case of Jacob and Esau as evidence that divine foreknowledge is simply God's knowledge of how God will respond to human choice and action, Fulgentius interpreted the same case as evidence of a predestination that is independent of all human agency. Again the Semi-Pelagian emphasis on human agency and the Augustinian emphasis on divine sovereignty have determined the interpreters' perspectives.

Fulgentius generalized from this example of Jacob and Esau that a good will and good work are, without exception, the gift of grace. They are freely conferred on those whom God has chosen as heirs. To these heirs God also grants

---

[136]*De ver.* 3.2.3.

[137]*De ver.* 3.4.6.

[138]*De ver.* 3.5.8.

[139]*De ver.* 1.4.8. For Fulgentius, as for Faustus, the transmission of original sin is not through sexual intercourse, which is the good gift of God, but through passion, which is the punishment of sin; cf. *De ver.* 1.4.10.

[140]*De ver.* 1.5.11.

perseverance in the good as well as reward for those merits divinely given.[141] As in Augustine, grace rewards grace. In the absence of such divine gifts, the evil will and evil work, entirely of human origin, are justly punished with eternal damnation.[142] No one at all deserves to be the recipient of divine graciousness; yet some are freely given salvation while the rest are justifiably condemned.[143]

It is in the context of such an understanding of original sin and the gratuity of election that Fulgentius dealt with the troublesome question of infants who die unbaptized.[144] He, like all other parties in this dispute, believed baptism to be necessary for salvation; therefore, those who die without it are damned. The cause of their damnation he attributed to original sin, not to divine foreknowledge of evil merit which they would have accomplished had they lived. Like Augustine, he insisted that God's foreknowledge is always of that which will actually happen. It does not pertain to that which would have happened under different circumstances. There is no divine foreknowledge of sins which will never be committed.[145] Future, but unrealized, good or evil merit is no more the cause of election or of damnation than past good or evil merit.

The question of why God did not effect the baptism of the infant is unanswerable, but whatever the reason, there is no iniquity in God. Nor is there room for chance. Whether a child is baptized is not an accident of human determination, not a matter of the piety or impiety of the parents, but an effect of the divine will.[146] Again for the Augustinian the hard case has become the paradigmatic case.

That divine will is never defeated. It cannot be resisted, changed, or understood.[147] When God wills parents to baptize their child, the divine purpose is accomplished without fail. Likewise, it is the result of divine judgment that God abandons the parents who, more fearful for the physical than the spiritual health of their child, do not bring the infant to baptism.[148] Similarly, it is a function of the divine will that some children, despite the solicitude of their Christian parents, die before they might be baptized[149] and that other children, despite the

---

[141]*De ver.* 1.6.12; 1.7.14.

[142]*De ver.* 1.6.12.

[143]*De ver.* 1.6.13.

[144]For a discussion of Fulgentius's views on baptism, see J. J. Gavigan, "Fulgentius of Ruspe on Baptism," *Traditio* 5 (1947): 313-22.

[145]*De ver.* 1.7.15.

[146]*De ver.* 1.9.18.

[147]*De ver.* 1.10.21.

[148]*De ver.* 1.10.22; 1.11.25.

[149]*De ver.* 1.12.26.

wishes of their infidel parents, are baptized through the instrumentality of the faithful.[150]

In none of these cases can there be any question of personal merit. As all are born in sin and infants have no opportunity to accumulate merit, there can be no diversity of causes for opposite outcomes. The cause always remains the inscrutable judgment of God.[151] Furthermore, that same cause is operative in the lives of those who live into adulthood, for in such cases once again personal merit is not the basis for election. All are members of the *perditionis massa*. A person who has been absolved and freed from sin recognizes in the new condition the prior work of grace. A person who is not so freed finds in damnation the actual guilt of Adam.[152] Fulgentius has undercut any human contribution to human destiny. He has also suggested, in contrast to Augustine, that knowledge of that destiny is available through examination of one's present condition. Evidence of the work of grace in one's life can relieve anxiety caused by the inscrutability of the divine decrees. This issue of assurance will be noted again later.[153]

In Fulgentius's affirmation that salvation is dependent on election and that all are not elected, a recurrent Augustinian problem arises: how can such an affirmation be harmonized with the claim of 1 Timothy 2:4 that God wills the salvation of all? Fulgentius had nothing new to add to the argument. Whatever God has predestined is accomplished; those whom God has willed to be saved are saved; no one resists the divine will. The term "all" is satisfied by the gift of salvation to every variety of person, i.e., people of all nations, conditions, ages.[154] Even the writings of Paul himself, as Januarius, Augustine, and Prosper had already noted, contain passages in which "all" is not to be understood as literally referring to all persons universally but in a less extensive sense. In such a way 1 Timothy 2:4 should also be interpreted.[155] The ministry of Christ himself argues against a universalistic interpretation of the term "all." The Savior spoke in parables which not everyone could understand. The impact of his method is clear: to those whom grace does not grant understanding of the truth, salvation is denied.[156] Divine sovereignty remains triumphant.

The conclusion is inescapable that for Fulgentius grace as necessary for salvation is not given generally to everyone but only to the elect. Yet even if that conclusion is accepted as an adequate resolution of the issues posed by 1 Timothy

---

[150]*De ver.* 1.12.27.
[151]*De ver.* 1.12.27.
[152]*De ver.* 1.13.28.
[153]See 193-95 below.
[154]*De ver.* 3.9.14; 3.10.15.
[155]*De ver.* 3.11.18; 3.12.19; 3.12.20.
[156]*De ver.* 2.2.3.

2:4, there are still other difficulties present in Fulgentius's understanding of grace. Its very dominance calls into question the genuineness of human agency. Fulgentius, of course, wanted to maintain the operation of both divine grace and human free will in human willing and action. He insisted that neither cancelled the other.[157] Yet it is questionable whether in his scheme there was any sense in which the will can be considered self-initiated. For Fulgentius, the fallen human will was defective and in need of the healing conversion which only grace can effect. The incapacity is so great that of itself the will cannot even desire conversion to the good. Either ignorance of its condition or pride blocks the way.[158]

The operation of grace on the elect must precede the operation of their own will for good. Grace chooses them and begins its work in the illumination of their hearts. Their will is thereby made good so that they might choose to value grace. That grace can even be desired and received at all is the result of its own unmerited operation.[159] Grace "makes itself to be known, loved, desired, asked for."[160] The change of the person's will comes about not by any human means but by prior divine mercy, just as the retention of the good will is through the continuing aid and governance of grace.[161] Prevenient and assisting grace are necessary for the beginning and the perseverance of a good will.[162] Stated differently, faith and its increase are the gifts of God. Apart from grace the human agent has only the possibility of infidelity.[163]

Fulgentius effectively disallowed the view that Cassian had suggested, i.e., that in certain cases the beginning of the good will might be of human origin.[164] The effects of the fall on human nature were far too devastating. Faustus, of course, had said that faith must always have its beginning in grace, but he had depicted this beginning primarily in terms of the operation of external expressions of grace, preaching and the law, upon the internal, still potent remnants of that grace given in creation.[165] In contrast, Fulgentius emphasized the internal character of the operation of grace. Faith has its beginning in the secret work of the Spirit on the human heart. It is not that grace does not work externally

---

[157]*De ver.* 2.2.3.
[158]*De ver.* 2.2.3.
[159]*De ver.* 1.15.33.
[160]*De ver.* 1.16.34.
[161]*De ver.* 1.16.34.
[162]*De ver.* 1.16.35.
[163]*De ver.* 1.17.36; 1.17.37.
[164]See Marianne Djuth, "Fulgentius of Ruspe: The 'Initium Bonae Voluntatis'," *Augustinian Studies* 20 (1989): 39-60.
[165]See 173-76 above; see T. A. Smith, 209-10.

through such means as preaching, but the illumination of the heart by God is necessary to help the otherwise inadequate hearing.[166]

Despite the undeniable dominance that Fulgentius attributed to the operation of grace, he still attempted to maintain the notion of the freedom of the human will. He insisted that all persons, good or otherwise, have a free will. In the justified this will has been properly ordered, so that it knows and loves the truth. In the rest the will either does not know what God commands and is unaware of its sinfulness, or there is knowledge of the command and a false confidence that it can be fulfilled apart from grace. Accordingly, good is done but in an evil way, for the person is seeking self-justification.[167] The command itself, as the gift of God, is good. It is given for human benefit. The fault lies with the person who believes it can be fulfilled apart from the assistance of grace.[168]

In a somewhat similar way Faustus had contrasted the works of the law and the works of grace. The former were unacceptable, for they were attempts to justify oneself by means of the law apart from grace, whereas the latter, as works preceded and attended by grace, were accepted and affirmed. The contrast to Faustus, therefore, does not arise on the issue of works performed apart from grace. The contrast lies in the fact that for Faustus the will of itself was able to choose the good. Grace would then assist the accomplishment of the good choice. For Fulgentius, the will was not even free to choose the good without the special preparation of grace.

Such special preparation comes only to the elect. In their case the divine command addresses the will and exposes its weakness. Humbled by self-knowledge, the person turns to grace for fulfillment of the demands of obedience. That grace may come through the instrumentality of the command gives proof to Fulgentius of the freedom of the will.[169] Such proof, however, is not entirely convincing. Those persons whom the law leads to grace constitute a group whose membership is externally defined, i.e., their membership is primarily the result of God's decision and is only derivatively their own action.

It is becoming clear that although Fulgentius spoke of the will as free, the description is somewhat deceptive. As a follower of Augustine he insisted that unless the fallen will is changed by grace it either seeks the evil or at least never seeks the good.[170] In other words, apart from grace the will is free only to serve evil. When the will has been changed by grace, it is free to serve the good and does so "willingly." That very willingness, however, is the gift of God who, in

---

[166]*De ver.* 1.22.45.
[167]*De ver.* 2.3.4.
[168]*De ver.* 2.3.4; 2.3.5.
[169]*De ver.* 2.3.5.
[170]*De ver.* 2.5.8.

converting the will, has equipped the person for good.[171] Such a freedom as Fulgentius described was hardly the neutral freedom of the crossroads to which Faustus had appealed.

Even Fulgentius's insistence on the voluntary character of the good will was strained at best. He pointed out that although the beginning of the will in faith and its continuance and completion in love are the gifts of grace,[172] the will itself must voluntarily accept these gifts in order to have them and use them.[173] This voluntary reception by the will does sound, in isolation, as if the human agent actually has some autonomous role; however, the context disallows any independence to the good will. The divine gifts of faith and love themselves prepare to assist the will for their own reception and use.[174] That the willing and acting are genuinely human seems dubious, unless, of course, to be genuinely human means to be the instrument of divine grace. The human person is necessary but only in the sense that the divine will requires embodiment. This possibility more and more seems to be what Fulgentius had in mind.

Freedom, rather than being the neutral condition of the will which it was for Faustus, is a specifically positive condition for which the will must be prepared by grace. This preparation consists in releasing the will from sin and empowering it for good. Thus prepared the will is finally free to cooperate with grace.[175]

Fulgentius has made grace the context of freedom, specifically freedom for good works. As a result of connecting good works inextricably to grace he was able to respond from several perspectives to the objection that the doctrine of predestination is detrimental to moral incentive. In so doing, he also effected several shifts in the Augustinian position. First, taking a new step on the Augustinian side of the controversy, Fulgentius expressed his conviction that if grace is operative in a person, that person will not do otherwise than carry out the works of grace.[176] There really is no choice in the matter, except the choice for the good. The logic of grace has been carried further than ever before. Human agency for the good is to its core the work of God.

Second, in this insistence on the unfailing character of the operation of grace Fulgentius does not appear to have taken into account the case of those who are called to faith and then allowed to fall away. He did speak of the multiform character of the work of grace and asserted that grace is not given equally to all or even to those to whom it is given.[177] On the other hand, he did not examine

---

[171]*De ver.* 2.5.8.
[172]*De ver.* 2.10.16.
[173]*De ver.* 2.10.17.
[174]*De ver.* 2.10.17.
[175]*De ver.* 2.12.19; 2.14.24.
[176]*De ver.* 3.6.9.
[177]E.g., *De ver.* 1.16.35–1.19.40; 2.1.2; 2.17.30.

the consequences of this inequality of gifts, and his statements regarding predestination so closely related the gifts of faith, perseverance, and eternal life as to leave the impression that the sequence is automatic.[178] Fulgentius's focus remained fixed on the necessity and sovereignty of grace; thus he either eliminated or simply ignored what had been for Augustine one of the most difficult instances of reprobation, that of graced Christians. Significantly, 1 John 2:19 ("They went out from us, but they did not belong to us; for if they had belonged to us, they would have remained with us. But by going out they made it plain that none of them belongs to us"), which had been important to Augustine's explanation of why some do not persevere, does not appear at all in the *De veritate praedestinationis et gratiae Dei*.[179]

Third, in another move beyond Augustine, Fulgentius argued that as the acts of praying and watching are effected by grace, they are to be recognized as signs of one's predestination.[180] Here for the first time, it seems, an Augustinian was offering assurance of election.

Fourth, Fulgentius asserted that the doctrine of predestination in no way obviates the duty of keeping the evangelical and apostolic commands. Christ surely knew from the beginning those who would believe; yet he gave commandments. Paul taught predestination; yet he also taught obedience.[181] Carrying this line of thought somewhat further than Augustine had,[182] Fulgentius used the authority of the *evangelica* and *apostolica mandata*, which everyone accepted, as an argument for the authority of the doctrine of predestination. Particularly, as Paul gave us both the commandments and the doctrine, to reject the latter is to attack the former as well. It is also to challenge the veracity of the apostle.[183] The grace of predestination and the duty of obedience are inseparable.

Approaching the relationship of predestination and moral incentive from several angles, Fulgentius attempted to cement the connection between grace, specifically grace as sovereign, and good work. In so doing, he somewhat revised the Augustinian position. Two of the modifications need to be examined further. They have to do with the vigilance of the elect and the assurance available to the elect.

Regarding the matter of vigilance, Fulgentius, as Augustine had done, distinguished between grace as given to Adam and grace as given to those who are in Christ. By grace Adam was given a free will by which he might either remain

---

[178]E.g., *De ver.* 3.2.3; 3.5.8.
[179]*De don. pers.* 8.19.
[180]*De ver.* 3.6.10.
[181]*De ver.* 3.7.11.
[182]See 65 above.
[183]*De ver.* 3.7.11; 3.8.12.

in the uprightness in which he had been created or depart from it. As a result of Adam's fall, his progeny are enslaved to sin. For those who are elected, prevenient grace is necessary to reform the will. To the extent that the will is corrected, the person is free; to the extent that the will remains captive, the person is subject to sin. As a result of this condition of partial freedom and partial servitude, the child of God must struggle against subjection to sin and pray for the grace of deliverance. Such grace is necessary to the "soldier" of Christ whose will has been weakened as Adam's had not.[184]

This internal struggle of the infirm will does not cease in this life for the saints. The liberty and peace that had belonged to Adam are available to his descendants in Christ only in the undisturbed security of the next life. For the present, the life of the saints is a battle in which they must be ever vigilant and prayerful. The loss of freedom and thus of virtue means that they must not only strive, but also must implore God to ascribe virtue to their efforts.[185] Echoes of Cassian, with the references to combat, and of Faustus, with the reference to grace being given to work, resound in all this monastic imagery of watching and praying. However, all such statements must be heard in the context of Fulgentius's Augustinianism. Despite the need for vigilance, the elect finally will not be conquered.[186]

Significantly, the very presence of this vigilance within the person is an occasion for assurance of election. Fulgentius offered a criterion that Augustine had not provided for distinguishing the vessels of mercy: "All who, having rejected material abundance, serve devotedly in faith and love, are vessels unto honor."[187] Those who give evidence of the gifts of faith and love in a life of good works--clothing the naked, giving hospitality to the stranger, visiting the sick and imprisoned--are surely vessels of mercy.[188] In Fulgentius there was a closer conjunction of the monastic ethos and the doctrine of election than in any other figure of the entire controversy.

Furthermore, there was in his treatise less uncertainty about perseverance than Augustine had shown. For example, he argued that Christ has already said that those persons who perform good works for his sake will receive eternal life. How then can their condition be construed otherwise?[189] The same holds true, as Scripture testifies, for those who suffer abuse in this world for Christ's sake, as do monks and laity who serve God.[190] At the same time, Fulgentius suggested,

---

[184]*De ver.* 3.15.24.
[185]*De ver.* 3.16.25.
[186]*De ver.* 3.17.27.
[187]*De ver.* 2.23.44.
[188]*De ver.* 2.23.44.
[189]*De ver.* 2.23.44.
[190]*De ver.* 2.23.45.

it is those within the church who persist in error who can be identified as the vessels of abuse.[191] The criterion by which one's standing before God can be discerned, Fulgentius believed, was the quality of one's life. Those who rejected the dictates of the world, as did the monks, were obviously chosen by God. Those who rejected the dictates of the church, as did troublemakers and heretics, were obviously rejected by God. In neither case did their behavior determine their standing before God. On the contrary, their standing before God determined the behavior that they willed and accomplished. If it is the human condition to be a vessel of abuse or of mercy, an instrument or container molded by its contents, then it should be possible to detect from external signs one's internal condition. One could examine one's own life for evidence of election. The importance of human agency appears to reside not in the person's actions in themselves but in these actions as they witness to the divine action within the person.

Since the basis for assurance about one's standing before God is not discernible from such signs as rank or achievement within or without the church but from evidence of the good which God is doing through the person, any sort of social elitism is undercut. Similar to Augustine's discovery, Fulgentius found the criterion for human worth to be located in grace.[192] This nonelitism which he espoused was fundamental to his understanding of the nature of authority. The problem, however, was that Fulgentius undercut one kind of elitism, that of rank, only to replace it with another, that of election, now dangerously ascertainable in the moral character of a person's life. It is an elitism of visible saints.

Fulgentius's assurance about the signs of election did cohere with his inattention, noted above, to the case of graced Christians who ultimately fall away. It can surely be construed as evidence that Fulgentius did not retain Augustine's distinction between predestination to faith and predestination to glory but, instead, took the two as one.

Fulgentius cited as authority for his doctrine of grace a wide variety of passages from Scripture, especially the experience of Paul.[193] Without making explicit reference to anyone except Augustine, he insisted that what he taught was consistent with the testimony of both the Greek and the Latin fathers, who themselves had been inspired by the Holy Spirit. Their testimony, in turn, was consistent with the apostolic tradition itself.[194] Presumably Fulgentius believed that the authority for what he said rested, not in the realities of monastic experience,

---

[191]*De ver.* 2.24.46.

[192]Cf. W. S. Babcock, "Augustine and Tyconius: A Study in the Latin Appropriation of Paul," *Studia Patristica* 18 (Oxford and New York: Pergamon Press, 1982): 1211-12.

[193]*De ver.* 2.15.25; 2.15.26; 2.16.27. Scriptural references include Rom. 5:3-5, 2 Tim. 2:3, 1 Cor. 15:10, 7:25, Phil. 4:12-13, Col. 1:29.

[194]*De ver.* 2.17.30; 2.18.31.

whether Eastern or Western, but in his faithfulness to what he believed to be the divine Spirit speaking through the tradition of the church.

In fact, Fulgentius's repeated warnings against pride, against the conviction that the good that one does is self-derived, may easily be construed as a criticism of the anthropological assumptions of monastic effort. Yet such a conclusion on our part is tenuous at best, for his attack was explicitly directed not at any monastic claims but at the notion that rank in this world is indicative of rank in eternity. In particular, he rejected the identification of the vessels of mercy with persons of high ecclesiastical or secular position and of the vessels of wrath with such undistinguished folk as clerics, monks, and the laity. It is clear that Fulgentius repudiated the idea that prominence within church or world is a sign of election.[195] Bishops and emperors are not to assume that they are vessels of honor but must live humbly and conscientiously in the service of God and their people.[196] Similarly, those who have abandoned the values of the world, monks and clerics who live godly lives, are not to be regarded as despised by God simply because of their low temporal estate.[197] Not rank but the gifts of grace, faith working through love, make one a vessel of honor.[198] It is not that Fulgentius held all bishops in suspicion. To the contrary, he listed a group of distinguished bishops from East and West, such as Innocent of Rome, Athanasius of Alexandria, Gregory of Nazianzen, Basil of Caesarea, Ambrose of Milan, John of Constantinople, and Augustine of Hippo, and insisted that no one could doubt that they were vessels of mercy. His point, however, was that the same valuation is equally true of certain holy monks lacking in ecclesiastical rank.[199] Election cuts across any temporal elitism.

Conclusion

In Faustus's *De gratia* the Semi-Pelagians' position had reached its fullest expression. Fulgentius in the *De veritate praedestinationis et gratiae Dei* presented the final thoroughly Augustinian argument. The controversy would remain unresolved until the Council of Orange in 529, but each side had stated its case as cogently as it ever would.

Faustus had given the argument for human agency. Although fallen in Adam, human nature is not so vitiated as to be unable to choose between the good and evil and effect its choices. The assistance of grace is necessary for the beginning and the accomplishment of the good, but in no way can grace be construed as

---

[195]*De ver.* 2.20.36; 2.21.37.
[196]*De ver.* 2.22.39.
[197]*De ver.* 2.22.41.
[198]*De ver.* 2.22.40.
[199]*De ver.* 2.22.43.

controlling human decision and action. The outcome, therefore, in reward and punishment, is a just recompense which is reliably given to human deserving. Furthermore, grace is presented as being available to everyone. God wills the salvation of all and makes that salvation a universal possibility, but the realization of that possibility remains dependent upon human choice and action. Faustus had attempted to steer a course between the extreme Pelagian emphasis on human agency to the denigration of grace and the extreme Augustinian emphasis on divine agency to the denigration of any human contribution. It was in this middle ground, with its recognition of the necessity of both human agency and divine grace, that he located the normative tradition of the church. Even in this middle ground, however, his aim was primarily to emphasize the significance of human action and, only secondarily, the necessary assistance of grace.

In contrast, Fulgentius had presented the argument for sovereign grace. The human condition as fallen in Adam is so thoroughly incapacitated as to be unable to will and to do the good apart from the transforming work of God. Good works necessarily depend upon the operation of grace. That operation is totally gratuitous and as such is completely determined by the divine will and choice. As a result, a person's good will and action and, accordingly, even final destiny are the outcome of divine agency as it elects human agents and then unfailingly works through them in correspondence with the divine will. The fact that not all are saved is evidence that God wills a particular rather than a universal salvation; however, assurance of one's own election can be derived from evidence of grace operating within one's life. Fulgentius had made the case for divine agency but at the cost of undercutting any human contribution in the attainment of salvation. A person's destiny is determined from beginning to end by the grace or judgment of God.

As we have seen, in the early decades of the sixth century, two fully elaborated positions were available. Yet it is obvious that in this stage of the controversy there were not any remarkable innovations on either side. Instead, the phase was typified by quite the opposite of novelty. The need to define and to secure an authoritative tradition markedly affected the character of the debate. Vincent, Prosper in the *Auctoritates*, Faustus, and Fulgentius, all in varying degrees, were seeking to locate and to clarify the standard by which doctrines on grace and human agency might be measured. As already noted, this activity of securing the tradition, positively, through citation and, negatively, through censorship or anathema was common to the time. Perhaps this particular passion can be seen as an attempt to maintain the continuity of the faith amidst the discontinuity and disruption of the age.

It should be noted, however, that despite the need for continuity, there was also some development in the argumentation. On the one side, Faustus effectively reinterpreted the concept of divine foreknowledge so that what had previously seemed to buttress the Augustinian position was now used to undercut it. For Faustus, foreknowledge pertains to merit and is thereby contingent upon the character of human agency. It operates to ensure a just divine judgment which is based on the quality of a person's action.

On the other side, Fulgentius contributed to the argumentation by his polemic against rank, i.e., social or ecclesiastical elitism, as evidence of one's standing before God and by his suggestion of another kind of elitism, that of visible saints. Not one's position in the church or the society but the quality of one's life could be considered as indicative of election. In contrast to Augustine, Fulgentius has allowed for the possibility of firm assurance among the elect.

Despite the absence of remarkable innovation, therefore, Faustus and Fulgentius were not simply repeating the tired arguments of a static controversy but were also advancing the discussion. In the end, however, these new points played no role in the resolution of the debate.

One change that would be of more lasting significance had to do not specifically with the argumentation but with the ecclesiastical context in which the controversy was now carried out. With Faustus and Fulgentius the lines between the monastic and the congregational setting, which had held prior to this time for the Semi-Pelagians and the Augustinians, were breaking down. Now both sides of the controversy operated in a monastic and a congregational setting. This combination of contexts would continue to be true of the last phase of the debate.

It was now time for the argumentation to draw to a close. The church lacked the resources for further disputation. Moreover, the affair over the Scythian monks had called into question the suitability of the South Gallic consensus on grace, as expressed by Faustus's *De gratia* and the Councils of Arles and Lyons for which he had written. Pope Hormisdas, through his recommendation, however restrained, of Augustine's teaching over that of Faustus, had effectively enhanced the authority of Augustine over the monastic theology of Cassian and Faustus. Augustinianism was gradually becoming the Western tradition.

Chapter 6

Caesarius of Arles:
The Culmination of the Controversy

Introduction

In tracing the development of the Semi-Pelagian controversy, several elements have been identified as recurrent in the formation of arguments on both sides of this debate. Foremost was the original theological issue of the relation between human actions and the outcome of these actions. The debate over this issue continued unresolved for over a century, and in its course certain secondary factors consistently recurred as the context in which the argumentation developed. These factors were not only theological in character but also ecclesiastical and social: the function and location of authority, particularly with respect to the identification both of tradition and of the ecclesiastical elite; the deterioration of social conditions resulting from the barbarian invasions and the emergence of the church as the primary institution of stability and continuity in an increasingly barbarized world; the emergence of Western monasticism as related to all of the other elements but particularly as the essential element without which there would have been no debate.

In the last phase of the controversy the truly remarkable phenomenon was the convergence of all these factors in the career of one man, Caesarius of Arles. A bishop who brought the authority of an ecclesiastical council to bear on the resolution of the debate, an educator who was ever-diligent that his flock be informed in Christian faith and morals yet was at the same time somewhat suspicious of the classical heritage, an effective activist who was responsive to the needs of a society crumbling about him, a monk who was trained at Lérins but also profoundly influenced by Augustinianism—Caesarius was all of these. As a result, his work was revelatory not only of the character of the church in the early sixth century in South Gaul but also of the dynamics of the last stage of the Semi-Pelagian debate.

Particularly illustrative of these dynamics was the relationship between the position taken at the Council of Orange regarding divine grace and human agency and the position taken on the same issue in the sermons that Caesarius disseminated throughout much of Gaul as well as in the short treatise that he wrote, the *De gratia*. The similarity of the council's theological stance to that found in

Caesarius's sermons and treatise indicates not only the prominence of the bishop of Arles but also the viability of the pastoral theology that he espoused. In order to interpret the import of these sermons, it is necessary that the context in which the sermons belong first be defined.

A Changed World and a Changed Church

It is chiefly through the sermons of Caesarius that we are able to become acquainted with the theology of the man who, in bringing the Semi-Pelagian controversy to a conclusion, effectively undercut the influence of those who opposed Augustinianism. Nevertheless, these sermons were not written primarily, if at all, to combat Semi-Pelagianism but rather to instruct the bishop's fellow Christians in the faith and its attendant morals. Caesarius was addressing the parish priests and the laity of the Gallic towns and countryside; thus the context in which these sermons were produced and heard differed markedly from the context in which the theological debate had been carried on. A brief look at this new context is necessary preparation, therefore, for an examination of the sermons. The political, social, and cultural circumstances of the Gallic church will be viewed from three perspectives: popular religious practice, the expansion of religious education, particularly for monks and clergy, and the life of Caesarius himself.

To understand popular religious practice during the episcopacy of Caesarius, it is necesary to realize that Christianity still had a relatively tenuous position in Gaul. At the time of the Germanic invasions and for a century or more afterwards, understanding of and commitment to this alien religion were far more extensive than intensive, especially among the poorly educated or illiterate rural population. Large numbers of people might have borne the name "Christian" as a result of the conversion of their patron, presumably an aristocratic landlord; yet the ancestral, community-based, folk religion of the native Gauls and of the Germanic immigrants was never far below the surface. Christianity definitely did spread among the unlettered masses, but its content was not only impoverished by the limited literacy of both clergy and laity but was also highly colored by the oral folk culture of these Gallic peasants and the Germanic invaders.[1]

---

[1]William E. Klingshirn, *Caesarius of Arles: The Making of a Christian Community in Late Antique Gaul* (Cambridge: Cambridge University Press, 1994) 1-2, 183-85, 202; James C. Russell, *The Germanization of Early Medieval Christianity: A Sociohistorical Approach to Religious Transformation* (Oxford: Oxford University Press, 1994) 134-82; J. Ropert, "Mentalité religieuse et régression culturelle dans la Gaule franque du Ve au VIIIe siècle," *Les cahiers de Tunisie* 24 (1976) 45-47; R. P. C. Hanson, "The Reaction of the Church to the Collapse of the Western Roman Empire in the Fifth Century," *Vigiliae Christianae* 26 (1972): 286. For a survey of Gallic religion prior to Christianity, see J. J. Hatt, "Essai sur l'évolution de la religion gauloise," *Revue des études anciennes* 67

The coexistence of Christianity and paganism is indisputable, particularly in rural areas. Two examples illustrate the geographically widespread character of this situation: a sermon from North Italy by Maximus of Turin (died sometime between 408 and 423) and another from Galicia or northwest Spain by Martin of Braga (520-580). Although Maximus's sermon was delivered in Italy approximately a century before Caesarius began his episcopate, there is little reason to suppose that the situation in the Italian countryside was significantly different from that in corresponding areas of Gaul a hundred years later.

Maximus was warning landowners who lived in Turin, thus away from their estates, that they themselves were corrupted by the idolatrous practices engaged in by those who worked their lands. It was the owner's responsibility to remove the idols and forbid the pagan practices.[2] The catechetical sermon of Martin of Braga, whose life more nearly overlapped that of Caesarius, reinforces the image of the coexistence of paganism and Christianity in rural areas. Martin's sermon was intended for those who lived outside the cities in the countryside, presumably primarily peasants. It enumerated specific pagan practices and traced their origins to the operation of the devil and his demons. Martin admonished his hearers to abjure these observances as totally incompatible with their baptismal renunciation of the devil and confession of faith in the triune God. The purpose of the sermon was to provide a remedy for the peasants' ignorance. It provided instruction concerning both the sinfulness of idolatry and the truth of the Christian confession.[3]

The first canon of the second Council of Braga (572) further attested to the presence of pagan practice in Galicia. It specified that the bishops had to instruct their people about the errors of idolatry.[4] Moreover, in the *capitula* that Martin offered as a Latin translation of canons of the Eastern church, there were several canons concerned with idolatry. As some of them had no precedent and all of

---

(1965): 80-125.

[2]Maximus of Turin, *Serm.* 107. English translation in *The Sermons of Maximus of Turin*, trans. Boniface Ramsey, Ancient Christian Writers 50 (New York: Newman, 1989) 236-37; *Christianity and Paganism, 350–370: The Conversion of Western Europe*, ed. J. N. Hillgarth (Philadelphia: Univ. of Pennsylvania Press, 1986) 53-55; W. H. C. Frend, "The Winning of the Countryside," *Journal of Ecclesiastical History* 18 (1967): 12.

[3]Martin of Braga, *De correctione rusticorum*. English translation in *Iberian Fathers*, vol. 1, *Martin of Braga, Paschasius of Dumium, Leander of Seville*, trans. Claude W. Barlow, Fathers of the Church 61 (Washington DC: Catholic University of America Press, 1969) 71-85; Hillgarth, 53-55; M. Meslin, "Persistances païennes en Galice, vers la fin du VIe siècle," *Hommages à Marcel Renard*, vol. 2, ed. Jacqueline Bibauw (Brussels: Latomus, 1969) 512-24.

[4]Stephen McKenna, *Paganism and Pagan Survivals in Spain up to the Fall of the Visigothic Kingdom* (Washington DC: Catholic University of America Press, 1938) 84.

them accorded with denunciations made in Martin's *De correctione rusticorum*, probably written soon afterward (ca. 574), there is reason to believe that Martin himself composed the canons on idolatry in reaction to prevalent local practice.[5]

Additional evidence of the presence of paganism, this time in southeastern Gaul, can be found in the sermons of Caesarius. He inveighed against various superstitions and pagan practices[6] and even encouraged physical punishment as a deterrent to such behavior.[7] The sermons suggest that it was not only the laity but also the clergy who at times fell prey to superstition.[8] Caesarius thus felt it necessary to instruct the ignorant and admonish the erring.

Explanations for the tenacity of paganism, particularly among the Gallic peasantry, suggest that the benefits that Christianity offered, such as forgiveness of sins and individual salvation, and the requirements that it imposed, such as adherence to doctrine and conformity to ethical standards, had little, if any, appeal to persons whose ancestral religion attended to their communal needs for material prosperity. For Christianity to attract such persons, they had to be convinced of the superior power of the Christian God to provide for the well-being of persons, animals, and crops.[9] Similarly, for Christianity to gain and to maintain the loyalty of the Germanic invaders, these peoples had to believe that the Christian God offered at least the same material security, including success in war, that the tribal deities had been depended upon to provide. As Wallace-Hadrill has argued, the Franks converted to a religion which they believed to be continuous with that of their ancestors. Strong familial ties inclusive of the deceased as well as basically constant religious values would have precluded too radical a shift in religious loyalties. Their conversion to Christianity was initially, at least, "the substitution of one kind of folk-magic for another."[10]

---

[5]See McKenna, 84-86.

[6]Caesarius, *Serm* 1.12; 13.3,5; 14.4; 19.4; 50.1; 51.1,4; 52.2,2; 53.1,2; 54.5; 184.4; 192; 193; cf. Henry G. J. Beck, *The Pastoral Care of Souls in South-East France during the Sixth Century* (Rome: Gregoriana, 1950) 281-83. Wallace-Hadrill, 14, has pointed out that the paganism with which Caesarius was concerned was not classical paganism but a popular variety. For a discussion of this paganism, see Klingshirn, 209-26. See also Rudolph Arbesmann, "The 'cervuli' and 'anniculae' in Caesarius of Arles," *Traditio* 35 (1979): 89-119.

[7]*Serm.* 13.5. For a discussion of Caesarius's views on coercion for religious purposes, see Klingshirn, 232-33, 238-41.

[8]*Serm.* 50.1; cf. Beck, 281n.100.

[9]Russell, 102-103, 180; C. E. Stancliffe, "From Town to Country: The Christianisation of the Touraine 370–600," in *The Town and Countryside*, ed. D. Baker, Studies in Church History 16 (Oxford: Basil Blackwell, 1979) 52-53. For a useful description of the characteristics of community or local religion, see Klingshirn, 46-47.

[10]J. M. Wallace-Hadrill, *The Frankish Church* (Oxford: Clarendon Press, 1983) 33-36.

Even as Christianization gradually progressed in the countryside in fifth and sixth century Gaul, traditional religious habits and beliefs of indigenous Gallic paganism and of Germanic paganism continued. What resulted were complex patterns of loyalties, with persons who identified themselves as Christians continuing to engage in ancient religious practices that had been designed to ensure such things as agricultural productivity or the recovery of health.[11]

An important factor that contributed to the persistence of paganism was the general decline of literacy. Whereas in previous times education had been a mark differentiating the upper and middle classes from the illiterate lower class, it now increasingly became a mark distinguishing the clergy from the laity. It must be acknowledged, of course, that some lay persons were highly literate and many of the clergy were barely so; nevertheless, the church, despite its suspicion of the classical heritage, gradually became the repository of learning. Specifically, it was in the church that written Latin was preserved, whereas in the secular, unlettered world a spoken, decadent, yet living Latin became the common language.[12]

As an example of the deterioration of the language, one might cite the preface of Gregory of Tours' *Historia Francorum* in which Gregory acknowledged his own lack of literary skill and bemoaned the fact that no one possessed sufficient training to chronicle the times. Such professions of literary inability and cultural inadequacy were a standard rhetorical device and thus cannot necessarily be accepted at face value; nevertheless, Gregory's own writing tends to confirm his self-evaluation.[13]

The decline in educational level could not but have affected the church. With the priests often minimally educated and bishops sometimes hardly any better off, their limited knowledge of Latin hindered the study and exposition of the Scripture, and their ignorance of the church fathers contributed to a general theological regression.[14] Furthermore, because the church had found it necessary to accommodate its message to the religious expectations of its Gallic and Germanic hearers, emphasis had shifted from such things as the reorientation of life through repentance and forgiveness of sins to the superior power of the Christian God over the material world. Entailed in this shift was greater attention than previously to the cult of the saints and religious relics as means of access to divine

---

[11]Klingshirn, 209-26; Ropert, 48-50; Frend, "The Winning of the Countryside," 8.

[12]Wallace-Hadrill, 50-53; Riché, 31-36, 48-51, 79-99, 184-89, 196-97; Auerbach, 250-58.

[13]*Historia Ecclesiastica Francorum, Praef.*; see Gregory of Tours, *The History of the Franks*, vol. 2, trans. O. M. Dalton (Oxford: Clarendon Press, 1927). For an assessment of Gregory's literary skill, see Erich Auerbach, *Literary Language and Its Public in Late Latin Antiquity and in the Middle Ages*, trans. Ralph Manheim, Bollingen Series 74 (New York: Bollinger Foundation, 1965) 103-12.

[14]Ropert, 54-56.

power. Such accommodation, in combination with the limited literacy of the clergy, resulted in a Gallic church the vast majority of whose membership was poorly educated in the doctrinal content and ethical norms of the Christian faith. The church, rather than necessarily serving to transform the belief and practice of its members, was to some degree itself transformed or even "Germanized."[15]

It is not automatically to be assumed, however, that this transformation was necessarily a matter of degeneration or paganization of the church. Peter Brown has argued that popular Christianity, such as evidenced in the cult of the saints, was neither simply the reemergence of the old pagan substratum now clothed in Christian garb, nor somehow different in practice from that form of Christianity observed by the ecclesiastical leadership. Nor was it the case that the leadership gave in to the force of popular pressure. Instead, what is to be seen in such phenomena as the cult of the saints was the attempt of both the elite and the masses to express a new form of piety based on significantly different presuppositions about the material world and the holy than had been held by their pagan predecessors.[16]

According to Brown, the shrine of the saint became the locus for the saint's *praesentia*, and around the shrines developed elaborate patterns of interaction with and dependence upon the holy, yet deceased, person. Proper observance of such behavior constituted *reverentia*; breaches in propriety toward the supernatural signaled *rusticitas*.[17] The latter quality could be as much an element of urban life as of rural life; nevertheless, inhabitants of the countryside tended to lack the ease of access to the shrines that the urban Christian possessed, and they typically were not so well trained in the manners of interaction with the divine. As a result, there was something of a division between urban and rural religion, but it should not be construed as a division between Christian and pagan. The division was within Christianity itself between loci of accessibility and inaccessibility to the holy.[18] From Brown's argument one might conclude that the goal of

---

[15]Stancliffe, 54-59; Ropert, 54-59; Russell, 4, 39.

[16]Peter Brown, *The Cult of the Saints* (Chicago: University of Chicago Press, 1981) 17-22. Wallace-Hadrill, *The Frankish Church*, 9, 78, has argued that the devotion to relics that rose to importance in the fifth century in Gaul, although it had pagan antecedents, was not only a decidedly Christian but also a predominantly aristocratic phenomenon. Similarly, the lives of the saints written in the late sixth century were intended by their lettered authors to capture the loyalty of the masses of people and to guide their worship. Their audience was popular, but their source was not.

[17]Brown, *Cult of the Saints*, 119-20. Wallace-Hadrill, *The Frankish Church*, 50, confirmed that the *reverentia* offered in the cult of a saint was a matter of manners and not of paganism. The contrast to *reverentia* was "boorish *rusticitas*," not some purer form of Christianity.

[18]Brown, *Cult of the Saints*, 121-22, 124.

Caesarius's sermons was to educate Christians, both urban and rural, in the etiquette of relation with the divine.

A second perspective from which the changed conditions of the time can be observed is in the evolution, however gradual, of religious education. As the enormity of the change which the West was undergoing was only slowly recognized, so the need for a greatly expanded educative role of the church did not immediately become obvious. The appearance of peace and stability belied the vast alterations in political reality. Of particular importance was the fact that the situation of the aristocrats seems to have remained remarkably stable during this time. The old nobility still maintained its position, property, and centuries-old opportunities for diversion.[19] Moreover, the illusion of imperial unity remained despite the division of the Mediterranean region into four barbarian kingdoms. The new borders offered little impediment to travelers or communication, and the situation was even improved after 507. At that time Theodoric, the Ostrogothic ruler of Italy, annexed Provence to his domain[20] and thereby restored partial unity.

Continuity with the classical heritage steadily degenerated, however. Some barbarian leaders early evinced interest in classical culture, but by the beginning of the sixth century, their numbers had dwindled to insignificance.[21] The barbarian governments were in need of bureaucrats whose training had prepared them for administrative service, but such training was almost entirely practical and required no knowledge of the classics. The careers of Cassiodorus and Boethius, whose remarkable classical education and literary accomplishments were utilized to the advantage of Theodoric's court, provided notable exceptions to this situation. On the whole, however, there was little use for Roman aristocrats who were proficient in literary and rhetorical skills. As a result, the incentive for educating Roman children in their heritage was diminished. Some nobles accepted the habits of the Germans and encouraged physical, even military, education over classical learning. Others sought refuge from the changed world by becoming clergy or monks and acquiring the peculiar kind of education that came to be available in the church.[22]

---

[19]Riché, 20-21; Samuel Dill, *Roman Society in the Last Century of the Western Empire*, 2nd ed. (London: Macmillan, 1899) 374.

[20]Riché, 18.

[21]Riché, 62, 64. The Vandal aristocracy in North Africa and the royal Amal family in Italy were exceptions. On the whole, the barbarians sought to maintain their own culture as a means of safeguarding their peculiarity and cohesiveness.

[22]Riché, 76-78. On early development of Christian schools in Gaul, see T. J. Haarhoff, *Schools of Gaul: A Study of Pagan and Christian Education in the Last Century of the Western Empire* (Johannesburg: Witwatersrand University Press, 1958) 175-97.

As indicated in the preceding chapters, the church had not always stood in opposition to classical culture or offered an alternative to it. Instead, it was only with the decline of the classical school that the rejection of that culture became outspoken within the church, just as it was partially as a result of that decline that Christian schools arose.

For the purposes of the church and its ministry, the preparation provided by a classical education simply ceased to be of much benefit. Such schooling increasingly stressed complication in form over richness of substance. Yet a complicated, highly stylized form of presentation was hardly suitable for communicating the gospel to a marginally literate audience. Evangelization and pastoral work required that the clergy be schooled in simpler, more engaging modes of discourse.[23] An example of such an effective style can be found in Martin of Braga's *De correctione rusticorum* which was addressed to peasants.[24] Of course, a needed shift in the preparation of the clergy was not the only reason for the emergence and development of a purely religious education. As in the past, accusations of immorality and error were leveled against the literary and philosophical components of classical instruction. Yet finally the impetus of change came from the church's own missionary and pastoral need to communicate its message.[25]

We shall return shortly to an examination of the preaching style that did emerge. For the moment, however, it is important to take note of the distinctly religious culture that arose first alongside of and later in place of the classical. This culture emerged initially within the monasteries. Its purpose was to provide a context in which the desires and behavior of the learner might be converted and perfection attained.[26] Reading served as a key feature of the pedagogy: common reading at meals, private reading, and the recitation of the Psalter. Of course, as some of the inhabitants of the monasteries were merely children, and others, although older, were unable to read, basic elementary instruction had to be provided. The materials used not only for this instruction in literacy but also for lifelong nurture were those suited for the formation of an ascetic culture. Secular writings of the classical tradition appear to have been by-passed,[27] although an obvious exception would have been Cassiodorus's *Institutiones divinarum et humanarum litterarum* which was originally composed about 562. Yet Cassiodorus wrote the *Institutiones* for the education of his own monks at Squillace. He

---

[23]Riché, 79-95.

[24]Martin of Braga, *De correctione rusticorum*, in Hillgarth, 57-64.

[25]Riché, 87-91.

[26]Riché, 100.

[27]Riché, 112-21. Riché, 118-19, includes among the materials studied the Bible, the Rules of Basil and Pachomius, the writings of John Cassian, and the works of the fathers.

intended secular learning to function in the service of their religious education: it was to contribute to the development of skills in biblical interpretation.[28]

Clergy, however, typically were not monks, and lacked the training provided in a monastery. In order to facilitate their separation from the secular culture and their preparation for office in the religious one, at least in a few instances, an episcopal residential community, *domus ecclesiae*, was formed for that purpose. Certainly not all who were to enter the ranks of the clergy had the benefit of such professional training and basic education while living in community, but for some the opportunity was made available, as in the home of Bishop Caesarius.[29] In rural areas a similar arrangement developed. Religious instruction was provided in the household of the parish priest.[30] Finally, in scattered cases, some training was available for those who wished to study and interpret Scripture by means of the tools earlier developed for the examination of classical texts.[31] Classical instruction of any sort for future clerics was the exception, however, and not the common practice. Those who entered the priesthood typically had not been schooled in the classics elsewhere.

It should be remarked that the various types of Christian educational institutions that existed in the early sixth century did so alongside of and not yet in place of secular education. They were founded to provide a specific kind of training unavailable in a classical school. Their purpose was to shape monks and clerics in a religious culture.[32]

As the altered social conditions were mirrored in the evolution of religious practice and religious education within the church, so also the social and ecclesiastical conditions of late fifth and early sixth century southeastern Gaul can be seen in the life of one of its foremost leaders, Caesarius of Arles. Specifically, the character of the changing times may be glimpsed in the peculiar kind of pastoral oversight that his episcopacy provided.

Born about 470 in Chalon-sur-Saône, reared in a Catholic, probably aristocratic, home, accepted into the clergy, presumably as a lector, at the age of seventeen, Caesarius entered the monastery at Lérins about two years later. There he was trained in monastic discipline for at least half a decade.[33] For reasons of

---

[28]Cassiodorus, *Inst.* 1.27.1; cf. James J. O'Donnell, *Cassiodorus*, 202-206.

[29]*VCaes.* 2.5-6; Hanson, "The Reaction of the Church to the Collapse of the Western Roman Empire in the Fifth Century," 281; Riché, 124-26.

[30]Riché, 128-29; Beck, 61-62. The Council of Vaison, 529, canon 1 (CCSL 148A) ruled that all parish priests would keep young lectors in their homes and instruct them in the Psalms, the holy readings, and the law of the Lord that they might provide worthy successors for themselves.

[31]Riché, 129-35.

[32]Riché, 134-35.

[33]Klingshirn, 16-32; Riché, 122-23; "Introduction," *Saint Caesarius of Arles: Sermons*,

health Caesarius went to Arles where he began but quickly abandoned the study of classical literature, presumably because of reservations regarding its appropriateness and adequacy in the spiritual formation of a cleric and monk.[34] The abortive character of this educational venture was later reflected in the nonclassical, even rustic style of Caesarius's own sermons as well as in his continuing suspicion of pagan literature. On the other hand, Caesarius was hardly unlettered. He taught Latin to Abbot Florianus of Milan, and his own work reflects an extensive knowledge of the church fathers.[35] In fact, his teacher of classical rhetoric, Julianus Pomerius who was himself an Augustinian, had a decided influence on the development of Caesarius's own theological views, including his views on grace.[36]

While he was in Arles, his abilities came to the attention of the local bishop Aeonius, who was also his relative. The bishop, recognizing that Caesarius could provide much-needed leadership for the Arlesian church, obtained his release from Abbot Porcarius of Lérins, ordained Caesarius to the diaconate, later made him a priest, then established him as the abbot of the local monastery for men.[37] Finally, he actively sought to ensure that, at his own death, Caesarius would succeed him. That succession does not seem to have been entirely smooth, but Caesarius was indeed elevated to the episcopacy of Arles in 502.[38]

It was in his capacity as bishop that this product of Lérins is of particular interest. As pastor of the most prestigious see in Gaul,[39] Caesarius assumed extensive responsibility, which he discharged with distinction. He was particularly effective in adapting his pastoral style and efforts to the vagaries of the age. Specifically, he not only functioned in the traditional role of the activist bishops

---

3 vols., trans. Sister Mary Magdeleine Mueller, Fathers of the Church 31, 47, 66 (Washington DC: Catholic University of America Press, 1956, 1964, 1972) 1:v-vii. (Most of the English translations of quotations from the sermons of Caesarius will be taken from Mueller; a fresh reading has been offered when appropriate.) For a somewhat different interpretation of the chronology, see Griffe, 3:321-22. *Sancti Caesarii Arelatensis Vita ab eius familiaribus conscripta, Sancti Caesarii Arelatensis opera omnia*, ed. G. Morin, 1.3-5, 3 (Maredsous, 1942): 1.3-5. For an English translation of portions of the *Vita*, see Hillgarth, 32-43.

[34]*VCaes.* 2.5-6. For a discussion of the reform movement in the Gallic church to which Caesarius's rejection of classical education was related, see Klingshirn, 18-19, 74-82.

[35]Beck, 13, citing Florianus, *Ep. ad Nicetium.*

[36]J. C. Plumpe, "Pomeriana," *Vigiliae Christianae* 1 (1947): 227-39; A. Solignac, "Julien Pomère," *Dictionnaire de spiritualité* (Paris, 1947) 8:1594-1600; Klingshirn, 72-82, 142, citing C. Tibiletti, "La teologia della grazia," *Augustinianum* 25 (1985): 489-506.

[37]*VCaes.* 1.11; cf. Beck, 47-48; Klingshirn, 83.

[38]*VCaes.* 1. 13-14; Klingshirn, 83-87, suggested that another may have briefly served as bishop after the death of Aeonius and before the episcopacy of Caesarius.

[39]Griffe, 2:190, 193, 237; Klingshirn, 51-71.

of the preceding century, but in a changed world he also developed means for the pastoral oversight of an increasingly illiterate flock. In other words, he accepted responsibility for securing both the physical welfare of his fellow citizens during the turmoil of the barbarian struggles and the spiritual welfare of his fellow Christians whose world had been radically reshaped by these struggles.

Hillgarth has described Caesarius as representing "the role the native Gallo-Roman bishops played in the confused century between the collapse of Rome and the assured hegemony of the Franks." As such he is credited with the "relatively peaceful transition [of Arles and Provence], first from Visigoths to Ostrogoths (508), and then (536) from Ostrogoths to Franks."[40] After the siege of Arles in 508-509, Caesarius ransomed captives from the Goths, at first by emptying the episcopal treasury and afterwards by the sale of valuable liturgical equipment and ornamentation.[41] In 513 clerical opposition, possibly to his sale of church assets for the benefit of the women's monastery that he had founded, led to his being arrested and taken to the court of the Ostrogothic ruler Theodoric in Ravenna. Caesarius, however, took advantage of the occasion to gain the support of both Theodoric and Pope Symmachus for the extension of the authority of the see of Arles.[42] He even used Theodoric's gifts to him to redeem prisoners taken by the Ostrogoths, including inhabitants of the city of Orange.[43] Other acts of charity in response to the needs of the times included the establishment of a hospital[44] and the provision of housing for former prisoners. His own home was even used for this latter purpose.[45]

Attention to the physical well-being of his people was only one aspect of Caesarius's episcopal leadership. The activist bishop never abandoned his training and allegiances as a monk. He composed *Regulae* for monks and nuns, required greater discipline of his clerics, and in Hillgarth's estimation, "represents the definite triumph of monasticism in the Gallic church."[46] Thus in Caesarius we

---

[40]Hillgarth, 21. For a discussion of Caesarius's lack of identification with the old Roman political and cultural order and his receptivity to the new order of competing barbarian kingdoms, see William M. Daly, "Caesarius of Arles, A Precursor of Medieval Christendom," *Traditio* 26 (1970): 1-28. See also, R. A. Markus, "The Sacred and the Secular: From Augustine to Gregory the Great," *Journal of Theological Studies* n.s. 36 (1985): 84-96; J. J. O'Donnell, "Liberius the Patrician," *Traditio* 37 (1981): 31-72.
[41]*VCaes.*1.32,33; Klingshirn, 114-17; cf. Beck, 340.
[42]*VCaes.* 1.36-38; Arnold, 272-81; Klingshirn, 123-37.
[43]*VCaes.* 1.37-38; cf. Beck, 340.
[44]*VCaes.* 1.20; cf. Beck, 334.
[45]Mueller, *Sermons* 1:x-xi.
[46]Hillgarth, 21; Klingshirn, 83, 102-103, 118-22, 186-88, 199-200, 251-52; Prinz, 76-84. *Césaire d'Arles, Oeuvres monastiques*, vol. 1, *Oeuvres pour les moniales*, ed. and trans. Joël Courreau and Adalbert de Vogüé, Sources chrétiennes 345 (Paris: Les Éditions du Cerf, 1988). For a discussion of the spread of the ascetic ideal in the churches of Gaul

find a clear confirmation of a tendency which was already apparent in Faustus and Fulgentius. That tendency was the merging of two streams which seemed at odds in the beginning of the Semi-Pelagian controversy: 1) bishop and congregation, of which Augustine was representative, and 2) monk and monastery, of which Cassian was representative. In this respect, he was, of course, preceded by a sequence of monk-bishops in Gaul going back to Martin of Tours.

Caesarius's episcopal work also included obvious administrative responsibilities. Throughout the fifth century the bishops of Arles had sought to gain and maintain for Arles metropolitan status, and the struggle to secure the city's ecclesiastical prominence continued throughout Caesarius's episcopacy.[47] At Caesarius's request in 513 Pope Symmachus confirmed his metropolitan status beyond his own province of Viennensis, and the pope named him as papal vicar of Gaul, a role that gave him the authority to "oversee papal interests" throughout Gaul, although the actual extent of his control was dependent upon the shifting fortunes of the barbarian kingdoms.[48] It was as metropolitan that he had the authority to call councils, including the Council of Orange over which he presided in 529. It was this council, ratified by Pope Boniface in 531, that was the final act in the drama of the Semi-Pelagian controversy.

The Council of Vaison in 529, which was also under his jurisdiction, proved to be a milestone in Caesarius's efforts to adapt pastoral oversight to the realities of the time. Congregations were desperately in need of instruction in the faith. Sermons were infrequent, particularly in rural congregations. In earlier days Gallic priests had preached, but their authority to perform such a function had gradually eroded. The responsibility and privilege of preaching came to reside in the bishops alone,[49] but, of course, the frequency of their visits to any one congregation was necessarily limited. In response to congregational need, therefore, the council restored to the priests the authority to preach. If the priest were unable, a deacon was to read from the fathers.[50] Caesarius's role in ensuring the implementation of the council's action can hardly be overestimated. He made collections of sermons available to priests in rural areas so that, even if they were poorly educated themselves, they could still instruct their people properly.[51] The sermons were both his own and those of the church fathers as modified by him for purposes of brevity, clarity, and suitability for the Gallic church. Caesarius

---

and Caesarius's role in this effort, see Markus, *The End of Ancient Christianity*, 199-228.

[47]Klingshirn, 65-71.

[48]*VCaes.* 1.42; Klingshirn, 127-32; Mathisen, 50n.37.

[49]Beck, 267-68.

[50]Conc. Vaison, 529, canon 2; *Serm.* 1.15; Klingshirn, 144-45, 229-32; Beck, 268-69.

[51]*VCaes.* 1.55; *Praefatio libri sermonum; Serm.* 1.15; Beck, 267.

also gave these collections to the bishops under his charge for use by their own priests and deacons; thus the sermons had widespread geographical distribution.[52]

The content of these sermons as it was relevant to the Semi-Pelagian controversy will be examined shortly; however, for the moment it is important to note the remarkable homiletic style employed by Caesarius and his contemporaries. In sermons intended for the instruction and nurture of unlettered people, Caesarius sought to present the truths of the Catholic faith in a manner that was not only theologically responsible but was also suited to the level of his hearers. The direct, yet vivid character of the sermons reveals that the activist bishop could also function effectively as the sixth century pastor of the semi-literate and illiterate masses in the city and countryside. His own preaching was, of course, primarily in the city, but the sermon collections were utilized in rural as well as urban churches.

Caesarius's homiletic style has been criticized for its lack of classical eloquence, but as Erich Auerbach has pointed out, the bishop's sermons had an eloquence all their own, peculiar to the development of a new genre. His unadorned manner of expression was not simply the result of his own aborted training in classical forms. Caesarius quite deliberately opposed the use of these forms as inappropriate for the communication of the gospel to the masses whom he served.[53] This responsibility for communication he took very seriously, and he warned his fellow priests that he and they would be accountable on Judgment Day for the pastoral oversight of their congregations, especially for informing the people of the divine demands upon their lives.[54] It was because of this conviction of accountability that Caesarius not only made sermons available for the use of his priests but also made certain that such sermons were in a form comprehensible to their listeners. The ideal of clarity over that of rhetorical embellishment goes back, of course, at least as far as Augustine.

The form Caesarius employed was straightforward, rather colloquial prose that elevated the matters of everyday life to a holy seriousness.[55] If the morality of human interaction were worthy of the divine attention and judgment, then personal responsibility and accountability were matters of enormous significance. Thus it was the responsibility of the preacher to inform the congregation of their

---

[52]Mueller, *Sermons* 1.xxi, xxii, citing G. Morin, "The Homilies," *Orate Fratres* 14 (1939–1940): 484-86; cf. *VCaes.* 1.55; Klingshirn, 9-15, 231-32, 281-86.

[53]Auerbach, 87, 92; Ramsay MacMullen, "A Note on *Sermo Humilis,*" *Journal of Theological Studies* n.s. 17 (1966): 108-12; Daly, "Caesarius of Arles, A Precursor of Medieval Christendom," 8-9; Carl Franklin Arnold, *Caesarius von Arelate und die gallische Kirche seiner Zeit* (Leipzig: J. C. Hinrichs, 1894; repr. 1972) 121-23.

[54]*Serm.* 1.4, 5, 19; 57.2; 115.5; 185.7; cf. Beck, 91, 261.

[55]Auerbach, 87, 92.

just obligations and rightful hopes before God. The sermon was an instrument of pedagogy.[56] Its purpose was to communicate the Christian faith in such a manner that the parishioner might consider it, discuss it, and enact it in daily life.[57]

The prominent emphasis that Caesarius placed on Christian responsibility was not without effect in the Semi-Pelagian controversy, specifically as it contributed to the resolution of the debate. Thus it is important for us to examine the character of the Christian life that was portrayed in his sermon collection. Such an examination should provide clues for understanding the relationship between the theology that actually functioned in South Gallic congregations and the theology that governed the formulation of the canons of the Council of Orange. In contrast to the theoretical statements of the council on the interaction of divine grace and human nature, the sermons were concerned almost exclusively with practical application.

As preacher and collector of sermons, Caesarius knew how to address his audience. It was the notions of fear, judgment, repentance, and charity that actually made contact with the congregations of South Gaul, and it was these concepts that Caesarius so skillfully elaborated for his people as he composed his own sermons and edited sermons written by others. The functional theology in South Gallic churches in the early sixth century was the theology preached, most conspicuously by Caesarius, and officially defined by the Council of Orange.

The Sermons of Caesarius

In the thematic description that follows I shall make no attempt to distinguish Caesarius's own sermons from those that he borrowed and edited. Despite the fact that his sources are as diverse as Augustine and Faustus, I have operated from two related assumptions. (1) Whatever Caesarius included from the work of others he must have thought appropriate for Christian preaching and teaching. (2) As his primary motivation in disseminating sermons was to provide instruction in Christian faith and practice, he prepared his own sermons and modified the sermons of others in ways intended to maximize their pedagogical effectiveness in Gallic churches. This editorial freedom included the adaptation of the arguments, illustrations, and emphases of other preachers in accord with his own views.[58]

---

[56]Auerbach, 93, 102.

[57]Beck, 263, 271, 274, 276.

[58]For an introduction to the sermons, see Marie-José Delage, ed., *Césaire d'Arles. Sermons au People*, vol. 1, Sources chrétiénnes 175 (Paris: Les Éditions du Cerf, 1971) 65-117. For examples of his adaptations of Augustine's sermons regarding the work of grace, see Klingshirn, 142-43, and Daly, 20-21.

Regarding the relationship of the sermons to the Semi-Pelagian controversy, it should be noted that although Caesarius was highly instrumental in bringing the controversy to a close through his work at the Council of Orange, it is not at all apparent from his sermons that this controversy was a matter of great concern to him. Some of the issues of the debate are certainly to be found in the sermons, such as the pervasive emphasis on human agency and the last judgment, the references to the law and to the role of grace, and the employment of biblical images such as the fall of Adam and the hardening of Pharaoh's heart. His investigation of these issues, however, appears to have been at some remove from the dynamics of the argumentation characteristic of the controversy itself. A possible conjecture is that his preoccupation with human responsibility, repentance, the imagery of judgment, and the motivation of fear stemmed more from the early stages of his own monastic training than from his concern for the Semi-Pelagian debate.[59] Be that as it may, the sermons presumably serve as an accurate indicator of his own theological interests and convictions and of his application of these to the situation of congregations in South Gaul.

Before considering the particular sermonic themes that relate to the controversy, it is important to recognize the existence of an overall theological scheme into which the individual issues were interwoven. Caesarius, concerned as he was with the pastoral oversight of souls entrusted to his care and at least to some degree influenced by the monastic theology represented by such men as John Cassian, used his sermons to instruct the congregations in the Christian faith and morals, to exhort them to a proper pursuit of the Christian life, and to assure them of the grace of God available in and for that pursuit. The emphasis throughout was on the living of the Christian life, for by means of such a life the transformation of the self is accomplished and eternal reward is attained. The overriding theological scheme, therefore, corresponded with the general monastic framework of human action, assisted by grace, receiving its just reward in eternity. The connection between action and its outcome held. Two sets of elements were critical to this scheme: last judgment and repentance, grace and free will.

Such a theological scheme must, of course, have had its own presuppositions with regard to the human condition. These presuppositions pertained specifically to the fall of Adam and its consequences. Although Caesarius rarely mentioned the fall in his sermons, references that he did make indicate that he believed that the difficulty of the human predicament stems directly from the sin of Adam. Human nature as created by God was pristine; undefiled by any vice, the heart was governed by virtues.[60] In the transgression of Adam, however, all sinned,

---

[59]One can also point to passages in Cassian, such as *Coll.* 11.7-13, which stress the motivation of fear in the initial stages of the religious life.

[60]*Serm* 114.3; 116.5 (CCSL) or 116.1 (Fathers of the Church).

with the result that all are now born into a condition controlled by vice.[61] As Adam had lived in paradise, he and his offspring were cast out into this world, which is a hell of sorts, a middle place between paradise and the lower hell of torment from which there is no return. In contrast to the latter, this earthly hell is meant to serve as a location from which one may merit a return to paradise, one's proper home.[62]

Life on earth, therefore, is something of a way station, a rather unhappy, yet necessary point of transition to one's final destination. It is necessary because the character of one's life while on earth, i.e., one's thoughts and actions, determine whether one merits return to beatitude in the homeland or to further and final separation from God in hell. Earthly choices, therefore, are of enormous consequence, for their outcome is either eternal bliss or eternal torment. These opposite possibilities furnish the incentives for the Christian life: blessing or terror, reward or punishment.

These assumptions regarding the human condition provided the foundation on which Caesarius elaborated his scheme for human action and its outcome in eternity. Two sets of elements within this scheme, last judgment and repentance, grace and free will, must now be considered.

Perhaps the most frequently employed image in the sermons is that of the last judgment, with Christ's judgment of the nations (Matthew 25:31-46) providing the most prominent contours of that image. Although the notion of judgment necessarily contains an element of fear, which, as we shall see, Caesarius did not fail to exploit, he underscored the essentially rational character of that judgment by his insistence on a direct cause and effect relationship between one's merits and the divine decision: God will reward good deeds and punish evil ones; therefore, one should live in such a way as to earn eternal reward.[63]

Reference to the last judgment served as a dramatic and vivid way of presenting a standard of value alternate to the standard or standards that ordinarily prevailed in human society. It also served as a means of insisting that this alternate standard would finally be forced upon all who did not, by repentance in this life, bring themselves and their behavior into conformity with it. The emphasis on the last judgment was, therefore, a way of evoking a transformation of the self on the part of the hearer.

Preparation for the last judgment, according to Caesarius, included self-examination, repentance, and acts of charity. Caesarius repeatedly called his lis-

---

[61]*Serm.* 59.1; 114.3.

[62]*Serm.* 149.4; 150.1.

[63]In contrast, see Ropert, 57-58. An illustrative but hardly exhaustive list of references to Mt. 25: 31-46 include *Serm.* 15.2; 17.2; 25.2; 27.3; 29.3; 31.5; 43.7; 98.2; 104.6; 131.2; 154.2; 157.1; 158.2,6; 183.5; 199.3,4; 224.4; 228.6.

teners to an examination of their conscience. If upon self-scrutiny they discovered themselves to love and to perform the good, they should recognize themselves to be agents of God, and should rejoice. If, in contrast, they discovered evil thoughts and actions, they should know themselves to be servants of the devil and should repent.[64] Such an emphasis on self-examination as revelatory of one's standing before God was far removed from the Augustinian inscrutability of the divine decrees. On the other hand, it did accord with Fulgentius's claim of the availability of assurance through self-examination. For Caesarius the quality of one's interior and exterior life was a reliable indicator of one's final destiny. There was a trustworthy connection, therefore, between one's actions and their outcome. Fear is appropriate but not fear of a judgment already passed or of the unknown or the arbitrary but a constructive fear of one's own sins, sins which might still be repented of before it is too late.

> Endeavor always to think of the day of our death and the terrible, dreadful judgment. No more useful remedy for wounds of all sins can be found than for each to think of the hour when we will leave this world.[65]

Repentance is the key here. It is a medicine or antidote for sin.[66] It involves confession of sin, amendment of life, and performance of good deeds. By all of these acts one may redeem one's own sins and prepare for divine reward.[67] In fact, one is not harmed by one's sins if repentance precedes death,[68] for God forgives the sins that are confessed and heals the one who seeks the divine aid.[69] To hate and to turn from one's sin is to be united to God.[70] Repentance thus serves as an anticipation of the last judgment by which one willingly enacts in this life what will otherwise be forced on one unwillingly by the divine judge, i.e., condemnation and punishment for sins. Repentance, the giving up of one's old standard of value and the taking up of the divine standard, is the present means of transforming the self and bringing it into conformity with God. Otherwise, through condemnation in the last judgment, conformity is forced upon the person to the person's pain, for condemnation is itself the final and irreversible triumph of the divine standard over any standard one might claim for oneself or enact in one's behavior. As already noted, Cassian had sounded a similar theme.[71]

---

[64] *Serm.* 98.2-3; 107.4; 160.2,3; 166.5.
[65] *Serm.* 56.1.
[66] *Serm.* 5.4.
[67] *Serm.* 10.3.
[68] *Serm.* 56.2.
[69] *Serm.* 59.1,5.
[70] *Serm.* 67.1.
[71] See 105 above.

As Caesarius taught that speedy and sincere repentance is efficacious, he also taught that there are degrees of repentance appropriate to the seriousness of one's offenses. For the minor, perhaps inevitable, transgressions of life, adequate repentance consists of the giving of tithes and, after provision for necessities, the giving of what is left, as well as charity towards friends and enemies. For more serious sins committed in ignorance, repentance is to become an orientation of life, even if such repentance does not occur until near death. What was important to Caesarius was the consistent performance of charitable works combined with a turning away from one's offenses. He questioned the efficacy of repentance deliberately delayed until death and unaccompanied by good works.[72] In fact, Caesarius had no confidence whatsoever in any verbal expression of faith that lacked a physical outworking in deeds.[73] Faith was not to be nominal but lived.

Repentance, of course, would be a manifestation of faith, for, according to the bishop, faith is comprised of belief in both the divine promises of reward and the divine threats of punishment. Stated differently, faith is belief in the divine standard of value, for the rewards reward what is good by that standard and the punishments punish what is bad by that standard. Evidence of this belief consists in the performance of good works in order to earn the reward and to avoid the punishment.[74] Thus both faith and its factual expression in works are necessary in order to withstand the judgment.[75]

In particular, he urged acts of charity, especially the giving of alms.[76] Two kinds of alms sufficed for the redemption of one's own sins. The first consisted in the giving of one's substance to those in need. Not only were tithes to be presented to the church but whatever remained after provision had been made for necessities was also to be given to the poor. The second kind of alms consisted in granting forgiveness to enemies. Caesarius also spoke of the maintenance of a good will or charity toward all as a third type of alms, but typically the third was considered inseparable from the other two.[77] Good will or charity were sufficient when material alms were lacking, but the reverse was never true: the gift of one's substance must be accompanied by a charitable heart. To receive the forgiveness of God one must first forgive the neighbor.[78] In other words, mere

---

[72]*Serm.* 60; 63.

[73]*Serm.* 12.5.

[74]*Serm.* 12.1,5,6.

[75]*Serm.* 209.2,3.

[76]For an examination of the teaching of the "redemptive power of almsgiving" in the early church, see L. William Countryman, *The Rich Christian in the Church of the Early Empire: Contradictions and Accommodations* (New York and Toronto: Edwin Mellen, 1980) 103-21.

[77]*Serm.* 25.3; 28.3; 30.2-6; 34.3,5.

[78]*Serm.* 38.5; 39.1-2,4; 197.4; 199.2,8.

performance is inadequate without the genuinely appropriate motivation. Almsgiving, finally, is a matter of transformation of the self, not simply of performing certain actions, for motivation arises from the disposition of the self.

In discussing almsgiving, Caesarius referred to the centurion Cornelius, a figure important to Cassian's argument in *Collatio* 13. According to Caesarius, Cornelius and his companions had offered alms which had been accepted by God. Through their offering and its acceptance they were to some degree made clean.[79] It may be inferred that Caesarius did not deliberately exclude the view that in this instance human initiative preceded divine grace. Yet it is unlikely that he was trying to score a point for the Semi-Pelagians with this reference, for as will be noted later, his comments made in other contexts insisted upon the priority of grace.

He was trying, however, in his repeated admonitions to almsgiving to stress the necessity of a particular attitude toward the neighbor: charity. As love for the neighbor has been commanded by God, Caesarius stressed that not only is such love possible but that those who do not possess it are without excuse, for God grants it to those who seek it.[80] Charity is the fulfillment of the law;[81] it is the means for obtaining forgiveness of sins[82] and divine rewards;[83] it is an effective impediment to further sin;[84] it leads to one's inheriting the Kingdom of God.[85] Finally, it consists in the fulfillment of the twin precepts of love for God and for neighbor.[86] First, one loves God, then one learns how to love oneself properly in order to know how to love the neighbor. When there is love for both friends and enemies, one comes full circle to a perfect love of God. From charity as a manifestation of repentance one progresses through the virtues to love for God above all else.[87]

This love for God with one's whole heart and soul Caesarius depicted as the other side of the terror. Belief in the divine promises of reward is the obverse of belief in the divine threats of punishment. Belief in the latter without belief in the former, i.e., fear without love, is insufficient, for it is out of love that one desires God[88] and seeks the reward of eternal life.[89] This integral relation between

---

[79]*Serm.* 176.3; cf. Cassian, *Coll.* 13.15.
[80]*Serm.* 37.1; 137.4-5.
[81]*Serm.* 23.3.
[82]*Serm.* 128.3.
[83]*Serm.* 23.5.
[84]*Serm.* 29.3; 151.7.
[85]*Serm.* 29.3,4; 186.2,4.
[86]*Serm.* 186.3.
[87]*Serm.* 173.5.
[88]*Serm.* 140.4,5.
[89]*Serm.* 137.1,2.

fear and love bears some similarity to the relation between these two states as described by Cassian, although for the latter there was a clear movement through stages: from fear to hope to love. For both men fear and striving were necessary elements in the attainment of salvation. Such a conviction was not shared by the bishop of Hippo.

This yearning for God, which Caesarius described, presupposed an idea mentioned earlier, that is, that this earth is not our proper home. Here there can be no genuine joy; one can only use this life as a preparation by which one merits a return to the homeland, paradise.[90] He employed varied imagery to depict that preparation. For example, he used the Augustinian, biblical image of two cities. Life is a journey for the Christian from the earthly city where the Christian can only be an alien to the heavenly city where the Christian is a citizen.[91]

Caesarius's image does differ from Augustine's somewhat in that for the latter the members of the heavenly city are always members of the heavenly city; thus in one sense their earthly lives are not journeys to the heavenly city because they are already in the heavenly city. In another sense, of course, their lives are journeys to the heavenly city because these persons are not yet present in that city in its final and fulfilled condition.[92] It is not clear that Caesarius utilized both of these senses. He did remind his hearers that they are members of that heavenly city and aliens on earth; yet he also urged them to strive so that they might merit such a heavenly citizenship. His imagery contained no hint of their having eternally been members of that city. In effect, he was exhorting his fellow Christians to strive to attain their eternal goal, with the assistance of Christ, because such a destination is where they finally belong rather than where they cannot fail to be.

If Caesarius borrowed from Augustine to describe the preparation of a Christian, he also borrowed from the militaristic imagery of the monastery. It is through combat that, assisted by divine grace, one earns eternal life.[93] The struggle of daily self-examination, amendment of life, and performance of justice and peace lead to everlasting joy.[94] Preparation for beatitude is finally a matter of repentance.

Caesarius repeatedly warned, however, that manifestations of divine mercy should not blind one to the reality of divine justice. Faith consists in a belief in both, and reliance upon the former to the extent of denial of the latter is the essence of false hope.[95] Divine patience in waiting for our correction does not

---

[90]*Serm.* 215.2-5; 137.1-3.
[91]*Serm.* 151.2,6.
[92]Augustine, *De civitate Dei* 14.28; 15.1.
[93]*Serm.* 215.3-5.
[94]*Serm.* 166.5.
[95]*Serm.* 12.4-5.

negate the divine justice but, in fact, means that should we fail to repent in the face of such mercy, the punishment will be even harsher.[96] On the other hand, one should not despair in the face of one's sins, either because of their seriousness or because of their great number. Only to fear justice and not at the same time to trust mercy is to fail in faith. Divine justice and divine mercy must be upheld simultaneously.[97] The pastoral dimension of the theme of repentance has thus been effectively tapped: Caesarius has not only struck against overconfidence but has also provided an antidote to feelings of helplessness.

It is also in regard to the tension between justice and mercy that Caesarius dealt with the troublesome question of whether God is responsible for hardening the human heart. The case of Pharaoh could not be ignored. Caesarius contended that as a result of the merciful patience of God, one may continue indefinitely in one's sins and refuse to repent. Eventually the ever increasing magnitude of wrongdoing may lead to despair and despair to hardening. On the other hand, as in the case of Pharaoh, the divine mercy may occasion pride and even further sin. Again the result is hardening. Early divine justice or correction might have prevented the hardening, but correction may be withheld when hardening is deserved or when God inscrutably chooses to withhold it.[98]

Such an interpretation of the case of Pharaoh had precedent, of course, in the interpretations given by Faustus and by Origen. Faustus had taught that hardening is the individual's response to divine action. The individual is accountable for that response, for the same divine action might have occasioned the opposite response even in the same person.[99] Origen had spoken of God's withholding correction until the time is ripe for repentance.[100] Caesarius's scheme may have lacked the complexity of Origen's description of the work of grace, but for both men the divine operation had its own timetable and rationale which, however mysterious, did not in any way preclude clear human accountability. Moreover, for both men divine justice as well as divine mercy could be understood as expressions of grace. For Caesarius, the divine justice that corrects the sinner and elicits repentance is as much an expression of grace as is the divine forbearance that patiently waits for repentance and the divine forgiveness of the one who does repent.

So far, however, in surveying Caesarius's sermons we have managed to say a great deal about judgment and fear and repentance without saying much at all

---

[96]*Serm.* 17.4.
[97]*Serm.* 64.1; 184.6-7.
[98]*Serm.* 101.2-6.
[99]Faustus, *De gr.* 2.1; cf. Paul Lejay, "Le rôle théologique de Césaire d'Arles," *Revue d'histoire et de littérature religieuses* 10 (1905): 224-31; see 169-70 above.
[100]Origen, *De princ.* 3.7-13.

about grace. It appears that Caesarius presupposed the necessity of grace but saw little need to discuss it. Perhaps the reason was that he was preaching, and his primary intent was to admonish, to urge. I would suggest, however, that the fundamental reason for the emphasis on exhortation at the expense of grace was that one central image governed this thought, overshadowing all else: the last judgment. In the light of that image one must always speak of human accountability. "It is put in our power how we will be judged on the last day."[101] The conclusion is inescapable that Caesarius believed that the determination of the last judgment lies squarely on the shoulders of the individual.

This pronounced emphasis on human accountability, the urgent reminders of the impending judgment, with its possible outcome of punishment or reward, would seem necessarily to presuppose a capacity on the part of the hearer to make a fitting response. It is with reference to this capacity that Caesarius's teaching on grace is to be understood.

Caesarius's God was by no means only a judge. As fallen in Adam, Christians have been given the gift of rebirth in Christ. Christ has recalled humankind, lacking in preceding merit, from bitterness, from evil works, and from barren good ones to sweetness, charity, and fruitfulness.[102] He has restored humanity from the incapacitation of sin to health so that the soul once again has control over the body.[103]

Baptism, however, is necessary if the benefits of eternal beatitude are to be attained.[104] As Caesarius insisted that the grace of Christ's work was unmerited, so he also argued that the grace received in baptism was undeserved. Vessels of wrath by a first, carnal birth are reborn as vessels of mercy through baptism, forgiven and cleansed of all original and actual sin,[105] their nature changed.[106] Freed from bondage to the devil, they are by baptism made the "temple of God," and Christ reigns within them.[107]

By baptism, "all sins and offenses have been banished";[108] no "original or actual sin remains";[109] the baptized have been "cured";[110] good has been imparted.[111] Responsibility now lies with the regenerated person to persevere and

---

[101]*Serm.* 39.1-2; cf. 98.3.
[102]*Serm.* 126.2.
[103]*Serm.* 171.1.
[104]*Serm.* 167.1; 129.4.
[105]*Serm.* 129.5-6; 181.2; 229.1.
[106]*Serm.* 167.1.
[107]*Serm.* 94.3, 4; 227.1.
[108]*Serm.* 81.4.
[109]*Serm.* 129.5.
[110]*Serm.* 81.4.
[111]*Serm.* 133.4; 97.4.

grow in the good; otherwise the benefits attained in baptism can be lost, and sin can once again gain control.[112] Caesarius's statements indicate that he understood baptism to be the means by which one returns to a condition resembling the supralapsarian state of Adam.[113] Through the salvific work of Christ, a person emerges from the waters of baptism purged of evil, freed from enslavement to sin, and equipped with a restored capacity for choosing the good, although the capacity for evil choice still remains. Lapses following baptism do not result in the enslavement of the will by evil, as had the fall, but instead in an entanglement of the will in the habit of evil, a habit that is susceptible to being broken by repentance and by exercise in the contrary habit of good.[114]

With his insistence that the capacity for good, given in baptism, must be vigilantly exercised in defensive measures to prevent and to atone for lapses as well as in the positive pursuit of virtues and the attainment of reward,[115] Caesarius implied that baptism intensifies one's accountability before God. He was convinced that the gratuitous benefits of baptism, if not properly employed, can lead to judgment rather than to reward.[116] Christ, having been the gracious benefactor, will finally be our judge. As Caesarius warned:

> He knows how much to demand in return, since He bestowed so much. . . . When He comes He will pay what He has promised, but He will also ask for what He redeemed; what He gave at His first coming, He will exact at the second.[117]

Thus it is to the baptized that Caesarius would have felt particularly compelled to address his warnings of the last judgment, his appeals for self-scrutiny and repentance, and his encouragement in the good, i.e., his reminders of the faith, the promises and threats of God. For although all persons are accountable before God, it is the baptized who possess the capacity to see to it that the account they ultimately render will be a good one. And significantly, the audience to whom Caesarius addressed his sermons and thus his admonitions consisted not of those outside the flock but those within, his fellow Christians, presumably most of whom would have been baptized.[118] Such an audience would have most benefitted by admonitions to prepare themselves for the judgment, for it was they,

---

[112]*Serm.* 12.4; 15.4; 81.1-2, 4; 94.4; 121.8; 170.4; 203.4.
[113]*Serm.* 116.1.
[114]*Serm.* 65.2,4; 167.3.
[115]*Serm.* 119.5; 121.8; 126.5.
[116]*Serm.* 104.6; 121.8.
[117]*Serm.* 89.5.
[118]*Serm.* 70.2; 129.5; 200.4-5; Beck, 163; Klingshirn, 211.

Caesarius believed, who were peculiarly empowered to engage in such preparation.

Despite the confidence that Caesarius expressed in postbaptismal capacity, he made clear that human agency is not adequate for perseverance and growth. Grace must assist human effort.[119]

> We believe that in mercy God will deign to inspire us in such a way that with God's help we may guard our hearts from bad thoughts and preserve our body shining with purity and moderation. Then when we merit to appear before the tribunal of the eternal Judge, we will not deserve to receive punishment for our evil actions, but eternal rewards for our good deeds.[120]

One indicator of his conviction of the ongoing need for grace can be found in the types of phrases with which he regularly concluded sermons: "with the help of our Lord Jesus Christ"[121] or "May he deign to grant this"[122] or "May the Lord in His goodness bring you to this."[123] As formulaic as such phrases may be, they, nevertheless, are invariably startling when located, as is frequently the case, at the conclusion of a sermon that is otherwise thoroughly admonitory.

The Christian life, as portrayed by Caesarius, is a continuous struggle with one's final beatitude not secured until death. Augustine had argued that the outcome could not be known in this life; yet for him it was already decided by the eternal decrees. Life on earth was merely an outworking of these prior determinations of God. In contrast, for Caesarius the issue was not to be decided until the last judgment. At that time a retrospective evaluation would be made of one's life and just recompense awarded for eternity.

As a result of this changed attitude, two fundamental doctrines of Augustine were transformed: perseverance and predestination. Perseverance was no longer understood to be the necessary effect of the divine decrees. In a sermon on the struggles of Jacob and Esau in the womb of Rebecca, the passage in Genesis 25 that was crucial to the predestinarian argument of Augustine, Caesarius spoke of Rebecca as a type for the church. The unborn Jacob and Esau, struggling within her, he interpreted as representative of two groups, the good and the evil, who struggle against each other within the womb of the church. In other words, Jacob and Esau represent those who exist between baptism and the final judgment, some pursuing good, others evil. Their final destiny is as yet undecided, for Caesarius insisted that the possibility still remains for the evil, by repentance and

---

[119]*Serm.* 45.5.
[120]*Serm.* 45.5.
[121]E.g., *Serm.* 10.3; 18.7; 19.6; 29.4; 31.5; 33.4; 35.5; 36.8.
[122]E.g., *Serm.* 7.5; 12.6; 13.5; 14.4; 15.4; 16.4; 20.4; 23.5; 25.3; 30.6; 34.6.
[123]E.g., *Serm.* 6.8; 26.5; 27.3.

grace, to join the ranks of the good.[124] Once among those ranks, one must struggle to persevere in good with the aid of grace, assured that "whoever holds out to the end escapes death."[125] The significance of human action is undeniable. Caesarius's interpretation of this key Augustinian passage in combination with the conviction evident throughout his sermons, that the baptized have it within their capacity, as assisted by grace, to determine the outcome of the judgment, would seem to disallow the Augustinian notion of an unfailing gift of perseverance or predestination to glory. Thus without having explicitly rejected this doctrine, Caesarius has effectively done so by virtue of other elements within his position.

On the matter of predestination to grace, Caesarius's views are even less accessible. In a reference to Ephesians 1:4 ("[God] chose us before the foundation of the world") Caesarius did say that "even before we were born in this world, we were taught by the Spirit and predestined." Yet he followed this statement with the admonition: "Let us, with God's help, labor as much as we can so that in return for such great benefits we may possess a reward rather than judgment."[126]

This admonition, which leaves open the possibility of either final reward or punishment, would seem to indicate that the predestination of which he was speaking was predestination to grace, certainly not predestination to an unfailing gift of perseverance. Whether or not the one predestined to grace actually will attain to glory remains an open question, to be decided by the individual's use of the initial gift.

These comments of Caesarius on Ephesians 1:4, in combination with his statements elsewhere that the benefits of baptism are unmerited, bestowed by the grace of Christ,[127] can certainly be interpreted as pointing to a doctrine of predestination to grace. Perhaps Caesarius chose to offer no explicit endorsement on this Augustinian doctrine, but at the same time left open the possibility that those who were aware of it and were so inclined might continue to embrace it.

That Caesarius should have seen the Christian life as a continuous struggle, with the necessity always present to break out of sinful ways and to grow in the good, was consistent with his overall theological scheme. For him the Christian life, and accordingly, the transformation of the self occur in the shadow of the last judgment. Before such a specter, the human person, mutable from creation and weakened in Adam, rightly responds with fear. The Christian life thus comes to consist primarily in repentance and striving in the sure hope that the grace

---

[124]*Serm.* 86.2-5.
[125]*Serm.* 156.6; 209.3; 233.2; 234.2; Mt. 10:22; 24:13.
[126]*Serm.* 104.6.
[127]E.g., *Serm.* 129.5-6.

given at baptism makes possible a good will, the maintenance of which the grace given thereafter, will assist but not ensure.

The Eastern, Origenist monastic theme of striving for perfection is clearly in evidence. One's efforts for the good, as assisted by grace, determine one's eternal destiny. Caesarius was instructing the Gallic laity in an understanding of human agency similar to that held by their monastic counterparts. The life he urged upon them may not have been so arduous, but the necessity for striving was the same.

From this survey of Caesarius's sermons one may surmise that if Caesarius were the leading Augustinian of his day, then by the early sixth century some of the bite had gone out of Augustinianism.[128] To make such a statement is not necessarily to say that Augustinianism had lost to Semi-Pelagianism. The priority and necessity of grace still remained. What had been called into question was the sovereignty of grace. In other words, grace makes possible but does not determine salvation. References to the divine decrees have been dropped, and the automatic quality of perseverance has been effectively rejected as the significance of human effort and the last judgment have regained reality and ascendancy. The scheme of grace, free will, last judgment, reward and punishment has become the norm. Because the connection between action and its outcome was basic to Caesarius's emphasis on instruction and exhortation, the importance of human agency, at least following baptism, was no longer subject to question.

One may conjecture that as Augustine had discouraged preaching of the overpowering character of sovereign grace and had encouraged moral exhortation, Caesarius was giving practical expression to the African bishop's advice. In so doing, he was providing a solution suggested by Augustine himself. On the other hand, perhaps one may find in these sermons not so much a self-conscious attempt at resolution of the long-standing controversy but a theological stance judged by its author to be most suitable to the needs of his hearers. In all likelihood, the badly deteriorating social conditions of the time as well as the need to inculcate Christian values in marginal Christians did to some extent dictate the character of his sermons.[129] Perhaps decades of pastoral experience had convinced him of his parishioners' desperate need for moral admonition. Certainly he continually exhorted his flock to self-transformation through repentance under the shadow of the last judgment. An Augustinian presumption of grace undergirded and colored his understanding of how self-transformation could be possible. An insistence on human agency inevitably limited the emphasis he gave to divine grace.

---

[128]See Jaroslav Pelikan, *The Christian Tradition*, vol. 3, *The Growth of Medieval Theology (600–1300)* (Chicago: University of Chicago Press, 1978) 81.

[129]Cf. discussion regarding Maximus of Turin and Martin of Braga, 201 above.

Caesarius's solution, if it were even intended as such, was his own. At least in the theological scheme expressed in his sermons, he can be seen not so much as a partisan in the debate but rather as a pastor seeking to instruct his congregation in Christian faith and morals in a manner appropriate to their understanding and needs. Perhaps for this reason, he operated to a considerable degree outside the actual terms of the controversy itself.

The Council of Orange

In the sermons of Caesarius a theological position is to be found which can be described as standing in some loose relation both to the understanding of grace taught by Augustine and the monastic understanding of human agency represented by Cassian and Faustus. As Caesarius prepared, collected, and distributed the sermons precisely for the purpose of their being preached in congregations, he must have intended them to be immediately relevant and useful to the churches of South Gaul. It seems reasonable to assume that the theological position taken in these sermons was Caesarius's pastoral solution to the kinds of questions regarding the interaction of grace and human agency that had been the subject of the long controversy. It was also the solution that, so far as one can tell, was actually functioning or at least Caesarius meant to have function in the life of the church at that time and place.

In addition to the sermons, the *Opusculum de gratia*, a brief treatise that he wrote almost certainly against the Semi-Pelagian position, provides access to his views. In contrast to the sermons, which emphasized human accountability, especially the accountability of those who have received the grace of baptism, the *De gratia* focused almost exclusively on the utter gratuity of that initial gift of grace. In the treatise Caesarius affirmed that the judgments of God are hidden but just, and he rebuked those who would make grace in any way dependent upon merit.[130] In the *De gratia* Caesarius did not speak of predestination; however, as his point was that the grace of conversion is unmerited, he, implicitly at least, allowed for the possibility of predestination to grace. The fact that, with the exception of one passing reference, his discussion of the gratuity of grace contained no reference to the operation of grace following conversion suggests that Caesarius did not consider this latter grace to be utterly gratuitous.[131]

---

[130]*Opusculum de gratia, Sancti Caesarii episcopi Arelatensis opera omni*, ed. G. Morin (Maredsous, 1937–1942) 2:159-64.

[131]Referring to Mt. 13:12, he stated: *Qui confitetur se per dei gratiam accepisse quod habet, additur ei; qui autem de meritis suis et de naturae bono praesumit, etiam quod videtur habere auferetur ab eo.* The passage does speak of a grace given after the initial gift of grace, but it is a grace given to the one who acknowledges the gratuity of the

The argument of the *De gratia* readily coheres with the scheme that we have already found in the sermons and, in fact, strengthens that scheme with regard to the gratuity of the initial gift of grace, a matter that had received far less attention in the sermons than had the issue of human accountability following baptism. As the sermons had effectively, although not explicitly, disallowed predestination to glory, or an unfailing gift of perseverance, the *De gratia*, by its silence on the matter, provided no occasion for a reconsideration of the issue.[132]

In contrast to Caesarius's unofficial pastoral stance, the Council of Orange provided the official ecclesiastical resolution of the Semi-Pelagian debate. As such, the decrees of the council reflected the previous history of the controversy and spoke within the terms and framework of the controversy more explicitly and more self-consciously than did the sermons.[133]

We must now consider the theological frame, concerns, and substance of the decrees and compare them with the theological frame, concerns, and substance of the sermons. An examination of the position of the second Council of Orange should indicate (1) the importance of Caesarius in the council's deliberations and (2) the relationship between the official theological stance of this regional council and the theology actually operative in the surrounding Gallic churches where Caesarius's sermons were heard. The later point may suggest the extent to which the decisions of the council were, in fact, intended as a workable pastoral solution to the questions raised by Augustine's predestinarian doctrine.

We do not know the precise circumstances surrounding the second Council of Orange, but it seems that in 528 a council was held in Valence.[134] Although the records of the council have been lost, it is reasonable to assume that in at least two ways, the council was intended to serve as a threat to Caesarius's authority. First, the council was convened by Julianus of Vienne and included

---

initial grace. Presumably the merit to which this latter grace is given is the humility of one who recognizes his or her prior lack of merit.

[132]This interpretation both of the treatise and of the overall message of the sermons is corroborated by the argument of a sermon of Augustine's (*Serm.* 333) that Caesarius borrowed and expanded (*Serm.* 226): the grace by which the Apostle Paul was converted was utterly unmerited; the crown that he received was earned through his own efforts that grace had made possible and assisted. See Mueller, 3:156n.1.

[133]The decrees of the council do have a curiously isolated appearance so far as the broader life of the church is concerned. This council was separated by some fifty years from the Council of Arles (473) and the Council of Lyons (474) and by some three hundred years from the next major outbreak of controversy on the question of grace and predestination. See Pelikan, 3:80-95, for a discussion of the debate surrounding Gottschalk at the Synods of Quiercy (849, 853).

[134]*VCaes.* 1.60. See D. M. Cappuyns, "L'origine des 'Capitula' d'Orange 529," *Recherches de théologie ancienne et médiévale* 6 (1934): 122; Carl Franklin Arnold, *Caesarius von Arelate und die gallische Kirche seiner Zeit* (1894; repr. Leipzig, 1972) 347-50.

among its participants suffragan bishops who only a few years earlier had been transferred from Julianus's jurisdiction to Caesarius's as a result of Ostrogothic geographical gains.[135] Second, evidence from Caesarius's *Vita* and from the letter of Boniface II, confirming the determinations of Orange, indicated that the Council at Valence affirmed the long-standing Gallic antipredestinarian sentiment and in so doing called into question Caesarius's own views on grace. The letter of Boniface II stated that "some bishops of Gaul . . . want the faith by which we believe in Christ to be from nature rather than from grace."[136] Caesarius himself did not attend, claiming ill health, but sent a delegation to present his case. The foremost of this group was Cyprian, bishop of Toulon, who, citing Scripture and the fathers for authority, argued that a person "could of himself grasp nothing of the divine perfections unless first he was called by the prevenient grace of God."[137] If we assume that Boniface's statement referred to the view that prevailed at Valence, then Cyprian's position, and thus Caesarius's, would have been rejected there. The meeting that Caesarius convened at Orange the next year would have served as a rebuttal of Valence and a successful reassertion of Caesarius's authority, as confirmed by the bishop of Rome.[138] The confirmation of the bishop of Rome would also have testified to Gallic conformity to Roman teaching on grace. This confirmation was not insignificant as the affair a few years earlier over the Scythian monks had focused unfavorable attention on Faustus and the Councils of Arles and Lyons (473–474). Their deviation from Augustinian teaching on grace, with which the Council of Valence apparently concurred, now called into question the doctrinal correspondence of South Gaul to an emerging Western tradition.[139]

If such be the case, then the following sequence of events seems likely. When Caesarius learned of the success of his opposition at Valence, he took advantage of the dedication of a church in Orange in that same year to hold another council which consisted of both bishops and laymen.[140] The presence of the laity was significant. At the beginning of this controversy in Gaul, as noted in the case

---

[135]Klingshirn, 136-37, 140.
[136]*VCaes.* 1.60; Boniface II, *Per filium* 1 (Caesarius, *Ep.* 20.1). All English translations of quotations from the proceedings of the Council of Orange, 529, will be taken from *Theological Anthropology*, trans. and ed. J. Patout Burns (Philadelphia: Fortress Press, 1981) 109-28. See also Klingshirn, 140-41; Harnack 5:258n.4.
[137]*VCaes.* 1.60.
[138]G. Fritz, "Orange, deuxième concile d'," *Dictionnaire de théologie catholique* 11/1 (1941) 1087-89; Klingshirn, 141; cf. Seeberg, 1:380n.2.
[139]Markus, "The Legacy of Pelagius," 225-26.
[140]*Canones Arausicorum, Praef. Concilia Galliae A.D. 511–695*, ed. C. de Clercq, *CCSL* 148A, 55.

of Prosper and Hilary, and now at its conclusion, clear participation of lay persons occurred only in the Augustinian camp.[141]

Some time prior to the gathering Caesarius had requested and received advice from Pope Felix IV. The pope sent him a series of *capitula* that presumably formed the basis of at least sixteen of the twenty-five canons adopted by the Council of Orange.[142] Canons 9 and 11-25, with some modifications probably made by Caesarius himself, had been drawn from the *Liber sententiarum ex operibus sancti Augustini delibatarum* of Prosper, which itself was a collection of around four hundred quotations from Augustine.[143] Prosper had compiled the *Liber* probably after he had moved from Gaul to Rome to serve as secretary to Leo I,[144] thus during the last, somewhat conciliatory period of his work when he wrote the *Auctoritates* and the *De vocatione*. The identification of the origin of the first eight canons continues to be the subject of considerable debate for which no clear resolution is in sight,[145] although their Augustinian nature is beyond question. The tenth canon probably came from Caesarius himself, as did the modifications to the *capitula* sent from Rome and the Definition of Faith that followed the canons.[146]

Significantly, references to baptism that would prove to be crucial to the peculiar outcome of the council's work are found in the Definition and in Canon 13. The latter was one of the *sententiae* taken from Prosper, into which a reference to baptism was introduced.[147] As baptism had proved to be a critical element in Caesarius's sermons, so it would in the document accepted by the council.

---

[141]For the significance of lay participation, see J. J. O'Donnell, "Liberius the Patrician," *Traditio* 37 (1981): 57-60, 71-72; see also Klingshirn, 141.

[142]D. M. Cappuyns, "L'origine de 'Capitula' d'Orange, 529," *Recherches de theologie ancienne et médiévale* 6 (1934): 121-26; Fritz, "Orange," 1089-92.

[143]Cappuyns, "L'origine," 126-27; G. Fritz, "Orange," 1089-92.

[144]Pelikan 1:327.

[145]For the influence of the Scythian monks, especially John Maxentius, See Cappuyns, "L'origine," 127-42; for an argument for their Gallic origin, see P. Nautin, "Orange 529," *École Pratique des Hautes Études, annuaire* 1959-1960 (Paris, 1960) 86-87; for the argument that they are from the *capitula sancti Augustini*, an anonymous document from fifth-century Gaul, see "'Capitula Sancti Augustini,' in Urbem Romam Transmissa," *Johannes Maxentius*, ed. Fr. Glorie with intro., *CCSL* 85A, 243-73; for the suggestion that Caesarius was the author, see J.-P. Bouhout, *Revue des études augustiniennes* 25 (1979): 377-79; for a succinct overview of this debate, including the possibility that these *capitula* were those to which Hormisdas referred in his letter to Possessor, see Markus, "Legacy," 225-26.

[146]Fritz, "Orange," 1092; cf. Cappuyns, "L'origine," 126n.15.

[147]Fritz, "Orange," 1096-97; Fritz noted that canon 13 reproduced sentence 152 of Prosper, with the addition of a reference to baptism.

The fact that most of the canons corresponded so closely to the list that would have been sent from Rome indicates that the document did not emerge from the deliberations of the council. Instead, it is far more likely that those who signed the document simply accepted what Caesarius placed before them.[148]

In spite of the fact that the church came to view the work of this council as the authoritative answer to the questions raised by the Semi-Pelagians, it is less probable that the council offered its decrees as a systematic response to specific doctrinal maneuverings in the century-long controversy than as a rebuttal to the position of the Council of Valence.[149] Nevertheless, it is possible to detect in these canons both an overall theological position and particular determinations relative to themes elaborated earlier in the debate.

Not surprisingly, the canons leave no doubt as to the thoroughgoing consequences of the sin of Adam. They affirm that both the body and soul of our first parent as well as of all his offspring were vitiated and made subject to death as a result of the fall, and they explicitly describe as Pelagian the notion that it was only the body and not the soul so afflicted (1, 2). Nevertheless, they also make clear that even if human nature had not been corrupted, it could not have remained in the good and attained salvation without grace; thus as fallen, human nature surely cannot receive salvation apart from grace (19).

Having established the fragility of the human condition, the canons left no doubt as to the necessity of grace. It is grace that evokes the request for grace (3) and the Holy Spirit that creates the desire for purity and the origin of faith (4, 5). To believe and to seek are the gift of grace as are the desire for the good, the consent to preaching, and the decision for baptism (6-8). Justification is neither of nature nor of law but of grace (21). The *ortus bonae voluntatis*, which had been a matter of such dispute, especially between Cassian and Prosper, was now unequivocally lodged in grace.

Grace, in effect, changes the faithful from the fallen condition of Adam to the better (15). It is the only means of being freed from difficulty (14). It is the source of all that one possesses (16), in particular, of any truth and justice (22). For example, the courage that is peculiarly Christian derives from the charity "poured into our hearts . . . through the Holy Spirit" (Rom. 5:5) (17). The only things that can be properly consecrated to God are things that have been received from God (11).

The priority of grace is undeniable. Nevertheless, the council also affirmed human agency. The purpose of the operation of grace is to make possible the performance of good work to which reward is owed (18). The critical transition

---

[148]Cappuyns, "L'origine," 122-23, 142; Fritz, "Orange," 1092; Klingshirn, 141-42.
[149]Seeberg, 1:380-81n.3.

occurs at baptism. Grace brings one to baptism, but the grace conferred in baptism restores the freedom of the will (13). One can hereafter choose either good or evil. Grace thus circumscribes its own role by conferring on human agency the capacity to choose between alternatives.

On this point the position of the council not only differed from Augustine's teaching, which attributed all to divine grace as it works unfailingly through human instrumentality, but it also differed from the monastic theology of John Cassian and of Faustus, which would locate the possibility of a good will in the human agent alone. In contrast to the former position, Orange opened the door for genuine human agency, but in contrast to the latter, it delayed this opening until baptism. This particular understanding of the effect of baptism on human agency did accord, however, with the view of baptism that we found in Caesarius's sermons.

In characterizing the relationship of grace to human agency following baptism, the council sought to maintain the freedom of the will yet always hold in sight the continuing necessity of grace. The canons made clear that although baptism frees the human will so that it can choose the good, the assistance of grace remains essential for the execution of the good: those who "have been healed" must pray for divine assistance that they might persevere (10). The canons upheld the voluntary nature of obedience to the divine will even as they reminded that it is God who prepares the will, commands it (23), and works within it for the accomplishment of the good (20). In a canon that would seem to qualify the genuineness of the freedom enjoyed by the baptized, God was said to work "in us and with us to make us work" (9).

Although the canons did try to sort out the respective divine and human roles, with dominance clearly given to the divine, what the canons, in fact, offered was the description of a relationship that was designed entirely for the benefit of the human partner. Inaugurated and sustained by deity, the relationship confers life (24) and love (25) and in the process accomplishes a transformation of the human agent that enables him or her to become worthy of the divine love that was itself the source of the relationship (12, 25).[150]

These canons were followed by a Definition of Faith, presumably written by Caesarius.[151] It asserted that as a result of the incapacitation of the human will through Adam's sin, love of God, faith, and good deeds are impossible without the aid of grace. Accordingly, even the faith of those saints who preceded the coming of Christ was of grace and not of nature. So also those who now seek baptism act not of themselves but through the grace of Christ. After baptism they can, with the assistance of grace, attain salvation. In every instance of faith and

---

[150]*Conc. Arausicorum, Canones.*
[151]Cappuyns, "L'origine," 124.

love leading to baptism, the beginning is of grace without any prior human merit; afterwards grace assists the performance of good. No one is predestined to evil.[152]

The Definition thus reaffirmed the frailty of the human condition as being such that the *ortus bonae voluntatis*, including the reception of baptism, is lodged in gratuitous grace. Baptism does empower the human agent to do what pleases God, although not without the further assistance of grace.

In the Definition as in the canons the influence of both Augustine and the monastic theology of Cassian was evident, although each in a qualified sense, and in a pattern that corresponded to the scheme found in the sermons and the *De gratia* of Caesarius. First, the council unequivocally endorsed the Augustinian emphasis on the priority of grace. The preparation and conversion of the will and the gift of faith that leads one to baptism are all the work of an utterly gratuitous grace that no merit can ever precede. Particularly in the *De gratia* Caesarius had made this same argument.

Second, the council made no explicit attempt to resolve the matter of predestination. The Definition specifically denied predestination to evil, but neither the canons nor the Definition mentioned predestination to good, either in the form of predestination to grace or predestination to glory. The implication would seem to be that the council rejected the doctrine of predestination altogether, but the silence should not be construed in such a way. The monastic theology transmitted by Cassian had, of course, disallowed predestination. It had done so by saying that the *ortus bonae voluntatis* might reside in the person, i.e, that in some instances faith might initiate the operation of grace. The participants at Orange, however, by maintaining the Augustinian doctrine that in every instance the beginning of faith lies in grace, eliminated the monastic notion of the *ortus;* thus they disallowed the monastic argument against predestination to grace. On the other hand, they did not explicitly affirm this form of predestination. Nevertheless, by providing no explanation of their own for the beginning of the work of grace, while at the same time insisting on its prevenience, they, in effect, gave tacit approval to Augustine's teaching that God chooses some to come to grace. Caesarius, of course, had done the same.

On the Augustinian teaching of predestination to glory, the silence of the council cannot be construed as consent. Both the Definition and the canons affirmed the significance of human agency following baptism. Having conferred free will in baptism, divine grace thereafter assists human effort for the good rather than determining it. The integrity of the human contribution, so important to monastic theology, was thereby maintained but only after baptism. On the other hand, the Augustinian notion of predestination to glory was implicitly

---

[152]*Conc. Arausicorum, Definitio fidei.*

disallowed. The participants at Orange made clear that salvation is the reward for those who, having been baptized, persevere in the good with the assistance of grace. Such an understanding excludes Augustine's teaching that God, without regard to merit, chooses certain Christians to attain glory through a gift of perseverance that cannot fail. In his own preaching on baptism Caesarius had attributed to the sacrament the same power as did the council and thereby undercut the possibility of predestination to glory.

According to the canons and Definition of Orange, baptism is a watershed, with grace dominant beforehand and human agency rising to the fore afterward. Baptism secures the connection between human action and its outcome, at least with regard to all that follows it. The enormous weight that the sermons of Caesarius placed on human accountability cohered precisely with the importance granted to human agency in baptism by the participants at Orange. In fact, Orange espoused what Caesarius had preached: Christians have only God to thank for the gifts that they have already received, of faith, forgiveness, and the freedom to do good. They must act on the basis of this grace to attain salvation.

The work of the council was dated July 3, 529 and signed by Caesarius, a number of other bishops, the Praetorian Prefect of the Gauls, and several additional men of note.[153] The action of the council received official standing in the Western church on January 25, 531 when Pope Boniface II decreed its confirmation. In his letter to Caesarius Boniface ratified the council's position. He concurred that all good, even faith itself, is the gift of grace and repudiated the arguments of those who would assert that faith can arise from nature.[154]

Upon receiving the confirmation of the bishop of Rome, Caesarius attached to the acts of the council a brief preface and a list of quotations from Augustine, Pope Innocent, Ambrose, and Jerome.[155] All citations were to serve as corroborative evidence for the position taken by the council. The citations emphasized the necessity and priority of grace, the operation of which enables rather than undercuts the freedom of the will.

Such a list was, of course, intended to show the canons and Definition to be consistent with the tradition of the fathers, at least those in the Western church; thus it is of note that the charge of novelty against which the Augustinians had repeatedly tried to defend themselves was finally overturned, ironically, by quotations from the one who presumably had initiated the novelty as well as from his contemporaries. A long century had passed, time enough for novelty, at least in qualified form, to become tradition and for Augustine and the Western ecclesiastical leadership of his day to have been robed in authority.

---

[153]*Conc. Arausicorum, Subscriptiones.*
[154]*Conc. Arausicorum, Ep. Bonifatii II ad Caesarium.*
[155]*Conc. Arausicorum, Praefatio* and *Capitula sanctorum patrum.*

Conclusion

What our survey has demonstrated is that the particular configuration of doctrine that characterized the work of the council cohered with the views of Caesarius as he expressed these in the sermons and in the *De gratia*. It was a configuration that has often been described as a modified form of Augustinianism. Perhaps one might describe it more specifically as a form of Augustinianism modified to some degree by the monastic theology of Lérins and perhaps even more so by the realities of preaching in early sixth century Gaul.

Its relationship to both Augustinianism and to Lérinian monastic theology can be summarized as follows. (1) In accord with both camps, it maintained the necessity of grace from the first movement of the will toward the good until the entrance into beatitude; (2) in contradiction to a key Semi-Pelagian tenet, it insisted that the movement of the will toward the good always originates in unmerited grace and not in human capacity; (3) in a departure from both camps, it ruled that the grace given in baptism restores the freedom of the will to choose either good or evil; (4) in a further departure from both camps, it refused to commit itself explicitly on the doctrine of predestination to grace or predestination to glory. Nevertheless, because of its insistence on prevenient grace, the Augustinian doctrine of predestination to grace can be presumed to have received implicit endorsement. At the very least, this doctrine remained within the realm of the allowable. On the other hand, because of its assertion of the restoration of the free will at baptism the Augustinian doctrine of an unfailing grace of perseverance, or predestination to glory, was undermined.

These results indicate that the influence of Caesarius at the council was pronounced. Although the *capitula* that formed the basis for most of these canons can be traced to Prosper's compilation of quotations from Augustine, Caesarius exercised the freedom to edit them, including the crucial addition of the reference to baptism. It was also he who provided the Definition of Faith and the quotations from the fathers. Clearly, he was imbued with Augustinianism, but it was a restrained Augustinianism in which the more difficult points either were left unstated or were quietly abandoned. Such restraint was hardly novel among Augustinians, as decades earlier Prosper of Aquitaine had advocated just such restraint in the *Auctoritates*[156] and had practiced it in the *De vocatione omnium gentium*.

What had been lost was the Augustinian sense of the grace of God as unfailingly effecting the inscrutable divine will through its continuous operation on the human heart. What had been retained was the conviction of human

---

[156]*Auct.* 10.

dependence on divine graciousness. What had been gained was a reliable, comprehensible connection, at least following baptism, between human actions and
the outcome of those actions.

It was, in fact, this connection between human actions and the outcome of
those actions that came to the fore in Caesarius's sermons and perhaps made
possible the success of the council. The fact that the decrees of the council
effectively ended what had been a prolonged controversy indicated that the
council's position, if it did not already enjoy wide acceptance soon gained it. Of
course, with the general disorder that prevailed at the time, there may have been
little energy available for further debate. On the other hand, one compelling
reason for the apparent lack of resistance to the position taken by the council
may have been the fact that it was eminently preachable, as evidenced by the
sermons of Caesarius. It provided a pastoral response to what was perhaps an
otherwise insoluble dilemma.

Chapter 7

Conclusion

The issues that a century earlier had first been raised in a secluded monastery in North Africa and then later more fully formulated in monastic communities of South Gaul, issues that in varying degrees had continued to disturb the Gallic church, had now received their official resolution. From the questions at Hadrumetum to the canons of Orange the fundamental issue, which had served as the catalyst for all the others, was the nature of the connection between human action and human destiny.

The issue had arisen because the Augustinian doctrine of the sovereignty of grace called into question the long-standing scheme of free will, last judgment, and reward or punishment, a scheme that was especially associated with forms of monastic Christianity influenced by Eastern, Origenist thought. As Augustine had worked out the implications of the doctrine of the sovereignty of grace, its logic had required a judgment of God made prior to and independent of any human merit. Furthermore, in accord with his conviction of the extreme consequences of Adam's fall, he had taught that no merit at all was achievable apart from the work of grace. The result of Augustine's holding these two presuppositions of the sovereignty of grace and human depravity was an understanding of salvation according to which the entire process from beginning to end was of grace. The human person simply served as an instrument for the operation of deity. The human agent was a medium in and through which God's purposes were accomplished.

The consequent unreality of human agency had two important implications. First, although Augustine retained the old scheme, the prior, predestinating judgment so overshadowed the last judgment that the latter lost its force. Second, as the prior divine decision utterly determined the human action and its ultimate outcome, the connection between the two appeared severed. The beginning of faith, the conversion of the will, perseverance in the faith, and the merit of eternal beatitude were all the outworking of predestinating grace. The connecting thread throughout was no longer human but divine.

John Cassian and the monastic theology of which his work was representative functioned to reestablish this connection. Cassian assumed that divine reward is given to human striving for the good. Action has a direct, reliable connection with its outcome. Human agency is of crucial significance for human life and destiny. Persons can direct and order themselves toward God even to the point of exercising control over their thoughts. Cassian was writing for monks. He was offering guidance in their pursuit of perfection. His instruction presupposed that the properly regulated communal life of a monastery provided a context propitious to the operation of grace. In contrast, the congregational setting with which Augustine had to deal lacked just such pervasive regulation. Accordingly, he identified a different arena for the operation of grace. The benefits of grace that Cassian could locate in the regulated community Augustine located in the outworking of the divine decrees on the human heart.

Yet the differences between Augustine and Cassian did not arise simply because Cassian moved within a monastic context with its peculiar set of questions and Augustine functioned as episcopal overseer in a congregation of very ordinary Christians. Cassian was also heir to the Eastern, Origenist tradition as it had been shaped by the experience and teaching of the desert fathers, particularly Evagrius Ponticus. As such, his teaching on grace, although somewhat influenced by Augustine, arose from a different theological framework. Specifically, grace was understood not in terms of its sovereignty or predestinating decrees that unfailingly effected their determinations in human life but in terms of its multi-faceted character, its innumerable adaptations to the condition of the human person. Even though both divine agency and human agency were fundamental to the monastic theology that Cassian represented, their operation was not elaborated from similar presuppositions or with similar concerns as those that governed Augustine's thinking.

The apparent similarities between Augustine and Cassian had the effect of blurring and distorting the differences. Misunderstanding arose on those points where vocabulary overlapped but intent and emphasis did not. As a result, argumentation became confused. Perhaps the most striking example of this confusion occurred in the tendency of Augustine's defender, Prosper, to judge Cassian by standards inappropriate to the latter's position.

Prosper, for his own part, gradually shifted from an early extreme Augustinianism to a more conciliatory position. He grew silent on the doctrine of predestination and attempted to find a way to uphold the doctrine of the divine will for universal salvation. The effort proved unsuccessful, however. His conviction of the necessity and efficacy of grace for the beginning of a good will in combination with his belief that this grace is not given to all undermined the possibility of a universal divine salvific will.

Faustus operated out of the context of Lérinian monastic theology, which was shaped by the Evagrian pattern as transmitted by Cassian. He sought to maintain the importance of human agency by arguing against Augustinian extremes. Accordingly, he rejected both the doctrine that human nature is thoroughly incapacitated by the fall of Adam and the doctrine that grace is sovereign in its predestinating decrees, its utter gratuity, and its unfailing efficacy. As a result, Faustus's position was far more directly a reaction against Augustine than Cassian's had been. The effectiveness of human agency as assisted by necessary grace was the position that he tried to establish as normative by virtue of its moderate character. Human action had a reliable connection to its outcome.

Fulgentius, in contrast, insisted upon the Augustinian extremes of a thoroughgoing fall and a sovereign grace. In his overriding concern to safeguard the divine prerogative, he diminished the significance of human agency. As with Augustine, Fulgentius allowed the dominance of grace to sever the connection between human action and human destiny.

Significantly, in Faustus and Fulgentius the monastic and congregational settings converged; thus it becomes apparent that both kinds of theologies could exist in both settings. With Caesarius not only did the contexts converge but the two theologies did as well, although in surprising form. The Augustinian theology dominated, but it came to the fore less in the language that was specifically designed for the congregational setting, i.e., his sermons,[1] than in the more abstract language of Caesarius's treatise, the *De gratia*, and of the decrees of the Council of Orange.

In contrast, the influence of monastic theology can be seen in the renewed attention to the last judgment and the consequent emphasis on human accountability that dominated his sermons. This sermonic language presupposed the connection between a person's actions and that person's destiny. The themes of last judgment and repentance, grace and free will that provided the overall framework for his sermon collection rested on the assumption that the reception of grace in baptism restores the free will. The baptized are thus capable, with the continuing assistance of grace, of living in a way that pleases God and thereby attaining salvation. As such a life is arduous, repentance is an ongoing necessity if one's sins are to be atoned for prior to the final judgment. Caesarius's sermons transferred the life of strenuous exertion from the monastery to the congregation.

The necessity and priority of grace dominated in the determinations of the Council of Orange; however, as in the sermons of Caesarius, the influence of monastic theology was evident. Orange made inescapably clear that grace is gratuitous and prevenient in preparing and converting the will and in bringing the person to baptism. Grace is also necessary throughout the salvific process. Although the council did not mention the notion of predestination to grace, it implicitly allowed for the doctrine by providing neither an argument against it nor an alternative explanation of why some come to grace and others do not. On the other hand, the council's position on the restoration of the will's freedom at baptism left no doubts as to the significance of human agency in the life of the baptized. This admission of human agency effectively disallowed the doctrine of

---

[1]*Serm.* 233-38 were addressed to monks; however, the vast majority of the sermons were intended for the laity.

predestination to glory. The Augustinian notion that God should choose to bestow on some among the baptized an unmerited gift of unfailing perseverance and thereby bring them to salvation had proved unacceptable. What took its place was the conviction that all baptized Christians have the power to exert some measure of control over the outcome of the last judgment. Assisted by grace, they can struggle to exercise their good will in such a way as to render an acceptable account on the last day. The eternal destiny of the baptized is a direct result of their actions.

In the sermons and treatise of Caesarius as well as in the decrees of this council over which he presided, both of Augustine's presuppositions were evident. First, the doctrine of the thoroughgoing consequences of the fall informed the theological scheme that we found in all of Caesarius's work. His insistence on the prevenience and gratuity of grace rested on this doctrine. Second, this scheme retained the doctrine of the sovereignty of grace, although in diminished form. Grace remains sovereign prior to and in the bestowal of the free will in baptism. In this restoration of human capacity, however, grace effectively limits its own role to that of assisting the will in its choice and accomplishment of the good. The unmerited gift of grace in baptism makes possible but does not ensure the achievement of merit by which salvation is won. Nevertheless, this attempt to maintain the integrity of human agency, so important to monastic theology, lacks a feature of the divine and human interaction that had been crucial to Origen and Cassian: the highly variegated adaptation of grace to the condition of the individual human agent. For Origen and Cassian it was precisely this adaptation that worked to safeguard human agency. Instead, for Caesarius grace operates in terms of stages in the human condition, i.e., before and after baptism, in a manner even less variegated than Augustine had taught.

On the matter of authority, Augustine and the Augustinian tradition carried the day. This fact has several notable features. First, to the extent that the conflict was one of an established Eastern, Origenist tradition versus a newly emerging Western tradition, the Westerners won. Such a result was not surprising, as the controversy was entirely played out on Western soil, and local heroes had the advantage. Second, it was really only within the circles of South Gallic monasticism that the Eastern ascetic tradition was considered authoritative. The involvement of the wider Western church precluded either a primarily Eastern or monastic settlement. In other words, not only did geography work against the monastic theology, but so did the demands of a universal church that had to include not only monks but also the average Christians of varying capacities and degrees of commitment. An inclusive church had to claim salvation as the gift of God, although without disallowing the rightful yet subordinate role of human striving. Third, authoritative tradition proved to be variable, for with the passage of time what had once been novelty could become so familiar as to merit the assumption of orthodoxy. Augustine had succeeded in constructing a tradition out of his own thought and the scattered corroborating evidence of others. These thoughts, particularly as they were selectively compiled by Prosper and to some degree modified by Caesarius, had now become authoritative doctrine.

In the end what carried the day was a pastoral theology that was fundamentally grounded in Augustinianism, but an Augustinianism that had evolved in its encounter with monastic theology of Cassian and with the realities of the wider Western church. The outcome was not without irony. Augustine had developed his predestinarian theology of grace while ministering primarily to lay persons in Africa, and it was lay persons who proved to be the strongest supporters of this theology when it came into conflict with the Gallic monastic emphasis on human agency. Yet the Augustinianism that finally proved workable, at least among the laity of southern Gaul, was a theology of grace that made no mention of predestination but laid great emphasis on human agency. The pastoral solution employed by Caesarius and officially accepted by the Western church confirmed the connection between human action, as prepared, empowered, and assisted by grace, and human destiny. Predestination had proved to be unpreachable.

Bibliography

Editions

Ambrose. *De fuga saeculi.* PL 14:597-624.

———. *Expositio in Evangelium secundum Lucam.* PL 15:1603-1944.

Athanasius. *Vita Antoni.* PG 26.

Augustine. *Ad Simplicianum.* CCSL 44.

———. *Confessiones.* CCSL 27.

———. *Contra duas epistulas Pelagianorum.* CSEL 60:423-70.

———. *De civitate Dei.* CCSL 47, 48.

———. *De correptione et gratia.* PL 44: 915-46.

———. *De diversis quaestionibus LXXXIII.* CCSL 44A:11-249.

———. *De dono perseverantiae.* PL 45:993-1034.

———. *De gratia Christi et de peccato originali.* CSEL 42:125-206.

———. *De gratia et libero arbitrio.* PL 44:881-912.

———. *De natura et gratia.* CSEL 60:233-99.

———. *De praedestinatione sanctorum.* PL 44:959-92.

———. *De spiritu et littera.* PL 44:199-246.

———. *De trinitate.* CCL 50-50A.

———. *Epistulae.* CSEL 34, 44, 57, 58. For correspondence pertaining to Hadrumentum, see also *Aux moines d'Adrumete et de Provence.* Edited by Jean Chéné. Volume 24 of Oeuvres de Saint Augustin.

———. *Epistolae ad Romanos inchoata expositio.* CSEL 84.

Cassiodorus. *De insititutis divinarum litterarum.* PL 70.

Caesarius. *De gratia. Sancti Caesarii Arelatensis opera omnia* 2:159-64. Edited by G. Morin. Maredsous, 1937–1942.

———. *Sermones.* CCSL 103-104. Césaire d'Arles, *Sermons au Peuple.* Three volumes. Edited by Marie-José Delage. Sources chrétiennes 175, 243, 330.

Cassian, John. *Collationes.* CSEL 13. *Conferences.* Three volumes. Edited by E. Pichery. Sources chrétiennes 42, 54, 64.

———. *De institutis coenobiorum.* CSEL 17. *Institutions cenobitiques.* Edited by Jean-Claude Guy. Sources chrétiennes 109.

Celestine I. *Epistola ad episcopos provinciae Viennensis et Narbonensis, Ep. 4.* PL 50:429-36.

Columbanus. *Instructio I, Sancti Columbani Opera.* Edited by G. S. M. Walker. Scriptores Latini Hiberniae 2.

Councils

    Concilia Galliae, A. 314-A. 506. CCSL 148.

    Concilia Galliae, A. 511-A. 695. CCSL 148A.

    Denzinger, Henrici. *Enchridion Symbolorum.* Friburg: Herder, 1955.

    Les Canons de conciles Mérovingiens (VIe–VIIe siècles). Two volumes. Edited by Jean Gaudemet et Brigitte Basdevant. Sources chrétiennes 353, 354.

Cyprian. *De bono patientiae.* PL 4:645-62.

_____. *De mortalitate.* PL 4:603-24.

_____. *De opere et eleemosynis.* PL 4:625-46.

_____. *De oratione dominica.* PL 4:535-62.

_____. *Testimonia.* PL 4: 4705-4810.

Evagrius. *De oratione.* PG 79:1165-1200.

_____. *Practicus. Traité pratique ou le moine.* Two volumes. Edited by Antoine and Claire Guillaumont. Sources chrétiennes 170, 176.

Faustus. *De gratia.* CSEL 21:3-96.

Fulgentius. *Ad Monium.* CCSL 91:1-64.

_____. *De veritate praedestinationis et gratiae Dei.* CCSL 91A:48-548.

Gregory of Nazianzen. *Oratio XLI in Pentecosten.* PG 36:427-52.

Gregory of Tours. *Historia Francorum.* PL 71.

Hilary of Arles. *Vie de Saint Honorat.* Edited by Marie-Denise Valentin. Sources chrétiennes 235.

Hormisdas. *Epistulae papae Hormisdae.* CCSL 85A.

Hypomnesticon. PL 45:1611-64. J. E. Chisholm, *The Pseudo-Augustinian Hypomnesticon against the Pelagians and Celestians.* Two volumes. *Paradosis* 20. Fribourg, 1967.

Lucidus. *Epistula 2 (Libellus subiectionis).* CSEL 21:165-68.

Martin of Braga. *De correctione rusticorum. Martini Episcopi Bracarensis Opera Omnia.* Edited by C. W. Barlow.

Maximus of Turin. *Sermones.* CCSL 23.

Maxentius, John. *Responsio adversus epistulam Hormisdae.* CCSL 85A:125-53.

Origen. *De oratione.* Edited by P. Koetschau. GCS 3.

_____. *De principiis.* Edited by P. Koetschau. GCS 22.

_____. *Homiliae in Numeros. Homiliés sur les Nombres.* Edited by A. Méhat. Sources chrétiennes 29.

Possessor. *Epistola ad Hormisdam.* PL 63:489.

Praedestinatus. PL 53:587-672.

Prosper. *Epistula ad Rufinum.* PL 51:77-90.

_____. *De ingratis carmen.* PL 51:91-148.

_____. *De gratia Dei et libero arbitrio liber contra collatorem.* PL 51:213-76.

_____. *De vocatione omnium gentium.* PL 51:647-722.

_____. *Liber sententiarum ex operibus s. Augustini delibatarum.* PL 51:427-96.

_____. *Praeteritorum episcoporum sedis apostolicae auctoritates de gratia Dei et libero voluntatis arbitrio.* PL 51:205-12.

_____. *Pro Augustino responsiones ad capitula obiectionum Gallorum calumniantium.* PL 51:155-74.

_____. *Pro Augustino responsiones ad capitula obiectionum Vincentiarum.* PL 51:177-86.

_____. *Pro Augustino responsiones ad exerpta Genuensium.* PL 51:187-202.

Salvian. *De gubernatione Dei.* CSEL 8:1-200.

Sulpicius Severus. *Vita Martini.* CSEL 1:107-37. *Vie de Saint Martin.* Three volumes. Edited by Jacques Fontaine. Sources chrétiennes 133, 134, 135.

Vincent of Lérins. *Commonitorium.* PL 50:630-86.

Vita Caesarii. Edited by G. Morin. *S. Caesarii opera omnia* 2:293-345.

Translations

Ambrose

Saint Ambrose: Seven Exegetical Works. Translated by Michael P. McHugh. Fathers of the Church 65. Washington DC: Catholic University of America Press, 1972.

Athanasius

Athanasius: The Life of Antony and the Letter to Marcellinus. Translated by Robert C. Gregg. New York: Paulist Press, 1980.

Augustine

Confessions. Translated by R. S. Pine-Coffin. Baltimore: Penguin Books, 1961.

St. Augustin: Anti-Pelagian Writings. Translated by Benjamin B. Warfield. Nicene and Post-Nicene Fathers f.s. 5. Repr. Grand Rapids: Wm. B. Eerdmans, 1971.

St. Augustine: Letters. Volumes 4 and 5. Translated by Sister Wilfrid Parsons. Fathers of the Church 30, 32. Washington DC: Catholic University of America Press, 1955–1956.

St. Augustine: The Retractations. Translated by Sister Mary Inez Bogan. Fathers of the Church 60. Washington DC: Catholic University of America Press, 1968.

Cassiodorus

Cassiodorus Senator. An Introduction to Divine and Human Readings. Translated by Leslie Webber Jones. New York: W. W. Norton, 1946.

Caesarius

Saint Caesarius of Arles: Sermons. Three volumes. Translated by Sister Mary Magdeleine Mueller. Fathers of the Church 31, 47, 66. Washington DC: Catholic University of America Press, 1956, 1965, 1972.

Councils

The Church Teaches. Translated and edited by John F. Clarkson et al. St. Louis: B. Herder Book Co., 1961.

Peter C. Phan, *Grace and the Human Condition.* Message of the Fathers of the Church 15. Wilmington: Michael Glazier, 1988.

Theological Anthropology. Translated and edited by J. Patout Burns. Philadelphia: Fortress Press, 1981.

Cyprian

Fathers of the Third Century: Hippolytus, Cyprian, Caius, Novatian, Appendix. Edited by Alexander Roberts and James Donaldson. Ante-Nicene Fathers 5. Repr. Grand Rapids: Wm. B. Eerdmans, 1957.

Evagrius Ponticus

The Praktikos and Chapters on Prayer. Translated and edited by John Eudes Bamberger. Kalamazoo: Cistercian Publications, 1981.

Gregory of Nazienzen

Cyril of Jerusalem; Gregory Nazianzen. Translated by Edward Hamilton Gifford and Charles Gordon Browne. Nicene and Post-Nicene Fathers s.s. 7. Repr. Grand Rapids MI: Wm. B. Eerdmans, 1978.

Gregory of Tours

The History of the Franks. Two volumes. Translated by O. M. Dalton. Oxford: Clarendon Press, 1927.

History of the Franks. Translated by Ernest Brehaut. New York: W. W. Norton, 1969.

Hilary of Arles

"A Discourse on the Life of St. Honoratus, Bishop of Arles," *The Western Fathers.* Translated and edited by F. H. Hoare. New York: Sheed and Ward, 1954.

Martin of Braga
Iberian Fathers. Volume 1. *Martin of Braga, Paschasius of Dumium, Leander of Seville*. Translated by Claude W. Barlow. Fathers of the Church. Washington DC: Catholic University of America Press, 1969.
Maximus of Turin
The Sermons of St. Maximus of Turin. Translated by Boniface Ramsey. Ancient Christian Writers 50. New York: Newman Press, 1989.
Origen
Alexandrian Christianity. Translated by John Ernest Leonard Oulton and Henry Chadwick. Library of Christian Classics. Philadelphia: Westminster Press, 1954.
On First Principles. Translated by G. W. Butterworth. Gloucester MA: Peter Smith, 1973.
Origen: An Exhortation to Martyrdom, Prayer, First Principles: Book IV, Prologue to the Commentary on the Song of Songs, Homily XXVII on Numbers. Translated by Rowan A. Greer. Classics of Western Spirituality. New York: Paulist Press, 1979.
Prosper
Carmen de ingratis. Translated by Charles T. Huegelmeyer. Washington DC: Catholic University of America Press, 1962.
St. Prosper of Aquitaine: Defense of St. Augustine. Translated by P. De Letter. Ancient Christian Writers 32. Westminster MD: Newman Press, 1963.
St. Prosper of Aquitaine: The Call of All Nations. Translated by P. De Letter. Ancient Christian Writers 14. Westminster MD.: Newman Press, 1952.
Salvian
On the Government of God. Translated by Eva M. Sanford. New York: Columbia University Press, 1930.
Sextus
The Sentences of Sextus. Translated and edited by Richard A. Edwards and Robert A. Wild. Texts and Translations 22; Early Christian Literature Series 5. Ann Arbor MI: Scholars Press, 1981.
Sidonius Apollinarius
Poems and Letters. Two volumes. Translated by W. B. Anderson. Cambridge MA: Harvard University Press, 1936, 1955.
Sulpitius Severus, Vincent of Lérins, John Cassian
Sulpitius Severus, Vincent of Lérins, and John Cassian. Translated by Alexander Roberts, C. A. Heurtley, and Edgar C. S. Gibson. Nicene and Post-Nicene Fathers s.s. 11. Repr. Grand Rapids: Wm. B. Eerdmans, 1978.

Secondary Studies

Abel, Maurice. "Le *Praedestinatus* et le pélagianisme." *Recherches de théologie ancienne et médiévale* 35 (1968): 5-25.
Amann, É. "Semi-Pélagiens." *Dictionnaire de théologie catholique* 14/2 (1941): 1796-1850.
———. "Scythes (Moines)." *Dictionnaire de théologie catholique* 14/2 (1941): 1746-53.
Anderson, P. *Passages from Antiquity to Feudalism*. London: NLB, 1974.
Antin, Paul. *Essai sur Saint Jérôme*. Paris: Letouzey and Ané, 1951.
Arbesmaann, Rudolph. "The *cervuli* and *anniculae* in Caesarius of Arles. *Traditio* 35 (1979): 89-119.
Arnold, Carl Franklin. *Caesarius von Arelate und die gallische Kirche seiner Zeit*. Leipzig: J. C. Hinrichs, 1894; repr. 1972.

Auerbach, Erich. *Literary Language and Its Public in Late Latin Antiquity and in the Middle Ages*. Translated by Ralph Manheim. Bollingen Series 74. New York: Bollinger Foundation, 1965.

Babcock, William S. "Augustine and Tyconius: A Study in the Latin Appropriation of Paul." *Studia Patristica* 18 (1982): 1209-15.

_____. "Augustine's Interpretation of Romans (A.D. 394–396)." *Augustinian Studies* 10 (1979): 55-74.

_____. "Grace, Freedom and Justice: Augustine and the Christian Tradition." *Perkins Journal* 27 (1973): 1-15.

Bachrach, Bernard S. "Barbarian Settlement in Southern Gaul." *Traditio* 25 (1969): 354-58.

Bacht, Heinrich. "Logismos." *Dictionnaire de spiritualité, ascétique et mystique* 9 (1976): 955-58.

Bamberger, John Eudes, translated and introduced by. *Evagrius Ponticus. The Praktikos and Chapters on Prayer*. Kalamazoo: Cistercian, 1981.

Bardy, G. "Gélase (Décret de)." *Dictionnaire de la Bible, Supplement* 3 (1928–): 279-90.

_____. "Les répercussions des controverses théologiques des Vᵉ et VIᵉ siècles dans les églises de Gaule." *Revue d'histoire de l'Église de France* 24 (1938): 23-46.

_____. "Prosper d'Aquitaine." *Dictionnaire de théologie catholique* 13/2 (1936): 846-50.

Bartnik, C. "L'universalisme de l'histoire du salut dans le *De vocatione omnium gentium*." *Revue d'histoire ecclésiastique* 68/3-4 (1973): 731-58.

Beck, Henry G. J. "St. Caesarius of Arles." *New Catholic Encyclopedia*. 1967. 2:1046-48.

_____. *The Pastoral Care of Souls in South-East France During the Sixth Century*. Analecta Gregoriana 51. Rome: Universitas Gregoriana, 1950.

Biarne, Jacques. "La Bible dans la vie monastique." *Le monde latin antique et la Bible*, edited by J. Fontaine and C. Pietri, 409-29. Bible de tous les temps 2. Paris: Beauchesne, 1985.

Bogan, Sister Mary Inez, translator. *Augustine: The Retractations*. Fathers of the Church 60. Washington DC: Catholic University of America Press, 1968.

Bonner, Gerald. *St. Augustine of Hippo*. Philadelphia: Westminster Press, 1963.

Bouhot, J.-P. Review of *Johannes Maxentius*, edited by Fr. Glorie. CCSL 85A. *Revue des études augustiniennes* 25 (1979): 377-79.

Brown, Peter. *Augustine of Hippo: A Biography*. Berkeley: University of California Press, 1967.

_____. *The Cult of the Saints: Its Rise and Function in Latin Christianity*. Chicago: University of Chicago Press, 1981.

_____. "Pelagius and His Supporters: Aims and Environment." *Journal of Theological Studies* n.s. 19 (1968): 93-114. Repr. in Brown, *Religion and Society in the Age of St. Augustine*, 183-207.

_____. *Power and Persuasion in Late Antiquity: Towards a Christian Empire*. Madison WI: University of Wisconsin Press, 1992.

_____. *Religion and Society in the Age of Saint Augustine*. New York: Harper and Row, 1972.

_____. "The Rise and Function of the Holy Man in Late Antiquity." *Journal of Roman Studies* 61 (1971): 80-101. Repr. in Brown, *Society and the Holy in Late Antiquity*, 103-52.

_____. *Society and the Holy in Late Antiquity*. Berkeley: University of California Press, 1982.

_____. "Town, Village, and Holy Man: The Case of Syria." In *Assimilation et résistance à la culture gréco-romaine dans le monde ancien*, 213-20. Paris: Les Belles Lettres, 1976. Repr. in Brown, *Society and the Holy in Late Antiquity*, 153-65.

_____. *The World of Late Antiquity*. Norwich: Harcourt Brace Jovanovich: 1971.

Buonaiuti, E. "Manichaeism and Augustine's Idea of 'Massa Perditionis'." *Harvard Theological Review* 20 (1927): 117-27.

Burns, J. Patout. "Grace: The Augustinian Foundation," *Christian Spirituality: Origins to the Twelfth Century*. Edited by Bernard McGinn and John Meyendorff. New York: Crossroad, 1987.

_____. *The Development of Augustine's Doctrine of Operative Grace*. Paris: Études Augustiniennes, 1980.

_____. "The Economy of Salvation: Two Patristic Traditions." *Theological Studies* 37 (1976): 598-619.

_____. "The Interpretation of Romans in the Pelagian Controversy." *Augustinian Studies* 10 (1979): 43-54.

Burton-Christie, Douglas. "'Practice Makes Perfect': Interpretation of Scripture in the *Apophthegmata Patrum*." *Studia Patristica* 20 (1989): 213-18.

_____. *The Word in the Desert: Scripture and the Quest for Holiness in Early Christian Monasticism*. Oxford: Oxford University Press, 1993.

Cappuyns, D. M. "L'auteur du *De vocatione omnium gentium*." *Revue Bénédictine* 39 (1927): 198-226.

_____. "Cassien," *Dictionnaire d'histoire et de géographie ecclésiastique* 11 (1949): 1319-48.

_____. "L'origine de *Capitula* d'Orange, 529." *Recherches de théologie ancienne et médiévale* 6 (1934): 121-42.

_____. "Le premier représentant de l'augustinisme médiéval, Prosper d'Aquitaine." *Recherches de théologie ancienne et médiévale* 1 (1929): 309-37.

Cavallera, Ferdinand. *Saint Jérôme*. Louvain: Spicilegium Sacrum Lovaniense Bureaux, 1922.

Chadwick, Henry. "The Ascetic Ideal in the History of the Church." *Studies in Church History* 22 (1985): 1-23.

_____. "Prayer at Midnight." In *Epektasis: Mélanges patristiques offerts au Cardinal Jean Daniélou*, edited by J. Fontaine and C. Kannengiesser, 47-49. Paris, 1972.

Chadwick, Nora K. "Intellectual Contacts between Britain and Gaul in the Fifth Century." In *Studies in Early British History*, 224-27. Cambridge: Cambridge University Press, 1959.

_____. "Note on Faustus and Riocatus." In *Studies in Early British History*, 254-63. Cambridge: Cambridge University Press, 1959.

_____. *Poetry and Letters in Early Christian Gaul*. London: Bowes and Bowes, 1955.

Chadwick, Owen. "Euladius of Arles." *Journal of Theological Studies* 46 (1945): 200-205.

_____. *John Cassian*. Second edition. Cambridge: Cambridge University Press, 1968; repr. 1979.

Chatillon, F. "Un certain Prosper. . . . " *Revue du Moyen Age latin* 10 (1954): 204-206.

Chéné, Jean. Introduction to *Aux moines d'Adrumète et de Provence*. Oeuvres de Saint Augustin 24. Bruges: Desclée dc Brouwer, 1962.

_____. "Les origines de la controverse semi-pélagienne." *Année théologique augustinienne* 13 (1953): 56-109.

_____. "Que signifiaient *initium fidei* et *affectus credulitatis* pour les semipélagiens?" *Recherches de science religieuse* 35 (1948): 566-88.

_____. "Le semipélagianisme du midi de la Gaule d'après les lettres de Prosper d'Aquitaine et d'Hilaire à saint Augustin." *Recherches de science religieuse* 43 (1955) 321-41.

Chisholm, John Edward. "The Authorship of the Pseudo-Augustinian *Hypomnesticon* against the Pelagians and Celestians." *Studia Patristica* 11 (1972): 307-10.

_____. *The Pseudo-Augustinian Hypomnesticon Against the Pelagians and Celestians.* Two volumes. Fribourg: Fribourg University Press, 1967.

Chitty, Derwas J. *The Desert a City: An Introduction to the Study of Egyptian and Palestinian Monasticism under the Christian Empire.* Crestwood NY: St. Vladimir's Seminary, 1966.

Christiani, Léon. *Jean Cassien: La spiritualité du désert.* Two volumes. Fontenelle, 1946.

Clark, Elizabeth A. *The Origenist Controversy: The Cultural Construction of an Early Christian Debate.* Princeton: Princeton University Press, 1992.

Collins, Roger J. H. "Faustus von Reji." *Theologische Realencyclopädie* 11:63-67.

Cooper-Marsden, A. C. *The History of the Islands of the Lérins: The Monastery, Saints and Theologians of S. Honorat.* Cambridge: Cambridge University Press, 1913.

Countryman, L. William. *The Rich Christian in the Church of the Early Empire: Contradictions and Accommodations.* New York: Edwin Mellen, 1980.

Courcelle, Pierre. *Late Latin Writers and Their Greek Sources.* Translated by Harry E. Wedeck. Cambridge MA: Harvard University Press, 1969.

_____. "Nouveaux aspects de la culture lérinienne," *Revue des études latines* 46 (1968): 379-409.

_____. "Le premier représentant de l'augustinisme médiéval, Prosper d'Aquitaine. *Recherches de théologie ancienne et médiévale* 1 (1929): 309-37.

_____. "L'origine des capitula pseudo-célestiniens contre le semipélagianisme." *Revue Bénédictine* 41 (1929): 156-70.

Crouzel, Henri. *Origen: The Life and Thought of the First Great Theologian.* Translated by A. S. Worrall. San Francisco: Harper & Row, 1989.

Daly, William M. "Caesarius of Arles, A Precursor of Medieval Christendom." *Traditio* 26 (1970): 1-28.

Daniélou, Jean. Introduction to *From Glory to Glory: Texts from Gregory of Nyssa's Mystical Writings.* Translated and edited by Herbert Musurillo. Repr. New York: Charles Scribner's Sons, 1961.

de Broglie, Guy. "Pour une meilleure intelligence du *De correptione et gratia*." In *Augustinus Magister* 3:317-37. Paris: Études Augustiniennes, 1954.

Dechow, Jon F. *Dogma and Mysticism in Early Christianity: Epiphanius of Cyprus and the Legacy of Origen.* Patristic Monograph Series 13. Macon GA: Mercer University Press, 1988.

Delage, Marie-José, translated and introduced by. Césaire d'Arles. *Sermons au Peuple.* Three volumes. Sources chrétiennes 175, 243, 330. Paris: Les éditions du Cerf, 1971, 1978, 1986.

De Letter, P., translation and annotation by. *Prosper of Aquitaine: The Call of All Nations.* Ancient Christian Writers 14. New York: Newman Press, 1952.

_____. *Prosper of Aquitaine: Defense of St. Augustine.* Ancient Christian Writers 32. New York: Newman Press, 1963.

de Vogüé, Adalbert. "Les mentions des oeuvres de Cassien chez saint Benoît et ses contemporains." *Studia Monastica* 20 (1978): 275-85.

_____. "Monachisme et église dans la pensée de Cassien." In *Théologie de la vie monastique: Études sur la tradition patristique*, 213-40. Paris: Aubier, 1961.

_____. "Pour comprendre Cassien: Un survol des *Conférences*." *Collectanea Cisterciensia* 39 (1977): 250-72.

_____, translation by and introduction to *Les règles des saints pères*. Two volumes. Sources chrétiennes 297 and 298. Paris: Les éditions du Cerf, 1982.

_____. "Sub Regula vel Abbate: The Theological Significance of the Ancient Monastic Rules." In *Rule and Life: An Interdisciplinary Symposium*, edited by M. Basil Pennington, 21-64. Spencer MA: Cistercian Publications, 1971.

_____. "Sur la patrie d'Honorat de Lérins, évêque d'Arles." *Revue Bénédictine* 88 (1978): 290-91.

de Vogüé, Adalbert, and Joël Courreau, translated and introduced by. Césaire d'Arles, *Oeuvres monastiques*. Volume 1. *Oeuvres pour les moniales*. Sources chrétiennes 345. Paris: Les éditions du Cerf, 1988.

Diesner, Hans-Joachim. *Fulgentius von Ruspe als Theologe und Kirchenpolitiker*. Stuttgart: Calwer, 1966.

Dill, Samuel. *Roman Society in the Last Century of the Western Empire*. Second edition revised. London: Macmillan, 1910.

Djuth, Marianne. "Faustus of Riez: *Initium Bonae Voluntatis*." *Augustinian Studies* 21 (1990): 35-53.

_____. "Fulgentius of Ruspe and the *Initium Bonae Voluntatis*." *Augustinian Studies* 20 (1989): 39-60.

Dodds, E. R. *Pagan and Christian in an Age of Anxiety*. New York: W. W. Norton, 1970.

Drewery, Benjamin. *Origen and the Doctrine of Grace*. London: Epworth Press, 1960.

Duchesne, L. *Fastes Épiscopaux* 1, 242-46. Paris: Thorin & Fils, 1894.

Duval, Paul-Marie. *La Gaule jusqu'au milieu du Ve siècle*. Paris: Picard, 1971.

Evans, Robert F. *Pelagius: Inquiries and Reappraisals*. New York: Seabury Press, 1968.

Evelyn-White, Hugh G. *The Monasteries of the Wâdi 'n Natrûn*. Volume 2. *The History of the Monasteries of Nitri and Scetis*. New York, 1932.

Fairweather, E.-R. "St. Augustine's Interpretation of Infant Baptism." *Augustinus Magister* 2:897-903.

Folliet, Georges. "Aux origines de l'ascétisme et du cénobitisme africain." *Saint Martin et son temps*. Rome: Herder, 1961, 25-44.

Fontaine, Jacques. "L'aristocratie occidentale devant le monachisme aux $IV^{\text{ème}}$ et $V^{\text{ème}}$ siecles." *Revista d'Istoria e Letteratura di Storia Religiosa* 15 (1979): 28-53.

_____. "L'ascetisme chrétien dans la littérature gallo-romaine d'Hilarie à Cassien." In *Atti de Colloquio sulla Gallia Romana. Accademia Nazionale dei Lincei, 10-11 maggio 1971* (Rome, 1973) 87-115.

Frend, W. H. C. *Martyrdom and Persecution in the Early Church: A Study of a Conflict From the Maccabees to Donatus*. Oxford: Basil Blackwell, 1965; repr. Grand Rapids: Baker Book House, 1981.

_____. "Paulinus of Nola and the Last Century of the Western Empire." *Journal of Roman Studies* 59 (1969): 1-11.

_____. "The Winning of the Countryside," *Journal of Ecclesiastical History* 18 (1967) 1-14.

Fritz, C. "Orange, deuxième concile d'," *Dictionnaire de théologie catholique* 11/1 (1931): 1087-1103.

Gavigan, John J. "Fulgentius of Ruspe on Baptism," *Traditio* 5 (1947): 313-22.

_____. "Vita monastica in Africa desiitne cum invasione Wandalorum?" *Augustinianum* 1 (1961): 7-49.

Geary, Patrick J. *Aristocracy in Provence: the Rhône Basin at the Dawn of the Carolingian Age*. Philadelphia: University of Pennsylvania Press, 1985.

_____. *Before France and Germany: The Creation and Transformation of the Merovingian World*. Oxford: Oxford University Press, 1988.

Gibson, Edgar C. S., translation and prolegomena by. "The Works of John Cassian," *Sulpitius Severus, Vincent of Lérins, John Cassian*. Nicene and Post-Nicene Fathers s.s. 11. Repr. Grand Rapids: Wm. B. Eerdmans, 1978.

Glorie, Fr., editor. *Johannes Maxentius*, 243-73. Corpus Christianorum, series latina 85A. 1978.

Godet, P. "Fauste de Riez." *Dictionnaire de théologie catholique* 5/2 (1939): 2101-2105.

Goffart, Walter. *Barbarians and Romans A.D. 418–584: The Techniques of Accommodation*. Princeton: Princeton University Press, 1980.

Gorday, Peter J. "*Paulus Origenianus*: The Economic Interpretation of Paul in Origen and Gregory of Nyssa." In *Paul and the Legacies of Paul*, edited by William S. Babcock. Dallas: Southern Methodist University Press, 1990.

Gould, Graham. *The Desert Fathers on Monastic Community*. Oxford Early Christian Studies. Oxford: Clarendon, 1993.

Greer, Rowan A. *Broken Lights and Mended Lives*. University Park: Pennsylvania State University Press, 1986.

Gribomont. J. *Histoire du texte des ascétiques de saint Basile*. Louvain: Publications universitaires, 1953.

Griffe, Elie. "Cassien a-t-il été prêtre d'Antioche?" *Bulletin de littérature ecclésiastique* 55 (1954)240-44.

_____. *La Gaule chrétienne à l'époque romaine*. Three volumes. Paris: Letouzey and Ané, 1964–1966.

_____. "Nouveau plaidoyer pour Fauste de Riez," *Bulletin de littérature ecclésiastique* 74 (1973): 187-92.

_____. "La pratique réligieuse en Gaule au Vᵉ siècle: *saeculares et sancti*," *Bulletin de littérature ecclésiastique* 63 (162) 241-67.

_____. "Pro Vincentio Lerinensi," *Bulletin de littérature ecclésiastique* 62 (1961) 26-31.

Griggs, C. Wilfred. *Early Egyptian Christianity From its Origins to 451 C.E.* Leiden: Brill, 1990.

Guillaumont, Antoine. "La conception du désert chez les moines d'Egypte." *Revue de l'histoire des religions* 188 (1975): 3-21.

_____. *Les "Képhalaia Gnostica" d'Evagre le Pontique et l'histoire de l'Origénisme chez les Grecs et chez les Syriens*. Patristica Sorbonensia 5. Paris: Éditions du Seuil, 1962.

Guillaumont, Antoine, and Claire Guillaumont, translated and introduced by. *Traité Pratique ou le moine*. Two volumes. Sources chrétiennes 170 and 171. Paris: Les éditions du Cerf, 1971.

Guy, Jean-Claude. "Jean Cassien, historien du monachisme égyptien?" *Studia Patristica* 8 (1963): 363-72.

_____, translated and introduced by. *Jean Cassien, Institutions cénobitiques*. Sources chrétiennes 109. Paris: Les éditions du Cerf, 1965.

_____. *Jean Cassien, vie et doctrine spirituelle*. Paris: P. Lethielleux, 1961.

Hanson, R. P. C. "The Reaction of the Church to the Collapse of the Western Roman Empire in the Fifth Century." *Vigiliae Christianae* 26 (1972): 272-87.

Haarhoff, T. J. *Schools of Gaul: A Study of Pagan and Christian Education in the Last Century of the Western Empire*. Johannesburg: Witwatersrand University Press, 1958.

Harnack, Adolf. *History of Dogma*. Seven volumes. Third German edition. Translated by Neil Buchanan. Repr. Gloucestr MA: Peter Smith, 1976.

Hatt, J. J. "Essai sur l'évolution de la religion gauloise." *Revue des études anciennes* 67 (1965): 80-125.

Hausherr, Irénée. "L'origine de la théorie orientale des huit péchés capitaux." *Orientalia Christiana* 30 (1933): 164-75.

Heinzelmann, Martin. "L'aristocratie et les évêchés entre Loire et Rhin jusqu'à la fin du VIIᵉ siècle." *Revue d'histoire de l'eglise de France* 62 (1975): 75-90.

Hengel, Martin. *Property and Riches in the Early Church*. Translated by John Bowden. Philadelphia: Fortress Press, 1974.

Herrin, Judith. *The Formation of Christendom*. Princeton: Princeton University Press, 1987.

Heurtley, C. A., translation and introduction by. "The *Commonitory* of Vincent of Lérins." In *Sulpitius Severus, Vincent of Lérins, John Cassian*. Nicene and Post-Nicene Fathers s.s. 11. Repr. Grand Rapids: Wm. B. Eerdmans, 1978.

Hillgarth, J. N., ed. *Christianity and Paganism, 350–750: The Conversion of Western Europe*. Philadelphia: University of Pennsylvania Press, 1986.

Hoare, F. R., translator and editor. *The Western Fathers*. New York: Sheed and Ward, 1954.

Hoch, A. *Lehre des Johannes Cassianus von Natur und Gnade. Ein Beitrag zur Geschichte des Gnadenstreites im 5. Jahrhundert*. Freiburg: Herder'sche, 1895.

Huegelmeyer, Charles T., translation, introduction, and commentary by. *Carmen de ingratis S. Prosperi Aquitani*. Washington DC: Catholic University of America Press, 1962.

Jacquin, M. "A quelle date apparaît le term 'semi-pélagien'?" *Revue des sciences philosophiques et théologiques* 1 (1907): 506-508.

––––––. "La question de la prédestination au Vᵉ et VIᵉ siècles." *Revue d'histoire ecclésiastique* 7 (1906): 269-300.

James, Edward. *The Franks*. Oxford: Basil Blackwell, 1988.

James, N. W. "Leo the Great and Prosper of Aquitaine: A Pope and His Adviser," *Journal of Theological Studies* n.s. 44/2 (1993): 554-84.

Jones, A. H. M. *The Decline of the Ancient World*. London and New York: Longman Group, 1966.

––––––. *The Later Roman Empire 284–602*. Two volumes. Oxford: Basil Blackwell, 1964; repr. Baltimore: Johns Hopkins University Press, 1986.

Jones, Leslie Webber, translation and introduction by. *Cassiodorus. An Introduction to the Divine and Human Readings*. New York: W. W. Norton, 1969.

Jourjon, Maurice. "Honorat d'Arles." *Dictionnaire de spiritualité ascétique et mystique* 7 (1969): 717-18.

Judge, E. A. "The Earliest Use of the Word 'Monachos' for Monk." *Jahrbuch für Antike und Christentum* 20 (1977): 72-89.

Keble, John. *The Works of Mr. Richard Hooker*. 2 vols. New York: D. Appleton and Company, 1845.

Kelly, J. N. D. *Jerome: His Life, Writings, and Controversies*. New York: Harper & Row, 1975.

––––––. *The Athanasian Creed*. New York and Evanston: Harper & Row, 1964.

Klingshirn, William E. *Caesarius of Arles: The Making of a Christian Community in Late Antique Gaul*. Cambridge: Cambridge University Press, 1994.

————. "The Influence of Augustine's Sermons on the Preaching of Caesarius of Arles." Paper presented at the American Academy of Religion, Southeast Region annual meeting, 1987.

Koch, Hugo. *De heilige Faustus, Bischof von Riez: Eine dogmengeschichtliche Monographie.* Stuttgart: Jos. Roth'sche, 1895.

————. *Vincenz von Lerin und Gennadius: ein Beitrag zur Literaturgeschichte des Semipelagianisimus.* Texte und Untersuchungen 31/2. Leipzig: J. C. Hinrichs, 1907.

Labriolle, Pierre. *Histoire de la littérature latine chrétienne.* Third edition, revised and augmented by G. Bardy. Volume 2. Paris: Sociéte d'édition Les belles-lettres, 1947.

Ladner, Gerhardt B. "St. Augustine's Conception of the Reformation of Man to the Image of God." *Augustinus Magister* 2:867-78.

————. *The Idea of Reform: Its Impact on Christian Thought and Action in the Age of the Fathers.* Cambridge: Harvard University Press, 1959.

Laistner, W. "Fulgentius in the Carolingian Age." In *The Intellectual Heritage of the Early Middle Ages,* edited by Chester G. Starr, 202-15. New York: Octagon Books, 1966.

Lampe, G. W. H. "Sin, Salvation, and Grace." In *A History of Christian Doctrine,* edited by Hubert Cunliffe-Jones and Benjamin Drewery. Philadelphia: Fortress Press, 1978.

Lapeyre, G.-G. *Saint Fulgence de Ruspe: un évêque catholique africain sous la domination vandale.* Paris: P. Lethielleux, 1929.

Latourette, Kenneth Scott. *A History of Christianity.* Two volumes, revised. New York: Harper & Row, 1975.

Lawless, George. *Augustine of Hippo and His Monastic Rule.* Oxford: Clarendon, 1987; repr. 1991.

Lebreton, Jules. "Saint Vincent de Lérins et Saint Augustin." *Recherches de science religieuse* 20 (1940): 368-69.

Lejay, Paul, "Le role théologique de Césaire d'Arles," *Revue d'histoire et de littérature religieuses* 10 (1905): 217-66.

Lemaitre, J., R. Roques, and M. Viller. "Contemplation: Contemplation chez les orientaux chrétiens." *Dictionnaire de spiritualité* 2/2 (1953): 1762-87.

Leroy, Julien. "Les préfaces des écrits monastiques de Jean Cassien." *Revue d'ascétique et de mystique* 42 (1966): 157-80.

Lesousky, Mary Alphonsine. *The "De Dona Perseverantiae" of Saint Augustine.* Washington DC: Catholic University of America Press, 1956.

Lienhard, Joseph T. *Paulinus of Nola and Early Western Monasticism.* Cologne and Bonn: Peter Hanstein, 1977.

Lorenz, Rudolf. "Der Augustinismus Prospers von Aquitanien." *Zeitschrift für Kirchengeschichte* 73 (1962): 217-52.

McClure, Judith, "Handbooks against Heresy in the West, from the Late Fourth to the Late Sixth Centuries," *Journal of Theological Studies* n.s. 30 (1979): 186-97.

McGiffert, Arthur Cushman. *A History of Christian Thought.* Two vols. New York: Charles Scribner's Sons, 1932-1933.

McGinn, Bernard. *The Foundations of Mysticism: Origins to the Fifth Century.* New York: Crossroad, 1991.

McKenna, Stephen. *Paganism and Pagan Survivals in Spain Up to the Fall of the Visigothic Kingdom.* Washington DC: Catholic University of America Press, 1938.

MacMullen, Ramsey. "A Note on *Sermo Humilis,*" Journal of Theological Studies, n.s. 17 (1966): 108-12.

MacQueen, D. J. "John Cassian on Grace and Free Will," *Recherches de théologie ancienne et médiévale* 44 (1977): 5-28.

Markus, Robert A. "Chronicle and Theology: Prosper of Aquitaine." In *The Inheritance of Historiography 350–900*, edited by Christopher Holdsworth and T. P. Wiseman, 31-43. Exeter: University of Exeter Press, 1986.

_____. *Christianity in the Roman World*. London: Thames and Hudson, 1974.

_____. *The End of Ancient Christianity*. Cambridge: Cambridge University Press, 1990.

_____. "The Sacred and the Secular: From Augustine to Gregory the Great," *Journal of Theological Studies* n.s. 36 (1985): 84-96.

_____. "The Legacy of Pelagius: Orthodoxy, Heresy and Conciliation." In *The Making of Orthodoxy*, edited by R. D. Williams, 214-34. Cambridge: Cambridge University Press, 1989.

Marrou, H.-I. "Le fondateur de Saint-Victor de Marseille: Jean Cassien." *Provence historique* 16 (1966): 297-308.

_____. *A History of Education in Antiquity*. Translated by George Lamb. Madison WI: University of Wisconsin Press, 1982.

_____. "Jean Cassien à Marseille," *Revue du Moyen Age latin* 1 (1945): 5-26.

_____. "La patrie de Jean Cassien," *Orientalia christiana periodica* 13 (1946): 588-96.

Mathisen, Ralph W. *Ecclesiastical Factionalism and Religious Controversy in Fifth-Century Gaul*. Washington DC: Catholic University of America Press, 1989.

Meredith, Anthony. "Asceticism—Christian and Greek." *Journal of Theological Studies* n.s. 27 (1976): 313-32.

Meslin, M. "Persistances païennes en Galia, vers la fin du VIᵉ siécle." In *Hommages à Marcel Renard*, volume 2, edited by Jacqueline Bibauw, 512-24. Brussels: Latomus, 1969.

Morin, G. "Arnobe le Jeune." In *Études textes, découvertes. Contributions à la littérature et à l'histoire des douze premiers siècles*. Volume 1. Paris: Picard, 1913.

_____. "Lettre inédites de S. Augustin et du prêtre Januarien dans l'affaire des moines d'Adrumète." *Revue Bénédictine* 18 (1901): 241-56.

_____. "Saint Prosper de Reggio." *Revue Bénédictine* 12 (1895): 241-57.

Mueller, Mary Magdeleine, translation and introduction by. *Saint Caesarius of Arles: Sermons*. Three volumes. Fathers of the Church 31, 47, 66. Washington DC: Catholic University of America, 1956, 1965, 1972.

Muhlenberg, Ekkehard. "Synergism in Gregory of Nyssa." *Zeitschrift für die neutestamentliche Wissenschaft* 68 (1977): 93-122.

Munz, Peter. "John Cassian." *Journal of Ecclesiastical History* 11 (1960): 1-22.

Musset, L. *The Germanic Invasions: The Making of Europe A.D. 400–600*. Translated by E. James and C. James. University Park: Pennsylvania State University Press, 1975.

Myres, J. N. L. "Pelagius and the End of Roman Rule in Britain." *Journal of Roman Studies* 50 (1960): 21-36.

Nautin, P. "Orange 529." *Étude Pratique des Hautes Études, Annuaire 1959–1960* (Paris, 1960): 86-87.

Nisters, Bernhard. *Die Christologie des Hl. Fulgentius von Ruspe*. Münster: Aschendorffsche, 1929.

Nodes, Daniel J. "Avitus of Vienne's Spiritual History and the Semipelagian Controversy." *Vigiliae Christianae* 38 (1964): 185-95.

O'Connor, William. "Saint Vincent of Lérins and Saint Augustine." *Doctor Communis* 16 (1963): 125-257.

O'Donnell, James J. *Cassiodorus*. Berkeley: University of California Press, 1979.

_____. "The Demise of Paganism." *Traditio* 35 (1979): 45-88.

_____. "Liberius the Patrician." *Traditio* 37 (1981): 31-72.

_____. "Salvian and Augustine." *Augustinian Studies* 14 (1983): 25-34.

Olphe-Galliard, Michel. "Cassien." *Dictionnaire de spiritualité* 2/1 (1937): 214-76.

Oulton, John Ernest and Henry Chadwich, translators. *Alexandrian Christianity*. Philadelphia: Westminster Press, 1954.

Outler, Albert. "The Person and Work of Christ." In *A Companion to the Study of St. Augustine*, edited by Roy W. Battenhouse. Oxford, 1955; repr. Grand Rapids: Baker Books, 1979.

Parsons, Wilfrid, translator. *Saint Augustine: Letters*. Volumes 4 and 5. Fathers of the Church 30 and 32. Washington DC: Catholic University of America Press, 1955, 1956.

Pelikan, Jaroslav. *The Emergence of the Catholic Tradition (100–600)*. Chicago: University of Chicago Press, 1971.

_____. *The Growth of Medieval Theology (600–1300)*. Chicago: University of Chicago Press, 1978.

Pelland, Lionello. *S. Prosperi Aquitani doctrina de predestinatione et voluntate Dei salvifica*. Montreal: Studia Collegii Maximi Immaculatae Conceptionis, 1936.

Phan, Peter C. *Grace and the Human Condition*. Message of the Fathers of the Church. Wilmington: Michael Glazier, 1988.

Phillott, H. W. "St. Prosper." *Dictionary of Christian Biography* 4 (1887): 492-97.

Pichery, E., translation and introduction by. *Jean Cassien, Conférences*. Three volumes. Sources chrétiennes 42, 54, 64. Paris, Les éditions du Cerf, 1955, 1958, 1959.

Plagnieux, Jean. "Le grief de complicité entre erreurs nestorienne et pélagienne d'Augustin à Cassien par Prosper d'Aquitaine?" *Revue des études augustiniennes* 2 (1956): 391-403.

de Plinval, Georges. *Pélage: ses écrits, sa vie et sa réforme*. Lausanne: Librairie Payot, 1943.

_____. "Prosper d'Aquitaine interprète de saint Augustin." *Recherches Augustiniennes* 1 (1958): 339-55.

Plumpe, J. C. "Pomeriana." *Vigiliae Christianae* 1 (1947): 227-39.

Portalié, Eugène. *A Guide to the Thought of St. Augustine*. Translated by Ralph J. Bastian. London: Burns and Oates, 1960.

Prinz, Friedrich. *Frühes Mönchtum im Frankenreich*. Munich: Oldenbourg, 1988.

Rees, B. R. *Pelagius: A Reluctant Heretic*. Suffolk: Boydell Press, 1988.

Riché, Pierre. *Education and Culture in the Barbarian West From the Sixth through the Eighth Century*. Translated by John J. Contreni. Columbia SC: University of South Carolina Press, 1976.

Rippinger, J. "The Concept of Obedience in the Monastic Writings of Basil and Cassian." *Studia Monastica* 19 (1977): 7-18.

Rist, John M. "Augustine on Free Will and Predestination." In *Augustine: A Collection of Critical Essays*, edited by R. A. Markus. Garden City NY: Doubleday, 1972.

Ropert, J. "Mentalité religieuse et régression culturelle dans la Gaule franque du Ve au VIIIe siècle." *Les cahiers de Tunisie* 24 (1976): 45-68.

Rousseau, Philip. *Ascetics, Authority, and the Church in the Age of Jerome and Cassian*. Oxford: Oxford University Press, 1978.

_____. "Cassian, Contemplation and the Coenobitic Life." *Journal of Ecclesiastical History* 26 (1975): 113-26.

_____. "The Spiritual Authority of the 'Monk-Bishop': Eastern Elements in Some Western Hagiography of the Fourth and Fifth Centuries." *Journal of Theological Studies* 22 (1971): 380-419.

Rouselle-Esteve. A. "Deux examples d'evangelisation en Gaule à la fin du IVᵉ siècle: Paulin de Nole et Sulpice Sévère." In *Béziers et le Biterrois*, 91-98. Montpellier, 1971.

Rusch, William G. *The Later Latin Fathers*. London: Duckworth, 1977.

Russell, James C. *The Germanization of Early Medieval Christianity: A Sociohistorical Approach to Religious Transformation*. Oxford: Oxford University Press, 1994.

Sanford, Eva M., translation and introduction by. *On the Government of God by Salvian*. New York: Columbia University Press, 1930.

Schanz, Martin. *Geschichte der römischen Litteratur bis zum Gesetzgebungswerk de Kaisers Justinian*. Volume 4. *Die römische Litteratur von Constantin bis zum Gesetzgebungswerk Justinians*. Two parts. Munich: C. H. Beck'sche: 1920.

Seeburg, Reinhold. *Textbook of the History of Doctrines*. Two volumes. Translated by Charles E. Hay. Grand Rapids: Baker Book House, 1977.

Smith, Thomas A. *De gratia: Faustus of Riez's Treatise on Grace and Its Place in the History of Theology*. Notre Dame: University of Notre Dame Press, 1990.

Solignac, Aimé. "Julien Pomère." *Dictionnaire de spiritualité ascétique et mystique* 8 (1947): 1594-1600.

_____. "Péchés capitaux." *Dictionnaire de spiritualité ascétique et mystique* 12/1 (1984): 853-62.

_____. "Semipélagiens." *Dictionnaire de spiritualité ascétique et mystique* 14 (1989): 556-68.

Stancliffe, C. E. "From Town to Country: The Christianisation of the Touraine 370–600." In *The Church in Town and Countryside*, edited by D. Baker, 43-59. Studies in Church History 16. Oxford: Basil Blackwell, 1979.

Stancliffe, Clare. *St. Martin and His Hagiographer: History and Miracle in Sulpicius Severus*. Oxford: Clarendon Press, 1983.

Stevens, S. T. "The Circle of Bishop Fulgentius." *Traditio* 38 (1982): 327-41.

Steinmann, Jean. *Saint Jerome*. Translated by Ronald Matthews. London: Geoffrey Chapman, 1959.

Teselle, Eugene. *Augustine the Theologian*. London: Burns and Oates, 1970.

Testard, Maurice. *Saint Jérôme*. Paris: Société d'édition les belles lettres, 1969.

Thompson, E. A. *Romans and Barbarians: The Decline of the Western Empire*. Madison WI: University of Wisconsin Press, 1982.

_____. "The Settlement of the Barbarians in Southern Gaul." *Journal of Roman Studies* 46 (1956): 65-75.

Trigg, Joseph Wilson. *Origen: The Bible and Philosophy in the Third-Century Church*. Atlanta: John Knox Press, 1983.

Valentin, L. *Saint Prosper d'Aquitaine: Étude sur la littérature latine ecclésiastique au cinquième siècle en Gaule*. Paris: Picard, 1900.

van Bavel, T. Johannes. "What Kind of Church Do You Want? The Breadth of Augustine's Ecclesiology." *Louvain Studies* 7 (1979): 147-71.

Van Dam, Raymond. *Leadership and Community in Late Antique Gaul*. Berkeley: University of California Press, 1985.

Van der Meer, Frederic. *Augustine the Bishop*. Translated by B. Battershaw and B. R. Lamb. London: Sheed & Ward, 1961.

Viard, Paul. "Fauste de Riez." *Dictionnaire de spiritualité ascétique et mystique* 5 (1964): 113-18.

Vogel, Cyrille. *Saint Césaire d'Arles*. Paris: Bloud and Gay, 1964.

von Dobschütz, E., editor. *Das decretum Gelasianum de libris recipiendis et non recipiendis*. Texte und Untersuchungen 3rd series 38/4. Leipzig: J. C. Hinrichs, 1912.

von Schubert, D. Hans. *Der sogenannte Praedestinatus, ein Beitrag zur Geschichte des Pelagianismus.* Texte und Untersuchungen 24/4. Leipzig: J. C. Hinrichs, 1903.

Wallace-Hadrill, J. M. *The Barbarian West: The Early Middle Ages, A.D. 400–1000.* New York: Harper & Row, 1962.

————. *The Frankish Church.* Oxford: Clarendon Press, 1983.

————. *The Long-Haired Kings.* Toronto: University of Toronto Press, 1962.

Warfield, Benjamin B., translator and reviser. *Saint Augustin: Anti-Pelagian Writings.* Nicene and Post-Nicene Fathers f.s. 5. Repr. Grand Rapids: Wm. B. Eerdmans, 1975.

Weaver, Rebecca H. "Augustine's Use of Scriptural Admonitions against Boasting in His Final Arguments on Grace." *Studia Patristica* 27 (1993): 424-30.

Weber, Hans-Oskar. *Die Stellung des Johannes Cassianus zur ausserpachomianischen Mönchstradition: Eine Quellenuntersuchung.* Beiträge zur Geschichte des alten Mönchtums und des Benediktinerordens 24. Münster: Aschendorff, 1961.

Weigel, Gustave. *Faustus of Riez: An Historical Introduction.* Philadelphia: Dolphin, 1938.

Wolfram, Herwig. *History of the Goths.* Second German edition revised. Translated by Thomas J. Dunlap. Berkeley: University of California Press, 1988.

Wormold, P. "The Decline of the Western Empire and the Survival of Its Aristocracy." *Journal of Roman Studies* 66 (1976): 217-26.

Zumkeller, Adolar. *Augustine's Ideal of the Religious Life.* Translated by Edmund Colledge. New York: Fordham University Press, 1986.

————. "Die pseudo-augustinische schrift *De praedestinatione et gratia*: Inhalt, Überlieferung, Verfasserfrage und Nachwirkung." *Augustinianum* 25 (1985): 539-63.

Index